Kearny's Dragoons Out West

Kearny's Dragoons Out West

The Birth of the U.S. Cavalry

Will Gorenfeld and John Gorenfeld

University of Oklahoma Press : Norman

This book is published with the generous assistance of the
McCasland Foundation, Duncan, Oklahoma.

Library of Congress Cataloging-in-Publication Data
Names: Gorenfeld, Will, 1942– author. | Gorenfeld, John, co-author.
Title: Kearny's Dragoons out west : the birth of the U.S. Cavalry / Will
  Gorenfeld and John Gorenfeld.
Description: Norman : University of Oklahoma Press, [2016] | Includes
  bibliographical references and index.
Identifiers: LCCN 2016007081 | ISBN 978-0-8061-5394-0 (hardcover) ISBN
978-0-8061-9096-9 (paper) Subjects: LCSH: West (U.S.)—History, Military—
19th century. | United
    States. Army. Regiment of Dragoons, 1st—History. | West (U.S.)—
    History—To 1848. | Kearny, Stephen Watts, 1794–1848. | Soldiers—West
    (U.S.)—Biography. | United States. Army Cavalry—History—19th century. |
    United States—Territorial expansion—History—19th century. | Indians
    of North America—West (U.S.)—History—19th century. | Indians of North
    America—Government relations—1789–1869. | Mexican War, 1846–1848—
    Regimental histories. | BISAC: HISTORY / United States / 19th Century. |
    HISTORY / Military / United States.
Classification: LCC F592 .G66 2016 | DDC 357/.1830973—dc23
LC record available at https://lccn.loc.gov/2016007081

To Suzanne Gorenfeld

But time has no beginnings and hist'ry has no bounds.
Gordon Lightfoot, "Canadian Railroad Trilogy"

Contents

Illustrations

Figures

Maps

Acknowledgments

As was the case for Kearny's dragoons, my roots go back to Leavenworth, Kansas. It was there that—around the turn of the last century—my grandfather Jake Gorenfeld raised a family and found work as an immigrant carpenter. His son, in turn, was my father, Abraham Gorenfeld, who was born in Leavenworth, moved to California, and in 1941, the year before my birth, was drafted into the 17th Infantry Regiment of the Regular Army. My father, although a pacifist, became a twice-decorated master sergeant, involved in five seaborne invasions in the Pacific.

The Pacific War was too painful for my father to talk about, as it was for most combat veterans. But my curiosity about his service whetted my appetite, as an army brat, for military history. While a senior at California State College at Northridge, I took an independent study course in which I wrote a paper on folk songs of the American army in the West. My faculty sponsors were two extraordinary professors, Dr. John Baur of the History Department and Professor Bess Lomax Hawes of the Anthropology Department. They guided me in tying together the notions of social anthropology, cultural history, and the westward movement. It was their inspiration and aid that set me on the course that resulted in this book.

My passion for history was fed during the years I spent working at California Indian Legal Services in Ukiah, California. It was during this time that I befriended Gloria Lockart, a person vastly knowledgeable in the culture and history of her tribe, the Sherwood Valley Pomos of Northwestern California. Gloria opened my eyes to their history, survival, and treatment by European settlers. She became chairperson of her tribe.

My case of dragoon fever gained momentum when I became involved with the living history program at Fort Tejon in 1992. It was at Tejon that I became friends with park ranger Sean Malis and the late George Stammerjohan, a California State Park historian. Sean taught me much about the training, life, arms, equipment, and duty of the typical dragoon. George took me under his wing and, over the next twenty-five years, gave me the benefit of his encyclopedic knowledge of California history and historiography. I managed to survive his boot camp. If there is anyone most responsible for my writing this book, it is George.

It was not long before my son John and I began writing articles for publications, beginning with the Fort Tejon newsletter and then for publications such as *Wild West* magazine and the Company of Military Historians quarterly. We became acquainted with Greg Lalire (*Wild West*) and Dave Sullivan (*Military History*), editors whose helpful suggestions further sharpened our skills. In 2002 we met Professor Durwood Ball. It was Professor Ball who not only gave us a graduate course in historiography but who also first suggested that we gather up our sundry articles and put them in a book.

Research efforts for this book were also greatly enhanced by the helpful staffs at the National Archives, the University of California at Berkeley's Bancroft Library, and the Indiana Historical Society. It was during our research for this book that we met, via the Internet, Barbara MacLeish and Tim Kimball. Both of these individuals have remarkable historical research skills and generously shared much of what they had discovered.

For his part, John would like to thank his grade-school English and history teachers—Robert Carney, Steve Pollock, Bob Pease, and Diane Dowler—as well as his brother Louis, our friend the late George Eichen, and his wonderful and best possible fianceé Dr. Mary Cavanagh.

In preparing the manuscript, I was aided by the exceptional proofreading skills and editing of Dr. Alisa Reich, Jehanne Moharram, and Steven Baker, whose invaluable assistance and hundreds of corrections helped us find a focus. The authors would also like to give their thanks to Suzanne Gorenfeld, Will's long-suffering wife and John's mother, who proofed draft after draft and provided invaluable inspiration and editing.

Finally, two other individuals deserve mention. The first is Private James Hildreth, who served in the regiment and in 1836 wrote the first book about the 1st Dragoons, *Dragoon Campaigns in the Rocky Mountains*. It is a valuable first-person history of what it was like to serve in the regiment in its early years. Eighty-one years passed before another book on the regiment was written. In 1917, Professor Louis Pelzer authored *Marches of the First Dragoons,* a book that does a remarkable job detailing the regiment's history from 1833 to 1848. Over the years, Pelzer discovered a number of rare journals and incorporated them into his book and related works. While others have found more since, until now, no historian, including us, has attempted to completely update Pelzer's seminal work.

Kearny's Dragoons Out West

Prologue

They made us many promises, more than I can remember. But they kept but one—They promised to take our land . . . and they took it.

Red Cloud (Oglala Sioux)

Even when the Indian ceded millions of acres by treaty in return for blankets, food, and trinkets, it was not a sale but the conqueror's will that deprived them of their land.

Tee-Hit-Ton v. United States 348 U.S. 272 (1955)

One day in 1839, a fatherless twenty-four-year-old sailor's son picked up a pen and wrote to Charles Dickens. He had been raised in a small Maine town whose cold fishing waters and herring-smoking houses marked the farthest point east in America from the western scenes of his violent future. The letter writer, a prolific literary hopeful, was James Henry Carleton. His inquiry was brazen: a militia man who wanted to become a famous writer, Carleton's dream was to publish stories about the Indians that would hold readers in suspense, as Dickens had just done during the spectacular two-year run of *The Adventures of Oliver Twist*. Americans were beginning to vex Dickens by reprinting unauthorized copies of his work, and now, almost as rudely, one was asking for favors. What Carleton proposed in his letter was that he might move to London and count on Dickens's friendship.

What came back in the mail was a long brush-off from Dickens, who urged him to go west and not east. To call a complete stranger his friend, Dickens said, "would be to prostitute the term." Besides, it would be next to impossible for Carleton to find success in the British publishing world. "I cannot but think that good tales—especially such as you describe, connected with the customs and history of [America]'s original inhabitants who every day become more interesting as their numbers diminish—would surely find some patrons and readers in her great cities," Dickens wrote.[1]

"Interesting"—yet only in proportion to their being doomed, as white Victorians like Dickens and Carleton saw the Indians in those days. Doomed—under this sentimental view of Indians as part of a vanishing wilderness to be conquered—to fading from the Earth rather than surviving as neighboring nations. That view found its expression not just here in Dickens's letter but also in *The Prairie Logbooks*, the serials Carleton would publish in the next few years. The *Logbooks* contained his accounts of what happened when he took Dickens's advice and went west in a time when the officers of pre-cavalry America spoke of "dragoon fever," the dream of winning a commission as sought after as the second lieutenantship Carleton secured with the Regiment of Dragoons.[2]

Installments of the *Logbook* were published in New York's *Spirit of the Times*, allowing Manhattan readers to imagine themselves at Fort Leavenworth, in present-day Kansas, lining up with the rest of the dragoons under the oaks in preparation for what Carleton describes in terms of a grand adventure:

Time: 10 o'clock. You are on the parade under those grand old trees. On three sides of the great square that surrounds you, are the quarters of officers and men. . . . Men in military garb moving hither and thither—some packing effects—some arming themselves—some shaking hands with, and apparently bidding good-bye to comrades who are to remain behind! . . . Did you hear that bugle!— it blew what is called a signal, "boots and saddles." Now look at the different quarters—see the men pouring from them like bees from so many hives. Don't you hear the clang—clang—clang of heavy sabres as they descend the steps—they are all completely armed and equipped.

The journeys of Carleton, like the regiment itself, provide a window into a forgotten moment of western army history in which diplomacy, exploration, and demonstrations of quiet strength were the order of the day. Though the assurances that brought tribes to peace councils were the stuff of which the proverbial broken promises to Indians were made, they often seemed, at least, to have been drawn up in good faith, the parties to treaties and agreements operating from a naïve view of a lasting "permanent Indian frontier" west of the Mississippi, where the army would protect Natives from hostile incursions by land hungry settlers. The military role of the early dragoons was a far cry from what the regiment would become after the mid-1840s. Under the nuanced command style of Colonels Henry Dodge and Stephen Watts Kearny, the first patrols of the 1830s found the dragoons acting as intermediaries between Indians and white settlers, often protecting Natives from the abuses of the latter and serving in a role that might surprise anyone more familiar with the era of Custer, the Indian Wars, and the later subjugation of western peoples.

Likewise, the *Prairie Logbooks* occasionally strike a note of the paternalistic concern then in vogue toward American Indians. Carleton, though degrading in his treatment of an "Indian dandy" whom he finds hilarious for wearing a calico shirt backwards, also admired the "splendid specimens" of the Pawnee in the same way he admired the compass flower. He had mailed the flower specimen the dragoons found to the poet Henry Longfellow (inspiring Longfellow to write of the plant as what "the finger of God has planted/Here in the houseless wild, to direct the traveler's journey.") The "Prairie Indian," Carleton writes, "with eyes like Eagles. . . . They were not of that dingy brown color . . . but of that red, so peculiar to all the full-blooded savages of the West." His sympathy for the "noble savage" comes when he places blame upon white settlers for the wretched condition of "*all* Indians who live contiguous to our settlements. . . . Wherever their race has come into contact with ours," he writes, "they have perished, and passed away forever."[3]

The painter George Catlin toured with the dragoons in 1834 and produced images that made their way back to eastern and even European audiences eager for glimpses of western landscapes and peoples. Catlin's *Comanche Meeting the Dragoons* captures a warm encounter between an Indian emissary and the dragoon Col. Henry Dodge. At the head of a column of riders under a gray sky, the Indian rears up on a "milk white horse," as Catlin recalled, "carrying a piece of white buffalo skin on the point of his long lance in reply to our flag."[4] In the years to come, after five such journeys across the West, Catlin toured Europe to demonstrate not just his paintings but a Wild West show of Indians themselves in the flesh.

Charles Dickens came away from one of these shows—where the English could pay an admission cost of one shilling to watch visiting Indians perform allegedly authentic war dances—with more embarrassment than compassion. In an uncharacteristically cruel 1853 essay—adopting the bemused tone of the brave observer who sees that the emperor has no clothes—the *Christmas Carol* author ridicules Catlin and his contemporaries for finding value in the "miserable jigs" of Indian rituals enacted by "mere animals." The Natives, he sniffs, were "highly desirable to be civilised off the face of the earth," and not a moment too soon.

By then Carleton, and the dragoon regiment itself, had undergone a shift toward brutality. By 1860 the earlier paternalistic spirit of Col. Stephen Watts Kearny—which had stressed diplomacy with the Indians and the avoidance of open warfare—had given way to collective punishment. That was the year Captain Carleton, blaming the small and scattered Pah-Ute tribe for the unsolved killing of travelers on the road between Los Angeles and Salt Lake City, unleashed a campaign of violence that extended to posting the heads of innocents on a scaffold overlooking the road between Salt Lake City and Los Angeles. Later, during the Civil War, he was determined to crush the Navajos and Apaches and told his officers: "There will be no council held with the Indians. . . . The men will be slain whenever and wherever they can be found." All of this foreshadowed his signature catastrophe, the Long Walk, in which Carleton forced Navajo captives to march across more than three hundred miles of desert to the Bosque Redondo Reservation, a diseased and barren piece of land near the Pecos River where more than two thousand natives died from the effects of malnutrition, sickness, and government corruption.[5]

In many ways so went the regiment. The regiment was at first remarkable in its record of averting and preventing violence. This was the more remarkable for going against the grain of its origins, as a fast-moving cavalry formed in reaction to white terror over the return of Chief Black Hawk, and led, in its earliest incarnation, by the oafish Indian killer and backwoods politician Henry Dodge.

Like Carleton, the regiment initially succeeded in accomplishing its bloodless mission. It then suffered mightily, losing key personnel during the War with Mexico and its aftermath. During these years the regiment battled with many of the very tribes with whom it had negotiated treaties. By the end of the Civil War its ranks were composed of unfamiliar faces acting in a new spirit of violence.

The dragoons had, by then, encountered and dealt with dozens of tribes on the Great Plains while avoiding battle. This was during a forgotten historical moment from 1832 to 1846 when the army in the West, and not just the dragoons, enforced a new western order of peace, a pax Jacksonia, without engaging in open warfare.

When the regiment was formed, the government in Washington, D.C., considered land west of the Mississippi River to be worthless and uninhabitable; or, in the words of army explorer Stephen Long, the "Great American Desert." In his October 1829 speech advocating the policy of Indian Removal, President Andrew Jackson cast the banishment of tribes to this region as a charitable act to protect the "children of the forest" from the evils of white society, a decision "not only liberal but generous," for "toward the aborigines . . . no one can indulge a more friendly feeling than myself." Happily for Jackson's political support, his professed benevolence coincided with hunger among voters for Indian lands soon to be cleared of possessors. But people already lived and hunted on the western lands where the eastern tribes were to be resettled. Tribes already living on the Great Plains and beyond had long fought over scarce resources that were about to become scarcer with the disruption of westward expansion.[6]

The Indian Removal Act of 1830 forbade displaced Native peoples from crossing the Mississippi to return to their ancestral lands.[7] Companies of the newly formed dragoon regiment, supported by infantry stationed at strategic posts along the "Permanent Indian Frontier,"[8] were to fulfill the primary role assigned them between 1833 and 1845: keeping Native peoples west of the Mississippi, consigned to the Great Plains.

Across the Wide Mississippi

> I bet any one of you never seen a picture of one of those old Pilgrims praying when he didn't have a gun right by the side of him. That was to see that he got what he was praying for.
>
> Will Rogers, quoted in *Will Rogers Speaks*, by Brian Sterling and Frances Sterling (1995)

From the start, English colonists generally regarded the continent's native peoples as impediments to the development of land: obstacles needing to be removed (i.e., killed or ethnically cleansed) from those places white settlers desired.[9] By the 1820s, the nation's ever-mobile white population had pushed westward into the fertile lands of the Mississippi Valley at the edge of the vast prairie, located west of the Missouri and Mississippi Rivers. A few adventurous mountain men, among them Jedediah Smith, James Clyman, Jim Bridger, William Sublette, Hugh Glass, Thomas

Fitzpatrick, and Kit Carson ventured beyond them to trap for furs and to trade with Native peoples.[10]

By 1833, the army and state militias had forcibly "removed" most tribes living in the East and relocated them to lands west of the Mississippi River, away from white settlers, as ordered by Secretary of War Lewis Cass. The secretary also instructed the army to prevent white settlers from squatting on those lands set aside as Indian reserves. In creating the dragoons, he envisioned a power that would frighten the removed Indians into compliance. To facilitate the anti-Indian policies of President Andrew Jackson, Cass planned to keep tribes banished west of the Mississippi from returning by constructing a military road and a chain of forts and creating a regiment of dragoons—the last, he believed, "a species of force particularly dreaded by the Indians."[11] The goal may have been intimidation of Native peoples by something like an occupying foreign army. But in marked contrast to their counterparts in the blood-spattered, thuggish 2nd Dragoons, which would see action in Florida, officers of the 1st Dragoons in the West conducted themselves again and again with diplomacy, restraint and, sometimes, even true compassion.

The dragoons were not unique in the regular army for averting battle with the dozens of tribes they dealt with on the Great Plains. With the end of the Black Hawk War of 1832 and until the Mexican War (commencing in 1846), and aside from the vicious Second Seminole War in Florida and a solitary 4th Infantry skirmish with Cherokees in North Carolina who were fighting attempts to forcibly move them to Indian Territory—no regiment in the U.S. Army engaged in battle.[12] This high standard was the result of the enlightened leadership of generals such Alexander Macomb, Henry Atkinson, Edmund Gaines, John Wool, Winfield Scott, and Ethan Allen Hancock.

But what sets the period of 1832 to 1846 apart for the dragoons is that, unlike other regiments that averted violence and served as peacemakers, their missions often dealt with unconquered western tribes that regularly battled both with one another and with whites, and conducted raids in Mexico. In contrast to the tribes that other regiments encountered, many of the tribes that the dragoons held council with were living hundreds of miles away from the nearest white settlement.

What Is a Dragoon?

> Our gay uniforms, flashing sabres and prancing chargers were universally admired, and many patriotic young men would fain have joined us.
>
> James Stevenson, *Boots & Saddles*

The word "dragoon" is of curious origin, having come into being some five hundred years ago on the battlefields of Europe. The dragoon fused firepower and mobility and fought in the gray area between infantry and permanently mounted cavalry. By the 1620s, gunpowder had already been in use there for two hundred years and firearms had improved in efficiency. Generals could now send sharpshooters riding into battle where, mounted or dismounted, they could use firelock guns where their permanently mounted predecessors would have wielded arrows.[13] Since the sideplate of this gun often bore a serpent or dragon, its design has been identified as the inspiration for the term "dragoon." But other etymologists find its origin in the Dutch verb *dragen*, "to support or carry."

Dragoons would remain a vital formation for the next three hundred years.[14] European generals employed them as shock troops equipped with sabers as well as firearms. During this period, the typical cavalry soldier carried sabers, swords, and lances— weapons of shock—but the dragoon, able to fight mounted or dismounted, carried long arms, riding to an important spot, dismounting, and fighting as infantry.[15] German historians credit the mercenary Count Ernst von Mansfeld with the creation of the dragoon as part of his vision of a "flying army." The mustached, lace-collared, pillaging nobleman, eager to avenge himself against fellow Hapsburgs who had betrayed him in the Thirty Years War, used horses to deploy foot soldiers rapidly. His "flying army," or *armée volante*, could seed battlefields with Protestant musketeers more quickly than could his former friends, who had made a dangerous enemy by cheating him of his inheritance.[16]

But the onslaught of Napoleon's wars and the widening use of longer-ranged shoulder arms forced a rethinking in military science that took European horse soldiers down a path sharply different from the one traveled by their counterparts in America. While Americans were adopting dragoon fighting, Europeans were rejecting it as beset with problems: dismounted, the soldier is encumbered by sword and spurs; he or someone must protect his horse rather than engage the enemy; and training men in two styles of mounted warfare wasted armies' precious time and funds. So in Europe, the classical mounted cavalry prevailed.[17]

Although the United States first copied the formations, tactics, and equipment of its colonial masters, the fledging nation slowly evolved its own dragoon strategy. Fewer than a thousand dragoons fought in the Continental Army, and these disbanded after the war. By 1789, the nation included no dragoons in the newly organized U.S. Army. To the Founding Fathers, the best army was one that disbanded quickest, for a standing army seemed to the Framers as a potential tyrant's arm of oppression. An elite mounted force especially smacked of the exalted cavaliers of King Charles I, the deposed ruler of the English Civil War. Further, it would cost more to maintain and train mounted troops than it would simple citizen foot soldiers. Rather, the Founding Fathers would entrust well-regulated state militia to protect the new nation. In 1792, Congress hastily authorized an explicitly temporary dragoon force that was disbanded four years later; two equally evanescent dragoon regiments were raised, one in 1808 and one shortly before the War of 1812.[18]

In that conflict several states raised mounted regiments. Although the federal government greatly increased the size of its regular army, it cited financial concerns to justify merely combining the two extant dragoon regiments into a single unit. And at the war's end Congress dissolved this mounted force, due equally to thrift and to the early dragoons' negligible contribution to the war effort.[19] In any event, for the third time in the country's short history, it lacked a permanent mounted force, and it would take seventeen years before the federal government could be convinced to field one.[20]

Everything changed once the expansion rationalized by the ideology of so-called Manifest Destiny reached the Great Plains and brought new difficulties for the conquering U.S. Army. The sluggish trek of foot soldiers and cannon proved ill-suited to western peacekeeping tasks: protecting settlers from highly mobile tribesmen mounted on horseback and protecting the removed tribes from settlers. The army required a standing mounted regiment capable of rapid deployment, and Congress complied in 1832 by first creating the Mounted Rangers, and then in 1833 by authorizing formation of the United States Dragoons.[21]

Such a regiment would serve many new functions. In addition to showing the flag to justifiably disobedient and resentful Natives and to overly ambitious whites, the military alone possessed the power to maintain peace—by force, if necessary—over the vast expanses obtained in 1803 by President Thomas Jefferson's Louisiana Purchase. The dragoons thus inherited multiple missions of investigating and mapping new lands in the tradition of U.S. Army explorers Meriwether Lewis and William Clark, Zebulon Pike, Stephen Long, and Benjamin Bonneville, missions that also brought writers, painters, and naturalists to the Great Plains.

Westward expansion, fueled by both commerce and conquest, motivated others to support the establishment of the dragoons. Missouri needed the lucrative commerce coming to it via the Santa Fe Trail, so guarding and preserving the peace on the trail became an increasingly popular strategic role for the dragoons. In 1845, when war with Mexico appeared imminent and most regular-army regiments rushed south to protect Texas from invasion by Mexico, the 1st Dragoons remained at their stations to patrol and pacify the Great Plains and Indian Territory. When the war finally broke out, the regiment served as President James K. Polk's tool of conquest: as the bulk of the army held the line along the Rio Grande border, Kearny marched west along the Santa Fe Trail to invade New Mexico and, later, California.

One man would be identified with the dragoon regiment from its inception until he left the regiment at the end of 1846: Col. Stephen Watts Kearny, who used his prodigious energy and powers to mold the regiment in his own martial image and brought it universal acknowledgment as an elite corps. Ironically, sending his expert contingent to seize the territory that would soon become the Golden State significantly weakened it. The regiment's losses of now–brigadier general Kearny and other key personnel, and its bitter, questionable victory, tarnished the glory its officers and enlisted men had won prior to any war. Before we get to the role of Colonel Kearny, however, we must first consider the role of the regiment's founding father, Col. Henry Dodge, and some of the enlisted men who first made up its ranks.

CHAPTER 1

Henry Dodge and the Birth of the U.S. Cavalry

Here is the bold Dragoon who laughs at care,
And crosses Prairies with unshorn hair
. . . .
He mounts his horse, his march begins
O'er river and mountains away he skims;
And the uncouth elk with sudden fear
Bounds from his haunts when the Dragoon's near.

From Capt. Rufus Ingalls, *Song of the Dragoon* (1854)

"By the Right Flank, March!": The Dragoon Enlisted Man

Pvt. Thomas Russell felt himself an absurd sight, standing on the grassy parade grounds of the Missouri army barracks. Instead of a uniform he wore civilian clothes—cotton shirt, wool trousers, black leather military fatigue cap—and carried a stick. He was under orders to pretend this stick was a rifle. The men stood on a rectangular piece of ground on a hill behind which lay the dull-red bricks of Jefferson Barracks, and the land dropped away to the vast and muddy waters of the Mississippi behind them. It was hot and humid. At the sergeant's command, Russell and the ranks of Company A snapped to attention to face west—aspiring horse soldiers without horses, uniforms, or sabers and, in place of rifles and carbines, scraps of wood from their menial and miserable construction projects.[1]

Russell tried to reconcile his situation with the one a prominent poster outside the Nashville, Tennessee, recruiting station
had promised. Passing by it often in 1833, Russell was finally
tempted into abandoning a secure future as a lawyer in the small-
town South for a thrilling role as a hero in the conquered West.
The magical, trackless land of the Indian and the bison, the high
country of the Rockies—he had expected to ride through these in
an elite order of knightly men seemingly taken from the pages of
Ivanhoe. Instead, Russell and the other young men found themselves little more than day laborers in a disorganized and unde-
requipped infantry.[2]

For this predicament, Russell blamed a twenty-seven-year-old
recruiter by the name of Thomas Tredway, the natty and affable
sergeant who had greeted him in the Nashville recruiting station
and who operated as the front line of the army's desperate effort
to staff its new regiment. The veteran Tredway's smart black shako
hat sported a dancing yellow braid that matched the trim on his
stately indigo uniform. Everything about him seemed to embody
the courageous and gentlemanly existence of a professional soldier who knew adventure. But in real life Tredway belonged less to
Ivanhoe than to the tradition of river con men later immortalized
in *Huck Finn.*

As Tredway smilingly described the glorious West, Russell
found himself drawn by that wild alternative to lawyering in
Greeneville, Tennessee. Yes, Tredway confided with momentary
gravity, he would be lying if he didn't allow that being a dragoon
wasn't all roses and did occasionally require "light duties." But, he
hastened to reiterate, dragoon life brought a world of opportunity
perfectly suited to a gifted, middle-class young man seeking the
possibilities of the rapidly opening West. Tredway described his
time in the service, during which he had to feed and groom his
mount, of course, but was otherwise at liberty, like Thomas Jefferson at Monticello, to browse a "Library of Scientific and Professional works which cost 15,000$ & [was] free to all enlisted men
[so] every winter I could read, having nothing else to do than to
attend to my horse."[3]

Warming to his theme, Tredway concluded with the disclosure that dragoons' special privileges flowed from their distinctive
status as the army's first regular regiment of mounted soldiers:
"Exploring the Rocky Mountains," Russell recalled Tredway
explaining, "we would not be subject to the strict laws which in
general govern the army." By day, he was led to believe, they would
investigate prairie and forest; by night, be quartered in comfort.

As an added incentive, the sergeant promised Russell that he
would be able to keep his own horse, a fine mount worth a substantial two hundred dollars. Tredway would be delighted to provide
the valet service of riding it over to the barracks, where the army
would allow Russell to ride his steed or would compensate him for
its full value. The young lawyer, to his "disgrace and everlasting
regret," signed up. Shortly after, the charming recruiter received
his own orders to report to Jefferson Barracks, caught a riverboat
to his new station, and deserted and vanished, along with Russell's
mount, which he sold to unknown horse traders. His horse stolen,
bereft of uniform and saber, Russell had nothing but a three-year
commitment to serve in the wretched dragoons.[4]

The stick drill came to an end. The drill sergeant assigned
them their next duty: building stables for the horses—should any
arrive. Every day after close-order drilling on foot, Company A
would march from the parade ground, armed not with gentlemen's muskets but rather with "shovels, pickaxes, hammers, saws,
and various implements of mechanical use, to a spot on the ground
of the barracks, for the purpose of building stables"—a chore
against which many voted with their feet and simply deserted.[5]
Regimental records document that sixty-five men got up and left
between September and the end of 1833.[6] The guardhouse filled
with captured deserters and other malcontents, upon whom the
officers inflicted severe punishment.[7]

Russell shouldered a shovel, wistfully looked west toward the
great prairie, and considered joining the deserters—three more
years of this was more than he could imagine! He quashed the
thought. Desertion would disgrace his proud, well-connected
family. Then it struck him that he could draw on those enviable

connections to escape this dreadful regiment. But until discharge came, he would soldier on.

While Russell and the other aspiring knights-errant swung pickaxes and hammers like a chain gang, a congressman who knew the family wrote directly to President Andrew Jackson. Ironically, though, the president's own policy of Indian Removal had necessitated the formation of the regiment in the first place. But the White House duly referred the matter to the secretary of war, who in turn dispatched a request to an adjutant general, whose inquiry arrived at the desk of the unlikely commander of the dragoon regiment, the burly and crude former militia colonel, Henry Dodge.[8]

Now Colonel Dodge had to deal with the Russell-Tredway recruitment matter. On April 5, 1834, Dodge reported to Adj. Gen. Roger Jones that he had no doubt that Tredway "made use of every Artifice resorted to by [other] recruiting sergeants" and had also cheated Russell "out of the Value of his Horse." He declared Tredway to be "a man of most infamous Character[,] a man every way calculated to deceive those with whom he had intercourse." Problem was, Dodge pointed out, Tredway had enlisted half of Capt. Clifton Wharton's company. Were he to recommend honoring Private Russell's discharge request, more than fifty other equally justified applications by A Company members would follow. So the army declined to assist Russell.[9] Private Russell decided to make the best of a bad lot and, once again, soldiered on.

Russell soon discovered much company in his misery; many others realized that they had been lied to by a recruiter and that army life, even as a vaunted dragoon, was a hardship. Despite his intelligence and education, trooper James Hildreth of Geneva, New York, born in 1813, had fallen for the exaggerated enlistment pitch. He was promised a regiment organized to search the land well beyond the Mississippi, "the wild regions of the West, prairies, Indians . . . all objects of intense interest to my romantic imagination."[10] Some months after joining the regiment, the disillusioned Hildreth reported having heard "the sad story of many a heart-broken soldier as he recounted the misfortune that led to his enlistment, and as the tear-drop has trickled down his manly cheek."[11]

In other cases, deception (or at least secrecy) originated with the recruit, as in other regiments. An anonymous dragoon hinted at some comrades' dark motivations for joining: "The Company was composed of many young men, some of them of good literary abilities and others of skillfull Mechanical attainments each having his own reasons for enlisting which their Comrades never inquired into. Indeed, it seemed a point of delicacy to let each one keep his reasons to himself."[12] The *St. Louis Gazette* in 1839 published the results of a surgeon's informal survey of fifty-five recruits from various regiments who were asked their reasons for enlisting: "Every man was called upon to tell his own story; it appears that nine tenths enlisted on account of some female difficulty; thirteen of them had changed their names, and forty-three were either drunk, or partially so, at the time of their enlistment. Most of these were men of fine talents and learning, and about one-third had once been men in elevated stations in life. Four had been lawyers, three doctors, and two ministers."[13]

Clearly, the Regiment of Dragoons also attracted its share of desperate souls seeking employment, food, shelter, and concealment. In the mind of one recruit, the thought of a "career of Adventure was exciting & fatiguing, but as a general thing pleasant, diverting my mind from previous troubles. The free air and exercise furnishing a remedy to the troubled mind as well as stimulating."[14] But what set the Dragoon Regiment apart was its substantial number of highly educated enlistees. It was not unusual for educated men such as Russell, Charles Parrott, and the Hildreth brothers, James and William, to be enlisted in the regiment. In the years that followed, a host of well-schooled men from comfortable homes signed up to fulfill their dreams of taming the West, and their letters and journals offer valuable insights into enlistee life. In contrast to most regiments, the dragoons boasted a significant proportion of well-educated men, reared in comfortable surroundings but bored with the East and seeking adventure in the Wild West.[15]

James Hildreth and his brother William were two such men, they would later write two books together, one nonfiction and the other fiction, describing the regiment's first years.[16] Another recruit, Charles Parrott, was born in Easton, Maryland, on May 21, 1811, and had learned his family's mercantile business. Employed in his uncle's paper factory in Wheeling, Virginia, he read accounts of military life with growing fascination. Parrott joined the regular army on February 10, 1834, and was assigned to the Regiment of Dragoons, which he later described as "the finest ever raised in America" by virtue of its assembling brilliant young men from aristocratic and wealthy families from the East.[17]

Even outside observers shared this opinion of the regiment's troops, including the artist George Catlin, who had gained consent from the War Department to accompany the dragoons on their 1834 expedition. Catlin found the regiment "composed principally of young men of respectable families, who would act, on all occasions, from feelings of pride and honour, in addition to those of the common soldier."[18] Charles Latrobe, an author who accompanied Washington Irving in the Indian Territory and wrote of his travels in a book entitled *The Rambler in North America, 1832–1833*, also pronounced the recruits "distinguished from the rag-tag-and-bob-tail herd drafted into the ranks of the regular army—by being for the most part picked, athletic young men of decent character and breeding. They were all Americans, whereas, the ordinary recruits [of other regiments] consist either of the scum of the population of the older States, or of the worthless German, English, or Irish emigrants."[19]

But there were more pressing reasons for establishing the dragoon regiment than the troops' romance with the West or boredom with their elevated upbringing. After all, in the first third of the nineteenth century the United States had used the army almost exclusively to drive the Indians away from the paths of white settlers. By the 1820s, pioneers had pushed their settlements into the fertile areas bordering the great prairie west of the Missouri and Mississippi Rivers, but had halted their wagons at the edges of the two great waterways. In the same era, President

James Monroe dispatched Andrew Jackson to Florida to fight the Seminoles in a campaign that even contemporary observers found inhuman. Monroe preached a peculiar nineteenth-century doctrine that the savage, however noble, must for his survival be forced through land policy to evolve through the stages of civilization, from hunter to farmer. The president believed that the Indian's progress could be ensured only by graciously dispatching him beyond the great rivers into the West.[20] Thus, in 1825, Monroe requested that Congress devise a "well digested plan" to accomplish this result.[21]

President John Quincy Adams and other northern Whigs initially opposed forced removal of the tribes, but at the same time allowed aggressive states such as Georgia to invade Cherokee lands.[22] Expansionists cheered Andrew Jackson's victory over elite East coast intellectual Adams in 1828, as it decisively doomed all Native American claims to ancestral lands lying east of the Mississippi.[23] Fueling Jackson's policy of Indian Removal was not just greed for land but also a thirst for retaliation against tribes who had allied with the British in the War of 1812. To the pragmatic and racist new president, the best solution to the strife between white and Native was to use the natural barrier of the Mississippi River to segregate them. Jackson's Secretary of War Lewis Cass exhibited the disingenuous argument: believing that the government had the paternalistic duty to remove the tribes to protect them from extermination by contact with whites.[24] It would be the role of the army to remove the tribes and keep them to the west of the great river.[25]

Others, like the correspondent for the pro-Jackson *Missouri Republican*, reflected with empathy and insight on the moral rather than the tactical problems of removal. Indians had been cast across the river "to starve or plunder for a livelihood" once tribe after tribe had been dispossessed of their "farms and orchards . . . without any prepatory arrangements." So the Natives "hate us, because they feel we have wronged them. They fear us, because they see we are strong enough to wrong them with impunity, and believe we will wrong them whenever interest prompts. Most of them are in squalid poverty—some die every year." Fueling this poisonous situation was the illegal sale of whiskey: "Some of the vilest of our own people, miscreants who would ruin a whole tribe of Indians and endanger the lives of our frontier women and children, for the sake of a few dollars, get a barrel or two of whiskey . . . and seduce the poor wretches to their ruin. . . . Our march upon them is one everlasting encroachment, our incessant demand is, land—land—more land! . . . Yet the next year they shall cede the remainder, renounce their improvements . . . and [we shall] remove [them] to a dangerous wilderness."[26]

Despite opposition from an enlightened faction including former president John Quincy Adams and Senator Daniel Webster, Congress passed the Indian Removal Act on May 28, 1830, by a vote of 102 to 97. During the ensuing years, the Osages, Winnebagos, Sac and Foxes, Ottawas, Pottawattamies, the Five "Civilized" Tribes and others would be deported west beyond their original territory. These once-powerful and self-sufficient peoples were now relegated to existing on unreliable governmental dole and starving on new lands.[27]

With the tribes duly removed, soldiers in a series of western forts were charged with preventing any Indians from returning across the rivers. By invoking the Indian Trade and Intercourse Act of 1790, soldiers also tried to stop unlicensed settlers from trading with the tribes and entering or squatting on Indian reserves west of the rivers. But at this same time, wagons and merchants began to travel the Santa Fe Trail between Missouri and Mexican settlements in New Mexico and Chihuahua. The federal government expected the artillery and infantry garrisons of frontier posts to provide adequate protection for those merchants crossing the barren reaches on the Santa Fe Trail.[28] Many Plains tribes, however, resided well beyond the reach of the forts' foot soldiers and were difficult to police or control. In 1829, for example, the Sixth Infantry proved incapable of chasing down mounted warriors who were raiding travelers on the Santa Fe Trail.[29]

The 1832 Black Hawk War, named after the Sauk chief who tried to lead his people back across the Mississippi to their ancient

home, underscored the insufficiency of slow-moving foot soldiers to police the expansive bowl of the Mississippi Valley. That
June 15, in the midst of the war, President Jackson signed into
law the act creating the Battalion of Mounted Rangers. Reflecting the traditional distrust by Jackson and many in Congress of
a standing military, this battalion was to be composed entirely of
citizen rather than professional soldiers. As his recent victories
had brought the rough-hewn militia colonel Henry Dodge and
his equally rough tactics into vogue, the War Department named
him—both a gifted negotiator and a brutal champion of Indian
Removal—as the commander of the Mounted Rangers.[30]

Of course, not everyone was so impressed with Dodge, the
"Old Hero." To genteel Easterners, the rise of the new Jacksonian Man meant a barbaric intrusion into a world properly led by
the landed and educated gentry. A formal education, many felt,
should be prerequisite to the seat of office and the officer's rank
alike.[31] But Dodge and his officers (such as Jim Clyman, surveyor
of the West with Lewis and Clark, and Nathan Boone, youngest
son of the famed explorer) looked just like common workmen
and farmers.

Here, however, the roughly 660 frontiersmen in six companies
looked even worse. Each enlistee had to serve a one-year term
and, in the interests of federal thrift, to supply himself with clothing, arms, tack, and horses.[32] So these barely drilled, indifferently
attired, bargain-basement warriors hardly resembled soldiers at
all. Military bearing conspicuously missing from both their training and dress, novelist Washington Irving described them as "a
raw, undisciplined band, levied among the wild youngsters of the
frontier."[33]

The loosely organized battalion lasted but a year and did not
even help finish the Black Hawk War. They did patrol the frontier to quell settlers' fears, and supported Major Dodge while he
negotiated the Winnebagos' surrender of eight murder suspects
at Rock River in Wisconsin. One company escorted a caravan to
Santa Fe, and three companies ventured onto the plains, at which
time the Wichita tribe kidnapped Ranger George Abby.[34]

In short, the Mounted Rangers experiment had failed.[35] Still, its brief, bloodless stint at last convinced Congress of the utility of a permanent professional mounted force that could move rapidly to maintain peace on the frontier.[36] Secretary of War Lewis Cass, in his annual report for 1832, declared to a Congress already disinclined toward more military expenditure that the price tag for the Rangers was $153,942.50 higher than the estimated outlay for a mounted regiment of regular troops. He therefore proposed the creation of a regular army mounted regiment, officered by both formally trained regulars and frontiersmen.[37] In addition, the secretary envisioned for it a purpose extending beyond constabulary in the West: "[I]t is desirable to preserve in our military system the elements of cavalry tactics, and to keep pace with the improvements made in them by other nations. The establishment of a regiment of dragoons would complete the personnel of our army, and would introduce a force which would harmonize with, and participate in, the esprit du corps so essential to military efficiency, and so easily and certainly created by military principles."[38]

Most congressmen still balked at expanding the army—even more at establishing an order of mounted government troops—for both economic and philosophical reasons. Thomas Jefferson's writings had taught American statesmen to distrust permanent standing armies, which might fall under the sway of a tyrant. And permanent *mounted* regiments? Aristocratic. European. To say nothing of cost.[39]

Yet the government heeded Cass's recommendation and the persuasions of influential politicians such as Senator Thomas Hart Benton to form the Dragoon Regiment as its first step toward creating a specialized cavalry capable of controlling the frontier. On March 2, 1833, Congress passed and Jackson signed into law an "act for the more perfect defense of the frontier." Blending the army's professionalism with the hardscrabble talents of frontier scouts, its mission was to ensure that whites and Indians did not trespass upon one another's lands—a cause neither purely of conquest nor purely of kindness, but a complex mixture of both. As Secretary Cass would later describe its function: "Possessing an abundant supply of horses, and with habits admirably adapted to their use, [raiders] can be held in check only by a similar force, and by occasional display among them. . . . We owe protection to the emigrants, and it has been solemnly promised to them and repressing and punishing every attempt to disturb the general tranquility can only fulfill this duty."[40]

Dodge and Kearny

While the men drilled outside like boys with sticks, in the colonel's office at Jefferson Barracks stood the six-foot Henry Dodge, who had earned his small measure of fame for service in the Indian Removal and in the Black Hawk War. Unpolished in manners and schooling, Dodge owned slaves, scandalized ladies with foul language, and squatted on profitable lands belonging to the Winnebago tribe, then refused demands by army officers and Indian agents that he leave. At one time or another he had been an Indian fighter, a sheriff, a miner, a duelist, a frontier scout, and a defendant in a treason case. In that case, a grand jury had indicted Dodge over plans to join Aaron Burr in distant territories and establish a separate nation in the Southwest. But Dodge, it was said, had persuaded the jurors to drop the charges by roughing up nine of them. Other stories swirled about him, too: that he had crushed Sauk chief Black Hawk's attempt to lead his people home with unconscionable cruelty, and that he slept with a knife at the ready. The army had taken quite a risk by entrusting such a man with the command of its first regular regiment of horse-mounted soldiers. Even if dragoons needed horsemanship and frontier lore as well as army discipline, was this the man to lead them?[41]

Yet plucked from a rogue's life into military leadership, Dodge would grow into a shrewd negotiator, who often chose to parley with Native peoples rather than resort to violence. It is said that his nineteenth-century brand of fair play helped steer the First Dragoons away from bloodshed for its first thirteen years.[42] In fact, very different stories had even cast Dodge as a humanitarian. One possibly tall tale had it that during the War of 1812 he had saved 150 surrendering Miami Indians from slaughter on the spot by a vengeful fellow militiaman, a Captain Cooper: "Gen. Dodge, hearing the clicking of the locks of the rifles of the Boone's Lick men, and fearing the consequences, but without ever turning towards them, drew his sword and thrust its point within six inches of Capt. Cooper's breast, and reminding them of his pledge to protect the Indians in their surrender, said that he would never consent to their being slaughtered in cold blood, and that if Cooper's men fired upon them Capt. Cooper himself should instantly suffer the consequences."[43]

The Black Hawk War, though, ensured his ruffian's reputation. In 1832, bold newspaper headlines in the Wisconsin region had boomed with warnings: "TO ARMS! TO ARMS! BLOOD AND CARNAGE MARK BLACK HAWK'S PATH!" Four years earlier the Sauk war captain Black Hawk, his head shaved but for a spray of red-tinted hair, had been forced by treaty, along with his people, to abandon their cornfields in southern Illinois for exile west of the Mississippi. Into the new land they started.

Then, at sixty-one, Black Hawk led hundreds of Sauks back across the river to resettle their homeland. Black Hawk came waving a white flag of surrender but touched off a cycle of distrust, scalping, and murder.[44] Resentful settlers called Black Hawk's group "the British Band" because they had aided the Redcoats in the War of 1812.[45]

Twenty years after that Miami encounter, Colonel Dodge again rode at the head of militia chasing Black Hawk and again found himself faced with a white flag of surrender. But now his actions were darker. Moving fast through the Illinois woodlands, the Sauks had frustrated initial efforts by foot-sore regular and irregular soldiers to catch up with them. Readying his troops for the chase, Dodge compared the Indians to sea pirates while urging his men to maintain sterling military discipline: "I am convinced," he wrote in a letter, "that we are not to have peace with this banditti collection of Indians until they are killed up in their dens."[46]

Dodge made good on his word. On the eastern banks of the Mississippi River, near the opening to Bad Axe River, troops commanded by Gen. Henry Atkinson and Dodge trapped Black Hawk's people between volleys of gunfire from multiple directions.[47] The Sauks' white flag was dismissed as a mere ruse. In breechcloth, the Sauks were crossing the river desperately—not just warriors but families with elders, youngsters, and women carrying children on their backs. Under Dodge's orders, the militiamen cut them down from a hillside: "Dodge is giving them hell," said the captain of the *Warrior* steamboat, watching the action while his ship pulled up to rain canister fire on the Indians. The eight-hour massacre was so complete that an observer called the ship captain "a second Nero or Calligula [*sic*]." On land, a volunteer described the scene. The militia "poured over the bluff, they each shot a man, and in return, each of the braves was shot down and scalped by the wild volunteers, who out with their knives and cutting two parallel dashes down their backs, would strip the skin from quivering flesh, to make razor straps of."[48]

Many army officers expressed their outrage at the slaughter. Lt. Philip St. George Cooke, later a dragoon officer, believed the war to be an "ungracious errand" and a bloodletting against a proud people who were seeking to return to their beloved homeland. He interceded to save the life of a Sauk woman. Lt. Robert Anderson and Capt. Gustavus Loomis took similar acts of compassion for the vanquished and were horrified at the brutality of the volunteers.[49]

It was the reverberations of the Black Hawk War that helped pressure Congress into institutionalizing Dodge's style of warfare in a dragoon regiment. He had earned the gratitude of the infantry commander Bvt. Brig. Gen. Henry Atkinson, whose forces lay ill with cholera in nearby Chicago while Dodge tracked the Sauks. After the final conflict, Atkinson believed that Dodge's dogged pursuit of Black Hawk had saved his own reputation.[50] But a shift in military thinking had occurred in the wake of this war, and the general's stock would sink as the reputation of the rough-riding Dodge climbed. Now, unlike during his service with the Rangers,

Dodge would be served by officers and enlisted personnel: a lieutenant colonel would act as administrative assistant to headquarters to handle government record-keeping, and a sergeant major and quartermaster-sergeant would help Dodge with paperwork as personal aides.

Lt. Col. Stephen Watts Kearny, who was to serve as Dodge's right hand as his second-in-command, came from a very different background. Scion of a wealthy New Jersey wine merchant who had sided with the British in the Revolution, Kearny had studied Latin at what is now Columbia University, joining the debate society and declaiming his favorite poems of Virgil ("One man excels in eloquence, another in arms") and Horace ("Force without wisdom falls of its own weight"). Importantly, Kearny was no outsider to the professional army and had lived a storied military career. Dropping out of college to enlist in the army, Kearny led a hazardous charge in the War of 1812 at the Battle of Queenston Heights and was captured by the British—he was displeased to find himself answering to a hulking miner who could barely pen a complete sentence. Indeed, Kearny's harrowing experiences had hardened his prejudice against untrained militiamen like those whose shambolic leadership he blamed for the defeat of his charge in October 1812, on a cold Canadian shore near Niagara Falls. As part of the American attempt to seize Canadian lands before winter, his formation of men clawed their way up a hill strewn with corpses, rocks, and brambles, and dark with night and with Redcoat gunpowder, musket balls, and grapeshot. While soldiers, including the company commander, fell all around, Kearny and two others took charge of the unit—"undaunted," his colleague Lt. Col. Winfield Scott said—rallying the men to reach the top by a route its defenders had presumed too steep. The Americans took the heights.[51]

And yet that costly victory slipped away, and Canadians could later raise a monument to British major general Isaac Brock's sacrifice and the American collapse. Expected reinforcements from the New York state Militia had failed to cross the river to secure the United States' gains. Humiliated, Kearny and Scott were forced to surrender and sail down the St. Lawrence to Quebec as hostages. Powers in Washington and officers quickly blamed the fiasco on the New York Militia rabble, whose thousand-plus volunteers had seen the American maimed and dead, had heard the Mohawk war shrieks, and had refused to cross the icy waters into Canada.[52] But even before that morning, the daring plan had disintegrated into a petty spat over who was in charge. In that era generalships were entrusted to amateurs with political power, like Brig. Gen. Alex Smythe, the haughty Virginia lawyer leading the U.S. Army at Queenston Heights, and the multimillionaire Gen. Stephen Van Rensselaer of the New York City Militia who was, on paper, Smythe's commanding officer. But the Virginian lawyer-general refused to cooperate with the New York millionaire-general, arrogantly ignoring requests to prepare the crossing and support the regulars. And the equally outrageous millionaire-general had, in turn, alienated his own men by threatening them with friendly fire, vowing that cowards who fled would "expiate their crime by the fire of the Artillery and Musketry of the Columns which shall be directed at them to their total Extirpation."[53]

On their way to the old citadel in Quebec, the captives Kearny and Scott could contemplate the lessons of Queenston Heights. Kearny spent his confinement where a gentleman's code dictated cordial treatment of enemy officers, if not of enlisted men—indeed, any such speaking with an Irish accent might be severely punished as a rebellious subject of King George III.[54] To Kearny's relief, he and other captives were shortly released by exchange for others. But the mortifying defeat rendered him a lifelong stickler who sermonized about discipline, wrote manuals on procedure, and obsessively drilled the troops under his command. Toward the end of the War of 1812 Kearny's federal infantry regiment was dissolved. But General Scott would not return an officer as talented as Kearny to civilian life, and transferred him to the Second Infantry, where Kearny's uninspiring assignment to recruitment duty occasioned his written complaint to the secretary of war. After the war, Kearny's taste for exploration of the West was piqued when he led a battalion of infantry accompanying Gen.

Henry Atkinson's Yellowstone Expedition by keelboat up the Missouri River to the Mandan villages.[55]

Patterning himself after Atkinson, Kearny learned how to avoid bloodshed with Native peoples. During his journeys west, Kearny demonstrated diplomatic skill, holding his men back from violence as long as he thought possible. He could also calm the anger of Native Americans. After an army major violently pistol-whipped a brave for merely touching a cannon, tribesmen became furious, but Kearny was able to talk the band into lowering their bows.[56] Despite having been bred a consummate Easterner, Kearny was fast becoming a man of the West. Indians, in whose ways he immersed himself, dubbed him the Horse Chief of the Long Knives. Before joining the First Dragoons, Kearny navigated the Missouri River, smoked pipes with tribal councils, and wrote of the scalps he saw hanging from lodges.[57]

The Clash of Officers

Gaining a commission in the dragoons excited Stephen Kearny with the possibility of staffing the regiment with the best regular officers then serving in the army. But it was not to be. Henry Dodge, Secretary of War Cass, and President Jackson, as did most Jacksonians, distrusted the well-connected elite and believed that government positions ought to be made available to both the educated and common folk on an equal basis. Besides, they were of the view that commissioning both regular and Ranger officers would give the new regiment a good mix of leaders—some learned in military principles and others pragmatically acquainted with frontier conditions.[58] But, however well appointed, this structure planted the seeds of discord between professional and civilian officers early on, despite their sensible intentions, and ushered in confusion and tension.

Promotion was slow in the regular army. Anxious for promotion, regular officers clamored for commissions in the new regiment.[59] Such an officer was Ethan Allen Hitchcock, an 1817 graduate of West Point, who embodied military professionalism by teaching at the academy, serving with the artillery and infantry, and holding an appointment as commandant of academy cadets. The highly talented Hitchcock gained the support of notable officers (including Generals Alexander Macomb and Winfield Scott) for a coveted captaincy in the dragoons.[60] But Hitchcock, denied an appointment, believed that Dodge was prejudicial against regular officers in favor of former Rangers.[61]

Indeed, the favored group, rewarded with the perk of the option to become company-grade officers in the dragoons, were those who had served in the Rangers. Those who exercised this option were the ones who won permanent ranks in the regular army. In practical terms this meant that civilian soldiers with less than a year of service were given preference over veteran soldiers, a situation Hitchcock objected to as "preposterous." Stephen Watts Kearny took exception in the strongest terms. "The idea, that [the Rangers] will make better cavalry officers, from having rode up and down the frontier once or twice, is too absurd to be entertained for a moment; and as to discipline, why! It is a perfect farce."[62] Regardless of Kearny's low esteem for Dodge's organizational abilities, however, he must have respected, grudgingly, his colonel's two years' diplomatic experience in dealing with Native tribes (and no less with professionally trained officers who neither respected him nor one another).

President Jackson also bestowed a major's commission on Richard Mason of the First Infantry, a Virginia blueblood who looked down his nose at nearly everyone else—even upon those whom the United States Military Academy had conferred privilege. One sergeant described Mason as "an aristocratic Virginian, a large portly man, six feet in height. He possessed all the peculiarities of a southerner, accentuated." President Jackson, ignoring Kearny's counsel to avoid granting officer's commissions to former Rangers, went out of his way to pluck as captains a number of them (Jesse Bean, Nathan Boone, Matthew Duncan, Lemuel Ford, and J. B. Browne).[63] From regular infantry regiments entered Captains David Perkins, Edwin V. Sumner, Clifton Wharton, Eustace

Trenor, and David Hunter, and among lieutenants taken from the regulars were the gifted cavalryman and Virginian Philip St. George Cooke, as well as the future Confederate president Jefferson Davis.

Davis certainly looked the part. A contemporary described him riding a dark brown horse and splendidly attired in white drill pants, narrow at the boot and wide at the thighs, with a dark blue undress coat.[64] He was educated at Transvaal College and in 1828 graduated twenty-third out of a class of thirty-three from the United States Military Academy, escaping near-dismissal for drinking at Benny Haven's Tavern, a legendary off-limits establishment outside West Point. He obtained the rank of second lieutenant in the First Infantry and served on the Northwest frontier in the Black Hawk War.[65] When the dragoon regiment was created, Davis applied for and, on March 3, 1833, received an appointment. He was promptly dispatched to Lexington, Kentucky, to gather recruits. As soon as the company was raised, he reported to Jefferson Barracks, where on August 29, 1833, Dodge appointed him first lieutenant, to serve on his staff as adjutant.[66]

Among those lesser lights appointed second lieutenant was James Schaumburg (spelled variously as Schaumberg and Schaumburgh), a notorious duelist, son of one of Jackson's longtime supporters. Schaumburg had previously served as a lieutenant in the Marine Corps, but was repeatedly court-martialed, and was ultimately cashiered on October 20, 1832. No matter, as he immediately gained a second lieutenant's commission in the Mounted Rangers, which placed him in position to secure the same rank in the Dragoons—which he did.[67] As we shall later see, the notorious Schaumburg, in a sense, would become the longest serving dragoon officer.

The Value of Sergeants Major

The dragoons remained beset by leadership problems, many having to do with many distant posts. The regiment, during much of this time, was frequently without a sergeant major. To be in this state, in the antebellum army era, was to lack a crucially important officer.

A sergeant major was then, as now, the top enlisted man in a regiment by virtue of rank and experience. Col. August Kautz specified that "[t]he sergeant major should be a model soldier for the rest of the regiment in his dress and military deportment. His example and punctual requirements of duty go far towards influencing a proper discipline in the regiment." As the highest-ranking noncommissioned officer he assisted in making up guard, fatigue, and formations for parade details and saw to it that they were properly equipped for such duties. Each morning the sergeant major took roll call and gave the first sergeants their orders for the day.[68] And his responsibilities hardly ended there. Among his significant administrative duties he had to superintend "the clerk, and assist him in making out the various returns, rolls, and reports required, and in keeping the books and records of the regiment."

Since its beginnings the U.S. Army has required of its formations veritable pyramids of paperwork. The headquarters of a typical antebellum regiment hummed with ceaseless chores of composing, copying, sending, and filing reports, official letters, orders, returns, and vouchers of every description. Before the advent of computers and copiers—even of typewriters—the army (as any agency) produced separate cursive documents. Each was to be many times hand-copied before being delivered or filed. In most regiments, including the Dragoons, adjutants and the sergeant major ensured the efficiency of staff scriveners.[69]

So the sergeant major vacuum, during the regiment's first months in 1833, proved just as damaging as the absence of horses, weapons, uniforms, or manuals fresher than the old ones it had from the War of 1812.When Col. Henry Dodge finally met the call and designated the regiment's first official sergeant major, the man, John W. Guernsey, served only six months after being designated in November 1833. When he left on May 4 the following year he was not immediately replaced.[70]

Dodge's securing a new sergeant major was delayed by preparations for the great, but precipitate, expedition to the Pawnee
villages,[71] and by the marching regiment's consequent inunda-
tion with convalescing or dying troops. Encamped on the Washita
River on July 1, 1834, Dodge reorganized his force, leaving his
weakened soldiers behind with a detachment under Kearny's
care, and appointed William Bowman as sergeant major for the
remaining fit men.

In 1837, with the dragoons under Kearny's command, the need
for more regiments to fight in the Seminole War brought with it a
demand for more officers. The shortage paved the way for enlisted
men to rise in ranks. One beneficiary was Sergeant Major Bowman. He and seventeen other noncommissioned officers, decry-
ing as anti-democratic the current system for gaining commissions
through political connections or West Point pedigree, petitioned
Congress for officers' commissions. On August 26, 1837, the Congress granted Bowman's petition; he became a dragoon second
lieutenant and resigned his post as sergeant major.[72]

Kearny picked William Houghton to follow Bowman as sergeant major, a post he held briefly until his discharge on September 24, 1838. On March 1, 1839, the colonel promoted William
Gamble, an Irish immigrant, to succeed Houghton. Gamble had
served a stint in the British army before enlisting in the 1st Dragoons in August of 1838, assigned to Company H, and held the
position of sergeant major until his discharge on August 6, 1843.
(As General Gamble he would win laurels for commanding his
Union cavalry brigade on its first day at Gettysburg, July 1, 1863.[73])
But even Kearny could dally in selecting sergeants major, and did
not replace Gamble until nearly two years later. In 1845, camped
at Bent's Fort on his return journey from the Rocky Mountains'
South Pass, Kearny named Cpl. John Walker from F Company to
the position.[74]

But that choice did not settle matters long. In the spring of
1846, President James Polk planned an ambitious march to California for Kearny and the Army of the West by way of Santa Fe. Just
before departure, though, Kearny discovered that Sergeant Major

Walker was experiencing unspecified "private circumstances not admitting of his re-enlisting." Giving Walker "great credit for the manner in which he has discharged his duties," Kearny was keenly aware of "the necessity of there being a Sergeant Major on the Expedition to Santa Fe now before us." On June 16, he accepted Walker's resignation and promoted Sgt. John Haley to the position.[75]

Sgt. Maj. John Haley was with the dragoons when the regiment invaded New Mexico and participated in the occupation of Santa Fe on August 18. When Kearny reduced his force to a small escort, he ordered Maj. Edwin Sumner, a group of other recently promoted officers, and the noncommissioned staff, headed by Haley, to return to Fort Leavenworth via Santa Fe. After a mule-killing, Indian-dodging, month-long adventure over the Cimarron route of the Santa Fe Trail, the group marched into Fort Leavenworth on November 20, 1846.[76] Haley immediately assisted with regimental records and with the training of dragoon recruits. He also helped train Missouri volunteers to prepared them for a march to New Mexico and, maybe, California.

On July 23, 1847, the Missouri volunteers elected the popular and competent Sergeant Major Haley to command their Company I of the 3rd Regiment of Mounted Missouri Volunteers. The *Missouri Republican* for July 23, 1847, described Haley as "a fine looking man, has always borne the best moral character, is intelligent and knows well the duties of a soldier: he would not only be an ornament but a very great advantage to the [Missouri] regiment."[77]

Alas, Haley was enlisted as a dragoon and would not be available during his term of enlistment. To secure a commission in the volunteers he had to secure permission from the departmental commanding officer. A correspondent for the *Missouri Republican* lamented: "[t]he company will leave in a few days, and he [Haley] will hardly have time to receive his discharge and join it, provided the Colonel sends it the moment he receives his application, but owing to the objections urged by the commanding officer here . . . in all probability colonel STANIFORD will not grant it, and he will thereby lose forever an opportunity to distinguish himself. . . . There should be no one in the army that *could not be spared*; it is true, this man (Haley) is very efficient, and the commanding officer would, no doubt, be put to considerable inconvenience with out him yet that should not debar him from a position which his very worth has won; he should on the contrary, be assisted in obtaining the reward he so justly merits"[78] (emphasis in original).

Company I of the 3rd Missouri was set to march within a few days. It was therefore necessary for Haley to secure a discharge from the Dragoons. Likely, it was Col. John Ralls of the 3rd Missouri who petitioned for Haley's discharge from Lt. Col. Thomas Staniford, commander of the 3rd Military Department, headquartered in St. Louis. Just the month before, Lieutenant Colonel Staniford had pirated Lt. Henry Stanton of the Dragoons to serve as his adjutant. Staniford then granted Captain Haley a discharge from the dragoons. Thus, Wharton came to lose the services of his prized aide.[79]

Confusion reigned at the undermanned dragoon headquarters. Most of the regiment's paperwork would have to wait until after the end of fighting.[80] When war with Mexico came there were to be manpower shortages. The October 1847 regimental return for headquarters of the 1st Dragoons at Fort Leavenworth consisted of Lieutenant Colonel Wharton, sixty-six-year-old Maj. Nathan Boone (sick and nearly blind), a quartermaster sergeant, principal musician, chief bugler, and seventeen privates—ten of them musicians in the band, three prisoners in confinement, and residing in the post hospital was poor bugler Robert Quigley, who had accidently wounded himself in the arm while returning from California with Kearny.

Assembling the Enlisted Corps

The new regiment was composed of ten companies, lettered A through L (there was no Company J, too easily confused with I in the florid script of the day). Each company was composed of seventy-two enlisted men, a captain and two lieutenants. Attached to most companies was a brevet (honorary) lieutenant—a recent graduate of the United States Military Academy and awaiting permanent assignment in the army.[81] In addition, every company would have a first or orderly sergeant, three other sergeants, four corporals, two buglers who also served as couriers, and a farrier-blacksmith to care for and shoe the horses.[82]

With the regiment created and funded, and its officers selected, it now came time to fill the ranks of enlisted personnel. The dragoon regiment was to be composed primarily of citizens, but recruiting Americans to serve in the peacetime military would not be easy. In the words of military historian Richard Winders, "Americans asked themselves why, in a land filled with an abundance of opportunities, any man willing would enter an undemocratic system where little chance of advancement existed. In the minds of some, men became soldiers only when they lacked the enterprise to do anything else."[83] Indeed, as seen in the case of poor Private Russell, recruiters deemed lies crucial to enlisting; they judged false advertising a crucial tool for enticing enlistees. Sergeants baselessly claimed that signers-on would rank with cadets at the U.S. Military Academy, have nothing to do but ride on horseback and explore prairies and forests, and would soon be well clothed and comfortably quartered.[84]

Typical of published advertising was an 1835 announcement (possibly furnished by the adjutant general or adapted from his general copy) purportedly authored by Dragoon Capt. Edwin V. Sumner. Its wording differs only slightly from that employed by Sergeant Tredway to deceive Russell and others, depicting the regiment "splendidly mounted and equipped" with "uniform and arms . . . of the most handsome and costly kind." Furthermore, the advertisement glorified and whitewashed its assignment "to protect the frontier by making an occasional display of force among the Indian tribes during the summer months, and in the fall and winter . . . [to stay] in comfortable barracks."[85]

Not surprisingly, such promises attracted a very fine class of man indeed. The *Buffalo Journal* described the dragoons as "the finest looking raw recruits we ever saw; all New Yorkers, selected by Capt. S. himself from the northern and western counties of the state, within the age of 25 years, and as nearly as possible 5 feet 8 inches in height. All possessing a good English education. Such youth, with such a commander, *who permits of no menial service from any member of his detachment,* and fares as they fare, cannot fail to prove useful and become an ornament to the service"[86] (authors' emphasis).

Capt. Nathan Boone, youngest son of the legendary frontiersman, aimed his sales pitch at Missouri lads in plainer fashion.[87] But 1st Lt. Philip St. George Cooke inflamed the imaginations of backwoods Tennessee youth with images of riding on "the far prairies on fine horses, amid buffalo and strange Indians; so much so, that they scarce listened to any discouraging particulars."[88] At Fort Wayne, Indiana, Capt. Lemuel Ford, a former Ranger, raised a company with the promise that by next summer the regiment would be out "on exploring expeditions to the Yellow Stone River and the Rocky Mountains."[89]

With such attractive depictions it proved relatively easy to gather some 750 men. The next step facing Dodge would be to fashion them into a fighting force. Jefferson Barracks, Missouri, seemed the obvious place to accomplish these tasks, so the army aimed to have all dragoon companies congregate there to be outfitted and prepared. On paper the plan appeared wise. Situated high on a scenic bluff on the west bank of the Mississippi south of St. Louis, the red-brick post, built in 1826, had been first commanded by none other than Capt. Stephen Kearny, 1st Infantry. From a number of directions, river steamers easily reached the base and made it a gateway to the West. By 1833, Jefferson Barracks boasted adequate housing, a spacious parade ground, and several warehouses.[90]

Yet problems materialized immediately. Since it was designated as a place to train infantry, the Army Quartermaster and Ordnance Departments had made no effort to build sufficient stables for the horses of a regiment of mounted soldiers, much less to send any horses, clothing, arms, and other equipment. Arriving from a number of directions, recruits—most dressed in their single suit of old civilian clothes—found no uniforms, gear, or mounts.[91] Within a few months of service, they gave the appearance of a ragtag battalion of beggars.[92] Colonel Dodge himself grew alarmed. Like most of the men, his superiors had led even him to believe that new uniforms, horses, and arms would await troops at Jefferson Barracks. On August 28, 1833, Dodge wrote to the adjutant general: "Permit me to call the attention of the General in Chief to the absolute necessity of ordering the clothing and arms intended for the use of the Dragoons. There are four companies at this post, and Capt. Sumner is daily expected with an additional company. The recruits are much in want of their clothing, and it is important we should have our arms, that the Dragoons may be drilled at target shooting, as well as to fire with precision on horseback."[93]

Most vital to the rapid training of recruits were its noncommissioned officers. Indeed, every regiment depended upon its cadre of noncommissioned officers; in the case of the dragoons, many of whom had been transferred there from artillery and infantry regiments.

Unfair treatment of veteran noncommissioned officers by the capricious Adj. Lt. Jefferson Davis contributed mightily to the plunging morale. Sergeant Parrott described Davis as one of the greatest tyrants ever: "He was a brilliant military man, of fine personal address, nearly six feet in height, affable towards his equals, but overbearing in disposition and inclined to show undue authority over his inferiors." Parrot emphasized that Davis had peremptorily removed a sergeant without cause. He also observed, in Dodge, a mixture of weakness and diplomacy when officers complained of Davis's habit of peremptorily removing sergeants: "Colonel, your adjutant has reduced my sergeant to the ranks without preferring charges." Dodge was conciliatory; this approach would expose him, at times, to the charge of weakness. Not wishing a confrontation with his punctilious adjutant, he would say: "Just let the thing rest quietly and I will give them new warrants in a few days." Dodge was as good as his word and eventually reinstated all of the reduced men.[94]

As competent as the noncommissioned officers were at drill-ing infantry, they and commissioned officers lacked experience instructing mounted troops since the army had never had a per-manent cavalry, and no officers, even those educated at West Point, had studied cavalry training and strategy. Only two outdated pub-lications from the War of 1812 covered the subject,[95] and not until 1834 did the army publish Winfield Scott's book, itself largely a translation of a French work on cavalry tactics.[96] Trooper Hildreth conjured up the risks occasioned by such instructors attempting to teach the recruits: "[A] newly recruited regiment, under march-ing orders to explore a wild and unknown region of country, per-haps to encounter superior numbers of an enemy whose lives have been devoted to the chase, and who are perhaps the most accom-plished horsemen in the world, with but about six months train-ing, and that under officers who know less of the maneuvers of a cavalry corps than some of the dragoons themselves."[97]

Charles Hoffman, who traveled around the frontier and wrote about westward expansion, echoed Hildreth's critique:

The omission of providing riding-masters and a school of practice for both horses and men is a defect that all the care and exertions of the accomplished and energetic officers of this corps can hardly remedy. The same pains should be taken with each individual here as in "setting up" an ordinary recruit before subjecting him to com-pany drill; and no private should be allowed to back the managed charger assigned to him before he has taken at least one regular course of lessons with the riding-master; nor should a single troop have been sent from the head quarters of the regiment before not only every squad was perfect in the drill, but every company in the regiment had maneuvered for months together. The omission of the necessary provisions in the bill reported by Congress, and the disposition of the regiment on the frontier as each company is recruited, almost forbids an approach to such a state of discipline.[98]

Recognizing his officers' unfamiliarity with cavalry training, Kearny specially recruited British-born Edward "Long Ned" Stanley, a former cavalry officer, and made him orderly sergeant in Company E to train the officers so that they could then drill the men in both mounted drill and saber. The sight of a lowly "sergeant instructing his superior officers in the very science with which, of all others, they should be most familiar" amused Hildreth: "It is rather a laughable fact, and one which reflects but little credit upon the accomplished graduates of West Point, that they should be compelled to receive instruction in swordsmanship from one of the enlisted members of the regiment." When Long Ned was not instructing the officers each afternoon, he assisted the regiment with the purchase of suitable horses. Lieutenant Colonel Kearny had recruited the imposing six-foot-four Sergeant Stanley with the understanding that he would seek for Stanley the position of either riding master or master of the sword. Congress, however, refused to create the special rank of master of the sword or riding master and in 1834, Kearny granted Stanley's request that he gain a discharge. We shall later read of Stanley's involvement in the Texas Revolution.[99]

Morale began to improve when horses and uniforms arrived at Jefferson Barracks in early October. The men were able to start mounted drill and officers had gained enough knowledge from Long Ned to teach tactics to the men. Hildreth reported that he was "drilled by Maj. Mason, and considering the many disadvantages under which we labored," he discovered that with "very little practice . . . we came off with credit."[100] Once horses arrived and after a few weeks of mounted drill, the powers in Washington felt confident that the regiment was prepared to move into the frontier.

Recruits were issued both wool and white cotton canvas fatigue uniforms. The short, dark blue woolen jackets were trimmed in yellow and had a high collar, and were generally worn on parade and patrol. Casual students of the antebellum army often ask why nineteenth-century soldiers stationed on the sweltering Great Plains consistently wore dark blue wool uniforms. Living in our age of lightweight, warm, and durable clothing, we can make no sense of it. Though lightweight uniforms of white cotton canvas were generally available for fatigue duty during the 1840s, commanders such as Cooke shunned them for troops on campaign. Wool was more expensive, but had the merit of being more lasting. True, cotton keeps one warm by trapping air heated by the body, but once it becomes wet it ceases to insulate because all of its minute air pockets fill with water. When the temperature cools at nightfall or in a windy rainstorm, a cotton-clad soldier fast becomes chilled and perhaps hypothermic and disoriented. In contrast, rather than retain water, wool wicks it away. Even modern-day backpackers know the maxim, "cotton kills."[101] But wool or not, a real downpour is none too comfortable for troops or animals.

"Proceed to Fort Gibson"

Secretary Cass was anxious to see the regiment's mission begin as soon as possible. No matter that two of the companies had yet to receive their horses, or that western Missouri and Arkansas were being overtaken by a bitter winter.[102] So, led by Colonel Dodge, five companies of the regiment paraded out of the post on November 23, 1833, on a 450-mile march to Fort Gibson.

Although the trek was exhausting and bitingly cold, Private Hildreth found the Arkansas scenery the prettiest he'd ever seen: "Mountains and valleys so richly thrown together; forests and prairies so beautifully interposed; the elm and sycamore towered high in the air; the ledges of broken rocks emitted forth their tiny torrents, which gently meandered on their course through the tangled foliage."[103]

On the third day of the march it snowed. Each successive morning brought weather more frigid. On December 15, 1833, troops riding across an extensive prairie neared Fort Gibson, situated in the bottom of a sinkhole, but could not see it until they got within a couple of hundred yards of it. In 1824 Col. Matthew Arbuckle had built the fort, named after Commissary Department head Col. George Gibson, on the east bank of the Grand River, located at the head of steam navigation.[104] The fort's setting on a fertile river bottomland was highly susceptible to flooding and, even worse, to unwholesome outbreaks of cholera, dysentery, and malaria. Only later would it be moved to higher ground.[105] Emerging out of the frozen fog, the shivering troops and animals looked forward to the fort's warm quarters, and quickened their pace.

The ramshackle wooded fort, compared with Jefferson Barracks, was hardly elegant, but would at least provide the regiment and its horses much-needed shelter from the winter—or so they thought. The garrison troops of the Seventh Infantry greeted the column of weary dragoons, but the army had not prepared quarters either for the elite corps or their animals, nor had it arranged rations or provender.[106] The bone-tired troops were compelled to settle into a camp of tents erected outside the fort.

Yet Dodge wrote to General Jones to defend the move: "I am still of the opinion that the move was a proper one and that the Dragoon horses will be better able to perform the contemplated march next season than if they had remained at Jefferson Barracks." He also wrote to superiors that he would have his troops build their own barracks and stables, and be "drilled both on foot and horseback, and [thus was] confident they will be prepared for any service required of them early in the spring." The dragoons' new post, located slightly more than a mile from Fort Gibson, was named Camp Jackson to honor "Old Hickory," the president.[107]

In contrast to Dodge's dogged defense of it, the men would be slow to forgive the dreadful trip. Hildreth neatly summed up their misery: "Truly I believe no dragoons of the command will ever forget the day of their arrival [at Fort Gibson]; weariness and extreme fatigue were depicted upon every countenance. . . . We would willingly have drained our pockets of the last copper for a morsel of bread. I never saw so many half-starved men together."[108]

A decade later, Captain Cooke criticized the hasty redeployment of the dragoons from Jefferson Barracks to Fort Gibson. To Cooke, there was no rational military motive behind the move; it solely served the political aim of pacifying a Congress hopelessly ignorant of the needed preparations. The army command, he railed, ordered the deployment of the regiment because "the corps having been raised for the defense of the frontier, would be disbanded if it remained inactive so far in the interior as Jefferson Barracks."[109]

Indeed, the change of stations worsened recruits' conditions. Private Russell, the hoodwinked dragoon from Tennessee unused to manual labor, suffered constant hunger, was nearly broke, dressed in rags and now, more than ever, wanted a discharge. He had written to his congressman—a friend of his late father— detailing his plight and that of his comrades:

> I have not been inured to hard labor, yet I have fatigue to undergo of which the stoutest complain and get some days a pint of wormy flour, sometimes a gill of Beans, & a little meat most irregularly issued to us & often not time enough allowed to cook & eat them. . . . The fact is this fatigue I undergo had already nearly broken my constitution & I feel that I cannot survive 3 yrs such life; The acquaintances & friends of my youth would weep to see the alteration that fatigue, privations & hard labor has made on me.[110]

Cruel winter conditions persisted into the new year. Some dragoons had been issued thick blue woolen overcoats before they left Jefferson Barracks; the less fortunate wrapped themselves in a government-issued blanket and their horse's saddle blanket, and huddled around bonfires set dangerously close to tents.[111] In harsh wind and cold, the troops worked furiously to build barnlike barracks to give themselves some shelter from the weather. More disheartening, a steamboat carrying the regiment's clothing, pistols, and sabers sank in late 1833; raising it from the muddy river bottom yielded nearly useless, soggy cargo that arrived at Camp Jackson the next February.[112]

Horses were also bereft of shelter and their meager supply of fodder soon ran out. The army's efforts to supply the woebegone animals were haphazard. Complaining on behalf of the previously corn-fed horses, Dodge wrote to the adjutant general from Camp Jackson on February 2, 1834: "The first week in January the weather became extremely cold, twelve degrees below zero. Grand River, about one hundred yards in width, was frozen six inches thick. The navigation of the river being stopped prevented the delivery of corn, and I was obliged to have the horses survive on sugar cane."[113]

The Dragoon Regiment Soldiers On

Winter finally passed and spring bedecked the land with the welcome beauty of flowers, foliage, and grass. The kind weather thawed Grand River and allowed steamboats loaded with precious food, forage, clothing, and weaponry to arrive at the fort. But with the fair weather, tensions steadily worsened between the men and officers, and desertions resumed.[114] Frictions, evident from the start between regular army and frontiersman officers, also began to damage the regiment's functioning. On April 18, 1834, Colonel Dodge, about to lead the regiment on its first mission, wrote to the adjutant general that two of his officers, regimental Adjutant Lieutenant Davis and Major Mason, were both subverting his power:

> I find more treachery and deception practiced in the army than I ever expected to find with a Body of Men who Call themselves Gentlemen[.] My Situation is unpleasant[.] [Jefferson] Davis who I appointed my adj[utan]t was among the first to take a stand against me[.] Major Mason and Davis are now two of my most inveterate enemies[.] The desire of these Gentlemen appears to be to Harass me in Small Matters. . . . [U]nless Harmony and good feeling exists in a Corps the public Service cannot be promoted and to undertake an Expedition with such men I should run the risk of Losing what Little reputation I have acquired.[115]

There were other sources of tension. While Dodge tended to eitheroverlook or delegate regimental matters, Kearny was a hands-on administrator, concerned with every detail of the regiment's weapons, saddles, musicians, training, and mission. The two disagreed even about the primary purpose for the regiment. For Dodge its purpose was solely to patrol the West and keep the plains tranquil. Kearny, the professional soldier, envisioned it not only as a peacekeeping force but as a mounted force-in-waiting, should war break out again with Europe. His dragoons were to serve as the "nucleus upon which a larger body of well-instructed Cavalry could readily & speedily be formed." In other words, an expandable army.[116]

In September of 1836, after he took command of the regiment, the punctilious Kearny complained in a letter to Gen. Alexander Macomb that "Col. D[odge] *never did, nor could* drill a Company or Squadron of Cavalry"[117] (emphasis in original). The constant abrasion between professional and frontiersman officers plagued the regiment during its first five years. Army headquarters was all too aware of the growing dissatisfaction among officers, as well as of complaints brewing among enlisted men. Brig. Gen. Henry Leavenworth issued an order on May 1, 1834, to be read to the troops. It expressed the general's understanding that in the wake of the bleak weather and indifference by the government to the needs of the troops, desertions had occurred, but promised, "as a friend to the soldiers," that they "will not occur again."[118] Trooper Hildreth observed that the reading of the order to the assembled companies brought a wry smile to the faces of many men; indeed, a few hours after its recital, four more men deserted. During the months of May and June, thirty-two men fled the dwindling ranks.[119]

Suffering awaited those caught for desertion or drinking. In a nation founded upon the Jeffersonian principles of liberty, justice, and equality, a European-style class system might seem out of place. But from the outset the army consisted of two very distinct social rungs: officers and enlisted men. In contrast to the volunteers and unlike most mid-1840s American institutions (other than slavery), the army was impermeably stratified. Each soldier had his place, rigidly determined by his rank. Commissioned officers, as a rule, thought themselves an aristocracy superior to those whom they commanded, and viewed the enlisted men as a servile force existing solely to ensure their status and execute their orders. In addition to this attitude, the entire structure of army laws and military courts enforced officers' authority and power.[120]

Unfairness often marred hearings against enlisted men: they were routinely denied the assistance of counsel; the triers of fact were officers; and the prosecuting judge advocate needed only a two-thirds majority to gain a guilty verdict. A contemporary soldier observed that courts martial of enlisted personnel were inherently biased, as most ofen the testimony of enlisted men was of little or no weight when given against an officer. Court-martial panels regularly deemed chronically drunk soldiers "worthless," ordered their heads shaven, and drummed them out of the regiment.[121] These courts sentenced those found guilty of drunkenness or disobedience to perform hard labor with a ball and chain attached to their ankles.[122]

Deserters fared worst. Former Dragoon James Hildreth in his book, authored anonymously, *Recollections of the United States Army,* wrote that the convicted deserter "was seized and bound to a triangle that stood upon the parade [ground], and the individual detailed for that purpose, commences with the rawhide. The prisoner receives the first ten lashes—not a groan is heard. Another man is ordered to take the scourge, and the gruff voice of the colonel is heard, '*[M]en, do your duty!*' [T]he flesh is seen to fall from his back in strips, the blood flows from his wound to the ground, the victim gasps, he has fainted, *he feels no more*"[123] (emphasis in original).

But even fear of such draconian punishment did not deter flight from the dragoons. It was only the coming chill of winter and removal to a distant post that would temporarily cure the desertion epidemic. But at least those dragoons who stayed no longer had to carry sticks in place of guns. During the winter, the army had scoured federal arsenals and managed to find several hundred condemned Harper's Ferry flintlock rifles, infantry-style leather cartridge boxes, and powder horns quietly reposing since the end of the War of 1812.[124] In early 1834, the Ordnance Department delivered 750 outdated pistols and an equal number of antiquated sabers,[125]—weapons that were, in the words of Lieutenant Cooke, "of a very rough, inferior quality."[126]

And then a miracle occurred. In the spring of 1834 the Ordnance Department delivered new Hall percussion-capped carbines to the troops. At the time, the .58 caliber smoothbore carbines were the very first breech-loading weapons widely issued to the troops of any nation. Prior to the end of the Mexican War nearly all firearms were loaded with a ramrod at the muzzle and primed with loose gunpowder placed under the flintlock hammer. This design required one to empty its contents of load and lead bullet, contained within a paper cartridge, down its muzzle by means of a long ramrod to secure the powder and ball deep down the barrel and into the breech. The flintlock then needed to be primed by pouring powder into the primer pan, and then the hammer was cocked, and only then could one fire—a clumsy, lengthy procedure nearly impossible to perform while mounted.

But "broken back" Halls were loaded though a raised breech-block receiver on a pivot. Pulling down on a lever raised the receiver and exposed the breech, enabling the soldier to manually position the powder and ball snugly. The soldier then snapped the receiver down so that it was aligned with the barrel. Igniting the charge did not employ an exposed flint and a pan of black powder as did most guns of the era, but rather a revolutionary primer ignition system using tiny brass percussion caps coated with mercury fulminate.[127] Breech-loading weapons such as the Hall gave a mounted soldier a decided advantage over a flintlock muzzle-loading foe, especially one attempting to load seated on a restive horse.

The 1833 version's barrel was 26 3/16 inches in length that was secured by two-barrel bands. It was furnished with a sliding, 25 1/4 inch-long bayonet. The bayonet was eliminated in 1840 versions of the carbine and the barrel reduced to 21 inches in length.[128]

Variants of the Hall carbine would serve as the dragoons' primary weapon for the next fifteen years,[129] but in 1834 the device was still untested in the field. Colonel Dodge thus left it to each company commander to decide whether to arm his men with the new Hall carbines or to retain traditional flintlocks. Two companies, those of Captains Boone and Bean, preferred the rifle and their companies H and K retained them for the coming campaign.[130]

Dragoons also packed a single-shot flintlock horse pistol in .54 caliber, secured inside the covered holster that hung from the pommels of their saddles. This foot-long weapon was wildly inaccurate, inspiring the only somewhat sarcastic advice that "it was never wise to choose for a mark anything smaller than a good sized barn." Like long-arm muzzleloaders, it was difficult to reload while mounted; worse, when fired pointblank, it endangered shooter as well as target.[131]

From the dragoon's white buff belt hung the Model 1833 saber. Troops complained that the thin leather belt, with its flimsy, unadorned brass buckle, broke readily once the soldier mounted. Patterned after the officer's version of the 1822 British Light Cavalry model and manufactured by the N. P. Ames Company of Chicopee, Massachusetts, the poorly designed saber was too light and would wrap "rubber-like around a man's head and was only good for cutting warm butter." In 1838, Inspector General George Croghan found many of their blades "entirely unserviceable."[132] The dragoon also carried on his person a leather cartridge box, a small pouch containing percussion caps (if armed with a Hall carbine), a haversack for rations, and a wooden canteen. Although the typical dragoon could now be considered a "moving arsenal and military depot," this weighty equipage posed considerable challenges to mounting, dismounting, and certainly fighting.[133]

Due to pressure emanating mainly from Congress to send the year-old regiment into the field, expeditions were scheduled to begin in the spring. The result of these demands would prove to be disasterous. True, on paper and from its well-armed and smartened-up appearance, the regiment looked ready to take to the field. But little time remained to drill the recruits in using the new weapons or to condition and nourish the horses for the marches to come. All too soon, the undermanned, badly supplied, and barely trained regiment of dragoons would undertake three separate forays to contact tribes and enforce federal hegemony over the plains.

CHAPTER 2

Dragoons on the Plains, 1834–1835

The First Expeditions

O' wild's the life that the Dragoon leads;
And a careless freedom marks his deeds;
And gay his Camp on Mountain stream
Where the White Man's foot was never seen.

From Capt. Rufus Ingalls, *Song of the Dragoon* (1854)

In the springtime, slumbering Camp Jackson threw off its blanket of snow to become a beehive of activity. Excitement sped preparations for the new regiment's first expeditions: laying in food and ammunition; fattening, shoeing, and conditioning the horses; oiling and polishing equipment and tack; hiring scouts and teamsters. By May, the camp was ready to welcome Companies F, G, and I, allowing the entire regiment to assemble for the grand expedition to the Pawnee villages. While Dodge waited for the tardy companies, he decided to send one of the present companies out on the Santa Fe Trail and a second to keep peace on the plains.

The First Mission: Wharton's Escort

The dragoon regiment's initial assignment called for Captain Wharton's Company A to escort a wagon train on the Santa Fe Trail as far as the Mexican border. The task was significant as it was the first military company on that route since the ill-fated 1829 infantry expedition, when well-mounted tribal raiders of the plains ran rings around the foot soldiers. Recalling that disaster, the army command acknowledged in its orders the possibility of combat: "[S]hould Captain Wharton meet the hostile Indians in battle, he will charge them, if possible to do so, as the best possible plan of defeating them."[1] In reality, little danger of hostilities loomed, for the Comanches and Kiowas were not then at war with wagons plying the Santa Fe Trail.[2]

The fifty men of Company A trotted out from Camp Jackson on the thirteenth of May, led by Wharton, son of a wealthy Pennsylvania family and, in a colleague's words, "one of the most elegant men and soldier-like officers of the army, who has won as a disciplinarian a high reputation in the service."[3] Most of the soldiers rejoiced at escaping dreary and laborious garrison life, including Private Russell, the dupe of his recruiting sergeant, who was completing his three-year term purely out of his sense of duty.

At the Cottonwood crossing, Wharton's dragoons met the wagon caravan captained by Josiah Gregg. On the eighteenth, as the wagons halted at Walnut Creek, Kanza hunters amicably approached the traders' camp. Captain Wharton wished to hold council with them and was irritated at having to subdue certain "irresponsible persons" of the caravan who preferred to attack any Kanza hunters attempting to enter the camp. Wharton realized that the presence of rough-hewn civilians would impair negotiations with the tribes, and drew the Natives aside: "Having shaken hands with these Indians I conducted them, from a regard to the view of the traders who objected to their approaching the Caravan, to a spot at some distance from the wagons and there had a talk with them."[4] Wharton concluded that the dragoons could peacefully deal with what most whites condidered to be primitive and dangerous savages. The circumstance proved to be an early example of what would pertain throughout much of the regiment's twenty-eight-year existence: settler aggression toward tribesmen jeopardizing dragoon efforts to maintain tranquility.

With his opportunity for peaceful conference frustrated by the teamsters, Wharton had little choice but to proceed as an escort. The wagons and soldiers resumed their march, and as they approached the Arkansas River a party of about a hundred Comanche hunters appeared on the horizon. Wharton immediately formed his troop into line, preparatory, if necessary, to a charge: "[W]e were on the very eve of a fight, both parties having formed the line, and the word of command 'charge,' being on my very tongue's end, when the Indians fired their guns in the air, some dismounted from their horses, and others threw their bows and arrows on the ground, while they begged for peace, and assured us of their friendship."[5]

Other chances to discuss peaceably would arise, and again the teamsters would scotch them. As Wharton was walking to a planned council, he learned that some in the caravan were moving a cannon toward the Comanches' camp, intent on firing it. An officer who tried to restrain them "received in reply much personal abuse with even threats of personal violence." Then Wagon Master Gregg took it upon himself to approach the Comanche peace delegation and advise them to leave, claiming that the soldiers would attack them. Later in the day some of the traders waved a flag to lure the Comanches back to the council, scheming to fire their cannon at them once in range.[6]

Wharton called General Leavenworth's attention to

the difficulty of preserving harmony between a military escort and a set of irresponsible individuals such as those who were concerned in the measure alluded to. . . . I had entertained strong hopes of effecting much good at the meeting. . . . [While it] is true I had no special authority to hold a council with, or to make overtures or promises to, the Indian tribes whom I might meet on the march, I conceived, however, it would not be transcending my duty on all proper occasions to endeavor to impress the minds of the Indians that they should be at peace with each other. In furtherance of this opinion it was my intention to have said to the Comanches, that our people and theirs have little acquaintance with each other, that we have heard of them, however, and desire to be their friends if they would act in such a manner towards our people as to justify our friendship. . . . I thought the occasion a most fortunate and opportune one, to promote what I conceive to be the views of the Government in the case, and to serve the cause of humanity. . . . But the opportunity to make these statements I lost.[7]

With yet another prospect of parley with the tribe spoiled, the dragoons dutifully followed the wagons across the Arkansas and into Mexico. On the twenty-eighth of June, at the crossing of the Cimarron, Wharton's dragoons turned back toward Fort Gibson.[8] Confronted on this return trip by a large Pawnee band, the cautious Wharton, trained in the Cromwellian notion of trusting in God but keeping one's powder dry, again prepared for battle but, now unencumbered by belligerent teamsters, succeeded at holding a conference: "[T]he Indians ran up and offered their hands—we had a council, and smoked the pipe of peace with them."

Despite accomplishing their escort assignment and minor ambassadorial successes, the company's sixty-eight days away from barracks had brought discomfort, hunger, and other privations, as well as diplomatic frustrations. In Wharton's words, written in a letter to a friend, "we 'bold dragoons' have not an easy time of it."[9] When Wagon Master Gregg asked for another dragoon escort in 1839, the army, claiming its troops were committed elsewhere, declined his request.[10]

Sumner's Diplomatic Mission

The dragoon regiment's next task came soon after the departure of Captain Wharton's company, when Captain Sumner, commanding Company B, took his men into the land of the Osage tribe in present-day Kansas to quell a heated disturbance between that tribe and some of its Kiowa neighbors. Before the arrival of the whites the once-powerful Osages had inhabited an ancestral homeland along the Ohio River in Kentucky, but they gradually moved west of the Mississippi River to dominate the region between the Missouri and Red Rivers, almost constantly at war with other tribes and later attacking white explorers and settlers who were moving into their region.[11] The succeeding years found the tribe's fortunes in decline.

By 1834 the U.S. government had moved them off their soil for eventual resettlement forty miles west of Fort Gibson. Prior to their exile, contact with whites brought waves of smallpox and reduced tribal population from 6,200 to about 5,200. Yet in 1834, the artist George Catlin described the Osages as "the tallest race of men in North America, either red or white skins; there being few indeed of the men at their full growth, who are less than six feet in stature, and very many of them six and a half, and others seven feet." He observed that they still preserved "their valor as warriors, which they are continually shewing [*sic*] off as bravely and professionally as they can."[12]

Despite Osage pride and bravado, Sumner skillfully acquitted his role as peacemaker and resolved the unrest. He then returned to Camp Jackson in time to join Colonel Dodge's expedition to visit the Pawnees.[13] On May 26, 1834, Capt.Eustace "Pat" Trenor's Company F, whose men hailed from Boston, trotted into camp at last, followed by Capt. Lemuel Ford's Company G, composed of Indiana men.[14] Capt. Jesse Browne's Company I, with recruits from Maryland, did not arrive until the second of June.[15] With the addition of the final three companies the regiment could at last conduct its large-scale tour of the plains, though much later in the season than intended.

The Grand Expedition

Dodge prepared to take the bulk of the regiment on a first major venture. The camp continued to bustle with blacksmiths, tailors, herders, and saddlers in "constant employment, and in fact no one has time to be idle."[16] Although the regiment was now nearly at full strength, it was ill-prepared to embark on an arduous frontier campaign. Trooper James Hildreth, suffering from an unknown physical disability, had secured a surgeon's discharge on June 1and would not depart with the regiment,[17] but his brother and correspondent William, who joined the regiment's Company C in March of 1834, would supply valuable material for James's first book on the dragoons.[18]

James continued to fret over the regiment's poor training— only six months of drilling "under officers who know less of the maneuvers of a cavalry corps than some of the dragoons themselves."[19] Lt.Philip St. George Cooke shared Hildreth's view, later warning in a June 11, 1835, letter to Gen. Alexander Macomb that the regiment was being "hurried off . . . quite unprepared for an expedition" and specifying that recruits in Companies C and G were too ill-trained "for an extraordinary march . . . over a desert."[20] Worse, the delay of the mission until the last three companies arrived from Jefferson Barracks would expose the untried troops to blistering heat, and would later earn Cooke's most stinging critique.[21]

Nine companies, nearly five hundred sabres strong and with Colonel Dodge in command, at last left Camp Jackson on the fifteenth of June to begin the campaign to the Pawnee village some 250 miles away at the Red River headwaters.[22] Dodge's instructions were to show Native peoples the power of the federal government; to persuade the Comanches, Wichitas, and Pawnees to respect the rights of tens of thousands of eastern Indians whom that government had relocated onto the plains; and to impress on them the rights of an ever-increasing number of white traders crossing the region. Finally, Dodge was also to find and—if they were alive—secure the release of the captured minor Matthew Wright Martin and Mounted Ranger George B. Abby, of Nathan Boone's company.[23] *Niles' Weekly Register* summarized the mission colorfully: "[T]o give the wild Indians some idea of our power, and . . . to warn those Indians who have been in the habit of robbing and murdering our people who trade among them, of the dangers to which they will be exposed in case they continue their depredations and massacres."[24]

The grand cavalcade in Dodge's column included scouts and delegates from the Cherokee, Delaware, Seneca, and Osage nations, as well as two women, a Kiowa and a Pawnee, who had been abducted by Osages and were to be returned to their families by Dodge as a token of peace. Rounding out the civilian presence were the artist George Catlin and the prominent German botanist Heinrich Karl Beyrich.[25]

Even for an expedition bringing along a scientist and artist, the journey would be no parade. Many of the troops already carried deadly diseases, likely cholera and mosquito-borne malaria contracted at their base camp.[26] Heat stroke and dehydration debilitated the column as the late march met a fast-approaching summer with 105° days. Many troops, raised in cool coastal climes, were miserably unused to the temperatures facing them for the next two months. After the first day's march, artist George Catlin wrote that "ten to fifteen [of the men] were sent back on the first day, too sick to proceed."[27]

In spite of illness and discomfort the column marched on, covering terrain which, while parched, struck many as just what their recruiters had described: a wondrous, burning sea of gold. On the twenty-fifth, with Colonel Dodge, his staff, twenty dragoons, and guides riding in advance, the column rendezvoused with General Leavenworth and his two infantry companies bivouacked at Camp Osage near the Canadian River.[28] General Leavenworth indicated his intention to take command from Dodge. It was at this camp that Dodge ordered twenty-seven soldiers with varied ailments to be left there under the care of fifty-two fit men. Among those too ill to proceed was a distraught Lieutenant Cooke.[29]

After a brief pause the expedition, now under the leadership of General Leavenworth, crossed the Canadian River. The troops rode with relative ease for thirty-two miles through land enriched with an abundance of small waterways. On June 27, Leavenworth, though in poor health, hunted buffalo with Catlin, Dodge, and Lt. T. B. Wheelock. During the hunt the general was thrown from his horse and injured,[30] but let it be known in no uncertain terms that he intended to retain command and would rejoin the troops upon healing.[31] On the march again, as the column began to near the Washita, scouts searching for a crossing spotted, in the distance, a party of Pawnees.

Catlin sensed a lust for retribution among many of the hot-blooded junior officers, over various recent acts by Plains Indians. A nine-year-old Texas boy, Matthew Martin, reportedly was being held hostage after natives had slain and mutilated his father, as well as holding a slave brought along on the Martins' hunting trip. Colonel Dodge managed to cool passions.[32] When the regiment reached the broad Washita River and set up camp along its banks, the surgeon declared that rapid marching in the heat had sickened another forty-five men and three officers. The heat was also taking its toll on seventy-five horses and mules. But even as the troops rested in the shade, preparations were initaited to ferry the command across the river.[33]

The ferrying across the Washita began on the Fourth of July. General Leavenworth continued to suffer a raging fever and was forced to relinquish temporary command of the expedition to Colonel Dodge.[34] As so many were too ill from the effects of heat, malaria, and dysentery to march, Dodge decided to rest and to reorganize the column at the riverside. Finding it best not to encumber the expedition with the infirm and with wagons, he ordered that these remain behind and that troops of Companies G and K be distributed among six remaining companies. At a site now designated Camp Leavenworth, the general, his escort, and Company F remained: two hundred and ten able men and ninety sick ones. Lieutenant Colonel Kearny would command this encampment,[35] and it was here that Dodge appointed William Bowman as sergeant major. Bowman had begun his military career as a lieutenant with the 21st Infantry during the War of 1812, received an honorable discharge at its end, and returned to civilian life. In 1833, he enlisted as a private in the Regiment of Dragoons and quickly rose to the rank of sergeant in Company D.[36]

Those deemed fit to continue eagerly anticipated the adventures before them. Wrote Sgt. Hugh Evans, "We mounted our horses with enthusiasm and apparent prospect of acquiring fame." With 258 of his healthiest men and freed of baggage wagons, Dodge continued steadily west over the seared landscape toward the Pawnee villages. As he drew closer to them, he began to worry about the possibility of an armed conflict, and ordered each man to carry eighty rounds of cartridges—twice the number ordinarily carried by a trooper while on patrol.[37]

On July 10, a welcome rainstorm cooled things. But leaving flat terrain and entering the region of the Cross Timbers, in present-day central Oklahoma, complicated the traverse. The dense, thorny thicket functioned as an informal boundary between the Plains Indians and their newly settled eastern neighbors. Wagon Master Josiah Gregg described the Cross Timbers as

> entirely cut[ting] off the communication betwixt the interior prairies and those of the great plains. They may be considered as the "fringe" of the great prairies, being a continuous brushy strip, composed of various kinds of undergrowth; such as black-jacks, post-oaks, and in some places hickory, elm, etc., intermixed with a very diminutive dwarf oak, called by the hunters "shin-oak." Most of the timber appears to be kept small by the continual inroads of the "burning prairies;" for, being killed almost annually, it is constantly replaced by scions of undergrowth; so that it becomes more and more dense every reproduction.[38]

From here it is difficult to discern the exact route traveled by Dodge. We do know that he entered into a land "lying between the Red and Canadian Rivers as far west as probably longitude 100 [degrees] 30' some seventy miles west of the Witichita [*sic*] Mountains."[39] Marching in three columns, the six companies slowly sidled their way through brambles. Emerging, they reached the edge of the Great Plains and for the first time viewed their vastness.[40] Coursing streams were nearly naked of trees, "with occasional sparsely set groves of cottonwood in the nooks and bends. . . . In fact, there is scarce anything else but cottonwood, and that very sparsely scattered."[41]

As the men traveled west, they continued to observe distant Pawnee and Comanche hunting parties that fled with the troops' approach. On the fourteenth of July the dragoons espied some forty mounted Comanches. Fearing an engagement, Dodge ordered the troops to form a battle line, with carbines at the ready. The Comanches slowly retreated though they were "armed with bows, well filled quivers, spears, knives and shields, and appeared to be accomplished and daring horsemen."[42]

Dodge did not wish or seek a confrontation. He halted the command, raised a white flag, and with a few of his staff and scouts, rode forward. Sergeant Parrott wrote, "'Twas a moment of anxiety and interest; on this evidently depended the issue of the expedition. Every voice was still and even the horses seemed instinctively to maintain order & silence."[43] Artist Catlin gave this vivid account of what happened next.

> The Indians stood their ground until we had come within half a mile of them, and could distinctly observe all their numbers and movements. We then came to a halt, and the white flag was sent a little in advance, and waved as a signal for them to approach; at which one of their party galloped out in advance of the war-party, on a milk white horse, carrying a piece of white buffalo skin on the point of his long lance in reply to our flag. . . . This moment was the commencement of one of the most thrilling and beautiful scenes I ever witnessed. All eyes, both from his own party and ours, were fixed upon the manoeuvres of this gallant

little fellow, and he well knew it. . . . He at length came prancing and leaping along till he met the flag of the regiment, when he leaned his spear for a moment against it, looking the bearer full in the face, when he wheeled his horse, and dashed up to Col. Dodge with his extended hand, which was instantly grasped and shaken."[44]

Sergeant Evans noted the warrior proved to be "a daring and resolute Spaniard (who had been taken prisoner by them when very young and adopted their customs) [and] approached us without fear." The warrior's peaceful gesture broke any tension. Hildreth's correspondent wrote, "The hand of friendship was cordially proffered on our part and accepted." Dragoons and hunters dismounted, and "the pipe was lit and passed around."[45]

Several Comanche hunters spoke Spanish and so could communicate with a Mexican guide.[46] Through them, Dodge informed the hunters that he had come to bring peace to the region, and accepted the Comanches' invitation to their camp. The camp was located in a senic valley that was described by Sergeant Evans: "a beautiful sight of the Comanche village looking like a great meadow with the small cocks of hay scattered promiscously over it; when on the hight [sic] of this eminence the beauties in looking down on the valley was truely [sic] grand and romantic."[47]

While the entire command rested and traded with the Comanches, artist Catlin busily sketched and painted portraits of the Plains people and their village, composed of two hundred conical lodges made from buffalo skin. After three days, though, Catlin and twenty-four men discovered themselves too ill to proceed. Dodge left them to be tended by their Comanche hosts and a small detachment of dragoons commanded by Lt. J. F. Izard.[48]

With the aid of a Pawnee guide the dragoons, now reduced to 183 men, led their horses through the rocky ridges of the Wichita Range. The country became "very broken and uneven, of granite rock. . . . [T]he mountains rose to an immense height, and the passes leading to the village through them were difficult to find, long and narrow, and would have been a dangerous road had the

Indians contested passage with the soldiers." Fearing an attack by the Pawnees at night, the troops fixed their sliding bayonets and "every preparation [was] made for a conflict."[49]

The trip through the "excessive rugged rock country" on exhausted and lame horses might have been difficult, but an unidentified soldier wrote that he found the attendant sights as inspiring as those of the Alps: "Here the gradual swell, the beetling precipice, the castellated battlement, the solitary tower, the glittering, roaring cascade, the shady vale and opening vista, disclosing in turn distant views of new grandeur—all, all the rich combinations of mountain scenery are here thrown together, forming an unrivaled whole." The writer predicted that "in years to come" these wondrous mountains "will be the goal of all travellers on earth."[50]

On July 20 the dragoons sighted the Pawnee village. But the gravely ill General Leavenworth, try as he might, would not live to view it: while valiantly attempting to follow Dodge, he died near the Cross Timbers on the twenty-first.[51] That same day, the reduced troops formed three columns and made their grand entry into the Pawnee village "with all [the] military pomp and splendor" that their impoverished "circumstances would permit." Indeed, the unidentified trooper correspondent wrote that the men's arrival at the village "was timely" as they were quite out of rations.[52]

Surrounded by two hundred acres of well-cultivated corn, the Pawnee village consisted of "two hundred lodges, in shape somewhat resembling a cone, generally about thirty feet in diameter, and from twenty-five to thirty feet high. They were formed with polls [sic] planted firmly in the ground, fastened at the top, and thatched over with prairie grass."[53] Sergeant Evans observed: "They had plenty of corn . . . pumpkins, [s]quashes, wáter, and muskmelons, together with dried buffalo and horse meat. For supplies of these articles we gave them tobacco, tin cups, buttons, the yellow stripes from our pantaloons &c, but when we offered them money, they laughed at us, for these unsophisticated beings knew not its value."[54]

The tribesmen offered the troops much food and much friendly curiosity. Evans continued: "They all appeared remarkable for their friendship and kindness particularly the squaws who appeared to admire the appearance of the Dragoons verry [*sic*] much more particularly those who have large whiskers & heavey [*sic*] beards; They perhaps never before have seen the face of a white man."[55]

After the troops secured much-needed provisions Colonel Dodge held a grand council with leaders of the Comanche, Wichita, Pawnee, and Kiowa tribes. Using his best diplomatic skills to underscore the need for all four tribes to maintain peace with the newly relocated Cherokee, Delaware, and Choctaw peoples, Dodge spoke: "We meet you as friends, not as enemies, to make peace with you, to shake hands with you."[56]

Then, turning to a delicate matter, the colonel inquired if any of the assembled tribesmen knew the whereabouts of Ranger George Abby and of the missing boy, Matthew Martin. Pawnee Chief We-ter-ra-dhah-ro indicated that Abby had been killed by a band of Comanches near Red River during the previous summer, and that his tribe had young Matthew Martin in their custody but hesitated to release the boy. Colonel Dodge told the Pawnee leader that there could be no further council until the Martin boy was released. As unease grew between the Pawnees and Dodge, troops "stood by their arms in readiness."[57] The chief, to demonstrate his desire for peace, then ordered the boy and an unidentified slave belonging to the Martin family released from captivity.[58]

Disquiet was renewed, though from another source, when a menacing group of armed Comanche and Kiowa warriors brazenly rode into the village. But a calm and collected Dodge courageously met the challenge. He stepped forward to greet the warriors warmly, and presented to them the Kiowa woman recently captured by the Osages, who told her people of the kindness shown her by the white men. Many of the Kiowas, hearing her words and seeing their tribeswoman returned to them, shed tears of gratitude and embraced Colonel Dodge for his humanity,[59] and one Kiowa chief wept and hugged Dodge for several minutes.

The dragoons were unmistakably moved by their commander's skills. An unidentified officer wrote to a colleague, "The excellent management of Colonel Dodge upon this occasion superseded the necessity and terminated the affair honorably to himself and his command."[60] Dodge might have been, as Private Hildreth once complained, a merely competent military man, but proved himself among the ablest diplomats ever to have negotiated with tribes. (Years later, Dodge's son, Henry, Jr., would display similar tact as a popular agent for the Navajo tribe.) Following Dodge's speech, gifts were exchanged and the council ended. Colonel Dodge proudly reported his having accomplished the expedition's main purposes and his readiness to bring his men back to quarters. Twenty tribesmen guided the homeward-bound troops to a more level route through the hills than the perilous one by which they had come.[61]

Mother Nature seemed to manifest her blessing on Dodge's undertaking. On the first day of the return trip "a delightful shower of rain fell, for which we had long and anxiously waited," and the week's march covered more than one hundred miles. Throughout the journey back Dodge stopped at various encampments where he had left sick troops to pick up survivors and their attendants.[62] Though now very ill, Catlin had filled his sketchbook and canvasses with dozens of detailed images of tribesmen, scenes, and events he had captured during the journey, and couldn't wait to share them with the public. And just as rations ran dangerously low and game hid from the oppressive heat, Nature seemed again to intercede when the scouts discovered a large herd of buffalo. The troops cheered as they made camp while parties hunted much-needed meat. Despite the return of hot weather, morale began to climb.[63]

Still, travel was grinding on the infirm.[64] Sergeant Evans commented, "Not having anything comfortable for the sick either in their transportation or anything comfortable for them to eat consequently they must of course dwindle and become weaker and much less able to endure the hardships of the prairie."[65] Catlin, who had caught malaria, was among the fortunate few who gained passage home in a wagon, and observed, "Many are now sick and unable to ride, and are carried on litters between two horses.

Nearly every tent belonging to the officers has been converted to hospitals for the sick; and sighs and groaning are heard in all directions."[66]

Now in late summer, the punishing prairie exposed the column, as it crossed back over the Washita on July 30, to the "hot and burning rays of the sun, without a cloud to relieve its intensity, or a bush to shade us, or anything to cast a shadow, except the bodies of our horses."[67] Lieutenant Wheelock chronicled the climate's effect on the men: "[T]he breeze comes against the face and hands with an unpleasant heat, so that one turns from it as from keen blasts of winter; water scarce and in pools; our men present a sorry figure; but one that looks like service; many of them literally half naked."[68] But with fresh meat every day, blessedly cooler breezes every night, and Fort Gibson neared with every step, the men reached inside for one last measure of fortitude. Most of the horses, however, suffered pitifully from unrelenting heat, hunger, and thirst; to save them from collapsing Dodge ordered healthy dragoons to walk beside their mounts every other hour.

From August second through the fifth, Dodge rested his exhausted command.[69] But back to marching on the sixth, Lieutenant Wheelock reported an "exceedingly warm" day and that the column had "passed many creeks[,] the beds of which were entirely dry; our horses looked up and down their parched surfaces and the men gazed in vain at the willows ahead, which proved to mark only where water had been."[70] On that same date Dodge wrote Lieutenant Colonel Kearny, in command of the invalid camp on the Washita, telling of his plight:

> I have on my sick list report 56 men, four of whom have to be carried in litters. My horses are all much jaded and would be unable to return by the route of the Washita and reach their point of destination this September season. This has been a hard campaign on all (we have been for the last 15 days living almost on meat alone). The state of the health of this detachment of the Regt. makes it absolutely necessary that I should arrive at Fort Gibson as

carly as possible as well as the difficulty of providing grain for the horses. I am well aware you are placed in a most unpleasant situation encumbered as you must be with sick men, baggage & horses, and regret exceedingly that it is not in my power to assist you.[71]

Two days later the expedition, having fought its way back through the Cross Timbers forest, reached the banks of the Canadian River. Here Dodge set camp and drew provisions from the infantry detachment stationed there. Pork and flour recouped the men's spirits, but riding stock were nearly all in poor shape. Wheelock lamented: "[I]t would be difficult to select ten horses in good order."[72]

Dodge's footsore and ragged troops proceeded slowly toward Fort Gibson for another week, gathering convalescing soldiers left behind on the westward march. On August 14, the threadbare, sick, starving, and worn dragoons approached the fort and camped on a high hill overlooking it. Ten days later, Kearny's collection of patients and caretakers stumbled in to join them.[73] But shelter did not bring the hoped-for recovery from malaria, dysentery, and extreme exhaustion for all the men. Sergeant Evans reported: "[T]here was a great number of sick. Our pale haggered [sic] and sallow complection [sic] and ragged appearance too plainly showed we had been on a long and hazardious [sic] Campaign."[74]

From his hospital bed in a room shared with Captain Wharton, likely suffering from an ailment he may have picked up on his expedition of the Santa Fe Trail, Catlin recorded that the unwell staggered into the fort by the dozens and were dying at the rate of two or three a day.[75] He found it deeply depressing "to hear the mournful sound of 'Roslin Castle' with muffled drums, passing six to eight times a day under my window, to the burying ground, which is but a short distance in front of my room."[76] Nearby, the botanist Beyrich was quietly and bravely dying. As soon as Catlin could walk and stomach some food, "against the advise [sic] of my surgeon and all officers of the garrison," he readied his horse.

Climbing into the saddle, pistols in his belt and precious sketch-book slung across his back, Catlin escaped "from the gloom and horrors of a sick bed astride his strong and trembling horse, carrying him fast and safely over green fields spotted and tinted with waving wild flowers . . . to his wife and little ones."[77]

On August 30, Maj. Richard Mason advised the army that sixty-two of the 156 men in his squadron were incapacitated; Dodge granted him permission to move Companies E, F, and K to a more healthful site twenty miles west of Fort Gibson.[78] And in early September Colonel Dodge sent an officer to return nine-year-old Matthew Martin to his mother in Louisiana. Respecting the property rights of slave owners in the era, he also returned her recaptured slave.[79]

Such housekeeping accomplished, no troops fit enough to march were allowed to linger long at Fort Gibson or Camp Jackson. On September 3, 1834, Dodge divided the dragoons into three squadrons: one under Major Mason would remain camped outside Fort Gibson, another group commanded by Dodge himself would go to Fort Leavenworth, and a third would follow Lieutenant Colonel Kearny to build a new fort in Iowa Territory. "Thus, in three distant positions," Lieutenant Cooke sarcastically observed, "the squadrons of the ill-treated regiment found some leisure to invent and practice as many different systems of tactics and duty."[80]

Lieutenant Colonel Kearny was to take companies B, H, and I to Fort Leavenworth before proceeding north to Camp Des Moines in Iowa Territory. An uneventful march brought them to the fort, and their hearts "lept [*sic*] with joy" when they discovered they were to be provided with comfortable quarters.[81] After a brief pause they set out on another march, arriving in Iowa Territory on the twenty-fifth of September.

Dodge's placement of the regiment's three divisions along the Mississippi Valley would remain up through the Mexican War. But two of these initial posts proved unsatisfactory. Similar to the experience faced the previous year at unhealthy Fort Gibson, the squalid condition of Camp Des Moines bitterly disappointed

Kearny's men, and Kearny was quick to complain to the adjutant general. As an anonymous soldier wrote, "[N]ot a log is yet laid for stables for our horses. We shall on the 28th go to work with all our disposable force, and I hope by the close of next month we may complete the buildings, tho' they will be less comfortable and of meaner appearance, than those occupied by any other portion of the Army."[82]

Colonel Dodge's plan for the permanent stationing of elements of his regiment might have been sound, but he took the primary blame for what he perceived as the disasterous expedition to the Pawnee Village. Writing to the adjutant general on October 1, 1834, Dodge admitted that the expedition to the Pawnee village had failed: "Perhaps there never has been in America a campaign that operated more Severely on Men & Horses. . . . I marched from Fort Gibson with 500 Men and when I reached the Pawnee Pict Village I had not more than 190 Men fit for duty. . . . I was [obliged] to Carry Some of my Men in Litters for Several Hundred Miles."[83] Unlike later failures of the regiment, this blunder occasioned no cover-up. The criminal neglect of the War Department and the resulting loss of lives was widely reported and condemned in language markedly acerbic for the era. The editor of the influential *Niles' Weekly Register* spoke for many when he argued for disbanding the regiment:

> [A]fter the expenditure of an immense sum of money—after the loss of an hundred men, and some of the most promising officers in the service—it must be evident, that this regiment has failed in all the essential purposes for which it was created, and ought to be disbanded, or merged into the equally effective ranks of the infantry. . . . [T]he dragoons returned to Fort Gibson, worn out and exhausted—seventy-five of them to die. They are now in winter quarters. Men will have to be recruited—new horses to be procured—and new service to be seen, before they can be rendered effective. Are the advantages they have conferred, or may render, at all commensurate to the waste

of life, the untold sufferings, the immense expenditure of money, which has attended, and must follow in keeping of this regiment in service? We humbly think not.[84]

The *Niles' Weekly Register* included another letter critical of the dragoon regiment, later reprinted in New York's *Evening Star*, which reported that the news

> from camp Des Moines, where three of the companies belonging to this ill fated regiment are stationed, mentions the death of assistant surgeon Hales, and also second lieutenant Vanderveer, both of which officers stood high in the estimation of all who knew them. It also states that the report of the three companies stands at that date, December 9, 89 present and 43 absent since the organization of this regiment, not yet two years since. The deaths among the officers in comparison has not fallen short of the mortality among the soldiers—1 general, 2 captains, 1 doctor, and 4 lieutenants, have died. Considering the little that could have been anticipated, and less that has been achieved, the expense of so many valuable lives and so large an amount of property, has been but of small avail.[85]

All in all, nearly one hundred dragoons, including a general, six other officers, and a physician, had died from diseases during, on, or shortly after the 1834 expedition. More than one hundred horses had been lost to or irreparably damaged by excessive heat and lack of forage.[86] The unit retained but 340 recruits who either longed to explore more of the American West, feared risking desertion, or desperately needed a job.[87] Cooke, with remarkable outspokenness, later summed up his frustration with the army's senseless dispatch of an unready regiment onto the unforgiving Great Plains: "It is painful to dwell on this subject. Nature would seem to have conspired with an imbecile military administration for the destruction of the regiment."[88]

Despite his primary acceptance of fault for the campaign's crushing human costs, Dodge believed it had built a meaningful peace based on continuing, respectful dialogue between whites and Natives and between Plains and exiled eastern tribes. On arriving at Fort Gibson, he sent runners to a number of regional tribes to invite their delegates to confer at the fort on the first of September.[89]

An anonymous junior officer, though, saw Dodge's performance from a different perspective. Viewing the Pawnees and Comanches as wily, dangerous, and perverse opponents, and entirely overlooking their notable generosity toward the dragoons, he extolled "Colonel Dodge, who displayed a degree of perseverance in marching us without food in an enemy's country to their very villages, and obtaining from them a supply of provisions to last us to the buffalo country, forming with them treaties of peace and friendship, and obtaining from them one of our people, whom they had in bondage, and supporting that part of his regiment which was under his command without any provisions from the Government for near sixty days, and that too in an enemy's country, upon their own resources and hunters."[90]

Of course, the glowing approbation earned from various members of Congress and especially from its primary sponsor, Secretary of War Cass, proved more instrumental to the regiment's continued funding than did any private opinion. Pleased with Dodge's command and his accomplishment of the fundamental task, Cass reported that the dragoons "performed their duties in the most satisfactory manner, and they encountered with firmness the privations incident to the harassing service upon which they were ordered."[91]

Yet even such praise and recognition of sacrifice did not remedy the War Department's continued neglect of the dragoon regiment. As late as October 10, 1834, Major Mason complained to General Jessup of the quartermaster's unreasonable delay in issuing clothing to his squadron: "Two of the Dragoon companies now here [at Fort Gibson] are almost naked; they left Jefferson Barracks last spring and have had no clothing since, the unissued clothing of those companies left at that place have not yet reached this [place]. Many of the men have their bare feet on the ground, without even a moccasin to cover them & are wearing buckskin leggings for want of pantaloons."[92]

In the opinion of historian Grant Foreman, the September 2, 1834, council arranged by Colonel Dodge at Fort Gibson "was probably the most important Indian conference ever held in the Southwest."[93] But George Catlin proved prescient in his fears that the conference would result in the unrestrained entry by white traders into Comanche land, and would bring "evil conse-quences."[94] Indeed, many of this expedition's diplomatic accom-plishments soon expired. The seemingly solemn promise of the Great White Father to respect and defend Native rights would be repeatedly ignored once railroads, miners, and white settlers showed any interest in a tribe's land or resources.[95] But at least for the fleeting present, Dodge and his dragoons could well be proud of the peace they had briefly brought to the Southern plains.

1835: Dodge Redeems Himself

In gratifying contrast to the previous year, when poorly clad troops nearly froze to death in tents at the periphery of Fort Gibson and endured heat and sickness on the plains, the year 1835 proved considerably easier on the men and beasts. Sergeant Evans, relieved to have left Fort Gibson, wrote from comfortable quar-ters at Fort Leavenworth, "The winter passed off with verry little occuance [occurrence] except our ordinary military duties which kept us tolerably busy employed." With the spring came orders for three of the four companies now stationed at Fort Leavenworth to accompany Colonel Dodge on a journey to the base of the Rocky Mountains.[96]

Meanwhile, outside of Fort Gibson, animosity would explode between Mason and Lt. Jefferson Davis. To begin with, morale did not ride as high among those shivering in their tents back on the desolate plains. Many in this detachment viewed their commander, Major Mason, as "a man severe to a fault,"[97] and nearly everyone noted the growing feud between him and Davis. By December 7, 1834, the falling-out had blown into full flower as Lieutenant Davis refused Mason's order to discipline Cpl. W. H. Harrison and Bugler James Reed for allowing a horse to break free near the stable. Lieutenant Davis protested that the two troopers had tried their best to calm the agitated animal and both were, in Davis's opinion, among the very finest soldiers in the squadron. Such remonstrance and defense of lowly enlisted men infuriated Mason, who immediately confined Davis to quarters,[98] and thus intensified the antagonism between these two.

A later incident ensured a lasting rupture. Throughout the morning of December 24 rain fell at the dragoon camp but, fair or foul, the troops of Company E dutifully left their tents to stand in formed ranks at morning roll-call. Lt. James Carleton would later describe the dreariness of a rainy morning at a dragoon encampment: "The bleak wind is blowing the smoke every way but the right one; the dull leaden sky overhead; the cold rain and fog, all tend to make it anything but pleasant. Everybody and everything seems to have the blues."[99] Lieutenant Davis, now field commander of Company E, declined to appear, preferring the warmth of his quarters. When summoned by Major Mason to explain his absence, Davis argued, according to Mason, "in a highly disrespectful, insubordinate, and contemptuous manner" that army regulations did not require his attendance in the rain. Mason promptly initiated court-martial charges. During the legal proceeding Davis tendered evidence of "Major Mason's manner to subordinates, and the wounding reception he gave officer's explanations of conduct which [he] deemed censurable." Among Davis's favorable carácter witnesses was Sgt. Edward Stanley, a.k.a. Long Ned.[100] On March 15, 1835, the court found Davis guilty of breaching military decorum, but imposed no punishment upon him.[101]

Nonetheless, when Mason's squadron took to the field that spring, Davis remained behind at Fort Gibson. Likely frustrated with Mason's arrogance and, possibly, with the constraints of army life, Davis tendered his resignation, which President Jackson accepted on June 24, 1835. A week prior, Lieutenant Davis had married Sarah Knox Taylor, the daughter of Col. Zachary Taylor, in Louisville, Tennessee.[102] Though he ignobly resigned from the dragoons, in later years his path would repeatedly cross that of the regiment.

Having seen that the regiment could extend the reach of federal authority far onto the plains and, possibly, even to the distant Rocky Mountains, army headquarters ordered expeditions in 1835 demanding even more extensive forays than before. These orders specified that the commands would depart from their respective posts as soon as the weather and ground permitted. To increase the influence and range of the regiment, the army broke it into distinct columns, ordering three of the four companies stationed at Fort Leavenworth under Colonel Dodge to march up the Missouri River, cross the Platte River, head for the Rocky Mountains, and return by way of the Santa Fe Trail—a round trip of 1,600 miles. The remaining Fort Leavenworth company was to march to the Osage village on the Neosho River.[103]

A third column was to march from Fort Gibson to Chouteau Creek to meet with Plains tribes: in 1834 Colonel Dodge had promised those tribes in the region of Fort Gibson that a peace council would take place the following year. Major Mason received instructions to contact the Comanches, Kiowas, and other western tribes and invite them to attend Fort Gibson for talks. Many of these tribes, however, were unwilling to meet at Fort Gibson. Thus, Mason and his men left Fort Gibson on May 18, and after marching 150 miles southwest, located a suitable campsite along Chouteau Creek just north of present Lexington, Oklahoma. Plains tribes heavily attended this council. On August 19, U.S. commissioners Montfort Stokes and Gen. Matthew Arbuckle arrived, accompanied by representatives of the transplanted Cherokee, Choctaw, Osage, and other eastern Indian Territory tribes. The Treaty of Camp Holmes was signed on August 25, 1835, and four days later the dragoons left and arrived at Fort Gibson on September 5.[104]

To the north at Fort Des Moines, three companies under the command of Lieutenant Colonel Kearny were to "proceed up the river Des Moines, to the Raccoon Fork, there halt, and reconnoiter the position, with a view to the selection of a site for the establishment of a military post in that vicinity: on which subject Lieut. Colonel Kearny will report on his return to his winter quarters at Fort Des Moines. After having made this reconnaissance, Lieut. Colonel Kearny will proceed with his command to the Sioux villages near the highlands on the Mississippi, about the 44° of north latitude: thence taking a direction to the westward return [to] his original position at the mouth of the Des Moines."[105]

Headquarters ordered the commanders of each column (Dodge, Kearny, and Mason) to leave "at each of the three Dragoon stations a sufficient number of officers and men, to take charge of the quarters and other public property at those stations. Invalids to be preferred for this duty." In addition, the army invested the three details with the authority to arrest and turn over to civil authorities "any unlicensed white persons in the Indian country, or any person whatever, acting contrary to the laws relating to intercourse with the Indians."[106]

Dodge's Companies A, C, and G, with 117 rank and file, departed Fort Leavenworth on May 29, 1835.[107] Following the approximate route explored by Maj. Stephen Long in 1820, Dodge's 1,600-mile quest would be the largest U.S. military operation, thus far, ever conducted into the Far West. Unlike his expedition of 1834, he did not burden his column with artists and naturalists, and he better provided for his men and horses. In contrast to the hasty preparations for the 1834 march, the dragoons now took great pains to ensure that they had adequate supplies and that their horses were wellgrazed and conditioned.[108]

Capt. John Gantt, able frontiersman, trader, and cashiered army officer, served as the expedition's scout and interpreter.[109] Anticipating possible combat, Colonel Dodge "thought it advisable that two swivels (three-pounders) [cannon] should accompany the expedition, mounted on wheels. I believed these light field-pieces would secure my camp should the Indians make a sudden attack on the command, and enable me to force my passage across rivers or difficult passes, should any attempt be made to stop me."[110]

The Region between St. Louis and the Rocky Mountains

This map depicts the row of forts which, in the 1830s and 1840s, marked the edge of the nation's white population and the beginning of the Great American Desert. In 1835, Col. Henry Dodge's expedition, as did Col. Stephen Kearny's in 1845, traveled overland along the Platte River to the Rocky Mountains. Also included in the map is the Santa Fe Trail, an important trade route and, in 1846, the invasion route taken by Kearny and his Army of the West.

Headed northwest toward the Platte River, the expedition got off to a poor start the first day with stampeding pack mules and driving rain, and the column covered but fifteen miles. On the morrow the companies were forced to remain encamped as their herd of twenty cows escaped the drovers. On the last day of May advance was again sounded, but rain, mud, and rising creeks slowed their march for the next several days.

If muddy trails slowed the column, crossing the unexpectedly swollen water courses nearly brought it to a halt. Heavy rains had so engorged the prairie creeks and rivers, ordinarily containing little water, that they were nearly impossible to ford. The Big Nemohaw, usually a shallow waterway meandering southeast into the Missouri, was at flood level and with a swift current. It presented Dodge with his first challenge: how could he get his ordinance and wagons across this raging river?

After much thought he ordered a bridge to be constructed of driftwood, solidly embedded in the muddy banks, and extended across the river—a seemingly "speedy and safe mode of crossing." A detail was quickly formed with men from each company and placed under the direction of Lt. Enoch Steen. In less than three hours the bridge was half completed, even while the river continued to rise. As officers and men standing on the banks began to congratulate one other, disaster struck: The bridge broke apart, and workers had to jump to safety as its shards "took up the line of march 'for New Orleans and intermediate ports'" down the furious river. Some other means would have to be found to get across. An officer offered a solution: perhaps his wagon might be caulked and become a small boat. In an hour the creation of the novel craft was done and, by attaching ropes to each end, the men drew the vessel from shore to shore. Meanwhile Scout Gantt slaughtered an ox and fashioned from its hide another boat that could carry six hundred pounds of cargo. In this manner the column's baggage crossed without the slightest loss, while the men riding on horses and mules swam the river.[111] This may have been the first time that the army, operating west of the Mississippi, had floated a wagon across a river.

On June 10 the expedition reached the valley of the broad Platte River and encamped until the seventeenth. During that week Dodge held councils with the Omaha and Otoe tribes, meeting with sixty of their principal chiefs and warriors, as well as with their agent, Maj. John Dougherty. Of these two tribes Dodge optimistically wrote that they were begininng "to feel the importance of turning their attention to the arts of civilization." All that the government needed to do was to supply them with corn and tend to their needs. He believed that if cattle should be provided "they could have a large quantity of stock for no country could be better adapted to that purpose."[112]

Three days later, following along the banks of the Platte for some seventy miles, the column arrived near the Grand Pawnee village. The Grand Pawnees not only farmed the rich soil, growing crops of grains and corn, but supplemented their diet with buffalo meat. Two hundred Pawnees came out to greet the troops, shake hands, and pass around a ceremonial pipe, and prepared a feast to honor Dodge and his staff. On the twenty-first and twenty-second Dodge held a council with the leaders of four Pawnee tribes to underscore his wish that they make peace with their traditional enemies, the Arapahos and Cheyennes.[113] On the evening of the twenty-fourth, the companies moved onward.[114]

The troops marched steadily until July 5, when Dodge held council on the south bank of the South Platte with leaders and warriors of the "Arickees" [Arikaras]. Observed Lt. Gaines Kingsbury, Dodge's oficial journalist, the Arikaras were "the wildest and most savage tribe West of the Mississippi . . . [who have] an inveterate hostility to whites, killing all they could meet . . . [and are] at war with most of the surrounding nations."[115] The colonel warned the Arikaras that they must cease their bellicose ways, and the Arikara leaders promised never again to kill "white men when they came into their country but to treat them as brothers and friends." The parties exchanged gifts, and the dragoons resumed their journey toward the Rocky Mountains at daybreak.[116]

As they slowly traveled west the land became even more spectacular. After following the south fork of the Platte River for two hundred miles they reached a beautiful space abundant in rivers and streams. One soldier described the scene as "an unbounded prairie, a broad river, with innumerable herds of buffalo grazing upon its banks, and occasionally a solitary tree standing in bold relief against a clear blue sky."[117] Here Dodge left the South Platte and turned the column southwesterly. On July 15 they espied from a distance the lofty, snow-covered peaks of the Rocky Mountains. The sight enchanted the men, who had spent their entire lives along low-lying regions east of the Mississippi. In his diary, Sergeant Evans called "[t]hese Mountains so much the subject of curiosity and amazement to the eastern world," and as the men approached them the peaks grew ever more stunning.[118]

By the sixteenth, the armed companies of explorers, sightseers, and diplomats began their ascent.[119] On the twenty-second they gained a footing from which they "could behold the beauty and sublimity of those Mountains . . . [that struck everyone] with astonishment and wonder." The breadth and grandeur of the Rockies fulfilled one of the promises commonly made by recruiters that "caused many young men to enlist and endure the many fateigues [*sic*] & hardships common to a prairie life."[120] For Private Russell and other deceived recruits, at least two enticements actually came to fruition: they beheld both the splendor of the Rocky Mountains and vast herds of buffalo.

The stunning beauty of these majestic mountains would lure at least one dragoon back to them. Lt. Lancaster Lupton, a New Yorker who had graduated in the U.S. Military Academy's Class of 1829, would prove to have been especially enthralled. On his return to Fort Leavenworth, Lupton got into a verbal altercation with fellow officers so heated, it earned him court-martial charges. Rather than risk the disgrace of being cashiered, he resigned his commission. Lupton returned to the idyllic Upper Platte River Valley, became a fur trapper, married a native woman, built a fur-trading site he called Fort Lancaster, and lived peacefully among the region's inhabitants until he moved to California in 1849.[121]

On July 26 the column reached the ridge top dividing the Platte and Arkansas Rivers, descended, and bivouacked for four days along the banks of the Arkansas. On the twenty-eighth they followed the Arkansas and then encamped at the foot of Pike's Peak. While most of the exhausted command rested, Sergeant Evans joined a party that climbed part way up the steep rock face to near its breath-taking 14,000-foot-high summit. After holding a brief council with Arapahos on July 30 the dragoons veered south. By August 6, the expedition reached Bent's Fort, near a large Cheyenne village. Two days later representatives of the Blackfoot, Gros Ventre, Crow, and Arapaho tribes arrived for a council to be held at the fort on the eleventh. At this council Dodge brokered an agreement between the tribes to stop fighting and live in peace with one another.

With supplies running low, the regiment commenced its return trip, passing amicably through a number of Cheyenne villages.[122] Lieutenant Kingsbury wrote that the command was "in a most perfect state of health—not a man upon the sick report; the horses in fine order, nearly as good as when we left Fort Leavenworth. The colonel had seen all the Indians he expected to see, and had established friendly relations with them all."[123] The morning of August 15 found the troopers casually grazing their horses and drying their clothes and equipage after a heavy storm the previous evening when, at about nine o'clock, they were startled by several distant gunshots fired by what appeared to be a war party. Because the Cheyennes did not carry firearms, Dodge believed the attack to have come from another tribe. He had the bugler sound assembly and the men fall in for battle. Dodge sent the intrepid scout John Gantt to ride under a white flag toward the mysterious horsemen. Gantt found these to be a Pawnee group, purportedly en route to visit a nearby Cheyenne camp. Their leader professed that he had meant the firing of guns as a token of friendship and not as a hostile act. Dodge, incredulous of his alibi, hurriedly convened another peace council and persuaded the Native parties to cease fighting.[124]

Dodge's expedition tracked the Arkansas River in a roughly easterly direction and, on August 21, crossed it where it intersected with the Santa Fe Trail. Once on the trail and on level ground, the expedition moved rapidly toward home, making forty miles on September 10. That same day, however, Pvt. William Anderson of Company A died of illness—the only death to darken the expedition. He was buried "on a high prairie ridge and a stone placed at the head of his grave with his name and regiment engraved thereon."[125]

The dragoons were now riding home on familiar terrain and about to fully accomplish their mission in good order. On September 16, after an absence of 112 days and a march of more than 1,500 miles, the troops arrived back at Fort Leavenworth.[126] In the words of Lieutenant Kingsbury, "[t]he expedition had exceeded the interest and success the most sanguine anticipated."[127] Gen. Edmund Gaines, commander of the Southwest Military District, jubilantly commended officers and men, praising "the very great vigilance, care, and prudence on the part of the colonel and his officers, and constant attention, obedience, and fidelity on the part of noncommissioned officers and soldiers."[128] Unlike after the disastrous foray to the Pawnee villages in 1834, the men and their mounts returned in good condition and with their mission completed, proving to many critics the utility and efficacy of maintaining a mounted regiment on the frontier.

Colonel Dodge had learned much from the deadly mistakes of the Pawnee expedition. His regiment was better equipped and trained for the trip to the Rocky Mountains than it had been on the prior expedition, and Surgeon Benjamin Fellowes had taken specific steps to ensure the health of the troops by packing a supply of quinine to combat exposure to malaria. A modern-day physician observed, "The markedly different health record of [Dodge's 1835] expedition and the disastrous one of 1834 . . . is explicable in one word, i.e., quinine. The army had at last learned a lesson, that civilians on the trail had known for many years, that to travel on the trail without quinine was to risk severe illness and deaths."[129]

Kearny Maps Iowa Territory

While Dodge headed for the Rocky Mountains, companies B, H, and I, under the command of Lieutenant Colonel Kearny, had the less glamorous task of exploring and mapping Iowa Territory to discover a place for a new fort. They needed to determine whether a proposed site commanded a strategic location suitable for grazing, gathering timber, local transport, and other requirements. On June 7, 1835, Kearny departed from Fort Des Moines, and though the troops initially encountered several severe rainstorms they welcomed the excursion north after having spent over six months in the hard labor of repairing and re-constructing their dilapidated fort.[130] And even the coldest, wettest weather was a big improvement over the oppressive heat that had confronted them during their 1834 campaign to the Pawnee villages.

Lieutenant Colonel Kearny's troops crossed the Missouri River at Boonville and, six days later, reached the rain-swollen, nearly frozen Des Moines River, which they crossed with some difficulty. Kearny held council with the Sioux tribe, then continued northeast to enter Minnesota Territory. He reached the upper Mississippi and met the steamboat *Warrior*, which maneuvered to a landing near Kearny's campsite and took some of the sick on board. Kearny managed again to hold council with a small delegation of Sioux on July 19, and two days later sent the troops on the return trip to Fort Des Moines.[131] The party consumed its last ration of pork on July 23 but, providentially, on the following day saw a herd of buffalo. The nameless chronicler of Company I, a veteran of the 1834 expedition, contemplated: "[M]any of our men are recruits from the north & never saw a Buffalo before & therefore to them a Buffalo chase was something remarkable."[132] Just as when Dodge's troops first beheld the majestic Rockies, another of the recruiting officers' usually specious promises was in fact fulfilled as Kearny's men were indeed traveling "the far prairies on fine horses, amid buffalo."

Reaching a large lake, which Kearny named Lake Albert Lea after the expedition's gifted topographical engineer, the dragoons discovered themselves to be traveling in the wrong direction for skirting it. Fortunately, a passing Sioux hunting party reoriented Kearny properly toward Des Moines.[133] But the journey had begun to wear upon his soldiers. An anonymous dragoon's journal for July 31 complained, "We are wandering about like half starved wolves & no person appears to know in what direction we ought to steer. Much [murmuring] by the men." Spirits rose when finally, on August 19, they found the spot whose suitability for a fort the army wished them to assess, just where Raccoon Creek spilled into the Des Moines River.[134] Kearny assigned Lt. Albert Lea to reconnoiter the site, which he did "by descending it in a canoe, to ascertain the practicability of navigation with keel boats [and] sounding all shoals, taking courses with a pocket compass, estimating distances from bend to bend by the time and rate of motion, sketching every notable thing, occasionally landing to examine the geology of the rocks. . . . [Lea] made the trip without an accident [and] arrived many days before the main body."

Ultimately, Kearny judged the proposed location unfit.[135] But upon returning to Fort Des Moines, on August 19, our anonymous soldier-journalist penned a favorable report of the whole endeavor: "Arrived there about 2 P.M. having been absent almost 3 months. Sickness and all Disease has been a stranger to the camp & all have enjoyed good spirits except that stupidity caused by the want of food & upon the whole I can say we have had a pleasant Campaign."[136] Lieutenant Lea's journal, likewise, remarked with praise that the command had "arrived in fine order, without the loss of a man, a horse, a tool, or a beef, which were fatter than at the starting, after a march of eleven hundred miles."[137]

1835: The Regiment Proves Its Value and Looks to the Future

Forays out of Fort Gibson covered less distance but were crucial to securing peace on the plains. Col. Matthew Arbuckle, Major Mason, Indian agents, and an escort of dragoons set out toward

Camp Holmes, situated on the western edge of Cross Timbers, to treat with the Comanches. At that same site in 1834, leaders of the powerful Comanche tribe had ratified a treaty granting the members of relocated eastern tribes unlimited rights to hunt upon the Comanches' traditional lands.[138] But within a few years the invasion of hungry and ambitious newcomers, along with drought, resulted in a scarcity of buffalo, and sparked renewed warfare between long-resident natives and transplanted peoples. Defeat in the Red River War finally reduced the once-powerful Comanches to abject poverty by the mid-1870s.[139]

Success crowned the dragoon regiment's 1835 efforts to establish treaties and to explore territories. For most companies of the soon-to-be-called 1st Regiment of Dragoons, the following few years held routine garrison duty, drills, patrols, and enforcement of the Indian Removal policy. In the years to follow, and in contrast with the newly created 2nd Dragoons, the 1st Dragoons were to be spared long expeditions as well as fighting in the war then raging in the Florida Everglades. The 1st Dragoons could recruit, drill, and perfect themselves as a mounted force. The experience of the early treks, polished by persistent drilling, improved equipage, and repeated expeditions, made them superior horsemen and soldiers.

Command changed as well. In 1836 Colonel Dodge took a leave of absence from the regiment to lobby for the position of governor of the proposed territory of Wisconsin. Dodge believed his connection with the region and his military and diplomatic experience would convince President Jackson to name him territorial governor. On April 20 Congress established the Territory of Wisconsin, and, as he had predicted, Dodge could formally resign his commission to accept new duties as governor of Wisconsin Territory.[140] Since promotion in the antebellum army primarily obeyed seniority in rank, Lieutenant Colonel Kearny now became colonel of the regiment, Richard Mason rose from major to lieutenant colonel, and Clifton Wharton, the regiment's senior captain, would now be its major.[141]

Kearny, having been absent from dragoon headquarters for two years, would quickly discover that Dodge had swept two years of organizational problems under the rug. The results of Dodge's poor management included broken-down stables, a lack of block-houses suitable to defend Fort Leavenworth, declining enlist-ment, lackadaisical training, and poor maintenance of weapons and tack. Indeed, it appeared the men of the infant regiment had suffered under Dodge's leadership. In 1834, eighty-nine enlistees had died, thirty-three were discharged for physical disability, and 138 had deserted.

And yet, despite his many deficiencies, Dodge's efforts had managed to lead the most powerful federal force ever to invade the Great Plains. Despite mismanagement, abuse, disease, and death, Dodge's dragoons had not only expanded the presence of the United States Army, he had proven that this regiment was to be indispensable in preserving peace—achievements won in the face of the worst conditions that a shortsighted Congress, a foolish military bureaucracy, and unforgiving Nature could collectively inflict.[142]

During Dodge's two expeditions he met and held councils with many of the tribes residing in the Great Plains region. These efforts culminated in two peace conferences: one at Fort Gibson in 1834, and another held the next year at Camp Holmes. These councils, for the moment at least, brought about years of peace between most of the tribes and the whites.[143]

In short, regardless of his failings, Dodge had fundamentally shaped and supported the regiment. As a result, the dragoons would at last be regarded with respect. Those in command had learned firsthand the human and material costs of taking a badly equipped and ill-trained column through the trackless and brutal wilderness. Unfortunately, history would repeat itself too soon and too often, and the pitiful condition of the earliest returning dra-goons and horses would prove a preview of future expeditions' out-comes, occuring during the war with Mexico. Yet, despite enlistees' and officers' vivid understanding of the risks, the regiment would, again and again, accept such challenges. The men remaining with the regiment could now take a measure of pride in the permanent, elite mounted force, whose necessity and worth they had proved. The next years would sorely test Kearny's talents at reorganizing and revitalizing the force. But it would now be his chance to envision, shape, and empower the regiment.

CHAPTER 3

1836

Kearny Takes Command

W hen the dragoons were formed, President Jackson saw to it that the officer corps of the regiment would be chosen from a mixture of professional officers and former Mounted Rangers. Whatever the regiment's true functions, flaws in its basic operations were floridly illustrated by Kearny's criticisms. In due time, however, he would see to it that few former officers of the Mounted Rangers remained in the regiment, and would remedy a wealth of organizational problems that Dodge had failed to address.[1]

In early 1837, General Gaines personally inspected and recognized the prompt efforts of newly installed Col. Stephen Kearny and staff to rebuild the 1st Dragoon Regiment, commending "the exemplary commandant—his captains and other officers, noncommissioned officers and soldiers, whose high health and vigilance, with the excellent condition of the horses, affords conclusive evidence of their talents, industry, and steady habits."[2]

Change wasn't easy. For over two years, Col. Henry Dodge's casual command had frustrated the professional Kearny at every step. The two diverged not only in leadership style but on the very purpose of the dragoon regiment. Kearny's letters to the adjutant general are evidence that the two men didn't get along. Perhaps it was only coincidental that, on the 1834 march to the Pawnee villages, Dodge detached Kearny from the main party and saddled him with overseeing a camp for diseased and dying troopers. Or that once the expedition returned to Fort Gibson, Dodge sent him to barely habitable quarters at Camp Des Moines. Or again that when Dodge marched the bulk of the regiment to the Rocky Mountains in 1835—a feat reaping wild public acclaim—Kearny had been packed off to a less glamorous patrol mapping the Canadian border.

So when Dodge resigned in 1836 to become governor of the Wisconsin Territory, Kearny grabbed the chance to undo the damage Dodge had ignored. It would take many years to remake the dragoons into the elite corps of which he dreamed.

From Mass Exodus to Dragoon Fever

Beginning in late 1834, Fort Leavenworth became dragoon headquarters. The post would play a vital role in westward expansion. Established as a camp by the late Col. Henry Leavenworth in 1829 on the western bank of the Missouri River, the fort was four days' distance by steamboat from St. Louis and, prior to the war with Mexico, the westernmost outpost of the United States. In 1854, an army doctor described it as being "a most charming spot, and surrounded by one of the richest agricultural regions in the United States." Yet, as was true of Jefferson Barracks, and Fort Gibson, Fort Leavenworth constantly drew deadly cholera and malaria epidemics.[3] A correspondent writing under the name of Philos in 1854 described it as

> without exception the most beautiful place on the [Missouri] river. . . . As far as the eye could reach on either hand, hill rose above hill in an almost endless series of undulations, beautiful streams were winding their sinuous course through fertile valleys, and the whole diversified with fine groves, gave to the view an air of enchantment. . . . At the foot of the landing is a large store-house, at which considerable business is done. On the summit of the bluff is a large plateau, on which the fort or rather village

stands—for it has far more the appearance of a beautiful village than fort. In the center are three or four large
buildings much like the "city blocks," in which the soldiers
have their mess and lodge. At a little distance from these
and at several corners are a number of fine houses, the
residences of the officers.[4]

In 1857, now–lieutenant colonel Cooke described the post as
hardly resembling a fort, but rather "a straggling cantonment, but
on an admirable site." Here

the Missouri, in an abrupt bend, rushes with wonderful
swiftness against a rock-bound shore; from this the ground
rises with a bold sweep to a hundred feet or more, then
sloping gently into a shallow vale, it rises equally again,
and thus are formed a number of hills, which are to the
north connected by a surface but slightly bent, to which
the vale insensibly ascends; every line of every surface
is curved with symmetry and beauty. On these hill-tops,
shaded by forest trees, stands Fort Leavenworth. On the
one hand is to be seen the mighty river, winding in the
distance through majestic forests and by massive bluffs,
stretching away till mellowed to aerial blue; on the other,
rolling prairies, dotted with groves, and bounded on the
west by a bold grassy ridge; this, inclosing in an ellipti-
cal sweep a beautiful amphitheatre, terminates five miles
southward in a knob, leaving between it and the river a
view of the prairie lost in a dim and vague outline.[5]

The post may have been scenically located, but Kearny, its new
colonel, felt alarm not only at Dodge's lackadaisical staffing but
at his seeming unconcern for the strategic development of Fort
Leavenworth. Although placed in what was then the Far West and
in the heart of Indian land, it lacked fortification. Kearny feared
that the increasing number of forcibly transplanted Native Americans might attack the fort and nearby settlements:

We have near us many nations of Indians, several of them powerful, brave, and warlike, and some of which without assistance of others, are able to drive from this position, four Companies of Dragoons . . . and should we by any chance, be attacked and defeated by any body of Indians, it would be a signal for all the others within hundreds of miles from us, to join, and lay waste the settlements. . . . The stables here are perfectly worthless—unfit for the accommodation of a decent horse, and so located, that a Party of Indians might go to them in the Night, kill the sentinel in charge of them, and carry off all Horses, without our knowing any thing of it, 'til Stable Call the Next Morning. I recommended to the Qr. Master Genl, that New ones be allowed, which are Not only Necessary for the comfort of the Horses, but for the economy of the Service—if we attain this they will be located with a view to defense and protection.[6]

In due time, funds materialized for the construction of two blockhouses and new stables at Fort Leavenworth.

Of course, declining strength was not unique to the dragoons. Before the Civil War only 30 to 40 percent of a typical army regiment's assumed force was in fact fit for duty.[7] But Kearny held it crucial that his dragoons not suffer a reduction in manpower. On July 28, 1836, he wrote to the adjutant general, emphasizing the importance of sending recruits directly to Fort Leavenworth to restore the regiment's full vigor, given clear threats to the security of the unfortified post—mere scattered buildings encircled by countless tribes. He reminded the adjutant general that "[t]his Post, the most important on the Frontier on account of its Position, & the great number of Indians around it, is decidedly weaker than any other I know of, in the Indian Country," and thus the army needed to supply it with adequate troops. Each morning roll call reminded Kearny how much the regiment's muscle had diminished, company by company, from disease, desertion, and death. Two years' exposure to the elements had sapped the verve of all but the healthiest and most motivated dragoons. The four companies garrisoned at Leavenworth had 163 men—121 short of its sanctioned strength; by the end of July 1836, the entire regiment, with an authorized force of 705, had only 444 soldiers, a deficiency of 261.[8]

In part, the shortage derived from the fact that by the time Kearny took command, the bloom was off the recruiting rose. Most of the eager enlistees of 1833 were completing their three-year tours of duty. And as survivors of freezing Fort Gibson and the deadly foray to the Pawnee villages, many had had their fill of glorious service, and either failed to re-enlist or plain deserted.[9] To aggravate the situation, a detachment of ninety-six recruits intended for the 1st Dragoons was hastily diverted to combat in Florida to serve with the newly formed 2nd Dragoons. Other troops deserted en route to their new companies. Lt. William Eustis, for example, had the ill fortune of losing to desertion twenty-one out of seventy-five men on the trip between New York and Fort Gibson.[10]

To rebuild the regiment to authorized strength, Kearny dispatched several captains and lieutenants to eastern cities to open recruiting stations. But they found far fewer takers than in 1833, and by late 1836 the number of enlistees froze at 433. Kearny admitted to Captain Ford that recruiting "has not been as good as I anticipated." Indeed, Ford's labors in Indiana failed to produce a single signer, and those of Captain Duncan in Hartford and of Lt. John Burgwin in Boston gained only a few. In their drive to meet their quotas, other recruiters accepted nearly anyone who showed up. Many of those sent to dragoon posts were immediately rejected as physically unfit. Upon reviewing fifteen new men at Fort Leavenworth, Kearny "determined upon discharging *Ten* of these Recruits, being utterly worthless and incapable of rendering any service"[11] (emphasis in original).

The editor of the *Army and Navy Chronicle* opined that insufficient pay explained soldiers' reluctance to re-enlist. Inspector General George Croghan attributed it to "discontent among the officers."[12] Kearny, characteristically, held that the dragoon regiment's low morale stemmed from poor equipage, weaponry, and training as well as the incompetence of officers, and instantly embarked on plans to redress all these deficiencies. Yet the cause of recruitment enjoyed markedly better success once aided by the highly encouraging economic collapse and record unemployment of the Panic of 1837. Worldwide travails helped swell enlistment rolls further, as social unrest in the German States and the Irish Potato Famine brought to the United States an unprecedented number of jobless immigrants to whom even the army looked good.

However, the feeling was not mutual. The army was not eager to accept non-English speakers—or English-speakers of maligned ethnicity—into its ranks. Of a detachment of 110 dragoon recruits received in 1840 at Fort Leavenworth, twenty were Germans who did not grasp a word of English. The flood of foreign-born recruits presented novel problems. A corporal drilling newcomers to Fort Leavenworth as late as 1846 complained, "I need not say it is a very serious task to be drilling a lot of green horns and especially when they are sometimes so Dutch as not to understand or be understood."[13]

Too many, under the prejudices of the time, were Irish. Inspector General George Croghan remarked, "It is no pleasant task to instruct raw recruits, but when those recruits are ignorant of your language, the task is ten times more tedious and disagreeable. I would suggest the propriety of forbidding the enlistment of all such persons for the future, taking care at the same time to issue a like interdict against the Irish, who (a few honorable exceptions to the contrary) are the very bane of our garrisons."[14]

But it was not only the down-and-out who rushed to the dragoon regiment in the 1840s. In late 1845, three well-educated men caught the same fever and enlisted in the dragoons. All three served in the Mexican War and participated in the invasion of New Mexico. Yet, as for Hildreth and Russell and most recruits, enthusiasm for dragoon life proved a chimera for the trio: one rose to the rank of sergeant major but soon died on duty, one was dishonorably discharged in 1847, and the third deserted in 1848 to become a successful doctor and prospector in California.

On October 17, 1845, one well-shod young man who, after touring Europe, was down on his luck, and without telling his parents, enlisted in St. Louis. Mathias L. Baker, a twenty-eight-year-old clerk from a good family in Middlesex County, New Jersey, and seven other recruits soon found themselves ascending the Mississippi River to Prairie du Chien, Wisconsin Territory, traveling westwards by land another forty-eight miles, and finally arriving at castle-like Fort Atkinson, Iowa Territory, on November 25, 1845. The eight recruits were now privates in Company B.

Nelson Archy had grown up in Dayton, Ohio, the son of a prosperous businessman. One day in December of 1845, the husky youth passed a dragoon recruiting station and, curious about the regiment's illustrious expeditions along the Santa Fe Trail and to the Rockies, entered. Lt. John Love greeted Archy. The gracious southerner filled the youth's head with riveting tales of his firsthand experience in the Snively Affair (see chapter 4) and Kearny's march to the Rockies—wild Indians, buffalo, scenic wonders. To Nelson these marvels sure beat working in his father's dreary mill. He was going to enlist! He asked how old he had to be to join, and was crushed to hear Love reply that a recruit must be twenty-one, or eighteen with a parent's consent. The eighteen-year-old knew his father would never agree to his enlistment, since the elder Archy viewed him as cheap labor for his mill. Crestfallen, he left the station. But a few doors down he luckily espied a public house, and a drink or two gave him the courage he needed to return to the station, lie about his age, and enlist for a five-year term of duty.

A few weeks later Love sent Archy by steamboat down the Ohio River, bound for Fort Leavenworth, with a gaggle of his other recruits. One of these was twenty-three-year-old New York native Erasmus Darwin French, who attended the Albion Seminary in Michigan and had some training in medicine. But like Archy, he could not heal himself from dragoon fever. In all likelihood, the recruiter Love had promised him he could gain valuable experience as a hospital steward in the army, and French enlisted in Dayton, Ohio, on January 3, 1846.[15]

Morale within the regiment rose steadily, and many were now inclined to re-enlist. Fayette Robinson, who served in the 1st Dragoons as a lieutenant from 1837 to 1841, boasted of the dragoon's attachment to his company: "The records of the proper bureau, it is said, show more re-enlistments in its ranks, than in any other corps in the service. It is, or was, no uncommon thing to see in the ranks of a company the third of the company wearing the chevron [on the sleeve] which denotes a second enlistment."[16] Kearny, though, did not stop haranguing his superiors to add more men. By the end of 1837 the regiment's strength had increased to 619 men and counting; by the end of 1838, Kearny could report his companies to be near full strength.[17]

From Disdain to "Dragoon Fever"

A second, related matter, however, hampered the regiment during its early years: the dwindling number of officers. Graduates of the United States Military Academy were usually assigned to serve in a branch of the service according to their class standing: top alumni obtained officer commissions in the engineers, next came ordnance, then artillery, followed by dragoons and, lastly, infantry.[18] But graduates, even at the bottom of their class, were hard to come by. Rumors of discord and disorganization in the dragoons had killed interest in joining. In 1836 just four graduates—and all at the bottom of their class—opted to serve in the dragoons, and three of them resigned in under a year. A desperate Kearny now sought Secretary of War Cass's encouragement of Congress to issue brevet lieutenant commissions for untrained officers who were "citizens of our country, young gentlemen of education & of character."[19]

But Kearny himself may have contributed to the short supply of officers. From the regiment's earliest days he had stated his disapproval of elevating former Mounted Rangers as captains. While there is no direct evidence that Kearny forced from the regiment Captains—and former Mounted Rangers—Browne, Duncan, and Ford, all three resigned in 1837. For a variety of reasons, few civilian appointees remained in the army for very long.[20]

Kearny was not alone in his scorn. Indeed, many Military Academy graduates looked down not only upon former Mounted Rangers but also the few enlisted men who had gained officer commissions in the regular army. One such dragoon enlistee who became an officer was former Sgt. Maj. William Bowman. The cranky Capt. Thomas Swords expressed typical scorn toward promoting enlisted men in a letter to Lt. Abraham Johnston: "We have just heard of the death of Bowman, a very unexpected thing with us—as he was looked upon as one of the toughest cases in the Regt . . . but perhaps no great loss to the service, as the fewer of that set we have with us the better."[21]

One former Mounted Ranger officer, in particular, was to attract the disdain of his fellow officers. While he was commanding officer at Fort Des Moines, Kearny placed the troublesome Lt. James Schaumburg under arrest pending a court-martial. Before a hearing could be held, Kearny had left to take command of the regiment at Fort Leavenworth. Captain Sumner agreed to allow Schaumburg to depart from the post if he would resign his commission. The lieutenant agreed to do so and left for New Orleans. Upon hearing the news, Kearny wrote to the adjutant general pleading that Schaumburg not be permitted to revoke his resignation.[22] Good riddance to a former Mounted Ranger, and worse, one who did not get along with any of the other officers. On June 23, 1836, the army accepted his resignation.

Alas, Schaumburg revoked his resignation and reported for duty. The War Department refused to recognize him as an officer and Schaumburg appealed the order. President John Tyler restored Schaumburg to duty. In 1845 the Senate passed a resolution declaring the president's act as illegal and removed Schaumburg from duty, and the army dropped him from the rolls. In 1849, the Senate repealed its 1845 resolution, ordered Schaumburg's restoration, and recommended he be appointed as a captain of dragoons. "Unfair," cried Ewell, Swords, and Capt. Henry Turner, among others, who actively opposed Schaumburg's restoration to rank. Turner wrote to Senator Cass:

> The 1st Reg't of Drag's will suffer great injustice if this act is done. I believe more Officers of this Reg't have fallen in battle in this War than any other Reg't of the service, but without pleading the services of the Reg't. and the claim they may give to the favor of the Govmt. I am sure you will consider that it ought not to appeal in vain to the justice of the Govmnt. . . . My interest in it is that Officers of the Reg't may not suffer the injustice and humiliation of having Mr. S placed over them in the Reg't from which he resigned near 12 years ago while they have served, without other reward for faithful services, than such promotions as the survivors have attained from the death of those who have died in service or fallen in battle.[23]

On April 3, 1849, E. V. Sumner, the lieutenant colonel of the 1st Dragoons wrote to Secretary of War George Crawford about Schaumburg, pointing out that the unfairness of his being restored to duty after being out of the service for thirteen years would be harmful to morale. The officers, meanwhile, "have been struggling on for years through difficulty, and danger, to attain their present ranks, and now at the close of the war, find themselves" subject to postwar cutbacks in funding. Sumner believed Schaumburg's return as a captain would erode morale among the officer class.[24]

More important, Presidents James Polk and Zachary Taylor opposed the resolution and refused to order Schaumburg reinstated. An unapologetic Schaumburg, writing on occasion of Kearny's untimely death in 1848, shed no tears at the general's passing, writing to the adjutant general: "[W]hatever of bitterness I have felt was produced of what I considered his unjust course towards me, prompted by personal animosity. I am not aware of having ever by any premeditated act sought to bring about or engendered this feeling."[25]

In 1853, as an added fillip, the combative Schaumburg shot and seriously wounded one of his creditors in a Washington City hotel. He was convicted of the crime and spent slightly over a year in prison.[26] This conviction, however, would not mark the end of Schaumburg's many attempts to receive back pay.

During the Civil War, President Abraham Lincoln made the mistake of appointing Schaumburg a colonel and paymaster in the Union Army. The newly minted colonel promptly illegally withheld a portion of army payroll claiming it as his personal compensation for dragoon service between 1836 and 1861. The Senate promptly negated his rank, removed him from service, and demanded repayment of the pilfered funds. For fifty or so years, undaunted and unforgiving, Schaumburg was to claim he was still in the army and to petition the courts in an effort to revoke his resignation and to obtain just compensation for his time in the dragoons. He died March 9, 1886.[27]

Thanks in part to Kearny's zeal for public relations—in elevated military circles, at least—by the 1840s many cadets of the Military Academy came to regard the United States Dragoons as a corps d'elite. On the eve of his graduation in 1840, Dick Ewell, ranked thirteenth in a class of forty-two, wrote to his brother Ben that although he'd be stationed at far-flung frontier posts, "[v]ery flattering accounts are given of the First Dragoons. Their duties are said to be more pleasant than those of most other regiments of the service, and the officers are reported to be some of the best specimens of the army." Ewell gained a brevet second lieutenancy with the 1st Dragoons.[28] In 1841, Leonidas Jenkins and John Love, who graduated thirteenth and fourteenth respectively in a class of fifty-two, preferred brevet lieutenant commissions in the 1st Dragoons to positions as engineers or artillerymen.[29] And in the year that followed, Cadet John Newton wrote to Second Lieutenant Love of something going around which he called "dragoon fever."

Corporal, this is a great riding master we have now. He'll learn us more in 20 days than McAuley would have done in 2 years—instead of the never varying formula, Trot, Trot out and Gallop—this old Fellow carries us in to the midst of things at once. We charge around in the D . . . house, with two rows of heads, and also rings to cut and point at. You get so excited that you don't care for anything. You don't think of your horse except to carry him up to them. The consequence you get a confidence in yourself; it accustoms you to maintain your seat, and to manage your horse. Old McAuley was arrested for being drunk on duty, and resigned in consequence. . . . How do you like the Dragoons. There is a perfect "dragoon fever" in our class which increases in virulence as June approaches.[30]

Being a dragoon turned out to be a passing fancy for Newton, who later called his "dragoon fever" a "mere humbug." Graduating second in his class, he elected to enter the Corps of Engineers.[31] But Sam Grant, graduating twenty-first in the Class of 1843, was sorely smitten and wrote he "was anxious to enter the cavalry, or dragoons, as they were then called; but there was only one regiment of dragoons. . . . I recorded, therefore, my *first choice, dragoons*; second, Fourth Infantry, and got the latter"[32] (authors' emphasis). With the 2nd Dragoons dismounted by the army and turned into a rifle regiment, openings in the 1st Dragoons were few. The army assigned Grant to the 4th Infantry. Undaunted, young Sam wrote from Jefferson Barracks in November of 1843 to the adjutant general: "Sir: I have the honor to apply for a transfer from the 4th Infantry to the Dragoons. I am encouraged to make application for a transfer to that arm of the service which was my first choice on leaving the Military Academy, from the fact that there is, at this time, no one of the graduates of the same class with myself holding appointment in this arm, and that there is one less number of Bvts. in the Reg. for which I apply than in the 4th Inf."

His letter bore several powerful endorsements, including those of regimental commander Kearny and Maj. Gen. Winfield

Scott. Yet the application was denied, as officers were in short supply in the 4th Infantry.[33]

Dragoon fever struck hardest in 1844, when top cadets Joseph Whittlesey, second in his class, and Alfred Pleasonton, ranked seventh, bypassed the Engineers to become brevet lieutenants of the 1st Dragoons.[34] After a slight respite in 1845 the fever revisited the fabled Class of 1846 when Clarendon Wilson, ranked ninth, opted for the mounted regiment.[35] While the war with Mexico raged in 1847, all graduates were placed either with the artillery or infantry, and when it ended in 1848 the dragoons embarked on a calmer chapter as frontier constabulary. As late as 1854, John Pegram of Virginia graduated tenth in his class and decided to be a dragoon;[36] but by then the charm had been broken, and cadets' dragoon fever had burnt out.

Improved Weaponry and the Goods of War

Kearny was determined to improve the regiment's armaments. The dragoons were initially armed with sabers manufactured by the Ames Company since 1834 and designed to be thrust into the enemy. But in 1838, Inspector General Croghan agreed with complaints that these weapons were of inferior design and quality, with blades of too soft a metal to be serviceable.[37] In 1840, the Ordnance Department ordered from France a quantity of sabers patterned after the Model 1822 French Hussar saber. This model, designed not to skewer but to slash, had a substantially longer and heavier blade than did the Ames. Slashing a mounted opponent would likely break his collarbone and effectively remove him from combat, while thrusting the Ames weapon straight into the enemy risked lodging the blade between his ribs and pulling the saber out of the dragoon's hand. Soon the Ames, Tiffany, and Horstmann companies began manufacturing heavier cutting sabers for the army. When the demand for the new model outstripped these manufacturers' production capacities, the army ordered others from Prussian companies. By 1842, most of the dragoon companies had exchanged their lightweight Ames sabers for more deadly versions.[38]

Kearny himself focused particularly on the flaws of the innovative but temperamental Hall carbines. In 1838 he complained, "[T]he light manner in which our [Hall] Carbines are made & the rough treatment they frequently receive from Mounted Dragoons, are the causes of so many requiring services during the year!" In fact, most officers were unimpressed by the Hall, despite its initial promise, as they discovered that a gap between the barrel and the chamber increased over time, damaging the weapon and, often, the shooter. Additionally, they noted that if a trooper neglected to close the breech securely before firing, the blast would ruin the wooden stock. In 1841, Lieutenant Colonel Mason complained that "[h]is carbines [routinely] blew off the stock and will not stand 20 fires."[39]

Colonel Kearny further specified that the Hall needed a device "for ramming the cartridge, instead of the little finger, which cannot force it down sufficiently tighter." Soldiers on horseback carried their loaded Halls barrel down, which drained most of the powder from the breech and produced a misfire approximately one time out of three.[40] In 1843, the Ordnance Department issued to the 1st Dragoons an improved and shorter model in .52 caliber. The new model cured some, but not all, of the complaints of the weapon.[41] Yet despite all of these defects, Chief of Ordnance Lt. Col. George Talcott concluded, "[I]f my honor and life were at stake, and depended on the use of the firearms, I would sooner take one of these [Hall] carbines than any other weapon."[42] Dragoons continued to carry Hall carbines until 1851, but the training manuals for their use were woefully inadequate. In the fall of 1836, the energetic Kearny drafted his own manual, published a year later, which competently instructed the troops in the use of the carbines.[43]

To appreciate how crucial Kearny considered functioning Halls to be for his regiment, consider the case of Pvt. George Allen of Company C. The twenty-eight-year-old farmer from Connecticut enlisted in January of 1837, possibly inspired by the tightening economy heralding the Panic of that year. On August 26, while Allen was on guard duty at Fort Leavenworth, Lieutenant Johnston noticed that Allen's Hall was nonfunctional due to its having a chamber that did not fit the weapon. At first the court-martial panel did not wish to hear the case, as more pressing cases of desertion and drunkenness crowded its docket, but Kearny insisted on the need to punish the private's careless behavior, arguing

> [f]rom my ideas of Military duty, & Serving as we do, in an Indian Country, where every Soldier should be at all times ready for Service against an Enemy, I Can Conclude of but few offences of more serious nature & more entitled to the Cognizance of a General Court Martial than that alleged in the Charge against Prvt. Allen (Viz) that having been inspected at Guard Mounting by an Officer, and pronounced ready & in Order for Guard duty, that he did after marching [to] the Guard House then as part of the Guard entrusted with the Safety & Protection of the Garrison, deliberately change a part of his Carbine, So as to render it unserviceable.

Kearny had Allen arrested. On October 15, 1837, a court-martial panel heard the case and ordered Allen to pay the sum of $1.00 out of his $8.00 monthly salary and to be released. A chastised Allen soldiered on and was honorably discharged in 1840, but his conviction, however, served as a warning to others who might allow their weapons to be broken.[44]

Even more serious than this were problems with the horse pistols: the mainspring, tumbler, and sear for the regiment's regulation horse pistol were defective and regularly injured or killed many a dragoon. As early as 1837 Kearny complained to Ordnance that "[t]he cock spring of the Pistol is too weak, which causes it very frequently to misfire." But Ordnance did little to address the matter. Worse were the injuries and deaths caused by other defects of horse pistols, often secondary to a weak tumbler and sear.[45]

On March 17, 1834, Lt. William Bradford, prior to commencing patrol, inspected the two flintlock pistols secured in his horse's pommel holster. As he returned one of the pistols to the holster, the tip of the hammer caught the top of the holster, drew itself back and then released, discharging the weapon. The ball mortally struck Bradford in his left breast.[46] On June 13, 1843, Lt. Abraham Johnston, commanding Company D, was severely wounded in the foot when a pistol slung across his saddle accidently discharged. Capt. Burdette Terrett, serving at Fort Scott, Missouri Territory, was killed on March 17, 1845: as he took "a loaded pistol from his [pommel] holster with his right hand and passed it to his bridle hand . . . the horse jumped to the right, the pistol was discharged and Capt. T fell to the ground." Exactly three months later, on the evening of the seventeenth of June, 1845, at "about tattoo trooper Howard of I company carelessly discharged his pistol and shot himself through the thigh about three inches above the knee, the ball passed through a tent just over a man's breast and finally wounded a third man (Adolphus Berry) of Co. B in the knee." On January 6, 1847, Pvt. John McNelly of Company C shot himself in the hand when his horse pistol accidently discharged. Another misfiring pistol caused Lt. Joseph McElvane, out on campaign near Albuquerque, New Mexico, on July 3, 1847, to shoot himself in the arm, which had to be amputated. The young officer died nine days later.[47]

Kearny had greater success upgrading riding equipment. When he took command the regiment was employing an English-style riding saddle, lightweight with low pommel and cantle. The colonel found it unsatisfactory as the men had difficulty not sliding off the saddle when fighting mounted. He therefore sought a deep-seated model patterned after the English hussar saddle. The new saddles were to be manufactured by John Fairbairn & Co. in Philadelphia.[48] Captain Sumner, at Carlisle Barracks, received delivery of the saddles and described how he came to appreciate them. While he found that they "fit well on horses of different forms," he did not like riding in them at first, feeling too contained by the high pommel and cantle. However, he gradually became accustomed to the design and acknowledged its superior safety: "I prefer it to the low saddles, and there is no comparison to the security of the seat, indeed with the greatcoat on the pommel, the valise on the cantle, and the shabraque on, it is almost impossible for a man to be thrown, while his horse keeps his legs."[49]

Not every officer approved of the new tack, and even though Kearny had many a disagreement with Lieutenant Colonel Mason, he heeded his complaints concerning dragoon equipage, including that the new saddles "break with the ordinary weight of a man and let the whole weight upon a horse's backbone." Mason also argued that he could "break his bridle bits with his own hands with the greatest of ease and the leather of his bridle reins is of a loose spongy texture ruining on being wet, etc."[50] The army itself was not completely satisfied with the 1841 saddle, and in 1844 adopted the Ringgold Saddle.[51] Colonel Kearny was immediately displeased with the Ringgold and began testing the Grimsley saddle in the field. He found it "far better suited for Dragoon service" than the Ringgold. By 1847, Grimsleys were issued to companies being refitted at Jefferson Barracks and Fort Leavenworth. These saddles were to be used until they were replaced by the McClellan saddle on the eve of the Civil War.[52]

No issue, large or small, escaped the attention of the indefatigable Colonel Kearny. Among the deficiencies he addressed was the lack of a chief musician and of two chief buglers, and he asked the recruiting service for such.[53] Over time the Dragoons would recruit a number of well-trained musicians and would eventually have one of the best bands in the army. In the meantime, though, Kearny exerted himself to gain the transfer of deserter Georg Henneburg.

In 1836 Henneburg, with his wife and three children, landed in the United States from Germany. Unable to find employment and not fluent in English, he enlisted in the newly formed 2nd Dragoons. The recruiter allegedly promised him he would not be sent to Florida to fight Seminoles, but would serve as the regiment's principal musician and be stationed at Jefferson Barracks. Alas, as we have seen too often, recruiters fib. In September of

1838 Henneburg found himself on board a steamboat bound precisely for New Orleans and then Florida. He deserted and returned to Jefferson Barracks a month later to surrender himself to General Atkinson. The general sent him to serve as a bugler with Company B of the 1st Dragoons, then at Fort Leavenworth. On January 27, 1839, Kearny wrote to General Jones asking that the talented musician be kept to serve with the regimental band:

> This man appears to me like a very respectable German and still understands our language very imperfectly. As I have been thus particular about his family, that the Comd. In Chief may himself judge, & I have no doubt he would agree with me, in crediting his story, that he was deceived in his enlistment when promised that he was to serve at Jefferson Barracks, & not to be sent to Florida where he is most unwilling to go, as it would separate him from those far removed as from the native Home and dependent upon him. I have now to recommend that he be transferred from the 2nd to the 1st Dragoons.[54]

Bugler Henneburg re-enlisted in the 1st regiment and on July 16, 1846, began service with Company F, under the command of Kearny's nephew, Philip. To secure his second enlistment, Philip Kearny promised to keep Henneburg with his family. But the departure of Company F to San Antonio, Texas, and the replacement of its alcoholic and (at least when sober) easygoing Capt. Philip Thompson with the junior but martinet Kearny, resulted in Henneburg's second desertion on September 14, 1846. This time, having had his fill of the army's broken promises, he did not return.[55]

The Second Seminole War and the Texas Revolution

Jackson's Indian Removal policy faltered when he attempted to ship the Seminoles, the enemies in his draconian 1818 invasion, from Florida to Oklahoma.[56] On December 28, 1835, members of the tribe ambushed and killed all but three of Maj. Francis Dade's detachment of 110 men. Regulars and volunteers from all over the country rushed to Florida to avenge the so-called Dade Massacre,[57] and the bulk of the federal army was drawn into Florida's troubled swamps. To suppress the Seminole uprising, Congress realized the army needed a second mounted force modeled after the 1st Dragoons,[58] and in 1836 created the 2nd Regiment of Dragoons. President Jackson appointed Col. David Twiggs commander, and went out of his way to name several civilians as officers. Three of them— Maj. Thomas Fauntleroy, Capt. Benjamin Beall, and Lt. George Blake—would, for better or for worse, gain command of the 1st Dragoons.[59] The new regiment's baptism by fire came on June 10, 1836, when a detachment consisting primarily of recruits initially intended for the 1st Dragoons was placed under command of 1st Dragoon Lieutenants William Tompkins and T. B. Wheelock, but fought near Micanopy as a company of the 2nd Dragoons.[60]

While the 1st Dragoons strived to embody military propriety, this sister regiment, in marked contrast, seemed to pride itself on being unruly, uncouth, and hard-drinking. Certainly, its fighting for nearly seven years (1835 to 1842) in the Second Seminole War under some of the worst conditions ever encountered by any U.S. military force might have contributed to the casual appearance and coarse manners of its officers and men.[61] Its men routinely flaunted regulations by sporting long tresses and facial hair, earrings, and nonregulation yellow bands around their fatigue caps, as well as by their devil-may-care attitude about protocol. Suffice it to say, their behavior fostered instant and utter disdain in officers of other regiments. In 1845, Gen. William Worth, journeying to Texas with the Army of Observation, wrote to his son-in-law from Corpus Christi, Texas: "On my left are the Second dragoons, an Augean stable; but I fear no Hercules to cleanse it."[62] But despite their impatience with decorum, this hard-riding regiment won repeated victories on battlefields.

A single, if major, event of 1836 would have long-term, profound effects upon two infant democracies and the recently created 1st Dragoons. On March 2, 1836, Texas declared itself independent of Mexico, setting the stage for its War of Independence and a decade of regional turmoil. Although the Republic of Texas had defeated Gen. Antonio Lopez de Santa Anna's forces at the 1836 Battle of San Jacinto and had wrung from him an acknowledgment of Texan independence, Mexico refused the new republic's demand to be recognized as a sovereign nation. Instead, Mexico considered her a rebellious state, and sought repeatedly to restore its control over her by force for the next seven years. President Jackson feared the unrest might draw in the United States during an election year. In all likelihood, Gen. Sam Houston begged Old Hickory to send troops to Texas, and the army responded by directing Gen. Edmund Gaines to issue an order to send observers to Nacogdoches on the Sabine River in east Texas, for his firsthand impressions and to ensure a measure of calm on the border with Mexico. Gaines selected companies E, F, and K of the 1st Dragoons, under the command of Captain Trenor, along with six infantry companies and a smattering of volunteers to bolster aid in his efforts.[63] The troops arrived in July and stayed until December in what was a full-scale invasion of Texas.[64]

Not all the eyewitnesses, though, were neutral. The new republic's offers of free land and military glory induced many U.S. soldiers to desert and to fight for Texas, and twenty-three of the deserters were from Kearny's elite 1st Dragoons.[65] In addition to these deserter-volunteers, the restless former sergeant Edward Stanley, discharged from the dragoons in 1835, recruited some two hundred men in New York City to participate in the Texas Revolution. Included among them were Algernon Thompson, later a prominent attorney in Texas, and James Perry, recently resigned from the U.S. Military Academy. The detachment of recruits sailed from New York only to be arrested by the British off the Bahamas for suspected piracy. Released from custody on March 2, 1836, Stanley and his men landed in Galveston. The rebels commissioned him as an engineer with the rank of captain in the Texas army. On May 22, 1836, an unfortunate duel at Fort Travis cut short Stanley's promising, if checkered, military career.[66]

Constabulary Duty

Although less grand than the expeditions of 1834–35 in terms of manpower, distance, and media interest, Kearny's array of missions from 1836 to 1839, enabled only by thinly spreading his companies, served to preserve the peace by disciplining whites, Natives, and, sometimes, officers. One problem dogging federal relations with the tribes stemmed from alcohol. When the federal government forced the tribes to move from their homelands east of the Mississippi, it promised to protect their new lands from encroachment by white settlers, whiskey peddlers, and other "worthless characters." Indian agent Tom Fitzpatrick observed, "It is the general opinion throughout the United States that Indians are very much imposed on by the white man who trades with them." Particularly damaging, Fitzpatrick specified, is "the introduction of spirituous liquors, and the evils arising out of its [sic] intoxicating influence."[67]

A typical attempt to curb the alcohol trade on Indian land and show the federal flag took place in 1836. On May 27, Companies C, D, and G departed Fort Leavenworth under the command of Lt. Benjamin Moore and visited the Pawnee villages on the Neosho River. The trip was uneventful and Moore returned to the fort on the twenty-eighth of June.[68] Kearny next dispatched Lieutenant Terrett into Indian country with instructions to arrest any sellers of whiskey and to destroy their product: "It has been reported to me, that Fallon & Premu have a quantity of whiskey near the Platte River, expecting to trade it all off with the Indians; you will examine into the subject and act as circumstances may require."[69]

Emblematic of the "worthless characters" entering Indian country was the notorious Heatherly family, a rough-and-tough group of cutthroats, footpads, horse thieves, and moonshiners living in the northwestern reaches of Missouri. In June of 1836 the Heatherlys crossed the Missouri River into Native land, discovered a Pottawatomie hunting party, stole some of the tribe's horses, and fled. The tribesmen tracked the thieves and demanded the return of their horses, which the Heatherlys refused to give up.

In the ensuing gun battle the Pottawatomie killed two members of the Heatherly gang. As was common on the frontier, panicked settlers reported that Native Americans were on the warpath and demanded protection and retribution. Missouri Governor Lilburn Boggs called out the militia, and a full-blown battle appeared imminent.[70]

On hearing such news Kearny dispatched Captain Duncan and Company C to prevent violence. Duncan called upon and arrested the four tribesmen who had been involved in the gunfight. After the investigation, Kearny had the prisoners released, and reported to General Atkinson that, given the Pottawatomie men were protecting their property from an "attack in Indian Country made upon them, by men who have no business there, and of the most worthless character," he was "unwilling to place them in confinement here." Assuring the governor that the dragoons would maintain the peace, thus ended the so-called Heatherly War.[71]

Between July 10 and October 27 of that same year Lieutenant Steen, in Company C, made two marches along the western boundary between Missouri and Indian land. Kearny instructed Steen to visit the tense region and "preserve peace" there, for which aim if "necessary . . . [white] intruders upon their land, should be driven away." His orders included destroying white settlers' crops "and burning their dwellings provided they are there without license, from the proper authority."[72] The troop removed the trespassing white settlers and helped restore calm to the region. Afterwards, Lieutenant Steen met with Captain Boone near Grand River to survey a more direct route between Forts Leavenworth and Des Moines.

Colonel Kearny ordered Lieutenant Terrett and Company G on July 31, 1836, to return four members of Little Dish's band of Yankton Sioux to the tribe—two women and two boys captured by Sac warriors. Terrett followed the example repeatedly set by Dodge of gaining respect and peace from a tribe by returning any of its number who had been captured by enemies. Kearny directed the lieutenant to tell the Sioux that as soon as the colonel heard that four members of their tribe had been taken captive, he made arrangements to have them safely returned to their people, "which will prove the friendship the American People had for and the interest I take in them. . . . You will advise them (or coming from the President of the U.S.) to keep peace with all their Neighbors[,] that they derive no good from Wars, when they engage in them, and that the Great Spirit is more pleased to see the Red Skins shake hands with, than to see them fighting each other."[73]

Meanwhile, the regiment received calls from the north. Federal officials and settlers near Green Bay claimed that members of the Menominee, Winnebago, and Kickapoo tribes were expressing hostile intentions, and sought the aid of the army to intimidate them. Companies B, H, and I, stationed at Fort Des Moines, trekked across Illinois to Peoria and Chicago and thence to Fort Howard near Green Bay. The three companies arrived at the troubled spot and accomplished their task without resorting to force, and after a 1,300-mile round trip, returned home to Fort Des Moines.[74]

But the fort would not shelter the dragoons for long, and military authorities began to implement plans to abandon it. That fall, Kearny feared an outbreak of violence among tribes relocated along the Arkansas River and decided to concentrate his regiment at Fort Leavenworth. In October, Companies B, H, and I traveled from Des Moines to Leavenworth and wintered there. Temporarily abandoned, Fort Des Moines was reoccupied in early 1837. But on June 1, 1837, Lieutenant Colonel Mason sent the fort's skeleton detachment of dragoons to Leavenworth and declared the post officially vacated.[75]

The actions of Lieutenant Colonel Mason at Fort Des Moines should rebut the popular belief that class distinctions ceased with the founding of the United States. Mason, a proud and privileged Virginian descended from British royalists, clearly felt affronted when exiled by Kearny to command dreary Fort Des Moines with scarcely even a corporal's guard. Judging it beneath a man of his means to spend the winter at such a spot, he violated direct orders that he remain there by summarily moving to St. Louis and tendering his resignation. Mason briefly returned to Fort Des Moines in the spring to preside over its formal closing, but immediately repaired to more decorous quarters in St. Louis.

Desperate for officers, especially field-grade ones such as Mason, Kearny was furious when he heard of Mason's antics and reported him absent without leave. His anger at Mason's unprofessional conduct did not dissipate when Mason returned to Fort Leavenworth while Kearny was away surveying a new military road to Fort Gibson. He returned to the fort to find Mason had, without any authorization, placed himself in command. Colonel Kearny immediately had the presumptuous Mason arrested and sought to court-martial him.[76]

General Atkinson, though, allowed Mason to rescind his resignation and ordered his release from house arrest. Kearny twice wrote to Atkinson, railing that no officer should be allowed to withdraw his resignation, "as it suits his own convenience; nor do I think that military offences committed by officers of high rank should pass unnoticed or rather be rewarded and those committed by officers of a junior grade be punished with severity." The stickler for decorum added, "I repeat that I had no personal feeling to gratify in pursuing charges against Lt. Col. Mason. He & myself for many years have served together with uninterrupted harmony, and on the most friendly terms. That harmony and that friendship are still in full existence (or at least on my part towards him)."[77]

When the insouciant Mason took a furlough that winter and spring, Kearny wrote to Adjutant General Jones on December 27, 1838, asking that he order Mason back to his post at Fort Gibson. Kearny's attempt to return Mason went to naught and Mason remained absent until the last day of May. But if Mason harbored any animosity toward Kearny for his arrest and other slights to his worth, he soon lost it; during Kearny's tense confrontation with mutinous John Frémont in California in 1847, Mason would side with Kearny and even challenge Frémont to a duel.[78]

If 1836 had been a year of reorganization, training, refitting, and limited forays, in 1837 the regiment spent even less of its time out on patrol. On September 1, 1837, Company H, under Captain Boone, ventured briefly from Fort Leavenworth as a body guard for a commission surveying the Western Military Road. Other missions that year included Company C's July 22 escort of a group of Pottawatomie removed from Indiana to their new reservation across the Missouri, and Company F's accompaniment of treaty commissioners out of Fort Gibson westward to Chouteau's trading post near the Cross Timbers. On another occasion, famished Osages had stolen settlers' hogs and the perennially panicked Governor Boggs had called out the Missouri militia. On October 29 Companies A, B, and D therefore duly rode south from Fort Leavenworth to force members of the Osage tribe to cease the alleged incursions on white settlements in western Missouri and to move them back across the Missouri River into Indian country.[79]

As the year 1838 began, six dragoon companies were concentrated at Fort Leavenworth and four companies lodged at Fort Gibson. Continuing his efforts to professionalize the regiment, Kearny wrote to Adjutant General Jones on February 18, seeking permission to create a special school for dragoon recruits at Carlisle Barracks: "By this means, I think, the Regt. can be splendidly filled & with good quality recruits. I despair of accomplishing the above in the ordinary mode of Recruiting." That spring the school would come to fruition with Captain Sumner in command.[80]

Kearny's interest in improving the mounted arm reverberated in Washington. The next year the army sent Lieutenants Philip Kearny, William Eustis, and Henry Turner to study the training, tactics, and equipage of the French cavalry in Saumur Military College. Their observations resulted in the publication in 1841 of Secretary of War Joel Poinsett's three-volume *Cavalry Tactics.*[81]

Early in the year Kearny took six of his companies up the Missouri River to the Pottawatomie reservation located near present-day Council Bluffs, Iowa, where they built a blockhouse designed to protect the tribe from threatened Sioux raids.[82] It was not long before the tribe at this reservation found itself in the path of settlers and traffickers in illegal whiskey. In a few months the government moved the band to Kansas where it was to join—forcibly in some instances—other branches of the tribe torn by the army from their lands in Illinois and Indiana Territories.[83]

Meanwhile, in what seemed a tragic replay of the Black Hawk War, the Osages, whom the army had compelled to return to their reservation in late 1837, continued to starve. They, too, cast hungry eyes upon their fertile ancestral lands to the east. In the spring of 1838 the Osages came to hunt and to steal from settlements in western Missouri; blood was shed, and they would brave the brutal attacks of a militia. On the last day of March Captain Sumner wrote to Governor Boggs, assuring him that the rumors of war were greatly exaggerated as the Osage tribe was "not prepared for any general outbreak, and they cannot be so mad as to attempt to face . . . an organized force."[84] Boggs nonetheless continued with his plan to fight them and amassed the militia.

But just as the militia, vastly outnumbering the tribesmen and determined to kill as many as possible, readied to strike, Kearny and two hundred dragoons crossed the Missouri and rode to the rescue of the Native peoples. Before the frontiersmen could re-enact the massacre of the Sauks that had taken place at the Battle of Bad Axe, the appearance of the dragoons abruptly ended the purported "Indian uprising."[85] Kearny crossed back over the Missouri with the "invading" Osages in tow. He met in council with Osage leaders at their village and demanded that they inflict corporal punishment upon those of the tribe who were guilty of any wrongdoing. Believing most members of the Osage tribe to be predisposed to peace yet in need of protection from vengeful settlers, the colonel left behind a detachment at the border and departed for Leavenworth.[86]

Other peacekeeping endeavors proved more complicated. Among the transplanted Cherokees near Fort Gibson, friction developed between a party opposing removal and those who had signed their agreement. During the winter of 1838–39 the majority of the tribe marched to their new lands along the infamous "Trail of Tears," during which a full quarter of their number died and the rest arrived at the most inhabitable reaches of present-day Oklahoma.[87]

The Trail of Tears experience fueled the anger of both Cherokee factions. The Cherokees requested a meeting with the Indian agent and with neighboring tribes to be held on September 15, 1838. Lieutenant Colonel Mason, hearing of the planned council, sent and published a letter to the ever-excitable General Gaines at St. Louis, claiming that the Cherokee groups intended to unify with one another and with Indians from the Red River to the upper Mississippi, and that, once joined, they would attack settlers in the spring of 1839.[88] Reading Mason's letter were frightened frontier settlers, who clamored for military protection.

As a result of this panic, the army deemed it necessary to build a fort in the Cherokee Territory. Thus on April 27, 1839, Special Orders No. 27 directed "Lt. Col. Mason, 1st dragoons, with the four companies of his regiment, stationed at Fort Gibson, to take post on the ground selected for the erection of the new work." Companies E, F, G, and K would build and garrison the new post on the Little Illinois River in northwestern Arkansas Territory near the Cherokee agency, with orders to intimidate the tribe.[89] When constructed, the new station, called Fort Wayne, would sit on a level plain near a bend of the river. Only a roadside marker notes its former location in present-day Adair County, Oklahoma, near the border with Arkansas. Major Hitchcock described the partially completed post in 1842:

> There is one two-story framed house finished, intended for two companies of Dragoons, with a kitchen at each end and the foundation for a similar house for two other companies; but the finished building is occupied as a store house and the men live in very low and rude log huts with dirt floors, etc. . . . Besides the buildings named there are frames erected for two-story buildings with piazzas for officers quarters. These have been standing uncovered several months, all work being suspended until the Government can decide upon the question as to the location permanently of the Fort.[90]

Lt. Richard Ewell and Company A were assigned to the post, where Ewell was appointed to the troublesome position of quartermaster. In this role he was charged with hiring contractors to build the post. Writing to his sister the young lieutenant complained of both the lack of female society and of having to deal with the contractors: "The brutes actually put me in a furor sometimes." And then there was the serious problem with the ready availability of alcohol in nearby Arkansas.[91] Fortunately for Ewell and others stationed there, the army abandoned the fort shortly after Hitchcock's visit due to the high incidence of malaria, and it was occupied by the Cherokee Nation.[92]

1839–1842: A Rebuilt and Fit Regiment Takes to the Field

A period of regular and generally uneventful patrolling ensued. In early May of 1839, 2nd Lt. William Bowman, the former sergeant major, led a detachment of forty dragoons out of Fort Gibson to escort a merchant caravan traveling along the Santa Fe Trail to Chihuahua. He met the traders at the Cross Timbers and accompanied them to the Mexican border near Bent's Fort.[93] During the trip, Bowman encountered a few friendly Comanches, whom he informally invited to discuss maintaining peace in the region.[94]

Soon after, on September 5, 1839, Colonel Kearny marched Companies A, B, C, and H, two hundred sabers strong, from Fort Leavenworth to investigate a potential fort location at Table Creek on the Overland Trail. Kearny was also to hold council with the Otoes to discuss their killing of two persons—Otoe Chief Ietan and a white man—as well as their destroying and stealing settlers' property and threatening war. He led the squadron at a leisurely pace, deploying a newly acquired inflatable India rubber boat to cross the broad Platte River:

> An opportunity was thus offered of testing the utility of Capt. Lane's admirable application of India rubber to purposes of military economy. A small box, of little weight, containing a boat capable of transporting about 1,500 pounds' weight across a rapid stream, having been brought

with us, the cylinders were inflated and the boat launched. It is almost superfluous, after the many testimonials in its favor, to say that the boat answered all the purposes of its invention, uniting with an ease of management and a readiness of transportation, which must give it entire precedence over every other kind of pontoon yet offered to the consideration of the military public.[95]

After the crossing, the troops encountered the bones, weapons, and equipage of Sergeant Evans, who had drowned there in 1836 on his way to return four members of the Yankton Sioux captured by Sacs. "The now useless sword and belt and cartridge-box, lying with their owner's remains, and marked with the letter of his company, and his number, identified the individual." Captain Boone saw to it the bones of the dauntless sergeant were placed into a box and buried with full military honors.[96]

A romanticized account of this event found its way into *Recollections of the U.S. Army.* William Hildreth, brother of the author James Hildreth who had been discharged for medical reasons in March 1837, was serving as the post sutler at Camp Des Moines when Evans's remains were discovered. William undoubtedly transmitted the information to his brother, who embroidered the story to taste: "The cap was upon the naked skull, confined there by its chin-strap; the eyeless sockets, and denuded bone of the face and jaws, grinned hideously at the beholder. The jacket was buttoned to the chin; over each shoulder were suspended the sabre and carbine; the legs were encased in boots, to which the spurs attached; and though the clothing and equipment of the rider decayed and defaced, there still was left the faithful semblance of the mounted dragoon astride of his steed, both were fallen on their side."[97]

Kearny's detachment continued to its destination. On September 15, Otoe tribesmen were alarmed to see Kearny and two hundred dragoons unexpectedly crossing the river and appearing at their village. The Otoes remained nervous about the blue-coated intruders as Kearny told the tribesmen that he had entered their country to put a stop to the tribe's misbehavior. Repeating the strategy he had used with the Osage tribe, Kearny recorded that he "selected three of their young Men, who had been amongst the most prominent of the bad ones, & told the Nation I intended to punish them severely which would as I hoped, serve as an example."[98]

But the Otoes refused Kearny's request and stated they would rather fight than give him the three accused men. As tensions increased, Joseph Hamilton, Indian agent, sutler, and frontiersman, spoke on behalf of the tribe, suggesting that if the accused men were turned over to him for a public whipping, such punishment should suffice. Kearny, employing the classic "good-cop, bad-cop" routine, feigned reluctance, and told the Otoe leaders that, if their people ever committed another act of misconduct, "his ears would be closed to all solicitations of their agent." Although this situation concluded favorably, the colonel observed in his report that "their Chiefs having but little control over their young men . . . I fear that nothing will keep them permanently quiet, but that establishment of a Military Post near them, which I have again to recommend."[99]

Kearny departed the Otoe village on the seventeenth and crossed the Missouri River to visit a Pottawatomie village, and held council there the next day. He explained to the assembled tribesmen the benefits of entering into a new treaty, which would provide them new lands to the south of the Missouri River. The leader expressed his tribe's reluctance to negotiate with the U.S. government, which had not fulfilled its obligations under the former treaty. Kearny agreed that his government had shortchanged them, and advised them not to accept any new treaty unless it complied with its promises under the former treaty. During this expedition Colonel Kearny especially noted the tribes near the Missouri frontier to be "suffering a great deal from the great quantity of Liquor Carried to them, part by the Whites, & part by the half Breeds, & Indians themselves, who purchase it from the Whites living near the frontier!" To stop this flow of spirits and other illegal conduct, he called for the imposition of martial law in Indian country.[100]

By September 25 the command, having marched four hundred miles round-trip, returned to quarters at Fort Leavenworth.[101] A couple of weeks later Kearny contentedly received one hundred recruits at the post with whom he could rebuild his six too-lean companies.[102] This came not a moment too soon, for on October 27, from among his pile of mail, the *St. Louis Republican* of August 14, 1839, screamed, "IMPORTANT FROM THE WESTERN FRONTIER—INDIAN TROUBLES" and the *Nashville Banner* of August 22, 1839, quoted a letter by General Atkinson on "ANTICIPATED INDIAN HOSTILITIES" in the Cherokee Nation. The long-brewing, long-feared internal Cherokee quarrel over removal to Indian Territory appeared ready to engulf the entire region. The murders of two prominent Cherokee leaders, John Ridge and Elias Boudinot, on June 22 foreshadowed a potential bloodbath.[103]

Kearny did not wait for orders. On October 27 he sent four companies, a total of 250 men, on the march from Fort Leavenworth to the troubled area some four hundred miles distant, which they attained on the eighth of November. Kearny doubtless saw this event as an opportunity to test the dragoons' strength in a long march and, if necessary, in combat, and welcomed it as good training for his new recruits.[104] Arriving in Indian Territory, Kearny learned "from various sources & to be relied upon, that there is no kind of probability of the Cherokees as a Nation or in any force resisting the Military in taking the murders of Ridge & Boudinot: & the command of Lt. Col. Mason being sufficiently large for that purpose. . . . [A]s there is nothing required of me, from yourself but to search after a few Indians, who if found, would not be assisted by others, in resisting the Military, I consider it my duty, to return to my Post [at Fort Leavenworth]."[105]

In fact, by 1840 most of the eastern and southern tribes were living west of the Missouri and Mississippi Rivers in a state of relative peace. Nonetheless, each year widespread white fears of massive Indian outbreaks—and some remarkably minor actual ones—resurfaced on the frontier. In 1840, the dragoons were called upon yet again by frightened citizenry to calm the scene of alleged unrest. Major Wharton responded to such reports by taking Companies A,

D, and G from Fort Leavenworth to Fort Gibson with orders to remain in the locality to prevent renewed conflict between the two belligerent Cherokee factions. At the same time, the Otoes, continuing to suffer from the combined effects of poverty and alcohol, regularly raided the villages of neighboring tribes. Not surprisingly, it was not long before some restless young Otoes joined with Ioways, crossed the Missouri River, headed south, and raided white settlements in Missouri. To manage this crisis, on March 25 Captain Boone led Companies B and I from Leavenworth for about one hundred miles, crossing the Missouri and continuing north to the valley of the Nishnabotna River in what is now southeastern Nebraska and straight into the tribal encampment. There he indicated to the Otoes that the time for negotiation was over and that if they did not leave immediately he was prepared to unleash his forces upon them. Realizing themselves outgunned and outnumbered, the hungry marauders returned to their designated reservation across the Missouri River.[106] Also during the same period, Company B, under the command of Lt. Enoch Steen, marched north from Fort Leavenworth to Fort Crawford in Wisconsin Territory. There his dragoons helped infantry troops remove the last of the Winnebagos from Wisconsin west of the Missouri to a reservation at Turkey River in northwestern Iowa Territory. The troops remained in the field until August 17, marching 1,700 miles without loss or "material injury to any of its horses."[107]

Finding there to be no war, just as he had in 1839, Colonel Kearny asked General Arbuckle to send Wharton's troops back to Fort Leavenworth. When Arbuckle refused, Kearny ordered Companies E, F, and K to return from Fort Wayne to Fort Leavenworth.[108] With the arrival of those three companies Kearny had sufficient manpower to undertake a mission to the Pottawatomie Reservation. On September 21, he set out with Companies F and K and eight days later they arrived at the Pottawatomie settlements, where they remained until the seventh of October. There, Kearny supervised the distribution of government annuities and assisted the tribe in its difficult decision of whether or not to permit 150 Ioway squatters to live on the reserve. Exactly one week later the dragoons were back at Fort Leavenworth.[109] Some months later, on December 11, 1840, a band of Kanza warriors swooped down upon an unsuspecting Pawnee village and took eleven women and children prisoner. Captain Trenor and Company F accompanied Indian agent R. W. Cummins from Fort Leavenworth to the Kanzan village on February 17, 1841, both to bring the tribe its annuity and to recover the captives. Not expecting a visit of military authorities, the agent reported, the tribe was "much alarmed at the appearance of the troops" and immediately turned over the prisoners. In March, dragoons returned the freed Pawnees to their people.[110]

The year 1841 passed for the 1st Dragoons without further events of consequence. On the twenty-fourth of June, Captain Sumner's Company B moved into quarters at newly established Fort Atkinson on the Turkey River in Iowa Territory. For the remainder of the year the dragoons performed routine patrols, chased away white would-be settlers who had crossed the Missouri to invade fertile tribal lands, and enforced federal policy by destroying the squatters' structures and burning their crops.[111]

By that same year of 1841, the army had come to realize that Fort Wayne, between its unhealthful location and the Cherokees' objection to its placement on their land, should be abandoned. Major Hitchcock specified that the tribe was upset that the fort sat upon "one of the finest portions of their country—in the midst of an orderly and industrious community—bringing with it a train of evils before comparatively unknown—exposing their women to seduction and even to violence and inviting the location of dram shops."[112] The army began to explore a new location for the fort. Thus on April 1, 1842, Capt. Benjamin Moore and Company C, accompanied by Major Hitchcock, rode from Fort Wayne to seek a salubrious site on the newly constructed Leavenworth–Gibson military road. About one hundred miles out they found a spot near where the road crosses the Marmaton River in what is now southeastern Kansas. The new post was to be named in honor of Commanding General Winfield Scott, and the army soon ordered men and materials to aid in its construction.[113]

Sgt. John Hamilton stayed behind to command a work party with orders to begin construction. Hamilton, recalling the cruel cold inflicted upon the dragoons at Camp Jackson during the winter of 1833–34, was not about to spend this winter in a tent, and promptly had his crew begin building crude, dirt-floored log barracks for the men.[114] Fort Wayne was abandoned and its garrison was transferred to Fort Scott. Capt. Thomas Swords, a former dragoon, became Fort Scott's post quartermaster, presiding over its construction. Determined to make the latest fort "the crack post of the frontier," Swords skillfully directed the soldiers detailed to build it. Relative peace in the region allowed the garrison to set up serviceable quarters before winter set in. It took eight years, but the fort eventually boasted a handsome set of lumber buildings that made it the most graceful of any post in the West.[115]

Throughout 1842 the dragoons continued to maintain the fragile peace on the plains. On April 18, Kearny trotted out of Fort Leavenworth with five companies bound for Fort Gibson to assist Gen. Zachary Taylor in pacifying relocated Cherokees' intratribal tensions. As in the past, the presence of troops intimidated hotheads and bolstered peacemakers.[116] In the same year, the Second Seminole War came to an end. It had been the young nation's longest war, costing 1,466 deaths in the regular army and leading to the forcible removal of most members of the Seminole tribe to Indian Territory. That spring a group of three hundred Seminoles, whose right to remain in Florida had been taken away, arrived in the Indian Territory but refused to settle in at their bleak reservation on the Canadian River, and instead crossed the Arkansas River to squat on Cherokee lands to its south.[117]

In response, Colonel Kearny met with the leader of the Seminole refugees on June 7 and demanded that his people leave the Cherokee lands. The tribal headman—schooled in resisting the white man by six years of war—agreed. Yet by noon the next day his defiant and proud followers remained south of the Arkansas. Furious at the deception, Kearny had his trumpeter sound "to horse" and assembled his troops. The colonel ordered, "If we come to blows, put your sabres well in; but on no account strike a woman or child."[118]

A short march brought the troops to the Seminole encampment, deserted except for a single brazen youth who, "regardless of the sabres flashing about his head," defied his potential captors. Not wishing to injure the brave boy, Kearny commanded that he not be pursued. The troops soon caught up with a few dozen Seminole refugees near the Illinois River, boarded them on a ferry, and deposited them on the north bank of the Arkansas. Though most were without horses, these resourceful people didn't remain where they had been placed but quickly scattered to lands south of the river.[119]

Kearny was more livid than before. It was late in the day, but Captain Cooke took two companies across the river to round up the fugitives. With some difficulty, one group of dragoons swam their horses across the river while others found a raft to cross. Against the setting sun, the soaked and hungry dragoons pursued the more ragged and starving Seminoles. The tribesmen, skilled at hiding in the Everglades, evaded detection and the soldiers had to cross the river again to arrive back in camp empty-handed. The next morning Cooke's troops got an early start. Well fed and in dry clothes, they sought anew the recalcitrant Seminoles, the chase disintegrating into a free-for-all. The dragoons, in the words of Captain Cooke, overran many miles of country and in a series of pell-mell charges, captured numerous prisoners, and reportedly gave one fugitive a saber wound. While for Cooke and the others this day represented one of glory, for the beaten and impoverished Seminoles it was yet another tragedy in their tribal history.[120]

Also in 1842, a series of company-sized patrols aimed at intercepting the flourishing illegal sale of liquor in Indian country. One such patrol, under the command of pious Calvinist and teetotaler Lt. John Gardiner, left Fort Leavenworth in early August. On the fourteenth Lieutenant Gardiner stopped two wagons carrying fifty-five barrels of whiskey, confiscated them, and arrested the traders.[121] But for every successful interception of spirits into

Indian Territory, there were dozens of wagon loads of contraband that got through and brought on the ruination of tribe after tribe.

Kearny: Enabling the Dragoons' Transformed Mission

Colonel Kearny had now commanded the dragoon regiment for over six years—time primarily spent equipping, recruiting, and training soldiers, and building a string of forts and a military road along the country's western frontier. Now the regiment pushed deeper into the Great Plains and the Rockies, and as tensions in the long struggle between the Mexican and Texan nations threatened to bleed into the United States, Kearny's dragoons managed any interference with the country's sovereign neutrality.

Between 1836 and 1842 the dragoon role had been essentially a constabulary one in the Mississippi Valley, keeping Native peoples and settlers apart and preventing intertribal warfare. But in 1843 the regiment began to move away from the Mississippi Valley and into distant westward lands to support the expansion of U.S. sovereignty in the Great Plains. The dragoons carried out the ideology of so-called Manifest Destiny, pushing Natives ever westward. That year, not coincidentally, also marked the beginning of the great movement of settlers along the Oregon Trail, largely motivated by Americans' discovery of the extensive, richly arable land beckoning them to the magnificent Pacific coast. While settlers would later flood California, at this period Oregon drew them. Fur traders and missionaries—as well as dragoon expeditions in 1835—had traveled the Oregon Trail before, but their revelations had not impressed those in the eastern United States until this time. Now, slowly but surely, ever-increasing numbers of settlers pursued the Oregon Trail to their dreams: the government's promise of free farmland in the Willamette Valley, or what other treasures they conceived.

By the beginning of 1843 the dragoons, along with other federal regiments stationed at posts along the frontier, had secured the frontier by keeping Natives from crossing the Missouri River to return to their homelands and whites from squatting on Indians' new lands or selling them liquor. Kearny's summers of long marches and tough diplomacy with a variety of tribes had earned, for himself and his regiment, the gratitude and respect of politicians and frontier settlers.[122] The ease and rapidity with which he moved his forces to troubled sectors and, when necessary, concentrated them as a show of strength, proved Secretary of War Cass's argument for creating the dragoons in the first place: the value of an elite mounted force to defend the nation against a foreign foe. The skills needed to become a crack mounted regiment had been slowly and dearly won, but under Kearny dragoon officers had finally learned how to train, equip, and lead their men effectively.

CHAPTER 4

The Snively Incident

Dragoons on the Santa Fe Trail

Mexico threatened war if the United States attempted to annex Texas—not an unreasonable scenario, as the U.S. Army had already become involved in a host of minor foreign relations matters in the area. Lt. James Carleton, for example, investigated claims by Texicans that Comanches were stealing their slaves and selling them in Indian Territory. He also looked into acts by Texicans crossing the border illegally to sell spirits to Native Americans.[1] But these peccadilloes paled in comparison with the international border-crossing of armed bands of Texican land pirates to raid Mexican traders on the Santa Fe Trail, which stretched the war into U.S. territory.

Throughout this period, both the Lone Star Republic and Mexico plundered each other's lands. In one such raid, in 1841, the Republic of Texas launched an expedition of merchants, escorted by soldiers, in hopes of securing its claims to parts of the Mexican province of New Mexico and gaining control of the Santa Fe trade. Mexican soldiers attacked the column, captured the invading Texican force, and marched its prisoners nearly 2,000 miles to Mexico City. They executed seventeen men, and many more died from wounds, disease, and starvation, or languished until U.S. diplomacy secured their release in 1844. It was no secret that the young republic wanted to retaliate for this outrage, for Mexican general Adrian Woll's September 1842 raid on San Antonio, and for the disastrous Texican military operation known as the Mier Expedition in November of that year. Recalling all these, the government of Texas called for reprisals.[2]

Early in 1843, the Texas government implemented plans to attack Mexican caravans on the Santa Fe Trail. On February 16, its president, Sam Houston, presented a colonel's commission to Jacob Snively and instructed him to lead his 176-man "Battalion of Invincibles" on raids against Mexican commerce on the Trail, thereby to "retaliate and make reclamation for injuries sustained by Texas citizens." The merchandise seized would be deemed a lawful prize, to be divided equally between the Republic and the raiders, and Snively's instructions ordered him "to be careful not to infringe upon" the territory of the United States. In his journal notes on the expedition Texican adventurer and later judge Stewart Miller remarked that the men were all well armed, "furnished generally with a rifle, brace of pistols, & Bowie Knife."[3] To support Snively, the Texas government commissioned Col. Charles Warfield to lead troops in similar incursions against Mexican trade.[4] Snively's detachment set out from Georgetown, Texas, on April 25. A month later, after a march of about 350 miles across what is now Oklahoma, they reached the Arkansas River. Warfield's force joined Snively on June 4, swelling the battalion to 190 men.

On June 19, at about sixteen miles from the Arkansas River, the two Texican forces met and easily bested a ragged one-hundred-man militia detachment from Taos. Governor Manuel Armijo, approaching with four hundred men to fight Snively, retreated upon hearing of the Taos militia's defeat.[5] In fact, the first effective repulsion of the Texican raiders came not from Mexico but from the United States. On June 30, 1843, four companies of the 1st Regiment of Dragoons splashed across the Arkansas, unlimbered their artillery, and formed a line of battle, sabers drawn and howitzers prepared to fire on the Texican position: "I find you are an armed body of men on the territory of the United States, and by the laws of nations I have the right to disarm you. . . . I now command you to lay down your arms," demanded Dragoon

Captain Cooke.[6] Texicans were used to bucking the odds, but they surrendered as these soldiers in dirty blue coats were from a friendly neighbor, not Mexico. President Santa Anna, of course, applauded the dragoons' actions, but the Republic of Texas most certainly did not. In fact, the Texicans filed a diplomatic protest claiming that its troops had not even entered the United States.

The War between Texas and Mexico
Impinges on the United States

At least for the time being, the United States did not wish to enter the conflict between Mexico and Texas. Claiming neutral status, the United States preferred to trade freely with both belligerents. From as early as 1821 commerce on the Santa Fe Trail had become an important source of wealth for the state of Missouri as well as for the Mexican province of New Mexico. By issuing letters of marque to Texican land pirates, the money-strapped Republic of Texas attempted to commandeer this exchange route for its own profit. U.S. neutrality notwithstanding, the dragoons would soon find themselves embroiled in international politics.

The ever-tenuous relations between Mexico and the United States were strained to near breaking when on October 19, 1842, Commo. Thomas ap Catesby Jones, mistakenly believing that war had been declared, sailed his naval squadron into Monterey, California, and seized the town.[7] Discovering his mistake, an embarrassed Jones sailed away. When the U.S. War Department began receiving reports, in the early days of 1843, that the new Texas Republic intended to raid wagon trains traveling the Santa Fe Trail, Secretary of State Daniel Webster requested permission from the Mexican government for the U.S. Army to escort Santa Fe-bound vehicles across the international border and into New Mexico. Gen. Juan Almonte, the Mexican minister in Washington, D.C., answered that he lacked authority to approve such a plan. But Almonte agreed that American forces could—if they deemed it necessary and if invited by Mexican citizens—cross the international border, and that Mexico would not consider such an armed escort to be an invasion.[8]

Col. Charles Warfield, commissioned by the Texas government, traveled to Missouri, where he recruited men to invade New Mexico. His recruits assembled around mid-May 1843, on the Santa Fe Trail, where they met Snively's Texican troops. The joint forces were then to raid commerce in New Mexico. Traders on the Santa Fe Trail heard of these efforts and, concerned for the safety of their caravans, requested army escorts. It was time for the U.S. Army to enter the scene and protect the trail from piracy.[9]

It did not take long for the attacks on wagon trains to begin. On April 10, about 240 miles west of Independence, Missouri, fifteen raiders, recruited mainly in that state and under the command of John McDaniel, pillaged two eastbound wagons and murdered their owner, wealthy Mexican merchant Don Antonio Chaves. Though associated with the Texican militia, McDaniel's gang probably acted outside the authority of the Texas government and certainly shared none of the booty with it. Supporters of Texas quickly repudiated the band as murderous outlaws who followed no orders but their own. No matter. It was high time for the U.S. Army to protect the Trail from banditry.[10]

Lt. Col. Richard Mason at Fort Leavenworth, on April 3, 1843, sent sixty dragoons under Lt. William Bowman in pursuit of McDaniel's detachment with instructions to arrest them. The marauders had a two- or three-day head start and Lieutenant Bowman, low on provisions, was unable to intercept them and returned to the fort. The *St. Louis (Mo.) New Era* would blame the U.S. dragoons for turning back; had the troops "kept on the trail one day longer, they would have" saved Chaves from his fate.[11]

Unleashing the Dragoons

News of the danger to American commerce posed by the McDaniel foray easily won Adj. Gen. Roger Jones's approval for U.S. Army troops to escort wagon trains leaving Missouri for Santa Fe. The

1st Dragoons, accustomed to travel on the Trail and having their primary bases near its eastern terminus, were the logical choice as military guards. Jones believed this mission would not only protect trade but also had "the advantages of keeping mounted forces in readiness to dash over the wide prairies as occasions require, or at least yearly, if only to exhibit themselves to the frontier Indians." Responding to the call, Col. Stephen Kearny quickly devised a plan to dispatch two of his three dragoon squadrons west on the Santa Fe Trail to protect merchants and, if necessary, to capture Texicans preying on commercial traffic.[12]

On May 14, 1843, Capt. Nathan Boone sallied forth from Fort Gibson in the Cherokee Territory with the sixty-two sabers of 1st Dragoon Company H. Among his men rode the 1839 enlistee John Flynn, a highly literate thirty-year-old hatter from New York City recruited by Captain Trenor, who would record his experience of this expedition, including being sixteen hours "in the saddle without dismounting, and on one occasion 3 days without food."[13] Four days later Lt. Abraham Johnston and twenty-seven others from Company D reinforced Boone's column. The squadron rode to the scene of the Chaves crime, but efforts to find his remains or to capture his killers proved fruitless. Boone's squadron continued the hunt westward on the Santa Fe Trail.[14] In the meanwhile, a posse of Missourians accomplished what the dragoons had thus far failed to do: capturing McDaniel and some of his party and bringing them back to St. Louis for summary trial. The judge rejected McDaniel's argument that the Missouri federal court lacked jurisdiction because the alleged crime occurred in Indian Territory; the jury convicted him and an associate, and had them hanged on August 16, 1844.[15]

On May 27, 1843, a second column of 160 dragoons under Capt. Philip St. George Cooke left Fort Leavenworth to support Boone's force and to accompany a large caravan along the Santa Fe Trail.[16] The party boasted the luminaries Capt. Benjamin Moore of Company C, 1st Lt. William Bowman of Company F, and 2nd Lts. Daniel Rucker, John Love, and George Mason.

Noteworthy was the fact that Cooke's dragoons were not attired as they would be when in garrison. For example, many were not wearing the white belts army regulations called for—a variance Kearny forgave: "It has been a custom of some Comp[anie]s of the Regiment (& which I have not thought necessary to change) when going out on duty on the Prairies to leave their white belts in store & to use black ones, which were equally serviceable, tho not as uniform."[17] Moreover, since former Secretary of War Joel Poinsett had found pistols useless for dragoons, many men serving with Cooke lacked them and only half of the men in other companies were so furnished.[18]

In the succinct words of military historian Durwood Ball, "Cooke was an eccentric soldier."[19] He was also a bully and could be mean spirited; he once called for the annihilation of the buffalo to bring peace to the plains. In 1838 the proud and well-educated Virginian shot his wife, wounding her—accidentally, he said.[20] Petty vindictiveness was not unusual for Cooke. In 1844 Cooke, commanding a squadron in the expedition, ordered Capt. John Burgwin, his subordinate, "to change their usual manner of attaching their Picket Ropes to their Saddles." Burgwin countermanded this order. Maj. Clifton Wharton, hearing the squabble, neglected to intervene. Upon his return to Fort Leavenworth, Cooke formally complained to Colonel Kearny of the insubordination on Burgwin's part and sought to court-martial him.[21]

In Solomonesque fashion, Kearny faulted Cooke for overstepping his authority in issuing the picket rope order, Burgwin for countermanding the order of a superior, and Wharton, for not stepping in as commanding officer and putting an end to the petty quarrel. Kearny did not select Wharton to lead another expedition, and left him behind at the fort on his next two missions.[22]

Years later, in 1851, brevet Capt. John Love was serving under his old commander at the mounted school located in Carlisle, Pennsylvania. Friction developed between the two men and on September 9, 1851, Cooke arrested Love and filed court-martial charges that the subordinate had acted disrespectfully and used

profane language when addressing the lieutenant colonel, in con-
travention of Articles of War III and XXXV.[23]

In the case of Captain Love, Gen. John Wool, commander of
the 3rd Military Department, felt Cooke was being petty-minded,
refused to files charges, released Love from arrest, and reinstated
him as post quartermaster. He found that Love's "error was one
of judgment and not of willful insubordination and contempt of
authority." The spiteful Cooke gained a measure of revenge by
dispatching Love as the only officer in command of a detachment
of ninety-one Carlisle recruits to Jefferson Barracks. Months later,
Love, fed up with petty army politics, resigned his commission and
entered into business.[24]

Up to now, the sociable Lt. John Love's military career could be
described as a series of pleasant companionships and dull duties,
punctuated by relatively uneventful expeditions to the plains and
the Rockies. But his agreeable existence would change as hostilities with Mexico tore away treasured friends and tossed him all
the horrors of war.[25] His journal preserves his impressions of the
1843 trip—the first of three he would make onto the Great Plains
before the Mexican War—and echoes most new recruits' excitement at seeing the widening country. To the untried lieutenant,
arresting Texican pirates appeared much less valuable than escaping the tedium of Fort Leavenworth:

> May 27, 1843, the day fixed for our departure. Of course
> there was a great deal of bustle & confusion preparatory
> to so long a march: here you could see an officer sending
> after his tobacco & segars [sic], which he had nearly for-
> gotten, & without which, the march from being a pleasure,
> would have become a bore; another just stuffing his last
> shirt in his saddle bags; a third packing up needles, but-
> tons, thread &c, but as one may expect without a doubt of
> veracity, that "all things have an end," so had the packing,
> &c about 9 o'clock the bugles call us, not to "war," but
> to the parade ground where the companies were drawn
> up in line in front of their quarters. . . . What a beautiful

sight as the long line of horsemen march down the parade [ground], each one as he passed some friend[,] waving him an adieu.[26]

On the early part of the journey they ambled along a path for wagons traveling either west to Oregon or south to Santa Fe and Chihuahua. But by noon, before they had covered more than nine miles, a tempest drenched the soldiers and made the way impassable. Digging the wagons out of mud holes and wrestling with unruly mules exhausted the men. Cooke, who had planned to meet the traders' caravan at Pleasant Valley Creek, became increasingly frustrated as the muck deepened: "The waggons [*sic*] did not get up till nearly night & as it still continued raining, we camped: every one wet to the skin & thoroughly disgusted; what added to our disgust were some of the horses, with a desire to warm themselves, breaking their 'lariats' & racing through camp, gaining recruits at each jump, until nearly half were loose. Took an early supper & went to bed, praying that morrow might bring a little sunshine."[27]

But that morrow brought only more rain and annoyance:

One of our officers was notorious for his dislike to rainy weather now on awakening he found his mortal enemy [*rain*] . . . but his celebrated horse Sir Charles Piebald, out in the field, that is to say, Sir Charles had absented himself from camp without permission. After a fruitless search he was reported a deserter. Fortunately for the owner, in passing through the Kansas timber, two officers feeling thirsty, left the column a quarter of a mile; in returning they saw among a thick patch of grape vines & in a herd of Indian ponies, a horse they felt certain was Sir Charles; but he looked so innocent, & was much at home, they began to doubt; on considering, however, that there could not be another horse living, like him, they concluded to drive him to the column, where on arriving their first sus- picions were confirmed: he was captured, & returned to the longing arms of, or rather legs, of his attached, but slighted, master.[28]

But the end of rain and a bright show of sun the next day cheered spirits. On the twenty-ninth Love wrote, "How delightful to feel once more the warmth of the sun & to see countenances beaming with smiles & good nature, looking as if with the rain had departed their only enemy on Earth."[29] The young lieutenant, soaking up the scenery, sounds, and even the discomfort, was in no hurry to leave this undisturbed site. By noontime, the column reached the junction of the Military Road and the Santa Fe Trail. Like many traveling into the wilderness of the prairie, Love found the milestone both bittersweet and eerie, having left friends and real towns behind and pressing into a vast, uncharted region. While the beauty of the plains enchanted him, fears emerged: "[S]ome of us were perhaps leaving our homes & friends to be buried on the desolate prairie. For on leaving the Military road it seemed as if the last link that bound us to our homes was broken. With me, every thing was new. I had no conception of the country over which we would pass nor of the character of the Indians we would meet nor of what we would have to encounter from sickness &c." Still, after several hours' march, the prairie's grandeur "relieved my usual spirits as I saw the beautiful extent of country before me was with such green grass & myriads of flowers looking for all the world like some neglected garden. I know of no other way of conveying my first impression of the prairie than by a remark one soldier made to another[,] 'we are getting pretty well out to sea'—in rear & on each side could be seen the dim outline of timber while in front nothing but a vast plain, the grass waving with the wind, scarcely distinguishable from water."[30]

Riding along the south bank of the Arkansas River, Pvt. John Flynn of Boone's Company H also admired the glories of the country: "Few scenes in Nature, and none in Art, can exceed the gorgeous splendor of some of the prairies, covered with flowers so bright and so innumerable that I suppose one half of them have never been classified or named by botanists." Spent after a hard ride, Flynn extolled the positively tonic air of a prairie dawn: "This fresh air indeed truly appears to bring health, vigor, strength, power."[31]

Cooke's column stopped for lunch at Bear Creek and an officer who fancied himself a big game hunter rode out looking for bear. Spying distant dark objects, he thought them to be his target: "[O]ff he started at full speed with the hope of killing the first game. The bear finding itself pursued ran for his life. For it was then the pursuer increased his gait, compromised his life & braced himself for the deadly combat, an occasional smile appears over his face as he finds he is gaining ground, at last the object enters a hollow, the pursuer rushing to the edge. Raises in his stirrups, looks over & with horror he finds he has been chasing a sow & pigs."[32]

Even in fair weather, even in peacetime, encampment of a mounted force on the march required soldiers to tend to horses, unload wagons, pitch tents, gather firewood and water, and cook. In hostile territory they also needed to post sentries and to guard cattle, horses, and mules. In addition, the column of three companies had brought with it two small mountain howitzers—lightweight brass cannon capable of rapid deployment—designed by the army to be either pulled across the flat plain by a team of two horses or mules hitched to a wagon or artillery limber or, in rough terrain, disassembled and carried by three pack animals. After two days the column had traveled a mere twenty-three miles. The path became "monotonous, without a stick of timber, and bad water." Love, nonetheless, gleefully described the way a mischievous team of horses pulling one of the howitzers, "with a desire to afford variety &c to their faults towards varying the monotony of the march, by some means got their driver [thrown] from the [limber wagon] box & commenced kicking, running, jumping &c. Here you would see their running straight to the column—every man giving way of course, then running on the road, then turning and coming back to the column, the command scattered about, each one on his own preservation, making in all quite an amusing scene."[33]

The year 1843 marked the beginning of the "Great Migration" of citizenry westward to Oregon Territory, with eight hundred people in 110 wagons. The relocations following in the wake of the Mexican War and the California Gold Rush would dwarf this one, but Love's entry for the last day of May shows he recognized the Oregon/Santa Fe Trail as an absolute river of humanity. To him, the Trail,

> which looked like a road leading into some large town, a person getting on it in ignorance would feel badly to find it after traveling 10–12 days growing smaller what made it so large & dusty. [It] was the Oregon Company passing over it, in addition to the Santa Fe waggons—a mile &c half further [we] came to Elm Grove, might have been a grove once certainly is no longer, only the remnant of its ancient greatness being a single tree, the top of that cut off for fire wood. . . . Very monotonous road for 15 miles, not a stick of timber on the road, but occasional groves varying from 2 to five miles to the right & left. Water very bad, day hot & only stagnant pools to quench out thirst.[34]

While on the well-traveled road Love described being overtaken by a single Oregon-bound settler who was "merely going out to see the country, if he did not like it would return next spring[,] talked as if he were about taking a journey of a few miles. He expected to overtake the Oregon Company who were a day's journey ahead & consisted of nearly 1500 [people]."[35]

Riding five more miles under the blazing sun, the party reached "Black Jack Grove, a most inviting place . . . most especially as there was a stream of water running through it." Here, at present-day Gardner Junction, the tracks split, with the Oregon Trail veering northwest while the Santa Fe Trail, and the dragoons upon it, proceeded due west: "Passed waggon road three miles before reaching Black Jack, a plain dusty road with a finger [pointing] just at the forks & the word Oregon."[36] Love had always felt excitement and interest when meeting travelers. On the second of

June, he welcomed the sight of a group of hunters returning from the Rockies with a load of buffalo skins and several buffalo calves. But the tale they told of losing ten of their number in a fight with the Indians put him on notice that his venture onto the plains might not be a delightful sightseeing trip.[37]

Riding quickly on the flat road, Cooke made up for lost time. At Pleasant Creek by June 3, the dragoons met the wagons they were to escort. Lieutenant Love described the site "like all timbered creeks, running through the prairies, looking more beautiful than you could suppose it. Without exception the coldest spring water I ever tasted. Impossible to tell you how much we enjoyed the water after a ride in the hot sun for two or three hours." But he was less impressed with the teamsters: "Got the first sight to-day of the people we were to escort. Not very prepossessing either in person or equipments. The men (Spaniards) the distinct, darkest and worst countenances for white people I have ever saw. Their mules like themselves, only half horrified."[38] Soldier John Flynn of Company H echoed Love's view: "The drivers of these teams are the refuse of all nations, Mexicans of the lowest classes, half breed Indians, White Men from the States who dare not to be seen there again, all of the degraded portion of humanity, nothing better could be expected."[39]

After a pause for lunch, men and wagons proceeded eight miles further to Council Grove. Situated on the banks of the Neosho, it was

> the largest body of timber on the road between Kansas River & Red River in Mexico. Here the Traders always stop to lay in an extra axle tree & tongue in case they break down on the Prairie. Found most all the Traders on the west side of the river camped in the usual order, the waggons forming a salient angle making a place of safety for their animals in case of attack. We also found a load of corn which our provident quarter master had sent before . . . as the grass was a month more backward than usual.[40]

The layover at Council Grove lasted several days. Lieutenant Love took the opportunity to sleep, hunt, and fish but Cooke, concerned that his force was nearing a confrontation with Snively, used the time to drill the gun crews. The appearance of Capt. Burdette Terrett leading twenty-five dragoons of Company A delighted the gregarious Love, who wrote that the chance meeting with a brother officer "from Fort Scott enlivening us all as an arrival is sure to do; our spirits were now very high: we had . . . questions to ask about all our friends at Fort Scott & he about his at Leavenworth."[41]

While camped, young Lieutenant Love got to know "Old Nick" Gentry, a famed mountain man who was also a guide and Santa Fe trader. Among his many adventures Gentry had smuggled a load of contraband tobacco to Santa Fe with Charles Bent back in 1829: "He amused us very much by his manner of expressing himself, if he wishes to describe any thing, he will do so, by drawing a comparison between it, & something else . . . [letting his audience] see him riding over the prairie all alone, without any protection for his face than his long bushy hair, which looks as if he had seldom been acquainted with scissors."[42]

The brief stay ended. Wagons and their escort resumed the trek westward on June 6. The weather suddenly turned chilly and wet and the men were grateful for their woolens. Despite the discomfort, Love continued to marvel at the magnificence he encountered:

> When about five miles from Little Arkansas saw to the left the Sand Hills of Great Arkansas, looking so much like a City as to consider it almost impossible to imagine yourself 200 miles from any house unlike sand hills generally, these just mentioned have groves of stunted timber amongst them which obscures a greater part of the hill, exposing to view in one place a single spot the size of a house which you could imagine a neat dwelling in the suburbs of the city, then another long ridge like the front of a square of brick buildings, taken all together a very handsome sight.

Still another day, but none killed yet. Soon after securing camp the axes began to sound & then blazing fires were made in front of the tents, each one forgotten the discomforts of the day, as he sat dozing & warming himself by a cheerful fire."[43]

But while Lieutenant Love enjoyed the sights, Captain Cooke scoured the prairie looking for both Captain Boone and Snively's outlaws. He found neither but discovered a note written by Boone fastened to a tree at a ford of the Arkansas River and informing him that his two troops had crossed the river and found no signs of the raiders, but had seen a herd of buffalo. Boone failed to mention that in fact the flanks of an entire herd of buffalo had run through his camp, crushing tents and making the horses stampede. Private Flynn, however, later recounted the event and detailed how the men had excitedly grabbed their carbines, "causing so much cross firing, that it was wonderful that they, the men, did not kill each other." One trooper claimed to have been tossed high in the air by a buffalo: "It was that in the ascent and descent with his carbine in hand, that he remembered his carbine was capped and cocked, and that when he fell and struck the ground the concussion would cause the cock to fall, and so explode, that he had sufficient presence of mind to take off the cap, let down the cock, this in his journey up and down." Flynn's quixotic account omitted grimmer facts: on the thirteenth of June Lieutenant Johnston shot himself in the leg while chasing buffalo, and on July 25 a rifle that a teamster had carelessly propped against a wagon was knocked down and discharged a bullet into Pvt. Benuel Bean's back, killing him.[44]

After reading Boone's note, Cooke judged it wise to wait for the wagons to catch up, and called a halt. He then detailed a thrilled Love to lead a party to hunt buffalo. And so Love merrily rode off—the hunter on his prancing steed, footloose on the prairie, tracking big game: "Now I thought my long cherished dreams of hunting were about to be realized & as I charged my cartridges & put my pistols in my holsters & mounted my trim built little horse felt as if not one of a herd could escape certain death . . . but was disappointed for they only saw an antelope. . . . When near the road some one pointed to the right & there sure enough I saw about 2 miles off a small hill covered with objects running to & fro." Then the smug hunter found something moving out there he didn't expect: "I had made many inquiries about the ways of Buffalo & had it in my head the regular rule for approaching & running them but when I saw them approaching me instead of my approaching it nullified all the rules & completely staggered me. I thought it very strange my informers had not told me what to do under these circumstances. . . . I did not wait long, for presently a yell was heard as if a thousand devils were let loose. I then saw that these were Indians." Indians, and lots of them, galloping toward the little band of dragoons! Miles from camp, Lieutenant Love and his five men trembled over their fate:

> On they came whipping, spurring & galloping. . . . [T]he whole Prairie seemed alive with them; they were naked from the waist up; had neither bridle nor saddle; but a piece of Buffalo hide in their horses' mouths. (A more alarming sight I never saw, to one unaccustomed to Indians as I.) The change from Buffalos to a Band of Indians was so sudden & unexpected as to throw me completely in confusion; after nearing a little I ordered my men to face them, see to their arms & a white handkerchief to be raised to indicate how much we were in favor of peace. I drew my pistols[,] put one in my belt & held the other cocked in my hand determined to sell out all my interest in the world as dearly as possible.

Overconfident, as were most officers of the era, Love believed he could withstand any assault: "With 6 men [we] could have kept off 500 Indians as they never approach within gun shot. By their notions deeming it a greater victory to kill one man & lose none in return than to kill fifty & lose one of their men, which system would of course prevent their coming to close quarters."

This belief had some basis; the dragoons had patrolled the Great Plains for ten years without having to battle any of the tribes living there. Love was also certain that these Natives feared the troops' firearms. Regardless, the shavetail lieutenant rejoiced to discover the bloodthirsty warriors to be but a peaceful hunting party from the Kanza (also known as Kaw) Nation, living on a reservation in what was to become Kansas.

Practicing the diplomacy he had learned from Colonel Kearny, Lieutenant Love nervously invited the Kaw hunters to visit the dragoon camp that evening. As the tribesmen followed him, Love realized how extremely vulnerable, and how blessedly fortunate, he and his men had been. Any interest he had had in buffalo hunting was thoroughly extinguished, and he was glad to arrive safely back at camp. The Kaws, meanwhile, proudly showed off their hunting and riding skills to the white soldiers, bringing them fresh buffalo meat. In exchange, Captain Cooke gave the Kaws tobacco and fat pork. In fact, neither the Kaws nor any Plains tribes were spoiling for a fight with dragoons. The real threat to the Indians came from other whites lurking nearby: the Texicans. And a possible threat extended to the dragoons themselves; a year later, men of Warfield and Snively's band admitted that they had long been spying on the dragoons in this part of the country.[45]

Especially after such a close call, Love, like all soldiers on the march, appreciated the warming refreshment of spirits and had carefully packed a cherished bottle. On the evening of June 11, however, disaster befell. Lieutenant Love and Capt. Benjamin Moore had settled before the inviting campfire and decided to enjoy a few drops of peach brandy: "We found the cork out of the jug & the liquor gone save 2 drinks," Love wrote mournfully. "Our feelings were too deep for immediate utterance, we gazed at each for some seconds in silent agony when the Capt. after relieving himself by a deep drawn sigh said who was the last one at the jug. Oh: if I could find him out, I would trash him so he would be ever after this afraid even to look at a *peach* to say nothing of the *brandy*"[46] (emphasis in original). Love and Moore had to resign themselves manfully to live on food and mere water for the remainder of the expedition.

Confronting Snively

Lieutenant Love's journal then ends abruptly, mid-page. Did he lose his pen or ink or paper? More probably, Love would from this time travel more as a soldier than a tourist, and abandoned his reporting for more pressing duties. A run-in with the Texicans loomed, so Love no doubt had to abandon his dream of a carefree excursion onto the plains. Cooke now called upon Lieutenant Love's company to return by the Trail posthaste and to provide a close escort for the lumbering wagon train.

Signs of the imminent clash multiplied daily. On June 14, 1843, the dragoons learned that the Texas Invincibles had easily routed a troop of Mexican irregulars near Taos. Governor Manuel Armijo, waiting to escort the westbound wagon train at the border with four hundred men, had heard the same report and was racing back to Santa Fe. Four days later news came from across the river that Boone's soldiers had spotted men on the Santa Fe Trail and that Boone believed them to be scouts from Colonel Snively's band.

Snively's ranks had suffered during their march west and morale soared upon reaching the river. On June 16, Snively and his men intercepted the wagon of Santa Fe merchant and fur trader Ceran St. Vrain, but let him proceed without incident once they saw he was an American. Six days later, St. Vrain informed Cooke that Snively's troops, reinforced by Warfield's detachment, were settled at the crossing of the Arkansas River and lay in wait to ambush the next passing Mexican caravan.[47] But Snively had erred fatally by encamping just south of the Arkansas crossing. He had mistakenly believed that the waterway marked the international border and that, therefore, the site belonged to Mexico rather than to the United States. Although in 1843 some confusion remained over its ownership,[48] under the 1819 Adams-Onís

Transcontinental Treaty the territory was firmly claimed by the United States.

With a hostile force now close at hand, Captain Cooke readied his troops. He had them practice swiftly changing their formation from "column of route" (a rectangular formation of troops on the march) into "order of battle" (a formation of two extended lines of horsemen). On the twenty-eighth, Cooke directed his artillerists to fire explosive shells into a herd of grazing buffalo, to give them "more experience of the range and effects of the howitzer." The shelling wounded a bull, which in turn wildly charged the soldiers and did not stop until struck by a full volley of shots from carbines and pistols.[49]

On the morning of June 30, near present-day Dodge City, Kansas, Cooke spotted three riders whom he thought to be Texican spies. He dispatched a sergeant and six men to follow them. The sergeant returned some twenty minutes later to advise Cooke that the riders had joined a large body of men. Officers and sergeants barked orders and bugles blared as Cooke formed his troops into a column of platoons and advanced at a brisk trot. Before long he observed "a considerable force of men and horses about a fine grove on the opposite bank" of the Arkansas River, but the Texicans soon raised a white flag. In response, Cooke halted his men on the north bank and dispatched Lieutenant Love, a bugler, and a guidon bearer across the river to ascertain whose men they were, how strong their force, and what purpose they pursued.[50]

Love shortly returned with Colonel Snively himself and the colonel's aide. Cooke thought little of the man, commenting with contempt that he was a mere "shopkeep's clerk, quite insignificant in appearance and demeanor."[51] In their morning meeting, Cooke questioned Snively: "Sir, it is the belief of myself and officers that you are in the United States, what is your business here? What force have you?" Snively replied to Cooke that he held a lawful commission issued him by the president of the Republic of Texas, and had not trespassed on the United States. Cooke disagreed, angrily asserting that Snively's collection of "cutthroats" and "outcasts," "without an indication of the form and customs of regular organization, outrages all rules of modern warfare, which scarcely allow the *incidental* destruction or robbery of property on land"[52] (emphasis in original). Snively, a trained surveyor, replied that the boundary in this region was ill-defined and he had not invaded the United States. Not so, Cooke insisted; the Texicans had most certainly violated international law by entering the United States and by conducting espionage north of the river.[53] To establish this fact, Cooke pointed out "a band of men who were then crossing the river and crossing to the south side" where the Texican camp was located.[54] He then demanded Snively's immediate and unconditional surrender and warned that, if the order were refused, he would attack with 185 dragoons and two mountain howitzers.[55]

Snively returned to his camp to mull over Cooke's dictates. Right on his heels rode Cooke's mounted force across the Arkansas. This mad dash by Cooke's warriors across a river might have made a glorious scene, but was a poor tactic: the artillery ought to have remained on the far bank to cover the mounted troops as they crossed. Having one's artillery cross water in the range of the foe's weapons was downright foolish. Far worse, deep water slowed the horses and the uneven river bottom broke up and slowed the men's formation, creating a conveniently massed target for the outlaws to pick off.

Fortunately for both sides, common sense prevailed and no Texican shot that day. Gaining the south bank, the dragoons reformed their ranks opposite the Texican encampment, unlimbered their artillery, smartly formed a battle line, drew sabers, lit matches, and readied the howitzers to fire on Snively's position. Cooke sent Company A with sabers drawn and dismounted troopers with carbines at the ready, along with a wagon to collect the Texican firearms. Snively immediately ordered his men to surrender their arms. But unbeknownst to the dragoons, they had hidden their best weapons in the woods and handed over just the pitiful ones they had recently seized from the New Mexico militia.[56] Cooke's squadron took possession of these inferior arms, discharged them, and stacked them in the wagon to cart off. Cooke then allowed Colonel Snively's supposedly disarmed men to return home, and a group of some fifty Texicans even accepted Cooke's courteous offer of a dragoon escort back to Missouri. But the rest of Snively's men chose to travel home without an escort—and secretly to regain their cached weaponry. Their perfidy proved prescient, though, as Comanches twice attacked them before they reached home.[57]

With the danger passed the caravan safely crossed the Arkansas at the Caches, entered Mexico territory, and continued to Santa Fe. The next day Cooke began the return to Fort Leavenworth, arriving there on July 21 with no loss of man or horse, his three companies "well & improved in discipline." Hearing the good news that Cooke had turned back Snively and Warfield, Boone could also return from the field. Along the way he took time to explore the legendary Great Salt Plains but, with rations nearly exhausted, rode hard for Fort Gibson. Crossing nearly barren land, Private Flynn, although himself gnawed by hunger, worried more about the horses, "already much reduced, having nothing to subsist but by browsing on a short, scrubby, unhealthy bush." At last, Boone's struggling detachment reached the Creek Nation where the tribe generously supplied the famished troops and animals with food, refusing any payment. After ninety-three days on patrol, Company H arrived home.[58]

The mild season seemed to invite a second expedition. To ensure the safety of caravans further, in late August Cooke led out six companies to protect yet another group of 120 wagons bound for Santa Fe. This time he met no raiders but encountered a driving rain, which let him progress only eighty-seven miles in twelve days. The only casualty on the excursion was a sentry who, while leaving Cow Creek, "shot himself: his carbine was sprung [open] and thus it was discharged as from a pocket pistol; the ball" wounding him in the shoulder. It was during this expedition that Cooke discovered the site of Chaves's murder. The captain wrote, "'Twas here that a cry to God, wrested by human fiends from brother man, fell unanswered—echoless on the desert air."[59]

On September 17, the dragoons hailed the lightened caravan of the last spring returning from a successful sales trip to Santa Fe. Cooke continued on, escorting westbound wagons to the international border at the Cimarron Crossing of the Arkansas River, where he was met by a troop of Mexican lancers. After exchanging proper military decorum, the wagons crossed into Mexico, but soon bad weather began to close in. The return trip featured poor forage, a buffalo stampede, and a brush fire that threatened the dragoon camp. On October 5 the dragoons urged their starving and worn mounts homeward in an effort to beat the fast-approaching freeze, and reached Fort Leavenworth by the twenty-fifth.[60]

International, National, and Military Consequences

The *Baltimore Sun* of August 9, 1843, summed up the general American opinion: "The prompt and effectual measures adopted by Capt. Cooke, for the dispersion of [Snively's] band of freebooters—for, after reading the piratical commission, nobody will think them worthy of a better name—deserve the public approbation, as, we doubt not, his conduct will receive that of the Government." Of course, while President Santa Anna also very much appreciated the U.S. Army's protection of Mexican commerce from Texas, that republic would hardly take it lying down. The incident on the Santa Fe Trail, although bloodless, created at least a minor international affair—and plenty of political squabbling within the United States—when on November 10, 1843, a Texas diplomat in Washington, D.C., filed a formal protest claiming Cooke's actions had interfered with Snively's lawfully sanctioned mission. Not surprisingly, the anti-Tyler and anti-Whig *Missouri Republican* newspaper embraced the Texican cause and excoriated both Cooke and Gen. Zachary Taylor:

> We have regretted the readiness with which the General [Taylor] commanding this division has led himself to the

furtherance of a false feeling upon the subject.—Some of
the expressions in his letter to the Secretary of War of the
27th of July in commendation of Capt. Cooke's conduct
appear to us effusions of old age, rather than a clear head
and calm judgment, of the hero of Fort Erie. It sounds as a
mockery to talk of the violation of "the long known laws of
war;" in a case where every principle of right and fair play
have been violated by our own commander, and where his
assurance of our messengers has been disregarded and *the
flag of truce* used as a means to ensnare and entrap unsuspecting men.[61]

The *New Orleans Times-Picayune* went even further, praising
Warfield and claiming, without foundation, that Cooke was motivated by his financial dealings with New Mexican traders.[62] Of
course, the State Department brushed aside Texican assertions
as wholly without merit. Also not surprisingly, on April 8, 1844,
an army court of inquiry, with Col. Stephen Kearny presiding,
cleared Cooke of all charges of improper conduct. Once the dust
had settled and President John Tyler concluded a treaty with the
Republic of Texas to annex it as a state, the Senate rejected the
move, denying Texas admission into the Union.

By the end of 1844, Private Flynn, having completed his five-
year enlistment and wishing "once more to reside among civilized
people, brick houses, paved streets lighted by gaslight," took an
honorable discharge at Fort Gibson. Traveling by wagon and
stagecoach he reached St. Louis on January 3 and booked passage
on a steamboat to Louisville, Kentucky. Seated in his cabin, Flynn
was surprised and touched to see his former commanding officer,
Colonel Kearny, walking toward him. The colonel, on business
in St. Louis, had heard that a man of his regiment was about to
leave town and, in a remarkable display of appreciation for a common soldier, came to wish him well. Flynn considered it "to be a
high compliment, for a Colonel then doing the duty of a General
in charge of the Department, to take the trouble to walk 7 or 8
blocks through the dirty streets and dirtier Quays of St. Louis, to

bid farewell to a person who had been only of the rank and file of his regiment. It must have been kind feelings and not interested motives that actuated him."[63]

The site of the Snively surrender became celebrated among dragoon officers passing it in 1845 and 1846. On July 19, 1846, Lieutenant Love numbered among Kearny's Army of the West setting off to invade Mexican-held Santa Fe, and once again found himself near the Caches crossing of the Arkansas River. Some brother officers asked him the location of the Jackson's Grove encampment where he and Cooke had demanded that Snively's Texicans surrender, and Love proudly took them across the river to show them where Cooke's detachment had won its laurels. William Emory, an army topographical engineer with the Army of the West, confirmed that the grove was, indeed, located within the territory of the United States.[64]

But many Texicans remained bitter for years about the incident. After the end of the war with Mexico, Brevet Lieutenant Colonel Cooke, now stationed at Fort Mason, Texas, with the 2nd Dragoons, received numerous threats and "considered his life in imminent danger . . . on account of the 'Snively Affair'" and requested a transfer to New Mexico—a request Adj. Gen. Roger Jones obligingly fulfilled. Perhaps residual concern for personal safety led Cooke, in his *Scenes and Adventures in the Army* (1859), to detail his second, generally uneventful 1843 escort but to omit much description of the first one in which he encountered Snively, other than to affirm that the encampment in Jackson's Grove was within the United States.[65]

Keeping a Fragile Peace

Captain Cooke and his men had prevented what might have become a deadly confrontation between Texicans and traders. The Texicans also deserve some credit, for if they had opened fire American blood might have been "shed on American soil" as early as 1843, rather than in 1846; trade on the Trail would have been suspended; and such events might have provoked the United States to wage war on the Republic of Texas.

For the regiment there were also benefits. The men and officers of two dragoon squadrons had tested their skills and mettle in the field. Young officers like John Love and Philip Cooke, the former on his first Santa Fe Trail trip, gained valuable experience and won the confidence of Colonel Kearny. During the war with Mexico, Kearny would place Love in field command of Company B, which he would lead in combat at the Coon Creeks and again at Santa Cruz de Rosales. And, having seen Cooke exercise leadership with talent and judgment in a potentially dangerous situation— once in preparing his men to confront Snively and then in the confrontation itself—Kearny would again rely on Cooke as head of the Mormon Battalion on its march from Fort Leavenworth to California during the Mexican War. During the Civil War, Cooke became a brigadier general and remained with the army until his retirement in 1873. As for the regiment, the deployment of two squadrons (eight companies), fully armed and combat-ready, convinced Kearny and his superiors that the 1st Dragoons were entirely capable of invading Santa Fe, and perhaps California—or, if necessary, of riding overland to protect the Oregon Territory and then seizing the British Northwest. It would take one further expedition along the Oregon Trail to convince the government of their readiness.

Captain Cooke's two missions, coupled with the execution of McDaniel for the Chaves murder, effectively brought peace to the Santa Fe Trail. Texican raids of commerce ended. Within three years of the Snively affair the United States conquered New Mexico and established hegemony over the entire trail. During the war with Mexico and in the years that followed, the heavy traffic over the trail brought constant warfare with Comanches. Cooke steadily rose in rank until, in 1858, he gained the colonelcy of the 1st Cavalry Regiment. He became a brigadier general at the start of the Civil War, but his wartime performance was less than sensational. He remained in the military service until 1873 and died on March 20, 1895.

And as for Jacob Snively? After the war with Mexico he successfully searched for gold in California and New Mexico until 1871, when Yavapai tribesmen killed him while he was prospecting near Wickenburg, Arizona Territory.[66]

CHAPTER 5

Soldiers Four

Sumner, Allen, Wharton, and Carleton

In the early 1840s four prominent junior officers of the First Dragoons modeled a wide variety of leadership styles as they managed their men and the challenges of Indian Removal. Capt. Edwin Vose Sumner personified the consummate professional burdened with a conscience; Capt. James Allen represented the West Point–educated, fortune-favored military man; Maj. Clifton Wharton epitomized the efficient executive; and Lt. James Henry Carleton embodied the intelligent but self-centered shavetail whose unmeasured acts brought him both scorn and fame. In the ensuing years far too many dragoons would ape Carleton's panache (though less often, his intellect), while far too few would embrace Sumner's principled restraint, Allen's warm humanity, or Wharton's careful administration.

Sumner: A Martinet Burdened with a Conscience

In 1843 and 1844, while the bulk of the 1st Dragoon Regiment busily protected the Santa Fe and Overland Trails, two of its companies performed constabulary duty in the Iowa and Wisconsin Territories. A portion of this area sheltered several Native American tribes, relocated from the East, which had only recently ceded certain of these newly granted lands for white settlement.[1] To strengthen its position in the territories, the army had already stationed a dragoon garrison at Fort Des Moines. But in 1841 this forlorn post was augmented by the spanking new Fort Atkinson, established near lands formerly occupied by the Winnebagos, who had been relocated from Wisconsin Territory across the Mississippi River. The new fortifications, it was hoped, would keep the Winnebagos from moving back east across the Mississippi as well as shield them from raids by the Sac and Foxes and the Sioux.

Fort Atkinson gazed upon the Turkey River from a lofty bluff. Completed in 1842, it boasted four two-story barracks, two built of stone and two of logs, around a large square parade and drill ground. A tall flagpole at one end of the parade ground towered above all. Commissioned officers and their families enjoyed one of the stone barracks, while noncommissioned officers and their families lived in a hewn-log one. Private soldiers occupied the other two barracks—the lower floor of their stone building housing the hospital and that of their wooden one contained quarters and a great room used as a chapel on Sundays and a school during the week. At the corners of the parade ground stood a stone-walled gun house, a stockade, a stone magazine or powder-house, and the quartermaster's storehouse adjoined by the sutler's shop. A tall log fence with loopholes enclosed all the buildings.[2]

As early as June 24, 1841, Captain Allen with Company I of the 1st United States Dragoons had arrived from Fort Leavenworth; a year later, Captain Sumner and Company B replaced Allen's force; and for the next six years various companies of infantry and dragoons served the new post.[3] While those two as well as Wharton and Carleton would all execute the Indian Removal policy as ordered by the War Department, the manner in which each did so revealed his personal character and professional ethic. There were those officers who rationalized that Indian Removal was unavoidable and served a humanitarian purpose of the tribes' survival. Other officers grappled with the conflict between duty and the morality of their role.[4]

A glance at Winnebago history since the advent of whites in their lands illuminates strategic and ethical complexities as well as human tragedy extant in the removal of all Native American tribes.[5] In the seventeenth century French explorers had encountered the Winnebagos (also called the Ho-Chunks) living in what would become the states of Michigan and Wisconsin. Contemporary estimates put the tribe at 3,800 members. But years of disease and continual warfare with neighboring tribes weakened them, and their fortunes steadily worsened as they found themselves in the path of westbound white settlers, although they actually kept more peaceable relations with the whites than with other Native groups.[6]

In 1825, the Winnebagos signed with the United States a peace treaty that ultimately led to a series of agreements, each of which forced them farther west and to decreasingly desirable grounds. The Treaty of Prairie du Chien, signed in 1825, had unmistakably specified the boundaries of their land. But when rich deposits of lead were found there, miners illegally poured in. Inevitably, violence broke out when the Winnebagos attempted to evict the trespassers. In 1826 the army arrested six tribesmen for the murders of members of the Method family. The army released four of the accused, but two suspects were slain while in Army custody. Seeking revenge for their deaths, the tribe shamed Chief Red Bird, a longtime friend to the whites, into forming a raiding party. On June 27, 1827, Red Bird and two followers went to the home of one Registre Gagnier, whom Red Bird knew, and shot him along with his hired hand. They also scalped Gagnier's three-year-old daughter, who survived. Next, Red Bird attacked keelboats and killed settlers on the Lower Wisconsin River. These crimes panicked settlers around Prairie du Chien, who not unreasonably feared a general uprising. Governor Lewis Cass (later the secretary of war) mobilized the militia and called for federal troops.[7]

Military authorities reacted swiftly. A 580-man expedition under Gen. Henry Atkinson left Jefferson Barracks by steamers and was joined by the lead miner and squatter—and soon, dragoon colonel—Henry Dodge and his militia cavalry. The combined forces wasted little time chasing Red Bird into the heart of Winnebago country, and on September 3 a detachment of U.S.

Infantry under Maj. William Whistler caught up with him. Starving, surrounded, and hugely outmanned, Red Bird and his chiefs surrendered and were confined at Fort Snelling, where guards executed him and a few followers.[8]

With the Winnebago people again suppressed by force of arms, lead miners and settlers overran and looted their territory. In August of 1829, at Prairie du Chien, the Winnebagos signed yet another treaty whereby, for $540,000, they forfeited rights to most of their lands south of the Wisconsin River. The U.S. government wished to move the entire tribe west of the Mississippi and designated for them a narrow strip of productive earth, called the Neutral Ground as it was to provide them a safe haven from warring tribes to the north. Ill-advisedly, this placement settled the Winnebagos in areas claimed by their traditional enemies. And akin to most treaties with Native tribes, this one would also be broken: settlers trespassed on enviable portions of new tribal land, and annuities were paid late, if ever. Certain Winnebagos left for the new area willingly, while others resisted relocation and remained on their Wisconsin grounds. In 1837, federal authorities brought a delegation of Winnebagos to Washington, D.C., to negotiate a further treaty. No matter that this group lacked authority to speak for the tribe and had been tricked into thinking their vacating Wisconsin was only temporary. Predictably, the tribe broke into two factions, one honoring this treaty, the other refusing it.[9]

The government began to grant white settlers permission to cross the Mississippi River and venture westward into what would become Iowa. By 1836 the white population had grown to 10,500, and just four years later more than 43,000 settlers filled the territory. As the numbers of whites burgeoned, relations between whites and tribes in Iowa Territory deteriorated, and the dragoons would be called on repeatedly to protect both parties.

Captain Sumner had not attended the Military Academy, but was a career soldier stationed on the frontier for most of his professional life. Having won a presidential commission at age twenty-one, Sumner, born in Massachusetts on January 30, 1797, entered the infantry in 1819 and gained a captaincy in the dragoons.

Colonel Kearny, in many ways his mentor, often counted on him in a variety of assignments, from training recruits at Carlisle in 1835 to exercising independent command. A scrupulous man fond of donning full dress uniform whenever possible, he was regarded by Erasmus Keyes, a colleague and later a Civil War general, as "the greatest martinet in the service" and "one of the best instructed line officers in the army," who went "by the book" and never questioned orders.[10] A lieutenant of the Mounted Rifles, undergoing training by Sumner, found him to be of the "old school, rugged, stern, honest, and brave [and] had a good conscience." Only slights to his rank and privilege would rankle: while stationed at Fort Atkinson, Sumner resented that his brevet (honorary) status of major allowed a former subordinate, Capt. John Abercrombie of the 1st Infantry, to be his superior. Sumner appealed this humiliation to the adjutant general, writing that he "could not endure the modification of serving under an officer, in the same garrison, in which he had been under my immediate command for nearly two years."[11]

During the War with Mexico, Sumner trained the Regiment of Mounted Rifles and then assumed field command of the 2nd Dragoons. After the war the government placed him in military control of the New Mexico Territory, and by 1855 he led the 1st Cavalry. A cousin of the famed abolitionist Charles Sumner, Edwin Sumner shared many of his views on the evils of slavery. He rose to the rank of major general in the Civil War, and following the Battle of Fredericksburg he died at home on March 21, 1863.[12]

There was a generous side to him, often overlooked. Sumner manifested tremendous decency toward the Native Americans he confronted. Reassigned from duties at the Carlisle cavalry school in 1843, Sumner now commanded his Company B at Fort Atkinson, and it was here that he found himself torn between duty to orders and pity at their effects on hapless tribes.

By that year many bands of Winnebagos were starving and had fled their Neutral Ground reservation, located near Fort Atkinson. Some eight hundred had wandered north, another group of more than two hundred had gathered on the Upper Iowa near the Mississippi, and only 756 were at or near the Turkey River agency. Attempts to teach them farming had, thus far, failed: all but one fourth of the 1,500 acres located on the Neutral Ground Reservation that had been broken up were under cultivation by tribesmen, but they greatly preferred hunting to farming. Many Winnebagos refused to leave their haunts along the Mississippi, while hundreds slipped back into Wisconsin. Deadly diseases brought to the region by the whites had ravaged the tribe, leading to the deaths of many. More predictably, and problematic, were the thirty-nine members of the tribe who had been killed in drunken brawls during the preceding fourteen months, often caused when crooked settlers gave them whiskey in exchange for guns, horses, provisions, and goods, then sold these necessities back to them at exorbitant prices when the Indians received their annuities.[13] As we shall see, this practice led to the tragic deaths of two unscrupulous white traders, an infant, and the severe wounding of two other children.

The dragoons proved reasonably effective at intercepting liquor smuggling into the reservation.[14] It was, however, impossible to prevent the Indians from going off the reservation to the white settlements and obtaining spirits there, and in March 1843 Sumner had to report a tragic but typical incident in which the sale of alcohol to Natives led to the murders of settlers. He and his soldiers trudged through the snow to Wilcox's Settlement in Fayette County to probe the killing of merchants Teagarden and Atwood and a child by Winnebago tribesmen at the men's frontier store.

Like many other settlers, Teagarden and Atwood routinely sold liquor to the Winnebagos, and a tribesman had wandered into their store and pawned his gun to buy whiskey from Teagarden. He later returned to redeem the weapon, but Teagarden had sold it. He placated the man by plying him with more whiskey. In an eerie parallel to the 1826 murder of the Gagnier family by Red Bird, on the afternoon of March 25 the cheated man and two members of the Winnebago tribe visited Teagarden and Atwood's store. Upon their arrival they and the two merchants consumed a considerable amount of spirits, and Teagarden and Atwood fell fast asleep on the floor. The Winnebagos took advantage of the merchants' condition, tied them up, and murdered them. They raped a little girl and cut her face with tomahawks, then attacked two other children with tomahawks, killing one and seriously wounding the other. Setting the store afire, the killers stole Teagarden's horse and buggy, and escaped into the night. The two badly wounded children fled the burning building into below-zero temperatures, two miles from the nearest neighbor, and lost their way in the frozen dark. Settlers rescued them the next morning and somehow both survived, though the girl lost all her toes and suffered severe facial scarring from tomahawk wounds.[15]

Shocked townsfolk reported the incident to Captain Sumner, who immediately ordered his men to horse. On the morning of March 26 his troops rode hard for some twenty-five miles on the ice-slick road to the Wilcox Settlement. Sumner quickly apprehended three suspects whom the children identified as the killers and locked them in the fort's guardhouse—prompt actions that probably prevented a replay of the Red Bird uprising.[16]

But in questioning the prisoners Sumner learned that the violence had hardly been one-sided and came to empathize with the accused despite the viciousness of the crime. The captives told him that theirs was an act of revenge; they said whites had recently killed four Winnebagos—three men and a woman: "[o]ne man by a Dr. Taylor at Stewarts settlement without the least provocation, another by a whiskey dealer on the Mississippi in a drunken brawl, another by a trap gun set in a house, and the woman, after being horribly used, after tying and beating her husband, by a number of soldiers near Fort Crawford." Having grasped the systemic nature of the problem, Sumner wrote to Bvt. Col. Henry Wilson at Fort Crawford, after yet another such incident, cautioning his superior that there would be continued bloodshed in the territory so long as white soldiers killed Winnebagos without provocation: "I mention this, colonel, in all frankness, knowing that you will not suppose for a moment that I intend to convey any reflection upon yourself or your officers. I am too old a soldier not to know the impossibility of controlling soldiers, at all times, when out of sight. I hope and trust there may be some mistake in the affair. It is plain that an instant stop ought to be put on such conduct on the part of the Whites, or it will be utterly impossible to keep the Indians quiet on the frontier."[17]

That August, the three Winnebago suspects in the Teagarden and Atwood murders were tried and convicted in Dubuque and sentenced to be hanged. While jailed, two of the convicts killed the third; they ended up in the penitentiary and were later paroled.[18]

Sumner and his dragoons would again travel to enforce federal law against tribal interests. Territorial Governor John Chambers worried that large numbers of Winnebagos had wandered off of the reservation and needed to be returned to it. In November, army headquarters gave Sumner and his company orders to remove wayward bands of Winnebagos from their hideaways. In a letter to General Jones dated November 9, 1843, Sumner wrote, "These Indians are dispersed over a large space, some of them are believed to be as far south as Rock river, while others are in the Black river country, nearly 200 miles further [sic] north. The northern part of that country is exceedingly rugged for military operations, in a favorable season, and of course, the difficulty is greatly increased in the winter. I shall, however, do all that men and horses can do to accomplish that order."[19]

And that order was hardly pleasant for body or soul. But for Sumner, orders were orders and his duty was not to reason why. He left Fort Atkinson with his company on November 10 as icy winter winds blew, crossed the Mississippi, and traveled to near the headwaters of the Black River. He observed that the desolate country was "miserable and can never be settled by whites. The soil is of the worst kind, and the whole surface is broken into abrupt hills and impassable marshes." In this region he found Chief Yellow Thunder and several Winnebago families but elected not to remove the sick or elderly.[20] This act of mercy was double-edged as the ill and old, left to fend for themselves, would most likely starve, and whoever of them survived the winter would be rounded up in the spring and brought back across the river to their reservation any-way. From this location Sumner dispatched Lt. Philip Thompson with a detachment to search further east for others of the tribe; they located and removed an additional thirty. The company then moved in the direction of Madison where Sumner again detached Lieutenant Thompson to proceed toward Lake Koshkonong and Rock River in southern Wisconsin, where the patrol found several more Winnebago families. Passing near Prairie du Chien, Sum-ner sent Lt. Leonidas Jenkins into the Kickapoo Hills where he gathered seventy-five more Winnebagos. Sumner had planned to proceed, as ordered, to the Black River, but judged his horses and men so worn that he decided to return to Fort Atkinson and await further orders. After being in the field for fifty-one freezing days, Sumner arrived at the fort on New Year's Eve, 1843, bringing with him 162 captured tribe members.

Despite his stringent allegiance to duty Sumner experi-enced—and expressed—profound anxiety over removing more Winnebagos in wintertime. He pointed out to his superiors that "movement at this season of the year will be attended with great suffering to the Indians," and aired doubts about the governor's requirement that captured Winnebagos be kept near Fort Atkin-son: "[T]his creates the absolute necessity of feeding them, for there is no game in this vicinity upon which they can subsist. No arrangement has been made by the Indian Department to meet this emergency, and when my extra supplies are exhausted (which will be very soon) I shall be compelled to release them from restraint, in order that they may repair to some place where they can subsist themselves by hunting."

In addition he explicitly noted the tribesmen's "strong induce-ment to return to the East Side of the Mississippi," as its abundant game contrasted with the scarce animal resources on their res-ervation; indeed, he stressed, the tribe's very survival demanded occasional crossings to their wooded homeland.[21]

Sumner reported no violence in this expedition and, given his sympathy and worry for his captives' welfare, it is doubtful that there had been any.[22] But the forcible return of the fugitives in bitter winter certainly caused anguish, as would later, even more painful maltreatment by an uncaring Indian Department. Its bureaucrats were unmoved by Sumner's reasoning or scruples, and he was forced to keep the captured Winnebagos near Fort Atkinson through the cold season. After the worst of it, the captain declared them "perfectly tractable, and even friendly," even in conditions of extreme hardship.[23]

On February 3, 1844, Sumner marched out in a second attempt to reach the Black River. At Prairie du Chien the troops faced severe weather, lack of forage, and crossings of nearly frozen streams and rivers. Sumner determined it unwise to proceed into the rough country ahead, and returned to his base, equally unwilling to witness the "extreme suffering" he would be causing the famished Winnebagos. Sumner wrote, "I have never performed so serious a duty" as the locating and removing "of these Indians from their winter retreat."[24]

Dark events for the dragoons as well continued to mark the sweeping away of Natives. In March Lieutenant Jenkins took a detachment to pursue the Winnebagos, during which expedition Pvt. William Williams drowned when his horse fell into the raging Cedar River. And in 1844 new problems arose, this time with the Sioux. On September 15, Sumner was to march his troops north to the St. Peters River, where they were to investigate the murder of a drover and apprehend his (presumably) Sioux killers.[25]

Allen: Inroads to the Unknown

Capt. James Allen could hardly have resembled the proud and persnickety E. V. Sumner less. Although the Ohioan, born February 15, 1806, was, like Sumner, a trained professional (having graduated the U.S. Military Academy in 1829, along with Robert E. Lee), his personal demeanor, dress, and manner of command were decidedly relaxed. Perhaps his informality flowed from his imbibing, but neither that habit nor his carefree style impaired his effectiveness in leading troops or inspiring their adoration.

Seventy-two years after Allen's death, a biographer described him as differing from

> the typical soldier of old romance. He valued "the bubble reputation" at its real worth. Free from Cromwellian ambition, he escaped "fame's damnation." . . . He chose a soldier's life and uncomplainingly lived that life. With soldierly equanimity, he accepted new situations, not quarreling with fate, and standing well with the Department. Without compromising his dignity or yielding one jot of authority vested in him by his Government he won the respect and love of his men. When he died, many tears were shed, and long after his death his name was mentioned reverently and lovingly, even by men of an alien faith.[26]

During the war with Mexico, Allen's rare combination of tolerance and military expertise made him the ideal commander of the Mormon Battalion. The Saints revered him. Unfortunately, he never led the battalion much beyond Fort Leavenworth, dying there of illness at the age of forty—the first of many competent 1st Dragoon officers to lose their lives in the Mexican War.[27] The August 31, 1846, edition of the *Missouri Republican* published a detailed obituary for Lieutenant Colonel Allen that provides insight into his character and the esteem in which he was held. Its reporter noted that Allen's

> death has thrown a gloom over every thing at the Fort to day, and every face indicates sincere distress. I understand that he was a noble soldier, and universally beloved by all who knew him. His battalion (which has been gone ten days) perfectly idolized him, and his death will be a severe blow to them. He was much attached to the soldiers in his command, had brought them under very superior discipline, and said before his death that he had never commanded a finer, or more orderly company. Indeed every one here (ladies too) speak highly of this battalion."

The obituary mentioned Allen's adopted daughter—now a grown woman, at whose home he died—and his personal servant as particularly grieved. Lieutenant Colonel Allen became the first soldier interred in the new Fort Leavenworth Cemetery, and the writer described the funeral procession, in which military trappings conveyed, rather than counterfeited, genuine feeling:

> He was buried this afternoon, at five o'clock, with military honors, by Company A of the first Infantry, Lt. Wm E. Prince commanding. This company made a fine appearance on parade. The flag of the United States was folded and laid over his coffin, which was preceded to the grave by the company of Lieut. Prince and one of the finest bands of music I have ever heard, belonging to the first regiment of dragoons. . . . In the procession immediately following his body was his beautifully spotted horse, led by his servant, Wells, caparisoned as if for battle. His boots and spurs were at the stirrups, his sword hanging at the side of the horse, and his pistols, bare and of dazzling brightness, hanging at the pommel of the saddle. His body was conducted to a high bluff overlooking the broad Missouri, whose waters lave its base, and thence deposited forever.[28]

A skilled cartographer, Allen spent much of his military career exploring and mapping what was then the northwestern region of the United States. After charting the northwestern frontier region of Lake Michigan, the Upper Mississippi, and Chicago in 1833, he gained a second lieutenant's commission in the dragoons.[29] The details of Allen's 1844 expedition show not only his talents as an explorer but also his gifts in diplomacy and leadership. On August 11, Allen's Company I—fifty-two enlisted men and four wagons heavily loaded with provisions—rode out of Fort Des Moines. The army instructed Allen to take his company "up the Des Moines River, and up to the sources of the Blue Earth River or St. Peter's [Minnesota] River; thence to the waters of the Missouri; and thence returning through the country of the Pottawatomies."[30]

A journal kept by an anonymous enlistee reveals the men's high spirits at the commencement of the campaign: True, some restive horses threw their riders, "but on the whole everything went well."[31] Yet progress was slowed as troops confronted punishing terrain, dense timber, and rainstorms. Attempting to stay as close to the river as the slopes and ravines permitted made it excruciating to pull the cumbersome wagons over the deep creeks and muddy ground bordering the Des Moines. The journalist wrote that the troops "toiled during the day over a terrible prairie full of the worst sort of slues [sloughs]. The waggons would sink to their axles and it repeatedly required the combined efforts of all our men and double teams to extricate them, some of them soft places extended for a hundred yards."[32] Allen himself confirmed that he "[f]ound the country so wet and the slues so numerous that our progress was slow and difficult; the wagons, being yet heavily loaded, cut deep into the wet ground, and stuck fast in every mire till pulled out by the main strength of the command; the men were all the time muddy and wet, and more fatigued than on any previous day."[33]

The dragoons pushed onward under a leaden sky and through thick sludge. But on September 3 the captain located the headwaters of the Des Moines River,[34] the skies finally cleared, and a week later the dragoons hunted buffalo. The dragoon journalist wrote of a comrade in a nonregulation hunting shirt with a red fringe killing four bulls. White men killed these fine animals primarily for sport and often ate only their tongues—a frontier delicacy—leaving the entire remains to rot. While chasing buffalo, Captain Allen established contact with Sioux hunters.[35] He recorded: "I was surprised at meeting with more Sioux Indians. We penetrated their country very far, saw numerous trails and other signs of them, but only came actually in contact with two small roving parties on the Big Sioux; and we came upon these so suddenly that they were forced to meet us. They were much alarmed; approached us with great timidity, and, notwithstanding our assurances of friendship, seemed to wish to get rid of us as soon as possible."[36]

Leaving the nervous hunters behind and marching west, Allen reached the Sioux River on the tenth of September.[37] When twelve horses and mules disappeared from his camp, Allen suspected the Sioux of committing the theft and sent a detachment to recover them. Instead of finding the missing stock, though, the troops discovered the magnificent Sioux Falls. Allen reported:

> These falls present a remarkable feature of the river and country; the river, until now, running nearly due south, makes about the falls a bend to the west, and round to the northwest, and passes the falls in a due east course, and continues below in a northeast course for six miles, when it resumes its former direction. The rock of these falls is massive quartz, and is the first rock formation, or rock in place, that we have seen since we left the St. Peter's River. . . . The fall, as near as I could measure it, is 100 feet in 400 yards, and is made up of several perpendicular falls—one 20, one 18, and one 10 feet. The rock . . . on the borders of the stream is split, broken, and piled up in the most irregular and fantastic shapes, and presents deep and frightful chasms, and extending from the stream in all directions. There is no timber here on the borders or bluffs, and only a little on a small island at the head of the rapids.[38]

The next day the dragoons started southeast on what would prove a strenuous march back to quarters. They kept an eye out for Sumner's column bound for Traverse des Sioux. This column included forty-nine dragoons and had left Fort Atkinson on September 15 to reinforce the 1st Infantry's search for Sisseton Sioux thought to have killed a drover. On October 11 Sumner conferred with tribal leaders at Brown's trading post at Traverse des Sioux on the St. Peter's River; the chiefs surrendered the miscreants and Sumner's troops started for home the very next day, returning to Fort Atkinson on October 31.[39]

In contrast to Sumner's efficient patrol, Allen's column slogged through the rugged terrain at eight to twenty miles a day. Wagons continually broke down, many dragoons showed signs of exhaustion, and nearly all their mounts were malnourished, forcing the command to dismount and walk beside them for most of the remaining trip. Unlike troops traversing the flat western plains, Allen's men stumbled through an array of sloughs, mud, ravines, woods, and rivers. In late September Allen noted in his journal: "Met another ugly prairie slue at the end of eight miles, which it took three hours to cross, when we came to a country full of marshes and old shallow grass lakes, like that of the Upper Des Moines. Encamped on the prairie among the marshes, and near an island of timber, that we could not reach for the ugly marsh that surrounded it. The frosts are becoming severe, and the horses are failing fast."[40] Three days later he added, "[t]he grass has been so much deadened by the many frosts, that it no longer gives the horses a good subsistence; the horses and mules have failed wonderfully since we left the Little Sioux, though we have walked (on foot) most of the way."[41] They had no choice but to press onward. After considerable effort of men and animals, the weary detachment completed its fifty-four-day round trip of 740 miles though the present states of Iowa, South Dakota, and Minnesota, and returned to Fort Des Moines on October 3.[42]

In 1845, Captain Allen reviewed the campaign, which he believed had proven the utility of the regiment for impressing the Sioux Nation with the power of the federal government and extending its sway deep into its interior: "This expedition, together with the almost simultaneous one made by Captain Sumner's company from Fort Atkinson, near the valley of the St. Peter's, and to the north of it, must have produced a great moral effect upon these wild Indians, as showing them conclusively that we can easily throw cavalry enough into the heart of their country to chastise them for any wrong they may do to our people and government."[43]

Similar missions to show the federal flag and intimidate the tribes elsewhere were equally successful. In 1844, a mere five thousand settlers traveled the Overland Trail, but during the following decade hundreds of thousands of Argonaut miners, farmers, merchants, and ranchers plied the same route. Whatever violence or thievery the tribes committed on the eastern (dragoon-patrolled) half of the Trail was slight. In fact, never before in recorded history had so many people trespassed lands without assault by the occupants. The dragoons' displays of force, and the diplomacy and restraint of their officers, had imposed a surprising degree of peace on the plains and prairies.[44]

Wharton: Efficiency and Indifference

Born October 22, 1801, into the prominent family that later endowed the University of Pennsylvania's Wharton School of Business, Clifton Wharton was the second son among the eight children of Lt. Col. Franklin Wharton. In July 1798, Franklin Wharton forsook a business career to become lieutenant of marines on the frigate *United States*. He was promoted to captain, and in 1818, President James Madison named the thirty-six-year-old Franklin colonel commandant of the corps. From his post in the Washington, D.C., Navy Yard, Franklin directed Corps operations during the War of 1812 and until his demise in late 1818.[45] Upon his father's death, New York native Clifton, then seventeen, entered the army—most likely needing a job—as a second lieutenant in the Light Artillery, and was promoted to a first lieutenancy in the 3rd Artillery. In 1825, he transferred to the 6th Infantry and won the rank of captain in 1826. When the dragoons were formed in 1833 he secured a captaincy there, too. In 1836, Dodge's new duties as governor of Wisconsin Territory elevated Lieutenant Colonel Kearny to colonel,[46] Maj. Richard Mason to lieutenant colonel, and the regiment's senior captain, Clifton Wharton, to major.[47]

As noted in chapter 2, a dragoon colleague considered Wharton "one of the most elegant men and soldier-like officers of the army, who has won as a disciplinarian a high reputation in the service."[48] More important, the reader will recall that Colonel Dodge entrusted him with the regiment's first mission on the Santa Fe Trail in the spring of 1834. Despite teamsters sabotaging his efforts to negotiate with the Plains tribes, and the hardships inspiring his own assessment that "we 'bold dragoons' have not an easy time of it,"[49] Wharton completed the mission skillfully.

Wharton was regarded well enough by Colonel Kearny to be given command of the 1844 overland expedition. He was to lead five companies to revisit the Pawnee villages, to impress the various tribes with the power of the U.S. military (as always) but additionally to convince the Pawnees on the Platte to move north of the river and to adjudicate their complaints about the Sioux. Further, Major Wharton was to locate a better trail for travelers to the Oregon Territory and, on his return trip, to meet with several tribes recently removed by the government to lands lying west of the Missouri River.[50]

That mission would reveal Wharton's inability to lead a large number of troops in the field. Still, Kearny remained convinced that Wharton could handle the regiment's administrative affairs at Fort Leavenworth while Kearny himself led the regiment west in 1845 and 1846. For while Wharton may not have been a superbly competent, principled martinet like Sumner, nor an endearing, talented golden boy like Allen, neither was he a loose cannon like Carleton, and by 1846 he would attain the rank of lieutenant colonel.[51]

It was the outbreak of the Mexican War that would sorely test Wharton's administrative skills, when virtually the entire regiment departed for the fight and he was left behind. That same year would inspire countless patriotic songs, one of the most popular of which, "Female Volunteer for Mexico," told of a woman who followed her lover and the courageous soldiers marching to Mexico.[52] Although Lieutenant Colonel Wharton's wife Oliveretta (née Ormsby) didn't quite rush off to bear arms against the foe, she unofficially provided crucial services for the army. In fact, on October 27, 1847, her husband complained to Adj. Gen. Roger Jones that, for want of a proper adjutant and sergeant major he was obliged to seek assistance from "a female member of my family"—by which he meant Oliveretta—to clear the crush of regimental administrative orders, official correspondence, returns, field reports, and dispatches.[53]And yet Wharton managed to handle those mundane, inglorious clerical matters that kept the regiment functioning in distant fields. Only two years later a worn-out Wharton would die of cholera, the same disease that killed Allen and so many others at Leavenworth.

Unusually heavy spring rains from March through June 1844 pelted the plains, marooned wagon trains, and derailed all but the most crucial journeys. Major Wharton's departure from Fort Leavenworth was delayed by the weather and further delayed by chaos in Nauvoo, Illinois, where a vengeful mob murdered the Mormon prophet Joseph Smith and his brother Hyrum on June 27. The army refused the request of the governor of Illinois for federal troops to restore order, but did place troops on standby duty. It wasn't until August that the civil unrest in Illinois cooled, the ground drained, and rivers subsided sufficiently for an expedition to set out.[54]

On the expedition an elderly Delaware tribesman, Jim Rogers, served as guide, as he had previously done for the "Pathfinder," explorer Lt. John Frémont. But it rapidly became clear that Rogers lacked knowledge of the central routes to the west. Six miles into the march, Major Wharton and Scout Rogers chose to abandon the circuitous Council Bluffs Trail in favor of what they thought was a shortcut. But soon neither the major nor the guide knew where they were and the expedition became lost on its first night.[55] Three wagons suffered damage on the uneven trail and the axle tree of a howitzer broke while its horse team became mired in quicksand.[56]

On August 27, 1844, after wandering in the wilderness for over two weeks on the foray to the Pawnee villages, Wharton's dragoons at last reached a ridge overlooking the distant Platte River, which the Overland Trail followed westward to the Rockies. The troops descended into the green river valley, and a lively debate ensued as to whether the first Pawnee village to be visited was upriver or downriver. Relying on a pure hunch, Major Wharton cast the deciding vote that the village was upriver to the west. Serving under Wharton, Lieutenant Carleton noted in his journal that the major's guess proved correct when the following day two Pawnee emissaries rode into the dragoon camp and welcomed the dragoons to their land.[57]

Carleton indulged his fascination with the customs, appearance, and behavior of the Pawnee people. But while he happily penned his experiences, Wharton held delicate council with leaders of the Pawnee villages south of the Platte River. He pointed out to them that in 1833 the Pawnees had promised to move to lands lying north of the Platte. The major additionally sought to have the leaders agree to cease warfare with the Sioux. But the Pawnee leaders were uninterested in either point, and were content to remain south of the river and to fight the Sioux. Indeed, just then a Pawnee scout arrived with news of a purported battle between the Sioux and Pawnee tribes, which brought the meeting to an abrupt end.

Wharton suspected the commotion was a trumped-up excuse to break off talks. Before leaving the village, in the time-tested method of Dodge and Kearny, Major Wharton ordered his troops to perform maneuvers and fire a few rounds of the howitzers "as a manifestation of our power."[58] Carleton pointedly recorded the howitzers' effect on the Pawnees as several shells exploded downriver: "The report of the pieces, and the roar and splash of the shot as they went ricocheting along, seemed to astonish the Indians very much. . . . [There] would be no defense at all against such terrible engines."[59]

Next, Wharton took his troops across the broad and shallow Platte River to visit Pawnee villages on the north bank. Despite the river's pacific reputation—"one mile wide, one inch deep . . . too thick to drink, too thin to plow"—a quicksand bottom made the passage difficult.[60] Nonetheless, the troops crossed the river, and on August 31 the major met with the leaders of the northern villages. He again spoke of the harmful consequences of thievery, warfare, and alcohol. In marked contrast to those living to the south, these Pawnees proved receptive. The major left flour and salt pork for the chiefs, and that evening tribe members honored the troops with a ceremonial dance.[61]

On the rainy morning of September 1, the command executed a few military exercises to impress the tribe and began its trip down the Missouri River. In the major's words, their progress over rugged terrain was "retarded by wagons that had been stuck fast in mud holes." On the third of September he noted, "Private Tierny of Company C shot himself through the hand last night while on Guard. Such accidents from Carbines are not of infrequent occurrence in the Dragoons."[62]

In 1843, about a dozen members of the Otoe tribe had fired musket volleys at two boats descending the Platte River and passing their village, wounding a man. They also had threatened their Indian agent, telling him to leave or suffer the consequences. Colonel Kearny wished to send a strong military force to the village "to convince the Otoes & Missouri Indians into a sense of their duty to the Central Government." Wharton's visit to the unhappy village resulted.[63]

Wharton held council with the Otoes on September 7 near the American fur trading post at Bellevue. If Lieutenant Carleton was impressed with the military bearing of these tribesmen, he scorned what he believed to be the clumsy translations of their interpreter. Wharton noted the paucity of game in the region, and that this once-proud tribe was "miserably destitute." After smoking pipes, Wharton told them of his sadness of hearing of the tribe's misdeeds, such as the warriors' shooting at passing fur trappers, and attempted to convince them to cease hunting and raiding and to rely instead on farming and living peaceably with their neighbors. At this point one of the tribal leaders refuted the wisdom of the major's plans for them: the corn crop had failed; he was angry that the government gave them no provisions; and he feared many of his people would soon starve.[64]

Wharton, however, was indifferent to the leader's impassioned plea for increased government assistance (perhaps muffled by the interpreter's incompetence), and he coolly recorded that "nothing but fear of consequences prevents them from more frequently and openly manifesting their dislike of the Whites and their propensities to plunder them." Worse, as he had done at the two Pawnee villages, Wharton left the Otoes little food, but simply relied on blustering language, the dragoons' firm presence, and the firing of rockets to intimidate the natives into compliance with the Great White Father's callous treatment.[65]

Satisfied with the success of his diplomatic routine, as he perceived it, Wharton continued to apply it with heavy-handed and seemingly unreflective consistency. On September 9, a group of Pawnees journeyed downriver to the agency to receive their annuities, and the major was pleased to see that, by their cautious approach, the Pawnees seemed cowed by "the evolution that our Squadrons went through when at their village."[66] Carleton noted that Wharton took care to express extreme anger when he discovered that a few members of this band had plotted to murder explorer John Frémont on his way home from California, and to reward with gifts tribe members who claimed they had prevented the assassination.[67] After this confrontation, Major Wharton purchased an old, leaky flatboat to ferry his troops, howitzers, and baggage across the broad Missouri and to send surplus provisions downriver to Fort Leavenworth. Stormy weather worsened the boat's already poor condition, and its decrepit state, limited capacity, and time-consuming repairs delayed the trip until September 11. As a final gesture intended, as usual, to astound the hundreds of gathered tribesmen, Wharton ordered the men to fire a volley of shells from the two howitzers before having them ferried across the river.[68]

That evening, the major held a council with the leaders of the Pottawatomies, another tribe the federal government had recently removed from productive land in Illinois and Michigan to settle in what is now Nebraska. To the credit of his intelligence, Carleton fully grasped the result of the Indian Removal policy: that once-independent people now wasted their lives in idleness, spent their annuity money on whiskey, and were, therefore, doomed to vanish, even with the most fertile new lands—"2,000,000 acres of the very best land in the West. But they cannot be induced to cultivate it to any extent." Carleton wished the Pottawatomies might be induced to cede their grounds to white settlers voluntarily.[69] But just as happened wherever self-reliant Native groups held valuable natural resources, the government found a way to wrest the new lands from the Pottawatomies, and in 1846, they were moved from these too-precious holdings.[70]

Wharton's expedition closed with the same meandering with which it had begun. On the morning of September 19, at the Great Nemaha sub-agency, Wharton held council with the Iowas and the Sac and Foxes, delivering the standard message: behave yourself or risk armed retribution. After the council ended, the dragoons executed a charge, followed by the firing of a great number of artillery shells. Company K briefly remained behind while annuities were distributed to the tribes. By two o'clock in the afternoon the troops of the other four companies were out of sight and fast bound for home. But the quartermaster wagons traveling on the trail before the troops took a wrong turn. Naturally, the troops followed, forcing men and wagons onto a tortuous path that added seven grueling miles to the journey. On the afternoon of September 21 the trail-worn troops and mounts at last reached Fort Leavenworth.[71] In Carleton's words, "We were met by the Band, and the whole column entered the square from the north-west sally port, and wheeled into line upon the exact spot where, forty-one days before, it had taken up its march for the prairies."[72]

In many respects the expedition was replete with poor leadership in the form of frequently getting itself lost and mishandling efforts at diplomacy with the tribes. If Kearny was displeased with Wharton's performance, the authors are unable find any written evidence of such.

The Adventures of Lt. James Carleton

Lt. James Carleton's service in the Indian Territory, coupled with his accompanying the expeditions of Colonel Kearny and Maj.

Clifton Wharton on the Great Plains, gained him a firsthand view of the deplorable condition of many tribes. Expressing a great deal of sympathy for the "noble savage," he placed the blame upon settlers for the wretched condition of Native peoples "who live contiguous to our settlements." A man of letters, he initially embraced army policy of the period, believing it to be the solemn duty of the army to treat the Indians fairly and to protect them from whites.[73]

While Sumner was preventing intertribal wars, Allen was mapping territory and negotiating with the northwestern Sioux, and Wharton was attempting to shock and awe Natives, 2nd Lt. James Henry Carleton was facing yet another court-martial. Not only was his situation highly unusual, but of all dragoon officers there was perhaps none as erratic as Lieutenant Carleton. On the one hand, he was a sentimental nineteenth-century gentleman who loved the classics, revered Nature, and penned scintillating accounts of military life. On the other hand, when it suited him Carleton became a rigid, even cruel, authoritarian who flouted the fundamentals of military conduct.

Left fatherless at fifteen, Carleton served briefly in his native Maine's militia during a bloodless border tiff with Great Britain presumptuously named the Aroostook War. Obtaining a presidential appointment as second lieutenant in the 1st Regiment of Dragoons, Carleton would undertake the study of a variety of non-military subjects: botany, geology, astronomy, archaeology, and meteorology.[74]

Despite his refined interests Carleton, quite early in his career, risked court-martial, and not once but twice: the first time in Indian Territory for helping a fellow officer accused of murder escape custody, the second in New Mexico Territory for abuse resulting in the death of a drunken enlisted man. Although he ought to have been cashiered for either of these crimes, he was likely saved by political friends and the general sentiment that the death of a lowly, drunken private was insufficiently grave to warrant dismissal of an officer. But many of his fellows considered him unworthy: Capt. Thomas Swords, for example, wrote in 1845 from Fort Scott, "We are to be cursed here with Carleton. I shall give him a pretty wide berth."[75]

Although James Carleton is most often remembered for loyalty to the Union, having helped save New Mexico Territory from a Confederate occupation, he did so at the cost of the civil liberties of the populace. Fanatically bent on securing the region against invasion by Confederate Texas, Carleton called upon his California column to crack down on even suspected Southern sympathizers. Through this abuse of power he imprisoned, on trumped-up charges, former army officers, including Sylvester Mowry (who had served with Maj. Edward Steptoe's 1854–55 overland march of dragoon and artillery recruits to the West Coast) and Archibald Gillespie (the marine officer wounded at the Battle of San Pasqual in 1846).[76]

And then there was Carleton's obsession with total victory, which turned even more inhumane later in his career when he dealt with Native Americans. In 1860 he brutally punished desert tribes in California for crimes they likely had not committed. As departmental commander of New Mexico Territory during the Civil War, he would resolve to crush, once and for all, the power of the Navajo and Mescalero Apaches. He ran Navajos off their lands and, supposedly to make them into good, peace-loving Christian farmers, he forced them on the infamous Long Walk over three hundred miles of desert terrain to the Bosque Redondo Reservation, a diseased and barren plot near the Pecos River. As a result, more than 2,000 Navajos died from malnutrition and sickness.[77]

Carleton's army career nearly came to an end shortly after his presidential appointment. On a cold January day in 1842, 2nd Lt. James Carleton found himself stationed at Fort Gibson under the command of punctilious and arrogant Lt. Col. Richard Mason. At this time Lt. Charles Wickliffe, a fellow officer and close friend of Carleton, was known as "one of the Kentucky family rather famed for acts of violence."[78] Indeed, it wasn't long before Wickliffe's temper got the best of him.

Wickliffe had demonstrated a special fondness for a Cherokee woman. Unfortunately, the lady whose affections he sought was already married. On the evening of January 8, her husband, Robert Wilkins, a local merchant in the Cherokee Nation,[79] returned home to find the lieutenant there in the company of his wife. After heated words and threats, Wickliffe departed in a huff. The cuckolded Wilkins, aided by a man named Clark, flogged Mrs. Wilkins for her sinful ways. After Wilkins left his house to attend to some duties at the fort, she ran to the fort herself for the protection of her lover-lieutenant. The vengeful Wickliffe returned to Wilkins's home and waited, pistol in hand, for his return.

When Clark showed up at Wilkins's home instead, Wickliffe soundly thrashed him and then returned to the fort. That evening Lieutenant Wickliffe spoke with his friend Carleton and the post sutler. The sutler claimed Wilkins could be dangerous when drunk, and that he was often drunk. Carleton proffered the sage advice that Wickliffe ought to kill Wilkins before Wilkins could kill him. He further counseled Wickliffe that, under the law of self-defense, the lover had "ample cause" to shoot the ornery merchant whenever and wherever he should encounter him.[80] According to Lieutenant Colonel Mason, however, Wilkins was hardly a threat. Mason told Major Hitchcock that, in his mind, Wilkins "was not so dangerous as an old squaw would have been: and at all events the interference seems to have come wholly from Wickliffe and that too on account of the woman said to have been a common strumpet."[81]

Frightened and clinging to his two friends' bad advice, on the evening of January 9, 1842, Wickliffe loaded a double-barrel shotgun with twenty buckshot in one barrel and fifteen in the other—a deadly short-range load. The lieutenant rode to Wilkins's home and pounded on the door. Wilkins answered and, seeing Wickliffe shotgun in hand, turned to flee. Wickliffe fired: BANG went the first barrel and BANG went the second. Lieutenant Wickliffe had shot the unarmed merchant in the back at a range of fifteen to twenty yards. The wounded man lingered horribly for a week.

Mason described Wickliffe to Hitchcock as a "young man and at best unfortunate" who rode three miles and then "shoots the man in his own door and that too in the back."[82] Hitchcock later met Wickliffe and found him to be "mild and placid, almost timid. How could he be induced to kill Wilkins—to shoot him in the back, Wilkins unarmed!"[83] As it appeared to be a civil matter, Mason placed Wickliffe under house arrest pending the territorial government's filing of formal charges. Wickliffe, fearing he could not receive a fair trial in the civilian court, packed his belongings and, late in the evening of January 28, silently saddled his horse and bolted from Fort Gibson. Carleton was with Wickliffe when he stole away from the post, and distracted some enlisted men who were walking near the stables lest they notice the escape in progress.

To allow Wickliffe time to distance himself from the fort, Carleton made it appear that Wickliffe was still in his quarters. Acting as post adjutant, he falsely listed Wickliffe "present, in arrest" in the morning report for January 29 and, to avoid suspicion that he had escaped, had the accused man's rations delivered to his quarters as usual. These tactics allowed Wickliffe such a thorough getaway that he was never tried for the murder.[84] But his escape and its cover-up now entangled Carleton in the machinery of military justice.

The adjutant general initiated general court-martial proceedings against Carleton. Following a twenty-day hearing, the panel adjudged Carleton guilty of "conduct unbecoming to an officer and a gentleman" and recommended that he be dismissed from the service. On March 17, 1843, President John Tyler modified Carleton's sentence to a six-month suspension.[85]

Once returned to active duty Carleton decided to employ his novelistic genius to glorify his regiment's campaigns—and to gain fellow officers' grudging acceptance. The opportunity surfaced in the spring of 1844 when army headquarters issued orders for five dragoon companies to march west under Major Wharton to revisit the Pawnee villages, manage their conflicts with the Sioux, convince them to relocate north of the Platte River, find a surer travel path to Oregon Territory, and hold council with other freshly removed tribes.[86] In the previous section of this chapter we read of Wharton's successes and failures to accomplish this mission. In the instant section we shall read of Carleton's observations.

Lt. John Love, the journalist of the 1843 Snively mission, was to serve with Captain Moore's Company C; Captains Cooke, Burgwin, and Terrett led companies; and other officers included Lieutenants Phil Kearny (nephew of Colonel Kearny), Andrew Smith, T. C. Hammond, and George Mason (son of Lieutenant Colonel Mason). Artist Charles Deas rode along with the expectation of painting great scenes of the untamed plains.[87] And among the officers on this expedition departing Fort Leavenworth on August 12 was budding *auteur* Lieutenant Carleton, fresh from his six-month suspension and with plenty to prove.

It was the first trip out on the plains for Carleton, put in charge of the commissary and acting as the expedition's unofficial journalist. Even better, he was free from the critical Lt. Col. Richard Mason and let loose onto the romantic, rolling prairie. Later, The New York *Spirit of the Times* would eagerly print Carleton's spine-tingling account of the 1844 expedition to the Pawnee villages. He began by asking Easterners to imagine themselves at Fort Leavenworth, lining up with the dragoons under massive oaks and preparing for grand adventures.

Carleton touched vividly on the difficulties faced by soldier journalists attempting, at day's end, to gather and preserve their thoughts:

> They are all nearly sitting upon the ground in front of their respective tents, and each has a little bottle of ink propped up beside him to keep it from upsetting, a steel-pen in his hand, and upon his knees a roll of wrinkled and dog-eared paper which, every time he makes a dive for a new supply of ideas, rattles and rolls over in the wind and duplicates the old ones in all sorts of inverse order on various parts of the paper. It is equally interesting—after he has speared a fresh lot—to see the way in which he glues them to the sheet. He scorns dressing them in anything like straight lines. But just sticks them down from left to right up hill,

down hill, serpentine, and zig-zag; as he dots the I's and crosses the T's, his head keeping the exact time with his pen, and in all the skirts of the y's and bonnets of the h's, moving up and down *pari passu*, he may be regarded as just naturally putting in what might as well be termed the intellectual licks in an exceedingly earnest and credible manner. As for the ink blots, they get to be a perfect drug, and for punching the pen through the paper and spattering ink right and left, is such an ordinary occurrence that it is not minded at all, notwithstanding the *tout ensemble* of page when completed is so extremely ornamented from those fortuitous causes. Then pen has to go through the final exercises of punctuation that are called for by a second reading; now cutting a quirl and quiddity on notes of interrogation—or making a punch and thrust on those of admiration; giving a single party *in quatre* on a comma— a stocckado and parry on a semicolon—two rapid stoccadoes on a colon and finally a grand lunge on a period. . . . At last, the letter is held out at arm's length, in order the better to regard its proportions and appearance, the ink bottle capsizes, and its contents seeking the lower level where the writer sits, apprise him of the accident, by soaking up through his clothes, what a fierce "Curse the luck!" announces for the time being a cessation of literary labors.[88]

He also let readers in on the manner in which the dragoons, out in the wilds, typically spot and make their nightly encampment:

The ground is usually selected by the Quarter-master, who generally marches with the Pioneers under his command, some mile or two in advance of the troops. In choosing it he has an eye not only to the beauty and strength of the position, but also to its convenience to wood and water. Above all, he must have the fine grass in abundance, amongst which to picket the horses and mules. . . . If the encampment is upon a stream, and generally is so—our Squadron is formed along its bank, and facing it. The next takes position on its right, facing outward—the next upon its left, also facing outward. The wagons and howitzers are parked upon the fourth side, under charge of the guard. . . . As soon as each Squadron has got its place the men are dismounted, when they immediately strip their horses upon the very ground they occupy, and then lead them out of the square. After finding them a good spot of grass in the neighborhood, each man there pickets his horse.[89]

Carleton had other untoward events to record as well. A number of the troops became ill with high fever. On August 14 trooper John Clough of Company K fell suddenly from his saddle, went into convulsions, and soon died.[90] He was buried with full military honors. Harry Thompson of Company G died on the twenty-sixth and his comrades buried him with honors on the summit of a small hill.[91] In all, twenty-four men became sick with what likely was an outbreak of malaria. But the disease left as quickly as it had gripped the command, and the troops moved on.[92]

Whether or not Carleton fully redeemed himself in the eyes of his fellow officers through his literary efforts, he did bring the public a romantic but fresh and vivid view of dragoon life. And despite his prejudices and utter self-centeredness, he depicted the costs of Indian Removal and its fumbling execution with astonishing clarity. Like most other northeasters he romanticized the vanishing race, but like most whites coveted the valuable land they were living upon. In this regard alone, the loss to Dickens's circle was the country's gain. Events in later years, especially his witnessing the dead settlers at the site of the Mountain Meadows Massacre, would harden his heart, and in 1860 and 1862 he participated in vicious campaigns against the Paiute, Apache, and Navajo tribes.[93]

But if the dragoon endeavors left the frontier reasonably serene, political events were moving fast and contentiously. In the presidential election of 1844 expansionist James "Little Hickory" Polk narrowly defeated Henry Clay. Following the vote, lame-duck

president John Tyler, attempting to anoint his lackluster administration with a smattering of glory, negotiated a treaty to annex the
Republic of Texas. As might be imagined, this action did not sit
well with his own party and sat even worse with the Mexican government, which regarded it as a declaration of war.

When Polk took office in 1845, he kept his campaign promise
to advance the admission of Texas. To defend the new state, Polk
sent troops under Zachary Taylor into Texas to protect it from
an anticipated invasion by Mexico.[94] President Polk also pushed
claims to lands on the Pacific coast as he devised schemes to
acquire Mexican-held California by purchase or conquest and to
make territorial gains in the Northwest, threatening war if Britain did not accede to the jingoistic cry "Fifty-four Forty or Fight!"
and cede to the United States much of its territory in the Pacific
Northwest.[95]

If there was going to be a war, Colonel Kearny knew his regiment would be in the thick of it. The only question in his mind
was: war with whom? But regardless of the actual enemy—more
important, regardless of the actual officer in the field—Kearny
had ensured, and would continue to ensure, the regiment's readiness. With proven company-grade officers such as Sumner, Allen,
Wharton, and Carleton, in addition to a solid cast of junior officers such as Henry Turner, John Love, Benjamin Moore, Philip
St. George Cooke, and Abraham Johnston, Kearny bet that his
dragoons were prepared. And now, there would be a true test of
it: the trip to the Continental Divide.

Fort Atkinson, Wisconsin Territory. Built in 1842, with four two-story barracks, two built of stone and two of logs, around a square parade ground. Commissioned officers and their families enjoyed one of the stone barracks, while non-commissioned officers and their families lived in a hewn-log one. Private soldiers occupied the other two barracks—the lower floor of their stone building housing the hospital and that of their wooden one containing quarters and a great room used as a chapel on Sundays and a school during the week. At the corners of the parade ground stood a stone-walled gun house, a stockade, a stone magazine or powder-house, and the quartermaster's storehouse adjoined by the sutler's shop. Sketch by Lt. Alexander Reynolds.

"Dragoons on the Prairie" is an 1846 woodcut taken from *Recollections of the United States Army*, a book of ambiguous authorship likely written by former dragoon James Hildreth. Author's collection.

2nd. Lesson – 2nd Part.

Loading in ten times.

Fig A   Fig.B.

Load.   *Cast About*

This drawing of the School of Trooper Dismounted is taken from Secretary of War Joel Poinsett's three-volume booklet *Cavalry Tactics* (1841). It shows a dragoon in dress uniform demonstrating the proper handling and loading of a carbine. Author's collection.

4.th Lesson,–1.st Part.

In Tierce – Point.

Another Poinsett drawing, this one demonstrates the way a dismounted dragoon should hold his saber high "In Tierce—Point." Author's collection.

Twentieth-century artist Randy Steffen drew this picture of a dragoon private in 1833 white-cotton fatigue wear with a black leather cap. Steffen, *The Horse Soldier*, vol. 1. Courtesy of the University of Oklahoma Press.

Another of Steffen's drawings depicts a corporal in a dress uniform while mounted. Steffen, *The Horse Soldier*, vol. 1. Courtesy of the University of Oklahoma Press.

Dragoons, armed with Hall carbines, in the field. Elting, *Military Uniforms in America*, vol. 2. Reproduced with permission from the Company of Military Historians.

Dragoons wearing full dress uniforms. Elting, *Military Uniforms in America*, vol. 2.
Reproduced with permission from the Company of Military Historians.

Kearny's dragoons on the march along Night Creek, New Mexico Territory, during their fall 1846 expedition to California. This is a drawing of the site by Topographical Engineer William Emory, included in his official report of the mission. Emory, *Notes of a Military Reconnaissance.*

"Pima Indians" is another Emory drawing of what is today Arizona. These kindly people graciously shared their food with the dragoons, allowing them to continue with their trek to California. Emory, *Notes of a Military Reconnaissance.*

Initially lacking knowledge of mounted drill and swordsmanship, dragoon officers were forced to turn for guidance to the seasoned mind of a former British cavalry junior officer: Edward "Long Ned" Stanley, who acted as the regiment's de facto first sergeant major. This woodcut of a fictional version of Sergeant Stanley is taken from Hildreth, *Recollections of the United States Army.*

Sickly James Allen, mapmaker, was another of Kearny's cast of trusted junior commanders. He spent most of his time in the Northwest Territory exploring the region and keeping the peace. Initially placed in command of the Mormon Battalion, his untimely death in 1846 cost the regiment one of its best officers. "Captain James Allen and Fort Des Moines," *The Annals of Iowa* 20 (1937): 546–48. Courtesy of the Iowa Historical Society.

Eng.ᵈ by A.H.Ritchie

Overlooked by many historians is perhaps the most valuable product of Kearny's march to California in 1846: William Emory's report, entitled *Notes of a Military Reconnaissance, from Fort Leavenworth, in Missouri, to San Diego, in California*, a detailed, 385-page account of the geology, plants, animals, peoples, and archaeological ruins encountered by the Kearny expedition between Fort Leavenworth and San Diego. Congress immediately viewed the work as important, and in 1848 ordered more than 10,000 extra copies published. Courtesy of the United States Military Academy.

188

In 1833, Andrew Jackson named Philip St. George Cooke a lieutenant in the dragoons. He soon became one of Kearny's most trusted subordinates. In 1843, Kearny placed Cooke in command of a patrol that disarmed the Texas land pirates under Jacob Snively. In 1846, following the death of Colonel Allen, Kearny ordered Cooke to command the Mormon Battalion on its march from Fort Leavenworth to California. *Harper's Weekly Journal of Civilization*, June 11, 1858.

Nathaniel Boone, the youngest son of Daniel Boone and a former officer in the Battalion of Mounted Rangers, proved to be one of Kearny's most valuable subordinates, in particular because of his firsthand knowledge of the tribes of the Southern Plains. Courtesy of the State Historical Society of Missouri.

Unpolished in manners and schooling, Henry Dodge owned slaves, scandalized ladies with foul language, and squatted on lands belonging to the Winnebago tribe. At one time or another he had been an Indian fighter, a sheriff, a miner, a duelist, and a defendant in a treason case. President Andrew Jackson named Henry Dodge as the first colonel of the dragoons. Courtesy of the Wisconsin Historical Society.

The only Mexican War general who lacked political ambitions, worn down by hard campaigning in New Mexico, California, and Mexico, General Stephen Watts Kearny died an early death in 1848. Courtesy of the Bancroft Library at the University of California at Berkeley.

Aztec Club medal. The Aztec Club was formed in Mexico City in 1847 for army and navy officers who participated in the Mexican War. Several dragoon officers became members including Kearny, Emory, Sumner, Cooke, Ingalls, and Swords. The medal illustrated belonged to George Blake, who became colonel of the 1st Dragoons in 1861. Author's collection.

CHAPTER 6

1845

Exploration, Peacekeeping, and Preparation for Conquest

As 1845 dawned, the nation faced war. With the granting of statehood for Texas, the army considered sending a sizeable number of troops to form the Army of Observation in Texas, and would do so later in the year, moving them across the Nueces River to congregate on the banks of the Rio Grande in Texas. At the same time, United States diplomats clashed with Great Britain over the Oregon Territory, and many Americans were seized by the jingoistic cheer "Fifty-four Forty or Fight!" To prepare for possible hostilities with Britain, other regular troops took up positions to protect East Coast cities and ports. To the 1st Dragoons would fall the unique mission of preparing for war with either England or Mexico by moving a large body of troops west, exploring the possibility of either invading New Mexico or holding Oregon Territory.

Despite such thundering, as in the 1836 war with the Seminoles in Florida, the 1st Dragoons were, since their creation, spared removal from their frontier posts. Army headquarters in Washington, D.C., considered it crucial for the regiment to remain where it could continue its missions to police the Mississippi Valley, protect commerce on the Santa Fe and Overland Trails, and explore the open territory. So the dragoon regiment's duties actually increased as infantry and artillery regiments departed from the Mississippi Valley for Texas or the northeast.

Freed from immediate wartime preparations, Col. Stephen Kearny planned a grand expedition for troops stationed at Fort Leavenworth and Fort Scott to explore the Overland Trail as far as South Pass in the Rockies. The pass was a wide, wagon-accessible, and reasonably low trail through the otherwise nearly impassable mountain range. As such it was of enormous value to settlers west-bound for Oregon to have the army explore and possibly improve the route west. The expedition would also place the regiment in position for action should war break out with either Mexico or England. On the return trip, Kearny and his troops were to head south and then travel east along the Santa Fe Trail.

This excursion would also allow the War Department to choose a location for a fort on the trail that could protect the swelling numbers of would-be settlers. And as usual, such a show of the Great Father's military power would serve, equally, to intimidate regional tribes and keep them from attacking wagon trains. But there were less peaceable reasons for the expedition as well.

It rained heavily throughout the night of May 17, 1845, but the weather was clear that Sunday when Companies A, C, F, G, and K—about 250 sabers—departed from the muddy parade grounds of Fort Leavenworth under Kearny's command. Two mountain howitzers, seventeen wagons, and herds of sheep and cattle accompanied the troops.[1] The guide for the expedition was the experienced and respected mountain man, Thomas "Bad Hand" Fitzpatrick, a trapper, who had ranged the frontier since 1823 and demonstrated a keen understanding of the native peoples who populated the plains.[2]

Lieutenant Carleton was again to serve as the commissary officer on the mission and would again act as correspondent for the *Spirit of the Times*, a duty he fulfilled with relish. For his New York readers, and to the delight of army recruiters, he supplied this superb account of a dragoon expedition on the march:

> First, the guide is seen by himself, some quarter of a mile ahead of all: then the commanding officer, followed by his orderly and the chief bugler: then the staff officers: then

a division, mounted on black horses, marching by twos: then another on greys [*sic*]—another on bays—another on sorrels, and a fifth on blacks again, with an interval of one hundred paces between each division [company] to avoid one another's dust: then the howitzers, followed by a party of dragoons to serve them under charge of the sergeant major: then the train of wagons, with a detail to assist them getting over bad places, under the immediate command of the quartermaster-sergeant . . . then a drove of cattle and sheep, followed by a guard of nine men under the command of a corporal—and lastly, the main guard, under an officer to bring up the extreme rear.[3]

The hard rain resumed the first night, and the men slept upon the same ground that had been occupied by Major Wharton's expedition the previous year—a somewhat unnerving reminder for veterans of that roundabout operation. Many must have known, however, that with the experienced Fitzpatrick as guide and the capable Kearny as commander, this mission would not go astray.[4]

One of Kearny's most important tasks was to locate a route from Fort Leavenworth to the Overland Trail that would replace the tortuous one found through Wharton's 1844 meanderings. Kearny would not make Wharton's mistake of leaving the established trail too early. Only after three days into the march did he veer from the rutted path and turn northwest to discover a fresh course. In changing direction he followed a "rolling & picturesque prairie richly covered" with grasses and trees. On the next day the column crested a ridge and observed below them the Overland Trail, coursing over the plains near the Blue River. Lieutenant Turner found "the trail quite large & [it] appears to have been travelled by large caravans within the span of two or three weeks."[5]

On May 24 the dragoons forded the river and overtook the first of many Oregon-bound emigrant trains they would encounter, one with fifty slow-moving wagons. These travelers were much relieved to have a dragoon escort. Off in the distance, the troops "espied on a distant ridge, the wagon-tops of the emigrants—dim, white spots, like sails at sea"—Manifest Destiny made manifest.[6] By the time the dragoons got to South Pass, they would have met, by Kearny's estimate, 460 wagons and 1,500 settlers.[7] And by the year's end, some 3,000 settlers would have traveled west on the Overland Trail.[8]

Lieutenant Turner recorded that each of the oxen-pulled wagons "appeared to be the property of some single family, which contained all their worldly goods besides the members of the family [walking alongside] on foot." He observed that the emigrants included men of all professions—priests, doctors, lawyers, and more—a social variety, which would let them set up an organized community wherever they might settle.[9]

The trail in late spring proved dry, hot, and dusty, but since heavy traffic had compacted the ground, the dragoons could quicken their pace. Turner complained that the grazing was poor, the region "having been previously occupied by parties of immigrants" and left "nearly destitute of grass." Carleton agreed, writing of the "dreary monotony that surrounded" the column as it plodded along the gritty, scorching trail, with "the clang of hundreds of sabres as they swung heavily to and fro against the iron stirrups." Some veterans of the previous trip may have wished for a return of the drenching rains that had plagued them in 1844. But relief, without rain or chill, came as the troops entered the lush Blue River valley, which Carleton declared appeared at sunset as the "Fairy Land of the West."[10]

Too soon the column left this delightful spot and reached the broad Platte River, which it would track westward to South Pass. Wrote Lt. William Franklin, topographical engineer, "The country between the Blue and the Platte is very barren, there are ranges of hills much like the undulating land which formed the rolling prairie but wanting the verdure with which these latter are clothed."[11] Lieutenant Turner estimated that the river was three-quarters of a mile to a mile in width, two inches deep, and studded with islands supporting groves of cottonwood trees.

Not to be outdone by the literary efforts of Lieutenant Carleton, Captain Cooke painted this account of the column's arrival in the valley of the Platte: "Between us and the river lay two miles of green savannas; the wide expanse of the great river was in part concealed by Grand Island and its woods . . . the squadrons were gliding, two abreast, along gentle curves, over the fresh green grass, which was brilliant in the slant rays of a clear sun. The horses had a gallant bearing;—fifty blacks led; fifty grays followed; then fifty bays; next fifty chestnuts—and fifty more blacks closed the procession: the arms glittered; the horses' shoes shone twinkling on the moving feet."[12]

Along the river's banks the dragoons came upon a wagon train that had stopped to bury a child.[13] On June 3 Colonel Kearny ordered that two of the column's wagons, loaded with unnecessary items. be sent back to Fort Leavenworth. Turner observed, "This gives all an opportunity of communicating with absent friends & much letter writing is in progress through out the camp." Marring the peaceful evening, Kearny's horses broke from their picket rope, which was attached to a heavy metal pin that they yanked out of the loose sand, and galloped away. Darkness prevented the men from overtaking the errant animals, but the next morning Scout Fitzpatrick and a party took off in search of the horses and, to the colonel's relief, returned with them in tow.

Along this portion of the South Platte the dragoons encountered numerous herds of buffalo. Kearny allowed some of his men to hunt and bring in fresh meat. Turner excitedly obtained a portion but found the flesh of the emaciated beasts unsatisfactory. Continuing the march beside the river, the column met a party of French traders coming downriver from Fort Laramie on flatboats loaded with furs and buffalo robes and bound for St. Louis. Turner noted that, despite the difficulties they had encountered getting past the shallow river, "these poor fellows appeared light hearted & cheerfully expressed delight at seeing us." After the traders told Kearny there was good grazing a few miles upriver, the command mounted and quickly located Ash Creek, a veritable oasis of sweet water and forage. Fitzpatrick recalled to Turner that he had camped here when he was scouting for the John Frémont expedition in 1842.[14] Soon after, on June 11, the column encountered the deep, sandy, and barren lands bordering the Platte. Here, they encountered another group of fur traders, struggling to progress downriver, who had resolved to return to Fort Laramie and wait until the level of the water rose in the now-impassable river.

The troops marched passed the landmarks Courthouse Rock and then Chimney Rock. The latter was a three-hundred-foot narrow limestone formation, "dull grey sometimes varying to yellow and in a few instances white," arising out of flat, windswept ground in modern-day western Nebraska.[15] The rock marked for travelers the end of the flat plains and the beginning of the gentle grade up into the Rockies. The troops left the valley for a region of bleak bluffs composed of "marly sandstone" presenting "the appearance of immense fortifications."[16] The next day the troops met a large encamped party from the American Fur Company whose flatboats had gone aground in the low water, and who hoped the river would soon rise so that they could resume their journey.[17]

Five miles farther to the west, a village of twenty-five lodges belonging to the powerful Brule Sioux became alarmed by the sudden approach of the dragoons. Scout Fitzpatrick crossed the Platte ahead of the column and assured the Sioux of their peaceful intentions. Tribal leaders and a few warriors crossed the river and held council with Colonel Kearny, who presented them with some tobacco. After giving the Sioux a tour of the dragoon camp, the colonel invited them to meet with him a few days later near the American Fur Company's trading post at Fort Laramie.[18]

The troops reached adobe-walled Fort Laramie (then known as Fort John) on June 14. In 1845, the fort was owned and operated by the American Fur Company but would be purchased by the army in 1849.[19] The imposing structure, with fifteen-foot-high rectangular walls "imperfectly constructed with sun-dried bricks," sat on a bluff above the Laramie River in modern-day Wyoming.

Lieutenant Franklin described the fort as a "hollow square . . . formed by the rooms of the fort, which are used for storing skins, Indian goods, &c. and as a residence for the voyaguers [*sic*]."[20] Called the "Gateway to the Rockies," this first sight of civilization was welcome to travelers on the Overland Trail. Good grazing and plentiful water surrounded the fort, where settlers could purchase supplies, obtain advice, and have their wagons repaired.[21] Leaving Capt. William Eustis and Company A behind to set up camp near the fort and to guard supplies, wagons, livestock, and spare horses, Kearny proceeded to nearby Fort Platte to hold council with 250 Oglala and Brule Sioux.

Intimidation and Protection of Native Peoples

The council absorbed a long, blustery day at Fort Platte. Kearny informed tribal leaders that he was opening a new road upon which numerous emigrant trains would pass. He cautioned the Sioux not to harm or steal from the settlers, and reminded them of past incidents in which Sioux warriors had killed white men. He forgave the tribe for these past acts, but gave warning that further incidents of violence would now be punished. Kearny also warned of the dangers of whiskey being brought into their country and advised the tribesmen to spill any they encountered onto the ground. To demonstrate the Great Father's generosity, Kearny distributed gifts: brightly colored cloth, beads, knives, tobacco, and blankets. Then, using the dragoons' time-tested display of military might, fired three shots from the howitzers and sent rockets flying into the blackened skies.[22]

Upon his return, Kearny was to write to General Jones of the effectiveness of the army's display of force. "And as these were the first soldiers ever seen by these Upper Indians . . . those who saw them were much struck with their uniform appearance—their Arms & Big Guns (Howitzers), it is most probable" that those who viewed the troops would relay and exaggerate to others their accounts of the "power & force" of the dragoons.[23]

Having accomplished his diplomatic mission with the Sioux, Kearny confronted two difficult situations in succession. Back on the trail to South Pass, at Horseshoe Creek, the guard brought in an Arapaho woman with two small children. She stated that they had escaped from a party that had been ambushed by the Sioux, sighted the detachment, and walked into their camp. Kearny arranged for two soldiers (F Company Privates Callahan and Buckner) to escort her to Fort Laramie where she would be able to tell her story through an interpreter and be protected. The next day, a Private Smith of G troop, while on guard duty, accidently shot himself in the right arm near the wrist with a Hall carbine. Surgeon Samuel De Camp immediately amputated the man's forearm to stop the bleeding, but the shock of the amputation and loss of blood caused the trooper the "greatest suffering." In Lieutenant Franklin's words, "The poor fellow bore his loss without a murmur, and even stood another amputation afterwards without flinching." Kearny ordered that the wounded soldier remain behind in the surgeon's care and, with an escort of seven men, be moved to Fort Laramie when he was in better health. De Camp was to remain at the fort and await Kearny's return.[24]

The column now began a slow climb following the Sweetwater River through the broken and desolate country leading up to the Continental Divide. The broad road to South Pass, although surrounded by majestic peaks, ran through inhospitable surroundings relieved only by stunted sagebrush. Kearny reported the land for some three hundred miles beyond Fort Laramie as "a barren sandy desert" with scarce grazing for the animals. The dragoons had arrived late in the season and during a drought, after large herds of buffalo and passing caravans had devoured most of the grasses along the route. The experienced guide Fitzpatrick had never seen such a paucity of grazing in this country. Turner feared that "[o]ur grazing must improve or [the horses] will scarcely be able to return to Laramie."[25]

By the twenty-second, riding half-starved mounts, they passed Independence Rock, enriched with the graffiti of many passing travelers. Lieutenant Franklin observed that the rock was covered with the names of emigrants and politicians as "far above all were the names of Martin Van Buren and Henry Clay . . . put here by some Democrat and Whig, who [though] far on their way to Oregon . . . could not forget their political prejudices."[26] The sun beat down as the expedition proceeded west through a narrow gorge of the Sweetwater River known as Devil's Gate. But if the days were hot, night now brought freezing temperatures. So many horses and cattle suffered from heat and malnutrition that Kearny again reduced his command, leaving provisions and sickly stock behind under the guard of twenty-seven men, and continued his march to South Pass. To seek fresh grazing, Fitzpatrick detoured the troops to a route not usually traveled by wagons.[27]

South Pass at Last

Consuming the last full measure of energy from every man and animal, the column at last gained the summit. On the last day of June, Turner recorded that "an almost impossible ascent brought us to the culminating point of the famous S. Pass." The troops crossed the 7,550-foot-high South Pass, 281 miles from Fort Laramie and 850 miles from Fort Leavenworth. Kearny assembled the men for a roll call near the headwaters of the southwesterly flowing Green River. He congratulated them warmly on being the first United States troops ever to muster on the Pacific side of the continent.[28]

Perhaps even more gratifying to the troops, it was now time to head for home. At seven o'clock the following morning the command, having reached the westernmost goal of their mission, began its return trip downslope to Fort Laramie.[29] On their way down the pass the column met a westbound wagon train, its oxen teams straining every muscle to pull the heavy wagons up to the summit. The emigrants entrusted the dragoons with letters home to loved ones, "the last these friends would hear of them, probably for many years."[30] It was the Fourth of July, and members of the Oregon-bound train requested that Kearny fire a howitzer to celebrate. The colonel acceded. Cooke noted, "Accordingly it was fired! and awoke echoes from the granite mountains they never had startled before the chamois themselves; and the shell exploding amid the far-off answers of rock to rock, produced a glorious confusion of sounds—more rare, if not more windy than all the oratories of the day combined, and the inebriate, but hearty shouts of excited multitudes."[31] The young nation was a year older. Traveling a few miles farther downhill, the command rendezvoused with the detachment left to guard the wagons, cattle, and sickly horses. Lieutenant Turner observed that the stock looked much improved by their respite and enjoyment of verdant grassland.[32]

Riding swiftly downhill, they arrived at Captain Eustis's camp near Fort Laramie on July 12. Man and beast were gratified upon returning to Laramie to find, in the words of Lieutenant Franklin, "everything just as we could have wished. Our poor horses have become fat, and the man who lost his arm had entirely recovered, and the squaw and her children had become domesticated in the camp and living very comfortable."[33] But the trip was not without accidents: A trooper of Company F was badly injured while attempting to mount a restive horse, and the guide Fitzpatrick narrowly escaped death when violently kicked by a horse. The stunned Fitzpatrick quickly recovered, but not so the dragoon tossed from his horse. He was placed in an improvised litter and suffered genuine agony as the litter jerked along the trail to Fort Laramie.[34]

Upon reaching Fort Laramie, Kearny received a visit from Sioux leader Bull-Tail, who had been deeply impressed by Kearny's earlier speech about the evils of alcohol, to inform him that Mexican traders were routinely bringing liquor into the region. Kearny gave Bull-Tail a paper upon which he had written that the bearer and his agents were authorized to confiscate and to destroy all spirits brought to the tribe.[35]

Kearny now prepared for the Santa Fe Trail leg of the trip home. Believing that the wagons, worn mules, and horses would not be needed further, he sent them back to Fort Leavenworth on the Overland Trail. The kidnapped Arapaho woman and her children sent earlier to the fort, having no place to go, accompanied Kearny. With the nights warming, Kearny granted the troops permission to abandon or sell their light-blue, thick woolen caped overcoats. Not surprisingly, quite a few jackets ended up being traded at the fort for bottles of spirits.

The troop's departure from Laramie proved much more sudden than Kearny had planned. A brush fire fed by the wind roared swiftly toward the dragoon campsite; trumpets sounded, "Assembly" and "To Horse!" and, sober or not, the troops threw together their gear, climbed into their saddles, and sprinted away. With the flames nearly upon them horsemen, howitzers, and supply wagons "galloped forward to leap the girdling flame, and pass[ed] the blackened but still fiery space beyond."[36] Having out-ridden the prairie fire to reach safe ground, the troopers assembled, repacked, formed ranks, and proceeded on their journey. They skirted the Laramie River and then turned southward along the dry bed of Chugwater Creek on the eastern slope of the Rockies. Heading south, Kearny held council with the Cheyennes on the sixteenth of July. As he had repeatedly done during his career on the plains, Kearny told his listeners that they were children of the Great Father who demanded that the tribe's leaders avoid harming whites passing through their land, and warned of punishment should they disobey. And as he had to the Sioux, Kearny delivered his stock prohibitionist speech on the dangers of allowing spirits to be brought onto their land. He distributed liberal gifts and then had his trumpeter sound "To Horse!" The troops smartly mounted, formed ranks, and proceeded down the valley.[37]

Passing along the front range of the eastern Rocky Mountains southward, the soldiers casually rode past Long's and Pike's Peaks, each towering over 14,000 feet in elevation. On July 18 a group of Arapahos came into camp to inquire about the woman and children whom they heard Kearny had rescued from the Sioux and were now traveling with the column. It pleased the warriors that the dragoons had treated the woman and the children kindly, and they rejoiced in their reunion with the returned captives.[38]

For the first time in months the dragoons came upon a lush meadow. Emerging from a pine forest below Pike's Peak on July 25, the troops found "a greener prairie than [they] had seen since leaving the Missouri frontier," in contrast to the "the arid & sun burnt plains" they had confronted for the past couple of months.[39] Four days later Kearny, tracing the Arkansas River, arrived at Bent's Fort in present-day southern Colorado. Built in 1833 by William and Charles Bent and Ceran St. Vrain, it was the furthest American outpost on the Santa Fe Trail and the only settlement between the crossing of the Arkansas River and Fort Leavenworth. The fur traders greeted Kearny with a two-gun salute fired from the fort's small field piece.[40] Lieutenant Franklin was surprised to find that the fur traders "had many of the comforts and a few of the luxuries of a civilized life about them."[41] Intended primarily to facilitate trade with the southern Cheyennes, the fort was a favored residence of mountain men, such as Christopher "Kit" Carson.[42]

By the time Kearny arrived at Bent's Fort, his provisions had run dangerously low. Fortune, however, smiled on the detachment. The army quartermaster had wisely cached stocks of rice and hard bread at the fort intended for, but not used by, Cooke's 1843 Snively expedition. Surprisingly, the aged food was stale but edible.[43] Equally fortuitously, at Bent's Fort Kearny used his men to intercept a supply of intoxicants headed for the tribes. Into the fort came an unsuspecting wagon that had hidden within it a barrel and a half of pure liquor. Kearny had the wagon searched and, finding its noxious cargo, promptly invoked the Indian Commerce Act, declared the spirits to be illegal contraband entering Indian Country, and destroyed the goods. Given the difficulty of taking the moonshiners back to Missouri for trial and producing witnesses, he did not arrest them.[44]

The Long Westward Reach of War and Politics

That night, Charles Bent and St. Vrain honored Kearny and his officers with a grand feast. They also provided them with valuable intelligence of current events in New Mexico province. Cooke and the other officers, spoiling for glory, eagerly contemplated the prospect of war with Mexico and of crossing the unguarded border to race west and capture Santa Fe. Cooke recognized "war with Mexico [as] so inevitable" and that their long march, if nothing else, was a good dress rehearsal for it. The next year's occurrences would prove Cooke prescient.[45]

The soldiers soon left their gracious hosts and moved on. Traveling briskly, they next encamped thirty miles below Bent's Fort on the east bank of the Arkansas River. On the return trip the dragoons met merchant trains on the trail, saw herds of buffalo, encountered Native Americans, and witnessed turbulent prairie winds and thunderstorms—in brief, they experienced places, peoples, and conditions that most of them had previously seen on the Santa Fe Trail. For them, long trips out on the plains, originally so exotic, were becoming routine and often tedious.[46]

Still, the toil did not grow easier to bear for men or beasts. Leaving the lush region near Fort Bent, the dragoons again confronted the dusty wasteland. Cooke, a veteran of some marches along the trail dating back to 1828, marveled at how well the horses bore this portion of the march, despite poor quality of grass and their heavily equipped riders: "with carbine, sabre, pistols, cartridges, two blankets, a great coat, picket rope, and iron pin, &c. But it must break down anything but a cast iron horse to march this incessantly for a hundred days!"[47]

It was here that Kearny would lose his capable guide. On August 4 an express rider sent by the explorer John Frémont, who had recently arrived at Bent's Fort, overtook the column, bringing with him a much-appreciated cache of mail for the company. He also brought a less welcome dispatch from Frémont asking Kearny for the services of Bad Hand Fitzpatrick, and the guide confessed to Kearny that he had always felt more comfortable residing in the

Far West. Given that many of his men knew the Santa Fe Trail well, Kearny no longer required, though he surely valued, the services of Fitzpatrick. Saying farewell to the scout and interpreter, turning their faces westward, the troops moved into what was, for many of them, familiar territory—the Santa Fe Trail.[48]

Kearny soon drew within five miles of the border with Mexico. It was at this location in 1843 that Cooke's squadron had confronted Colonel Snively's Texas Invincibles. Kearny, who had headed the court of inquiry panel that found in favor of Cooke, thought it provident that he gain a firsthand inspection of the site of Cooke's actions. He dispatched Lt. William Franklin, the topographical engineer, to Jackson's Grove, where Cooke had disarmed the Texicans, and bade him use his instruments to confirm that the spot was located in U.S. territory; it proved indeed to be a full twenty-five miles east of the Mexican border.[49]

Riding steadily along the trail, passing caravans and immense herds of buffalo, the men came closer to their destination with each beat of the horses' hooves. On August 7 they knew that civilization was near when an escaped slave wandered into the dragoon camp. Wrote Turner, "he confessed that he ran off from his master & that it was his object to get if possible into New Mexico; that he had been treated badly by his master, he was willing to encounter any danger or privation rather than return."[50]

Here we witness a heartbreakingly common example of the great societal problem that afflicted the nation since its creation: the "peculiar institution" of slavery. Concerning the Arapaho woman and children enslaved by the Sioux, Kearny's sense of justice, along with that of the majority of Americans, dictated that she be set free—and she was. Those views, however, did not in Kearny's mind, and in the minds of a majority of citizens, extend to the case of an escaped slave of white men. The escaped slave was the property of his owner, and the law required that he should be duly returned to his master upon the troops' reaching the Missouri settlements—just as in 1834, Dodge had returned to his owner's family the African-American slave who had been captured by the Pawnee. Two days after being captured by the dragoons and put into the service of an officer, the man somehow escaped again. That Kearny may have had a change of heart is suggested by the lack of any attempt on his part, this time, to pursue the runaway. Indeed, the only dragoon pursuits that day were not of humans but of buffalo.[51]

The long trek gradually wore down the mounts. By the time the column reached Council Grove an increasing number of the horses had become unable to carry their riders. When the troops reached camp on August 20, three horses, including one of the colonel's, died from exhaustion. Four days later, the troops struck the familiar military road at a point ten miles from Fort Leavenworth. With darkness and rain beginning to fall, they dismounted and led the horses for the last miles. Travel-worn themselves, the troops assembled on the parade ground where they received the genuine commendations of their colonel, and were then dismissed,[52] with his final exhortation to tend to their horses' needs before their own.[53] For, even after so magnificent a mission, when mounted troops arrived at the end of a day's march they had to feed, water, walk, and otherwise tend to their horses before they themselves could rest. Such was the duty of a dragoon.

The army hierarchy had committed five companies—25 percent of its precious mounted arm—on a risky, difficult expedition deep into the county's interior. In this task, Colonel Kearny and his men performed well beyond their superiors' expectations. And the colonel was rightfully proud. He had lost but one man (though two had been badly crippled) and nine horses and mules, and had traversed a vast territory in ninety-nine days—proving once again the ability of his regiment to cover great expanses of unforgiving terrain rapidly. In his report, Kearny entered a simple, heartfelt tribute to his column: "Great credit is due to the officers and enlisted men who composed this command. They have all proved themselves what their ambition is to be—good soldiers."[54]

Of course, in less than a year's time, their abilities would be even more sorely tested in the Mexican provinces of New Mexico and California. But for now, the accolades flowed. General-in-Chief

Winfield Scott, upon reading Kearny's report, had nothing but praise for the men and officers of the 1st Dragoons. Scott wrote that the tribes with whom Kearny treated were obviously struck with the "fine appearance of the troops as well as by the wide and humane admonitions of their commander."[55]

A Return to Policing

The admirably successful Kearny expedition overshadowed—and may have encouraged—a number of less useful dragoon activities taking place in 1845. War jitters or not, the continuing need—sometimes, the perceived need—for the dragoons to act as a frontier police force in the Mississippi Valley manifested itself scattershot throughout the region. In fact, largely as a result of the dragoons' show of military force and their genuine diplomacy, the frontier would remain calm as the nation prepared itself for war with a foreign foe.

In January 1845, Creek immigrants battled Osage and Wichita warriors. Some panicked Creeks and traders fled to Fort Gibson for protection. Captain Boone took Company H to the mouth of Little River in February; finding calm in the region, he returned his troops to the fort.[56] Soon after, rumors of a Chickasaw tribe uprising brought Company D to the scene of alleged turmoil. That company finding no sign of war in the region either, it also returned to its station at Fort Washita on April 1. On the twenty-third of the month a report that Indians had attacked Warner's Station made Company D once again saddle up and march out of Fort Washita to cross the Red River into the soon-to-be-annexed state of Texas. Again discovering no conflict, they returned on the twenty-fifth. In October Captain Boone, with forty men from Company H, departed Fort Gibson and entered Texas to escort U.S. treaty commissioners to a meeting with leaders of the Comanche Nation. As the Comanches didn't appear at the conference, the troops returned to Gibson.[57]

Keeping International Borders: American and British Spheres

Other dragoon actions were more constructive. While Kearny was away on his expedition, a tumult over immigration roiled to the north in Sioux county in Iowa Territory (present-day Minnesota). "Half-breed" mixed Native and British Canadians known as *Metis* had for decades crossed the international border to hunt buffalo, and the Sioux had long expressed their dismay at these aliens from British settlements despoiling the herds. Now, with an English–American war lurking in the shadows, the War Department thought it necessary to display the presence of the U.S. military in the region, even if it consisted of just two companies of dragoons. Consequently, the army ordered troops to push the Metis back into Canada, thereby demonstrating the power of the Great White Father not only to resident Sioux but to illegal British subjects and the British government in London as well. Thus, it came to pass that Companies B and I marched from their respective posts at Forts Atkinson and Des Moines to meet at Traverse des Sioux on the St. Peter's (later Minnesota) River and from there to deal with the Metis together. The army issued orders to Captain Sumner, the senior officer, to assume command of the squadron.

Many of the troops in Captain Allen's Company I did not relish soon being placed under the authoritarian Sumner. The company was composed of freewheeling men accustomed to Allen's informal leadership style. An enlisted man expressed the general sentiment in his journal: "strong speculations as to how we shall get along with Capt. E. V. Sumner all expect to be blown up like the devil."[58]

Bad luck dogged preparations. As had happened in the previous year, heavy June rains flooded the area and greatly hampered troop movement.[59] Narrow, muddy roads became impassable for wagons, and one of the B Company vehicles overturned and was smashed to pieces. On June 13, the two companies made contact with one another. But while Sumner and Allen prepared for the upcoming confrontations with the Metis and Sioux, a careless trooper Howard of Company I, on June 17, 1845, accidently discharged his pistol and shot himself through the thigh, leaving him disabled. To top it off, the bullet passed through Howard's tent and struck trooper Adolphus Berry in an adjacent tent, seriously wounding him.[60]

Upon their arrival at Traverse des Sioux, Sumner found a boat plying upstream on the St. Peter's River. It had been sent with supplies for him from Fort Snelling, and its manifest included two mountain howitzers. But Captain Sumner was not pleased to discover that, though he had ordered thirty-one barrels of flour, the quartermaster had sent but seventeen, and some of them moldy. Sumner realized that unless he could purchase flour along the trail, the shortage of flour sharply curtailed the time the column could remain in the field. In the end, the scarcity of flour did not impair his operation.[61]

On June 22, the two accidentally wounded men left by boat downriver to Fort Snelling. The next day, to impress the Natives, Sumner fired his new brass mountain howitzers and shot rockets into the evening sky.[62] He departed Traverse des Sioux on the twenty-fifth and five days later he and the troops encamped on the St. Peter's River near Patterson's Falls. The following day, Sumner met with the Sisseton Sioux. His message was the standard one: the powerful and vengeful yet loving Great White Father would protect and care for the tribe so long as it did not harm any whites; if it did, his avenging hand would punish it severely. And he punctuated the communication in the usual way as well, with fired canons and distributed gifts. But characteristically, Sumner reported to his commanding officer that these gifts did more harm than good as they were so paltry compared to the gifts the British government had formerly showered upon the tribes. Accordingly, he suggested that the U.S. Government suspend the practice of gift-giving in this part of the frontier.[63]

The command next marched to Lake Traverse, crossed the Sheyenne River, and headed for Devil's Lake. Along the way Sumner met with a party of Sioux on July 6, gave them presents, and delivered the customary exhortation about the tribe's need to remain peaceful. Still headed toward Devil's Lake on July 8, the column came upon a small Sisseton Sioux encampment. While holding an informal council "from the saddle," Sumner noticed three men whom he had arrested for murder the previous fall but had escaped from custody at Fort Snelling boldly wandering into the camp. He promptly re-arrested them and had them bound in chains. The captain's action resulted in "a good deal of excitement for the moment," but Sumner restrained the outnumbered Sioux by commanding his force to hold their carbines at the ready. Sumner firmly declared that he would not discuss the matter of the arrests. The prisoners were later convicted by a civil court of murder in Dubuque, but once again escaped from custody.[64]

The primary object of the expedition remained: the trespassing Metis. Stifling heat and dysentery temporarily felled some of the men, including the frail Captain Allen. Nonetheless, the troops pushed on and reached Devil's Lake on July 18. Here Sumner held council with the Metis. True to character, he knew he was powerless to stop them and was moved by their plea to be allowed to continue hunting in this region as they had for generations. Sumner, lacking the authority to grant them permission to stay, suggested that they write to the federal government to request that they be allowed to continue to cross the border for one or two more years. For his part Sumner wrote to his superiors that the Metis did not represent a military threat to the United States, and that realistically "[i]t will be a difficult thing to keep these people out of the country, if they should determine to disregard the order; not from any resistance on their part, but on the contrary, from the confidence they will place in it. They know very well that their families and themselves will always be safe with United States troops, so long as they do not resist them." Indeed, the captain expected the Metis to leave when the troops showed up, "but the moment we left it, they would return again."[65]

Sumner viewed his mission as completed and turned for home. He retraced the same route he had taken up to Devil's Lake, boldly showing the flag to the Sisseton band to whom his prisoners belonged, daring them to resist or harass the expedition. Our anonymous enlisted journalist, hoping to view new territory, recorded his dismay at seeing the same scenery a second time, though he looked forward to being back at Fort Des Moines within four short weeks. Headed home, the troops were in high spirits, but on the twenty-eighth Captain Sumner, having difficulty locating his former trail, lapsed into "one of his slow moods," causing the dragoons to "hold in our impatient steeds, but in doing so there was tolerable hard swearing."[66]

Sumner encountered several Sioux hunting parties on his march south. At Lac qui Parle he met a northbound wagon train that brought mail and news. Most of the troops were cheered to learn that Texas had been annexed as a new state, but all were saddened to hear of wounded trooper Berry's death on July 16 from the freak gunshot wound he had suffered in his tent.[67] Arriving back at Traverse des Sioux on the afternoon of August 7, the regiment was met by a party of Sioux. The next day, the captain arrested yet another Sioux, whom he suspected of having stolen Captain Allen's Company I horses the previous summer. Sumner saw to it that the chained suspect was shipped by boat for trial at Fort Snelling, believing it more appropriate to turn him over to military rather than civil authorities.[68]

At 7 o'clock in the morning of August 11, Sumner broke up the combined squadron. Retracing the trail to Fort Atkinson, he delivered his men there eight days later.[69] Captain Allen employed a Sioux guide, hoping to find a better route home; he didn't. With his company they rode through woods, rivers, and muddy sloughs, battling ferocious swarms of mosquitoes, until they reached what they believed to be a fork of the Des Moines River on August 16. That evening, Mother Nature treated them to a tremendous downpour and lightning storm.[70] The anonymous trooper-journalist wrote of a grand feast of pancakes, pork steak, doughnuts, and coffee that Allen's men prepared for their final breakfast before returning to the fort. The sunburned dragoons, as they arrived at the fort midday on the twenty-eighth, were greeted by shouts of joy from the pale, sickly-looking garrison troops of the 1st Infantry.[71]

In the fall of 1845, land disputes between settlers and transplanted Cherokee factions broke out in the vicinity of present-day

Evansville, Arkansas. Fearful of an explosion of violence, Captain Boone led a squadron consisting of Companies D, E, and H with orders to keep the warring parties apart. Company H remained near Evansville until October of 1846, after the commencement of the War with Mexico, with a federal commission sorting out conflicting property claims. On March 30 G Company traveled to help maintain calm at the Six Indian Nations Agency; H Company remained camped near Evansville to help settle disputes over land and did not return to Fort Gibson until the nineteenth of October.

Sumner's Company B had barely regained their barracks after the difficult expedition near the Canadian border when they received new orders to remove yet another group of Winnebagos who had left their reservation on the Neutral Ground in Iowa Territory. Lt. Philip Thompson, having returned from recruiting duty on December 22, cleaned himself up, found a fresh fatigue uniform, and departed with twenty-six enlisted men. The mission was quickly accomplished and the detachment returned to the fort.[72]

Meeting the So-Called Mexican Threat

Since its founding in 1833, the 1st Regiment of Dragoons ranged widely across the Great Plains, gaining knowledge of a territory little known to other Americans and their government that would enable future pioneers to reach and settle in the West. The dragoons met in countless councils with tribes and, as best they could, settled their disputes and protected them from unauthorized encroachments and sale of spirits by whites. They also kept these proud peoples from crossing the Mississippi River into white settlements east of these rivers. This relatively small body of well-disciplined soldiers was led by insightful officers who accomplished these missions without any reported harming of a single individual—save one Seminole youth who was cut by a saber in Cherokee Territory.[73] Through their acts, the dragoons of 1833–45 earned the respect of Native peoples. But this splendid regimental tradition would soon end. On December 29, 1845, President

Polk signed a measure admitting the former Republic of Texas as a state into the Union, thereby precipitating the nation's bloody war with Mexico.

James Polk was one of the few presidents who managed to keep not just one, but two, campaign promises. A firm believer in the nation's imperial destiny, he promised, if elected, to settle the Oregon territorial question with Great Britain and to acquire California. He did both, with acquisition of New Mexico and the Southwest tossed in for good measure. Hoping to provoke a prideful Mexico into war, he sent Gen. Zachary Taylor's force across the Neches River, the recognized international boundary between Texas and Mexico, and south to the Rio Grande territory, which Mexico regarded as her own.[74] It was only a matter of time before the shooting would begin.

Colonel Kearny's primary concerns at this time were the possibility of war and the pending loss of several of his best officers to the newly authorized Regiment of Mounted Rifles. Captain Cooke, among other officers, was shopping for a higher rank in the new regiment. Even the colonel's wealthy nephew Phillip Kearny had resigned from the army to gain a commission in the Rifles. Kearny also wrestled with the continued violence resulting from Cherokee intertribal warfare and the army's demand for his troops to build a new post at Table Creek on the Overland Trail.[75]

By the end of 1845, the 1st Dragoons had been toughened by their many expeditions and campaigns on the prairies, to South Pass in the Rockies, into Wisconsin Territory and the Canadian border, and along the Santa Fe Trail. If there was to be war, the skills they had acquired, along with the resolve of both man and horse, were never more ready for the test.

CHAPTER 7

Kearny and His Dragoons at War

General Kearny is a rough old man and if we only know;
He marched some 800 miles to fight Old Mexico.
                    "The Colonel Doniphan March" (1846)

B y 1846 the 1st Dragoons—hardened by expeditions on the prairies, to South Pass in the Rockies, through Indian Territory, and into Wisconsin Territory up to the Canadian border, as well as by campaigns along the Santa Fe Trail—were ready to face wartime challenges. Kearny had not only trained his troops brilliantly but also carefully instructed his subordinates not to subject the regiment's all-important animals to the kind of negligence and harm they had suffered on the 1834 mission to the Pawnee villages. Writing to Assistant Quartermaster Joshua Brant in 1837, he acknowledged, "The Campaign of '34 was a disastrous one, to the Regiment, not only to the officers and soldiers, but to the horses of it, & we need not expect such another during its existence." But try as he might, Kearny could not possibly imagine the risks that lay ahead for men and mounts in the coming war, much less adequately prepare for a march of nearly 2,000 miles across a land as dry as bones.[1]

Although a possible war with Great Britain or Mexico, or both, loomed on the horizon, the year began as had most of the regiment's first twelve. In February 1846, a platoon at Fort Crawford,

under the month-old command of Lt. Philip R. Thompson, proceeded to Muscoda to tend to some trouble between settlers and
wandering Winnebagos. They camped and made excursions in
the vicinity to capture and remove the Indians. As soon as the settlers' fears were allayed, a portion of the platoon marched farther
to Baraboo River, where the troopers apprehended Dandy, a chief
who had persistently refused to move to Iowa. He was retained
as a hostage until spring freed the streams from ice and his band
could remove itself. On February 28, Mos-e-mon-i-ka, leader of
the Rock River band, was captured near Eustis Rapids on Rock
River and retained in custody with the same view. During much of
the month the weather stayed below zero, and the snow was from
eight to twelve inches deep.[2]

Judging from the correspondence contained in the regimental letter book, the commander of the 1st Dragoons was primarily concerned over administrative matters, such as the building
of a fort at the mouth of Table Creek and the Missouri River in
present-day Nebraska. During the prior thirteen years, Kearny and
his men, having explored much of the Southwest, had gained a
keen appreciation of the difficulties of moving troops through the
area. In a letter dated March 4, 1846, Kearny offered Secretary of
War William Marcy what he thought to be the best invasion route,
the trail that was traveled in 1839–40 by a group of Chihuahua
traders led by Henry Connelly, a Chihuahua physician and merchant.[3] Significantly, he did not think that there was to be a land
invasion of California via the Santa Fe Trail. Of possible interest is
Kearny's hinting that his suggested invasion of northern Mexico
would commence from forts in which dragoons were stationed
and be possibly led by him.

If it is the intention of the War Department to occupy
the Rio del Norte [Rio Bravo del Norte or Rio Grande],
allow me to suggest for your consideration the expedi-
ency of establishing some Post near the mouth [of the Rio
Grande], another at or about Santa Fe, and a third about
midway between those two, viz at a point opposite to the

Presidio del Norte (North Fort), which is at the mouth of the Rio Conchos—that point is about 100 miles N. East of the City of Chihuahua & where is a pass for a fine Waggon Road thru' the Mountains, leading from the direction of Forts Smith & Washita in a direct line to the City of Chihuahua, making this particular point on del Norte one of much consequence in a military view, as well as for commercial purposes. . . . The importance of occupying this point of the Rio del Norte may be found in the fact that we know of no other on that River where we are certain of having a good pass from the plains for a Road thru the mountains which lie on this side of the del Norte & from the further fact, that there is none other on that River where a Fort could be placed which would so readily command an entrance for our troops if ever desired to march upon the city of Chihuahua, & from thence (with baggage and ordnance) to most of the other Southern Cities, & to the City of Mexico itself.

There are several Mexican settlements near that point on the East side of the del Norte & between there & Santa Fe, & the Country is represented as good, producing fine wheat and other grain.

The starting place at this time for our troops to get there would be Fort Gibson on the Arkansas, & via Fort Washita on the Red River.[4]

Drawing toward War

As the year started out, it looked to some as if the United States were going to war with Great Britain—at least most of the officers thought so.[5] On April 16, Captain Cooke, recently returned from Washington, D.C., wrote to Lieutenant Love, "The news is warlike from Mexico . . . [but] most persons in Washington seem to think there will be war with England."[6] But in the spring of 1846, political and military events swiftly drove Mexico and the United States into conflict. Peace with Great Britain appeared to be attained when, on April 17, Congress began hearings to ratify a treaty fixing the border between the United States and its former ruler.

President Polk could now turn his full attention to securing Mexican territory by purchase or war, and ordered Taylor's small army to move south from the Nueces River and occupy to the north bank of the Rio Grande. In protest, Mexico sent its own troops into the region it claimed and demanded that Taylor leave. On April 25, Mexican cavalry at Rancho de Carricitos overwhelmed and defeated a patrol of Capt. Seth Thornton's reinforced company of 2nd Dragoons, killing eleven soldiers. Mexican artillery next bombarded Fort Texas, across the river from Matamoros. On May 8 and 9 General Taylor fought and won the battles of Palo Alto and Resaca de Palma. The cry went out that American blood had been shed on alleged American soil, and Polk got what he wanted when Congress formally declared war on Mexico on May 13, 1846.[7]

Kearny's two hotspurs in waiting, Captains Cooke and Sumner, fearing that the war might pass them by, penned their views to Gen. George Brooke, the commander of their military department, urging him to include their companies in the conflict. Sumner wrote: "I have been so long in service and on a peace establishment at that, it would be particularly mortifying to me to be left up here, if the rest of my regiment takes the field."[8] Cooke pointed out the unique skills possessed by the First Dragoons that would prove valuable on the field of battle. "The 1st Regiment of Dragoons have steadily matured & perfected a system of tactics and discipline of cavalry, its equipment for, and the art of making, long and active campaigns without disorganization or deterioration. The Mexicans are understood to be strong in this arm, (which must be met by its like,) and it is precisely that which cannot be created on such a sudden requisition as the present war, which takes the most time & pain for sufficient organizations."[9]

During the winter Fort Leavenworth had retained its normal relative calm. Author Francis Parkman visited the sleepy fort early in 1846 and was surprised to discover that "Fort Leavenworth is in fact no fort, being without defensive works, except two block houses. No rumors of war had as yet disturbed its tranquility . . . [and] the men were passing or repasting, or lounging among the trees; although not many weeks afterwards it presented a different scene; for here the very off-scourings of the frontier were congregated to be marshaled for the expedition against Santa Fe."[10]

Indeed, the stillness soon ended. During the ensuing weeks the fort burst into activity as detachments of Kearny's Army of the West—composed of regular dragoons and Missouri volunteer troops, artillery, supply wagons, and cattle—gathered and prepared to leave on their mission to conquer Santa Fe. Upon his late spring arrival, Pvt. John Hughes of the 1st Missouri Volunteers wrote to his hometown newspaper in Liberty that Fort Leavenworth proved "full of life and good humor."[11]

It took some time for the official news of the declaration of war to reach Fort Leavenworth. But on the mere whiff of war, Kearny took no chances. For one of his opening gambits, on May 26, Kearny ordered Captain Moore and his company, who were building a new post at Table Creek, to return posthaste to the fort.[12] Two days later, he sent George Howard, a civilian employee of the War Department, on a mission along the Santa Fe Trail to warn caravans of the impending war. He was escorted by Lt. Julian May of the Mounted Rifles, Sgt. Elbridge Towle, and six dragoons, and guided by Shawnee and Delaware scouts.[13]

Though he had received barely any military training, the would-be physician Pvt. Erasmus Darwin French, one of Love's 1845 recruits from Dayton, was included in the party. While en route, Howard discovered that merchant Albert Speyer's wagon train was carrying arms and ammunition to Chihuahua, Mexico. He reported this intelligence to Kearny, who ordered him to overtake and detain Speyer's wagon train. Speyer's ten large wagons, each pulled by ten mules, had a good head start, having left Independence on the twenty-second of May.[14]

Ten days later, Kearny gained information that Governor Manuel Armijo had a wagon train containing $70,000 worth of goods on the Santa Fe Trail. Kearny decided to intercept both this train as well as Speyer's. He reinforced Lieutenant May's detachment. Moore's company arrived at Fort Leavenworth on June 4 and Kearny promptly ordered them to take to the trail.[15] With only eight hours' rest, refitting, and notice, Captains Moore and Burgwin, scout Thomas Fitzpatrick, Companies C and G, two mountain howitzers, and two companies of newly recruited Missouri mounted volunteers thundered out of Fort Leavenworth on the fifth of June and raced madly over the familiar dust of the Santa Fe Trail to Bent's Fort. On June 13 Kearny ordered Lt. Pat Noble and fifty men of Company I to reinforce Moore's command. Moore's men made the 564-mile forced march in eleven and a half days. Although these troops could not overtake Armijo or Speyer's caravans, they once again demonstrated the dragoons' unique ability to deploy in force very rapidly to a distant field. Having been unable to intercept the two trains before they crossed into Mexico, Captain Moore decided to withdraw to Pawnee Forks and to stop all westbound freight wagons until the Army of the West arrived.[16]

While portions of the dragoons were chasing Armijo and Speyer over the plains, Colonel Kearny was making personnel changes in his regiment. On June 4, 1846, he ordered Company F broken up, nephew Philip Kearny placed in command, and its privates transferred to other companies. Private Archy, recruited in 1845 by Lieutenant Love in Dayton, was transferred from F to Capt. John Allen's Company I. Then the colonel placed Allen on detached service and assigned him to organize the Mormon Battalion. Kearny next put Company I under the command of Lt. William Grier.[17] During the ensuing weeks various elements of the 1st Dragoons were detached from the regiment for the war effort in Texas. Adj. Gen. Roger Jones ordered Companies A, stationed at Fort Scott, and E, stationed at Fort Gibson, to march south and become part of Wool's Central Division, set to invade Mexico from San Antonio, Texas.[18]

Clarendon Wilson, a recent top graduate of the Military Academy who had chosen assignment to the 1st Dragoons as a brevet second lieutenant, arrived at Fort Leavenworth just in time to witness the departure of troops and supplies destined for New

Mexico. In a letter to a friend he captured the flurry of movement that had, in a few short months, replaced the quietude of Parkman's visit:

> I found here more than two thousand troops (if these untamed volunteers deserve the name), but the number is daily diminishing as they are put en route for Sante [sic] Fe. This place is, at present, a perfect Bedlam—the damnedest noisy, dusty place that I have ever met with. You can hear nothing; for the teamsters are breaking mules and oxen to the wagons, and cursing, yelling at and thrashing them incessantly. The Mormon force are [sic] getting under headway today. . . . The Mormons are the most orderly of the forces that I have seen at this place. I think that they are more likely to do credit to themselves, if brought into action, than the other volunteers.

Wilson detailed the items he would take for the coming campaign:

> The outfit is an extensive one in the line of articles necessary for a prairie life, such as cooking utensils, blankets, knives, axes, oil-cloth (to protect against the expected long rains), quantities of woolen clothing, horses or mules, &c, &c, &c. . . . Myself and friend had to purchase 5 horses between us, one apiece to ride in order to spare as much as possible our parade horses, the other for our servant: it being absolutely necessary to get a servant at any rate of hire. . . . [I]f the Comanches undertake to carry the stores off, they'll catch hell or I'm mistaken.[19]

Kearny's Army of the West en Route

To conserve grass and water along the route, the departure was spread out over two weeks. As Wilson (and everyone) appreciated, the Army of the West would require a considerable amount of supplies, so the quartermaster's wagons left first. By June 16, some one hundred wagons were en route to Bent's Fort, and six days later, troops of Kearny's Army of the West left Leavenworth. On the twenty-second, portions of the Army of the West attempted to use the path Kearny had pioneered in 1845. This new road went from the fort to the Overland Trail and soon intersected with the Santa Fe Trail. Although many of Kearny's detachments following the poorly marked course missed the intersection with the Santa Fe Trail and for a while continued on the Overland Trail toward Oregon, at least the bulk of the Army of the West was finally on the move to conquer New Mexico. On June 30, Kearny and his headquarters staff departed Leavenworth. Company B from Fort Atkinson and Company K from Fort Crawford traveled by river to Fort Leavenworth, arriving there on July 6 and immediately hitting the Santa Fe Trail to Bent's Fort.[20]

In a ragged and somewhat disorganized march that was especially hard on the volunteers and their mounts, the detachments, one by one, reached the adobe walls of Bent's Fort. Awaiting them were Companies C, G, and I, along with Lieutenant May's detachment escorting War Department employee Howard.[21] Private French, among that escort when Kearny arrived, eagerly awaited fulfillment of his recruiter's promise of a chance to use his medical training. Once the troops arrived, however, he found himself assigned to serve as Kearny's personal escort,[22] not exactly what he had bargained for in Dayton, but not an altogether bad duty—thus far.

Before entering New Mexico, Kearny learned that Governor Armijo had issued a proclamation calling upon all male citizens between fifteen and fifty to take up arms to repel the American invaders.[23] To meet this challenge, Kearny resorted to the strategy he repeatedly employed to impress the Natives and would continue to use throughout the march to Santa Fe: he made sure that any spies or casual observers witnessed the massive military power of the Army of the West so that they might bring the fearsome information to Governor Armijo.[24]

The day of invasion, July 31, 1846, dawned. Kearny assembled the Army of the West at Bent's Fort, regulars and volunteers alike. The various components of Kearny's army had been camped miles to the east of the fort and were now on the move. Hearing the distant rumble of wagon wheels and muted hoofbeats, Lt. William Emory of the Topographical Engineers, encamped nearby, observed, "I looked in the direction of Bent's Fort, and saw a huge United States flag flowing in the breeze, and straining every fiber of an ash pole planted over the centre of the gate." He could also see a rising cloud of dust to the east moving toward him with "about the velocity of a fast walking horse—it was 'The Army of the West.'" Emory saddled his horse and joined the march. "A little below the fort," he noted, "the [Arkansas] river was forded without difficulty, being paved with well attritioned pebbles of the primitive rock, and not more than knee deep." As early as the second of August, Kearny's army crossed the Arkansas River and had invaded Mexico. But all would not be easy. Turning left, they left the river and entered an arid, elevated plain; within two days the draft horses began to fail "away in an alarming manner."[25]

The land beyond the Arkansas River would prove unusually hard on the horses. Mules gradually came to replace the exhausted steeds as draft animals as the columns slowly climbed 7,500-foot high Raton Pass. Descending slowly down from the steep, rocky pass, they reached a flower-strewn valley Lieutenant Emory called "the paradise of that part of the country between Bent's Fort and San Miguel."[26] During his slow march down the valley, Kearny carefully showed off the might of his force to some distant riders who he believed were spies.[27] His scouts brought five of them into camp. Emory thought that, mounted on small burros, "they presented a ludicrous contrast by side of the big men and horses of the first dragoons. Fitzpatrick, our guide, who seldom laughs, became almost convulsed whenever he turned his well practiced eye in their direction." These captives, having viewed the might of the invading force, would be released once the rear guard of the Army of the West had passed.[28]

On the fifteenth of August Kearny received word from a captured Mexican lieutenant and four lancers who warned of six hundred Mexicans in a gorge two miles outside the pueblo of Las Vegas, all set to block his advance.[29] As he prepared for battle the next morning, Kearny met Maj. Thomas Swords, Capt. Richard Weightman, and Lt. Jeremy Gilmer, who had ridden pell-mell from Fort Leavenworth eight days prior in hopes of joining the battle. Swords carried with him a dispatch announcing that Kearny had gained a commission as brigadier general, that Mason was now colonel of the regiment, with Wharton as its lieutenant colonel, and that the alcoholic Captain Trenor, left back at Leavenworth, should henceforth be addressed as major.[30] The same order deprived the 1st Dragoons of other gifted members in favor of the 2nd Dragoons, then stationed in Texas, by promoting Capt. Edwin Sumner to the rank of major and elevating Bvt. 2nd Lt. Bezaleel Armstrong to a permanent second lieutenancy with that regiment. Kearny ordered Sumner and Armstrong, promotions notwithstanding, to remain with the Army of the West.

Kearny now released the five Mexican soldiers bearing his warning: "Say to General Armijo, I shall soon meet him, and I hope it will be as friends."[31] A few miles down the road the dragoons entered Las Vegas. Newly minted Brigadier General Kearny then climbed a rickety ladder and loudly proclaimed from a rooftop that the territory now belonged to the United States. He announced that the inhabitants were absolved from all allegiance to Mexico and promised to protect them from Apaches and Navajos as well as to respect their right to practice the Catholic faith.[32]

It was now time for Kearny to deal with the danger from Armijo. Although Kearny had consistently avoided bloodshed since the War of 1812 and preferred to scare off the enemy with an overwhelming show of force, he now readied his army for combat. Excited at the prospect of seeing his first battle, Lieutenant Emory wrote: "The sun shone with dazzling brightness: the guidons and colors of each squadron were for the first time unfurled. The drooping horses seemed to take courage from the gay array. The trumpeters sounded 'to horse' with spirit and the hills multiplied and re-echoed the call. All wore the aspect of a gala day; as we approached the gorge, where we expected to meet the enemy, we broke into a brisk trot, then into a full gallop, preceded by a squadron of horse. The gorge was passed, but no person was seen."[33]

Crestfallen but relieved, the troops furled their flags and resumed plodding the trail to Santa Fe. Yet Governor Armijo continued to threaten the use of military force. Kearny received news that Armijo had collected a large contingent, poised to block the road to Santa Fe at Apache Canyon. This time Kearny would try reasoning to convince the governor of the folly of such deployment of troops. On the last day of July, Kearny had dispatched Santa Fe merchant James Magoffin and Capt. Philip St. George Cooke, commander of the force that in 1843 had successfully disarmed the Snively land pirates, to talk some sense into Governor Armijo.

Magoffin and Cooke spent much of their time in New Mexico being entertained by local traders and politicians, attempting to convince them to surrender the territory without a fight.[34] Many historians would later charge that, using the good offices of Magoffin and Cooke, Polk bribed Armijo to allow Kearny to conquer the territory. This may have been so, but as historian Justin Smith wrote, "Kearny had no money to use in this way, and in the absence of substantial evidence there seems to be no good ground to suppose the merchants had a sufficient reason for buying him."[35] Smith, however, overlooks the fact that Congress later reimbursed businessman Magoffin $30,000 of personal expenses in the New Mexico campaign.[36] It may take a full squadron of researchers, if ever, to resolve this debate, but a bribe of that magnitude would have had to be paid in gold, and $30,000 in gold bullion in 1846 would have weighed approximately one hundred pounds—a considerable weight for a mule or wagon to carry to Santa Fe, especially when bullets, blankets, powder, forage, water, tack, and food would have taken precedent.

But since Governor Armijo still appeared to want a fight, Kearny would give him one. Rather than rushing helter-skelter into conflict, he carefully formed his men as if for review. Bugles sounded, ranks were formed, and the troops marched out smartly to battle the Mexicans they expected two miles down the road.

The truth is that Armijo was never anxious to confront Kearny's considerably more powerful force. Besides, as a wealthy merchant who had long dealt goods with Missouri, he stood to profit handsomely by the increased trade that annexation by the United States would bring. It was good old greed rather than a bribe, Magoffin would suggest (and he was probably right), that convinced Armijo to surrender. Of course, much of the population, with little profit but much national pride at stake, wanted to resist the invasion. Led by Diego Archuleta, they pressured Armijo to put up a fight. And for the moment he moved his forces into a solid defensible position at Apache Canyon and then most oddly ordered a retreat, with the governor-general and his personal guard in the lead.

After handily marching past those once-strong places where Armijo's quickly dismissed battalions had recently stood, the five companies of the 1st United States Dragoons and the regiment of Missouri volunteers marched about fifteen miles east of Santa Fe to Cañoncito, or Apache Canyon. Perched at nearly 7,000 feet in the Sangre de Cristo Mountains, the canyon is a narrow, timbered gorge at the emergence of the Santa Fe Trail from Glorieta Pass. The ever-cautious Kearny feared that Governor Armijo was occupying the pass with his announced force of 1,800—in fact, this force consisted of but a few soldiers, a few cannon, and a swarm of poorly armed volunteers and Indians. But however badly armed and led they might have been, the steeply walled canyon provided an ideal position from which to impede an invasion.

Anxiously anticipating an ambush, Kearny carefully led his men, in combat formation, into the tight canyon. An advance guard of six rode ahead to ferret out the enemy; one hundred yards behind came General Kearny, his adjutant, a bugler, a trooper carrying a red and white swallow-tailed guidon, and a half dozen men of the general's guard. Behind this advance guard rode the five companies of dragoons and, following them, the

Missouri volunteers and the artillery. (This would be, on a smaller scale, the same way Kearny would later approach San Pasqual in California.) With every hoof beat, their hearts beat faster as they neared the awesome guns and poised bows of the defenders.

And then, from the western entrance to the canyon, appeared a small mule bearing a large man. New Mexico Secretary of State Nicolas Quintaros rode forward to deliver the astounding news that Armijo had, at the last moment, mysteriously disbanded his force and fled south to El Paso del Norte with an escort of ninety Mexican dragoons.[37] Once again, Kearny's tactic of brandishing intimidating force (and maybe a bit of *mordida*—that is, a bribe), accomplished his military objective without resort to combat. The road to Santa Fe was open.[38]

Late on the afternoon of August 18, the invaders crested a hilltop and surveyed the great prize in the valley below. As Kearny's men rode into Santa Fe they were uniformly unimpressed with the starkness of this legendary town. Cpl. Mathias Baker of Company B recorded that he was "much disappointed" with the city, "bare of wood and water, mountainous and the only parts they can cultivate is [*sic*] a few of the valleys that are watered by springs and small streams from the Mountains. . . . They raise corn, wheat, onions, [but] no potatoes, have thousands of goats, sheep, some cattle, plenty of asses and mules with some fine Pony horses."[39]

Riding into the town plaza, Capt. Benjamin Moore described the houses as "built of sun dried bricks, covered with the same material, and flat on top." He observed the other buildings of the town: "They have two large churches in Santa Fe, in character with the rest of the buildings in the town. The area of the public square consists of about three acres of ground around which the buildings are arranged, the palace and barracks for one side of the square. The other three sides have stores, dwellings &c."[40]

With twilight descending, certain elements of Kearny's force ingloriously entered into the defenseless, nearly deserted Plaza of Santa Fe: dusty and unmilitary looking invaders, burdening the backs of broken-down horses and worn-out mules.[41] After the

ceremonial firing of twenty-eight blanks from the two artillery batteries posted on a hill overlooking the town, Kearny raised the
Stars and Stripes over the governor's palace in the Plaza. That
evening, he and several officers accepted the dinner invitation of
a retired Mexican officer.[42]

On the following morning, the general overstepped his
bounds in a second formal speech, in which he declared New
Mexico to be part of the United States and subject to its civil laws.
He immediately set about creating a provisional military government, selecting businessman Charles Bent as acting territorial governor, and ordering a team of lawyers serving among the Missouri
volunteers to draft a civil code for the territory. The War Department would later declare these "Kearny Codes," along with his
proclamation of conquest, illegal as unauthorized by federal law.[43]
Almost too easily, Kearny's Army of the West had ridden some
eight hundred miles, taken possession of enemy territory without
a firing shot, and rose to the zenith of its glory. General Kearny
could now place his sights on conquering Polk's grandest prize:
California. Believing that the New Mexico citizenry was unlikely
to rebel, and finding a rumored northward movement of Mexican
soldiers unfounded, the general ordered a regiment of Col. Sterling Price's 1st Missouri Volunteers, along with two companies of
dragoons, to remain behind as a garrison. He sent Col. Alexander
Doniphan's newly arrived 2nd Missouri Regiment south to reinforce Brig. Gen. John E. Wool's force, thought to be advancing
on Chihuahua. Realizing that most of his horses were unfit for
the thousand-mile journey to California, Kearny mounted three
hundred of his best men on healthy mules. He directed that most
of the regiment's precious steeds be sent out for grazing and, their
health restored, herded back to Fort Leavenworth.[44]

Serving with the dragoon detachment at the grazing camp
was twenty-nine-year-old Cpl. Mathias Baker. It is unclear why
Baker left the comforts of his wealthy Middlesex, New Jersey, family without leaving any forwarding address and, in 1845, enlisted
in the dragoons. The army assigned him to Captain Sumner's
Company B. Typical of the soldiers marching with Kearny, Baker

believed that Mexican troops were cowardly, based on (or justified by) his own observation and that of his comrades that upon "the approach of the American Army, [the Mexican army] retired and totally dispersed. The whole country gave up without a gun being fired, if I except the firing of the American Artillery (blank cartridges) on this day of the entry into Santa Fe." Baker, like most, assumed the war would end quickly because all "our troops have to do is to march from our part of the country to the other for the Mexican Army will not fight." The corporal cast an eye at the available resources in that inhospitable land and concluded there to be little of value save veins of silver and gold, of which "no doubt before long Yankee skill & perseverance will bring many to light, as yet undiscovered. The Americans have heretofore been afraid to hunt for and work the mines on account of the Indians, who had been the Real masters of the country. But the American Dragoons will soon learn them to keep quiet."[45]

Kearny's New Mexico Chapter

Kearny would now attempt a military tactic not tried on the North American continent since 1540, when Francisco Coronado led an invading army over nearly 1,000 miles of harsh southwestern desert seeking, but never finding, the fabled Seven Cities of Gold.[46] Unlike Coronado, Kearny, about to invade territory that he believed to be in the hands of an enemy force, could not afford losses of men and animals. Moreover, the desert regions of the Gila River and Mojave Desert to be coursed by Kearny were far more inhospitable than those traveled by Coronado.

On September 26, 1846, Kearny's five dragoon companies, staff, and a detachment of Emory's topographical engineers commenced the march to California. The army assistant surgeon, Capt. John Griffin, observed that "all of the men are mounted on mules—some of them devilish poor at that. One or two gave out on the first day." The expedition's supplies were loaded into wagons, each pulled by eight mules. They followed the Rio Bravo

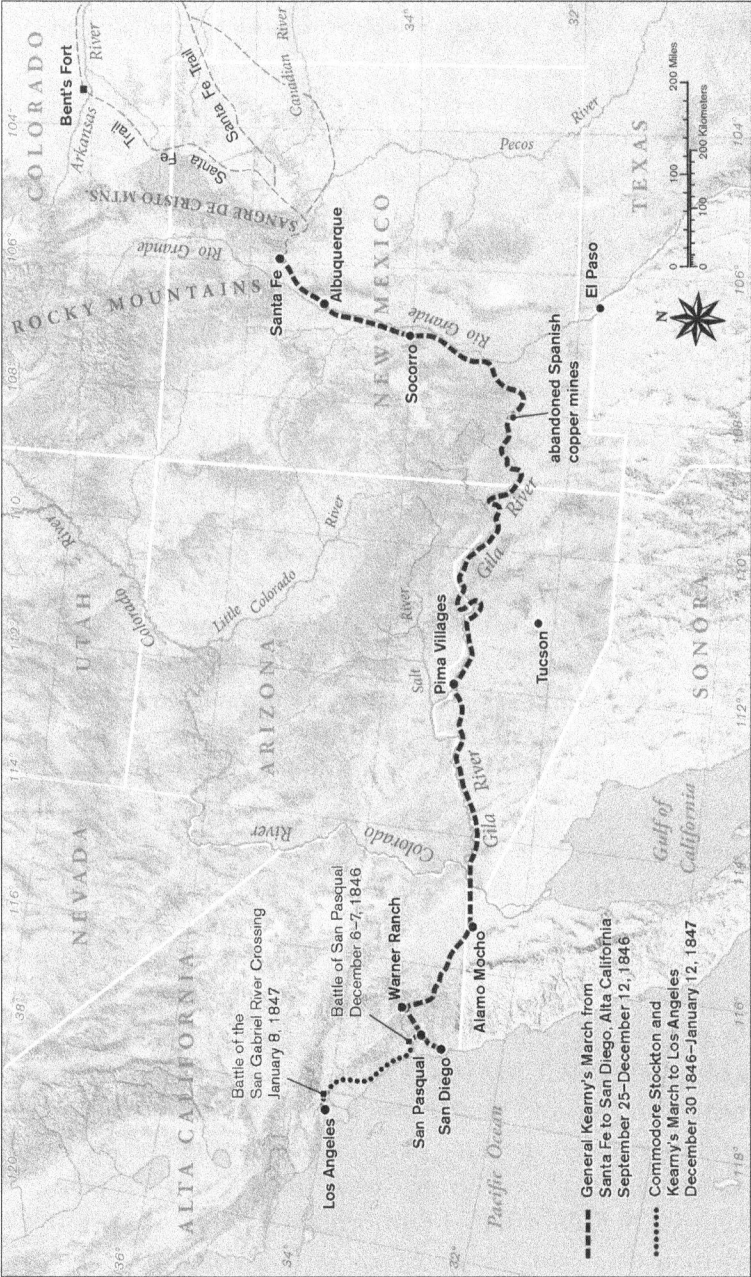

Kearny's March to California

After seizing Santa Fe, General Kearny, on September 25, 1846, led his staff and two companies to Alta California. Traveling south along the Rio Grande Valley, he followed the desolate Gila River westward to the Colorado River, thence across the Mojave Desert to his battle with Andres Pico at San Pasqual on December 6.

(Grande) south past the hamlets of Albuquerque and Las Lunas to the headwaters of the Gila River, where Kearny veered west on the trail to California.[47]

On October 2, a courier rode into Kearny's camp with the news of the death of Lt. Col. Allen of the Mormon Battalion. General Kearny needed to secure a replacement for Allen quickly. He didn't have to look very far: Captain Thompson was in Santa Fe, with orders to take command of the Mormons. But Thompson's heavy drinking was troubling to Kearny. He selected Captain Cooke, currently leading Company K, to ride back to Santa Fe to take command of the Mormons.

There is no doubt that the "promotion" to the rank of lieutenant colonel to command a battalion of unsteady volunteers came as a bitter disappointment to a career warrior such as Cooke— he would miss out on fighting in a mounted battle in California. Once again Kearny, as in the Snively campaign when he made a vital assignment, paid Cooke the highest of compliments—he was well suited to independently lead a battalion of troops.[48]

Four days later, the column was south of the village of Socorro when there occurred another event that was to have a significant effect on the expedition. Off in the distance to the west, Kearny's scouts spotted seventeen riders approaching. Scout Bad Hand Fitzpatrick recognized their leader as his old friend, Kit Carson, with the Delaware scouts; they were carrying reports from California bound for Washington, D.C. The dispatches announced that a mismatched collection of Capt. John Frémont's explorers, American residents of California, and members of the U.S. Navy had easily wrested California from Mexican control.

The bearer of these missives hardly resembled the Kit Carson of popular legend. This fellow was "a short, stoutly built man, with mild eyes, smooth face and long brown hair . . . modest and unassuming, seldom or never speaking of his exploits, except in answer to direct questions."[49] He confirmed what had been reported as having occurred in California. This information left Kearny more convinced than ever that the Mexicans were a cowardly bunch who would not offer any resistance.[50]

Still, Carson freely related to the officers that it would not be an easy trip. He warned Kearny that the trail to California along the narrow canyon of the Gila was treacherous and rocky. Carson mentioned to Dr. Griffin that he never knew of a party traveling along the Gila "that did not leave it starving, this [the doctor was] fearful will be our case before we leave." Carson told Captain Turner that the rough trail they were on, passing the Red Buttes, was like "a turn-pike road to what we must face arriving at the Gila."[51] After hearing Carson attest to the scarcity of forage and water on the proposed march, Kearny decided to reduce his large and burdened military formation to an escort of one hundred men from Companies C and K, along with staff and topographical engineers. Given that California was safely in Yankee hands, Kearny knew he no longer required five companies to march there. Kearny ordered Sumner to take command of Companies B, G, and I, and to return to Fort Leavenworth by way of Albuquerque.[52]

Corporal Baker, along with Privates Archy and French, had come this far with their companies as part of Kearny's Army of the West. Now, for the California leg, Kearny assigned French to serve in his personal escort, ordered Archy and his Company I to garrison in New Mexico, broke up Company B, and distributed its privates to the other companies. Corporal Baker would return with the company's other noncommissioned officers to Fort Leavenworth to help Lieutenant Love reorganize Company B. For many of the officers, Carson's news dealt a crushing blow to their expectation of armed combat and glory before the end of the war. Surgeon Griffin expressed the feelings of the officers and of the many enlisted men in the column: "[M]ost of us hoped when leaving Santa Fe—that we might have a little kick up with the good people of California but this totally blasted all our hopes, and reducing our expedition to one of mere escort duty."[53]

In contrast, the peaceable Kearny felt deep relief: the trip to the Pacific would be hard enough without having to engage in battle upon arrival. He took possession of Carson's dispatches and ordered him to be a scout for the expedition. Kearny then placed the dispatches in "the hands of a safe person [trusted scout Tom Fitzpatrick] to carry [them] on" to the nation's capital, then called Washington City. Kearny continued with his escort toward what he confidently expected to be a victorious and placid arrival at the western shore.[54] Several of his remaining officers and men had known one another since the regiment was formed in 1833, and others had served together for years. They had jointly suffered the deprivations of the early missions, which, through trial and error, had molded the regiment into what they rightly believed was the finest in the entire army. Thus they also cheerily anticipated the fresh laurels they and the regiment were sure to gain in California.

Yet, within the span of a year, the loss of men the regiment would sustain irreparably tarnished its sterling reputation, and ensuing years would see a continuous bleed of key personnel.[55] On October 7, the two columns prepared to ride on their separate missions over 1,000 miles apart. Old friends shook hands, exchanged pleasantries, and marched away in opposite directions. Many would never see one another again, some dying in California, some dying in New Mexico.

Kearny's first mistake was attempting to take along supply wagons and two howitzers. The expedition made barely seven miles between 8 A.M. and 5 P.M. on the first day. Convinced that wagons could not make the trip, Kearny sent Corporal Clapin with a Mexican guide to ride back to Major Sumner in Albuquerque, request that he take the wagons back, and provide the requisite number of pack saddles instead for the heavy freight like food, forage, ammunition, and tents.[56] Lt. Rufus Ingalls, in command of the wagon detachment, duly received orders to return the wagons to Albuquerque. The two howitzers, lighter than wagons and needed for protection, remained with the column. Emory wrote that the dragoons "parted with our wagons, which were sent back under charge of Lieutenant Ingalls and, in doing so, every man seemed to be greatly relieved." Engineer Emory made sure that plant specimens he had collected and carefully placed in the wagons would be delivered to one of his scientist friends, botanist John Torrey at Princeton University,[57] and continued to identify and gather further plant specimens on his way west.

The command piled the goods and supplies taken from wagons upon the ground and carefully transferred them to pack mules. Dr. Griffin recognized that the loss of wagons meant the men would have no replacements for the garments and boots they would wear out: "Oct. 10th. . . . We remained in camp all day, reducing our baggage so that it might be packed—it had already been cut down to the lowest point, at the camp & Santa Fe. I suppose by the time we arrive at Monterey if we have the Georgia uniform on it will be as much as we can reasonably expect."[58]

New Mexico Explodes in Violence

With Kearny's departure, Colonel Price became the conquered territory's military commander. The number of troops available to him decreased steadily: the year-long enlistment of many of his Missouri Volunteers was drawing to an end and most volunteer troops would be sent home; Doniphan had marched his 2nd Missouri Regiment to Chihuahua; dragoon companies G and I left behind by Kearny were forced to campaign on foot and on mules; and the remnants of Company B were back at Fort Leavenworth enlisting, refitting, and training raw recruits. Price faced increased raiding by the Navajo tribe and, worst of all, had heard that a number of citizens were fomenting rebellion.

Settling into garrison duties that fall, Colonel Price sent Companies G and I south toward El Paso to escort a wagon train heading to Chihuahua. It was on this trip that the 1st Dragoons let fly the only shots fired in battle to date. On November 12, 1846, a patrol from Company I, led by Capt. William Grier, encountered Navajo tribesmen who had stolen some 3,000 sheep from local settlers. Grier and Lt. Clarendon Wilson were upon fine horses, but most of the enlisted men rode mules. In a small-scale foretaste of what was to happen to Kearny's detachment less than a month later, the swifter horsemen foolishly rode too far in advance of their support and fell into an ambush. Lt. James Abert detailed the engagement:

[W]hile the companies were on their march down the river, some Mexicans rushed hurriedly up to them, crying out that the Navajoes had just been into the village, murdering the people and carrying off their flocks and herds. Captain Grier immediately set off in pursuit, and soon came in sight of the bold marauders. In a little while the Indians began to abandon the cattle they were driving off, until at last 400 head had been left along the route. So warm and exciting was the chase that the officers, who were well mounted, heeded not the want of their men who were unable to keep pace with them, but they pressed on, anxious to recover the immense "cavalgada" of sheep the Indians were yet driving. Suddenly they saw they had rushed into an ambuscade, for the Indians rising up from their concealment surrounded Captain Grier and his three brave companions. With horrid cries and shouts of "Navajoe," the Indians sprang forward to the combat; they were dressed for war, being ornamented with paints and plumes, and mounted on good horses, and armed with bows and arrows, and lances; but, fortunately, they were so crowded that they feared lest they shoot each other. At length, one of the chiefs came alongside of Lieutenant Wilson; their horses were on the gallop, each one waiting until the horses should jump together, when, at the same moment, Lieutenant Wilson and the Indian fired; the officer's pistol did not go off, and the arrow of the chief only cut off a coat button, and lodged in the saddle blanket of Captain Grier. As the Indian turned his horse, a Mexican, who had started at full speed, came in contact with him, and rolled horse and rider in the dust; the Indian was immediately upon his feet, and rushed up to a dragoon soldier, who had a [Hall] patent carbine, such as loaded at the breach, and had, unseen by the Indian, reloaded it, and the Indian coming up within two or three feet, the soldier shot him dead. One other Indian was killed, when Captain Grier ordered a retreat, and the four, drawing their sabres, cut their way out and rejoined their company, while the Nava-joes succeeded in carrying off 3,000 head of sheep.[59]

With this brief skirmish, the dragoon regiment had engaged in its first, but hardly its last, engagement with a foe. More was soon to come.

Young Private Archy was likely involved in this fight but, mounted on a slow mule and unable to keep up with Grier, he avoided fire. He may have written home about the adventure, which might have turned out far worse for his comrades. But somehow, around this time his family found out about his enlist-ment and took steps to secure his release from the army. Nelson's father wrote to President Polk pointing out that his son had been underage when he enlisted, and argued that allowing the boy to enlist deprived Archy Sr. of assistance highly valuable to "a man as poor as I am." He insisted that his son's service "belonged to me, no one had a right to it but me. I have given it to the govern-ment & ask nothing in return but an honorable discharge." The president forwarded John Archy's request to the War Department. On June 18, 1847, the assistant adjutant general wrote to the elder Archy noting that, although Nelson Archy lied about his age when he enlisted, given the present state of war with Mexico, "the inter-est of the Service will not justify the granting of an order for his discharge."[60]

In a letter to the press, most likely written by Captain Burgwin from Albuquerque in December of 1846, the writer sensed the "feeling of discontent existing among the people of the province." And yet he looked forward to battle: "If this should be . . . we may yet have the satisfaction and enjoyment of a battle with these peo-ple. Of the fatigues and hardships of a *quasi* war, the 1st Dragoons had enough, but we cannot boast the honor of having been in a 'stricken field.'"[61] Captain Burgwin's wish for a fight and being in a stricken field would soon come true.

On January 19, 1847, the tensions between Mexicans and Americans exploded in a violent uprising by Mexicans of all economic classes, joined by Pueblo Indians in Taos, Arroyo Hondo, and spreading southeast to Mora.[62] Rebels in Taos seized and executed Territorial Governor Charles Bent and five others. The insurrectionists killed seven *Norte Americanos* at Turley's Mill in Rio Hondo and then murdered two more on the Rio Colorado.[63] In Mora the insurrectionists attacked a military grazing camp, resulting in a vicious action and the ultimate destruction of the town by angered Yankee troops.[64] In the words of Colonel Price, "[T]he object of the insurrectionists [was] to put to death every American and every Mexican who had accepted office under the American government."[65] It was time for the former congressman, left by Kearny in command of what had been a placid territory, to gather his scattered forces and confront the uprising.

Price assembled a scratch force of 353 men, composed primarily of Missouri volunteers and white settlers, and left Santa Fe on January 23, following the Rio Grande northward. He sent orders to Captain Burgwin to march his two dismounted companies of dragoons north, specifying that Burgwin leave one company to garrison Santa Fe and bring the other to join Price's advance on the rebel stronghold in the Pueblo de Taos. Burgwin decided to take Company G with him and have Lieutenant Grier with Company I remain behind to guard Santa Fe.

The day after he departed Santa Fe, Price faced stiff resistance at the hamlet of La Cañada, where rebels attacked his supply wagons. He unleashed his artillery and advanced his infantry. In the ensuing battle, Price's men killed thirty-six of the enemy, including Jesús Tafoya, one of the leaders of the insurrection. With darkness fast descending, Price called his men to rest. That evening Burgwin's tired dragoons joined Price, and with these reinforcements, Price now had 479 men under his command.[66]

Price continued north. Before long he discovered a large enemy force awaiting him in the highlands south of Embudo, blocking the road to Taos. He dispatched 180 men under Burgwin and Capt. Ceran St. Vrain to march overland and flank the enemy. Scaling steep canyon walls, the dragoons and volunteers flanked the rebels' position and forced them to retreat.[67] With the dismounted company of Burgwin's dragoons in the lead, climbing ridges and crossing through deep snow, Price's men continued along the narrow canyon of the Rio Grande toward Taos.

Arriving at Pueblo de Taos on February 3, they found the rebels poorly armed with only a few antique flintlock muskets, spears, or just with bows and arrows. The defenders had fortified themselves well, however, inside the village's thick adobe buildings, and provided each *Nuevo Mexicano* strongpoint with interlocking zones of fire. Price surveyed these positions and decided to assault them from the west.[68] Augustine Demarle, a German immigrant serving as a sergeant in a Missouri volunteer artillery company, observed the rebels' position and reported to a newspaper in St. Louis:

> The whole place is like a fortress, and these people knew that it had never been conquered. At the front as a strongpoint was a high, very stout church surrounded by a wall; behind the church, sheltered from outside fire, were houses and an enormous open plaza and beyond that a towering building that looked like their citadel. The houses were very intriguing, like an old robber baron's castle from the middle ages. Five or six stories in form of terraces, one on top of another, each entered by a small ladder from the preceding one, so that when the ladder was pulled up, access was impossible; with simple methods they had made the place almost impenetrable.[69]

Price's artillery immediately went into battery. For two and one-half hours the cannon furiously banged away without effect at the solid walls of the San Geronimo Church. Running low on ammunition and with night coming on, Price called a cease-fire, and retired for the night in the comfort of Padre Antonio Martinez's home in the nearby town of Taos. His troops, meanwhile, spent the winter night on cold, wet ground. The well-rested general returned to the battlefield the next morning at the civilized hour of nine and courageously ordered his men to renew the attack.

The cannon fire resumed, but still could not breach the church walls. After two hours of shelling, Price ordered an assault on the church, planning to have Burgwin's dismounted dragoons, supported by a company of Missouri Volunteers, attack it from the west while the rest of the command advanced to the northern wall behind the church.[70] While Price ate his lunch, well out of the range of enemy weaponry, he watched dragoons and volunteers charge over open ground. Burgwin's dragoons reached the relative safety afforded to them by a wall near the west side of the church. From there they tried to break the walls with axes. When this attempt failed, Captain Burgwin decided to lead his axe-wielding men around to the front of the building and break down the front door. Exposed to skilled sharpshooter crossfire from a nearby house, Burgwin and three of his men immediately fell seriously wounded.[71] Fire from the insurgent riflemen was to have been suppressed by volunteers who were to advance from the south, but Price's amateur troops, in the opinion of a dragoon combatant, "did little service" to protect the exposed dragoons, whose casualties steadily mounted.[72]

Prompt thinking by Lt. Clarendon Wilson, the recent Military Academy graduate, brilliantly and viciously silenced the shooters. He ordered Sergeant Demarle's 6-pound field gun to fire grapeshot at the snipers' positions, effectively turning the cannon into a huge shotgun, each round of which hurled dozens of deadly, scattering spheres. Having muffled the foe's fire, Wilson's men shoved the cannon to within sixty yards of the church and fired twenty rounds of explosive shot, point-blank. The cannon was too close for its ammunition to be fully effective, but the repeated battering of cannonballs finally punched a small breach in a church wall. A frustrated Lieutenant Wilson raced forward and tossed a lighted cannonball into the church, and others threw in plenty more. Dense smoke filled the church's interior and the Nuevo Mexicanos abandoned it, leaving behind dozens of their dead.[73]

After losing the church, many guerrillas abandoned their positions in the western portion of the town and fled overland to the north, only to be slaughtered by St. Vrain's waiting volunteer mounted troops. Others took refuge in nearby buildings on the east side of the village. From this position one insurrectionist frantically waved a white flag. Many of the volunteers continued to fire their muskets and shot the flag and its bearer to pieces. An anonymous dragoon observed, "It was a shameful act [but] an excuse can be offered as the men were exasperated by the death of their comrades and had no thought but that of revenge." As night fell, shooting ceased.[74]

The next morning a white flag was again flown over the east half of the town, and was this time honored by Price's men. The insurrectionists laid down their arms and surrendered. By four o'clock in the afternoon, the dragoons had secured quarters and counted their losses: Sgt. George Ross, and Pvts. Eldridge Brooks, Nelson Beebe, and Michael Seviey. Pvt. Jacob Hunsaker died of his wounds on the following day, and Captain Burgwin and Pvt. Isaac Truax languished in pain until they died, mercifully, three days later. On February 10, Pvt. Frederick Schneider succumbed to wounds. The volunteers had lost seven men. Price estimated the rebels lost over two hundred men.

The anonymous dragoon observed that it was "[a] victory, indeed, deeply purchased by the single death of our brave, our dauntless and our ever good Captain. But his own 'G' [Company] proved itself and has won laurels and as far as was in our power, revenged his death, and fellow soldiers who fell with him."[75] With Burgwin's passing the dragoons lost, through either death or transfer, their seventh capable officer within the first year of the war. The depletion of such officers and of talented noncommissioned personnel was ultimately to lower the élan and effectiveness of the regiment.

On April 6, a drumhead court-martial convicted rebel leaders Pablo Montoya and Tomás Romero. A soldier murdered the latter in his cell and the former was executed the day after his "trial." While executions of other suspected rebels continued for the next month, the crippled Company G walked back down the long road to Albuquerque, where it reorganized and awaited further assignments.[76] But the rebellion continued throughout the territory, with numerous bloody raids, skirmishes, and executions until July of 1847.

The Gila Is a Hard Road to Travel

In the meantime, Colonel Kearny was marching west to California—a march that would take its brutal toll on man and beast. Blissfully unaware of the Californio rebellion, he envisioned a conqueror's welcome at the Pacific shore, which he thought was aptly named.

Kearny's column struggled along the steep canyon the Gila River had cut. Onward, ever onward, through a strange, bare, arid land, past ruins of old Spanish and Pueblo Indian towns, abandoned mines, and empty Indian lodges and camps they marched. At the end of this march the dragoons would encounter Californio vaqueros and face them in a battle at an Indian village known as San Pasqual. But to first get there they needed to cross the nearly 1,000 miles of harsh terrain that lay between Santa Fe and the California settlements.

To ensure this novel route would be properly mapped, a road built, and the economic promise of the region detailed for future expeditions, the War Department tapped Lt. William Emory and his staff of skilled topographical engineers, as well as Philip St. George Crooke and his Mormons, to make changes to the original route. They fulfilled their duty beyond the War Department's wildest hopes.

On October 18, 1846, the men came upon the ruins of copper mines near Santa Rita del Cobre. Here the dragoons met and held council with the Apache chief Mangas Coloradas. Engineer Emory, an eager student of the emerging science of anthropology, compared these exotic people to "antique Greek warriors" who always mounted in a "light and graceful manner."[77]

Leaving the Apaches, the dragoons continued to follow the Gila, although the sheer trail, winding over sharp rocks blanketed in volcanic dust, proved terrible for mules and impossible for wagons. Emory sent scouts back to advise Cooke, following with his Mormons, to avoid this route and seek an alternative to the south. He also warned him that temperatures in the region fell precipitously low at night. Cooke did secure an easier path and improved the passage west for his men and for those who would later travel southward to California.[78]

The troops quickly discovered how brutal the trip to California would be on the two howitzers and their wooded carriages. Attached to wheeled limbers and each pulled by a two-mule team, the howitzers broke down repeatedly and lagged well behind the column, slow-moving as that was. On October 21 Dr. Griffin wrote, "The howitzers have not come up yet, and it is now 8 P.M.— poor Davidson, he has a sweet time of it."[79] As Lieutenant Emory penned, by the time these guns left the Gila River canyon, "nearly every part of their running gear [had] broken down and [been] replaced."[80] The damage the weapons sustained would seriously impair the men's ability to fight at San Pasqual.[81]

As the expedition continued down Gila River Canyon, Emory recorded the topographical features before him, not only out of duty but also in hopes of proving his belief that the Aztecs had once inhabited the region, having become fascinated by the evidence of such ancient "busy, hardworking people." At one point he found the ruins of a magnificent three-story antique structure possibly built by the Aztecs, and named it Casa Grande. He also came into contact with members of the impoverished Pinos Lanos Apaches band, with whom Major Swords traded goods in exchange for several mules.[82]

After a torturous twenty-six-day trek through the pinched Gila River Canyon, the troops emerged onto a wide, grassy plain where they grazed their horses and mules while waiting for the decrepit, slow-moving howitzers. Dragoons and mounts were equally ragged and hungry from the ordeal. Noted Emory, "[N]o one observing our cavalry at this moment would form notions favorable to the success of the expedition." They were still five hundred miles from their objective. And as bad as their condition was at this time, they would suffer graver deprivations during the second half of the march.[83]

But for now, after winding slowly through what today is southern Arizona, they arrived at the junction of the Salt and Gila rivers to a very welcome sight. On November 11, Kearny reached the Pima and Maricopa villages, whose inhabitants greeted the troops generously with ample beans, tortillas, and pumpkins, as well as a number of cattle and horses. Having borne the searing desert sun since leaving Albuquerque, many troopers eagerly traded their woolen overcoats and jackets for food. As the troops refreshed themselves with the tribes' victuals, Emory drank in their culture, history, and agricultural technology. Restored after their three-day respite at one of the villages, the dragoons resumed their journey to California.[84]

"I have seen the Elephant"

But just a few miles west of Pima they immediately plunged back into the unforgiving wastelands of the Mojave Desert. Quartermaster Swords reported, "After leaving the Pimas the country assumes a very different character. . . . [G]rass becomes scant, and it was with difficulty that our tired animals could find enough to give them strength to proceed on the journey." Dr. Griffin's entry for the fourteenth of November specified that "[t]he mules were nearly mad for water and something to eat—but we were obliged to drive them out though this was attended with great difficulty." Mules began to die. Fast losing his riding stock, including his own horse, Kearny was forced to ride a mule and issued an order dismounting half the troops and assigning the remaining mules to pack service.[85]

As the column approached the Colorado River, the suffering became intense. "Most of the men were now on foot," recorded Emory on the twenty-second, and "a small party, comprised chiefly of the general and staff, were a long way ahead of the straggling column, when, as we approached the end of the day's journey, every man was straightened in his saddle by our suddenly falling on a camp which, from the trail, we estimated at 1,000 men." They thought it must be Gen. José Castro's army marching north from Sonoma. If so, Kearny believed it to be too great a force for his band of 110 to fight. He ordered fifteen men under Emory to scout the suspected Mexican position. The lieutenant discovered the camp to belong to a party of Mexican vaqueros herding some five hundred unbroken horses and mules south to Sonora, and approached the peaceful vaqueros bivouacked near the Colorado River. But his initial relief evaporated with their disquieting news that rebellious Californios had regained possession of Alta California, and that the horses belonged to General Castro. With a keen eye for horseflesh and eager to despoil the property of the Mexican government, Lieutenant Emory resolved to confiscate the best portion of the herd. Unfortunately, he very soon discovered that his "captured horses [were] all wild and but little adapted for immediate service." Kearny arrived and, suspecting these herders were nothing but common thieves, purchased twenty-five half-broken horses and allowed them to leave with the bulk of the rest.[86]

Kearny let his command relax along the river while the stock browsed its foliage. After exchanging their broken-down mules for confiscated Mexican horses, Emory, engineer William Warner, and artist John Stanley rode south to explore the region where the Gila meets the Colorado. As they approached the junction of the two rivers, Emory detained a well-mounted Mexican horseman riding east from California. Suspicious, the lieutenant took the man back to General Kearny. The general had the fellow searched and discovered messages he was bearing to General Castro detailing how the Californios, under Gen. José Maria Flores, had recaptured Los Angeles, though the Yankees maintained control over San Diego. These missives confirmed rumors of an uprising that had cleared the Americans from Santa Barbara and the Pueblo de Los Angeles. Emory neatly resealed the courier's dispatches and allowed him to ride away. The information determined Kearny to aim for San Diego rather than for Los Angeles as originally planned.[87]

Yet there was one slight glimmer of good fortune: Emory's and Kearny's recent acquisitions of Californio steeds gave the dragoons possession of approximately twenty-five reasonably—albeit not entirely—broken, fresh horses. Indeed, Captain Johnston noted that many of the dragoons were "remounted on wild horses, on which never man sat, they got many tumbles, but they stuck to the furious animals until they succeeded" in breaking the mounts into ersatz riding stock. Most of these animals seemed strong enough to carry a rider and his equipage to San Diego. They were not, of course, trained to perform cavalry maneuvers—a defect which became apparent a few days later when the troops engaged in a mêlée with well-mounted Californios.[88]

The dragoons were poised to enter California. Before them lay the western Mojave Desert—nature's final obstacle in their 1,700-mile, six-month odyssey from Fort Leavenworth to the Pacific. The twenty-sixth of November found the command, having forded the Colorado River, riding their horses and mules into the desert, each mount with a large bundle of river grass tied to the saddle. Captain Swords observed that they were crossing "the great desert, ninety miles without either grass or water, except a scant supply of the latter, obtained by digging wells through the loose sand."[89] After riding twenty-three thirsty miles over deep sand drifts, the troops located a promising well. To little avail, the men spent the entire evening digging deep into it with an empty champagne basket from the officers' mess to catch the drops more precious than any liqueur. Luckily, before long Captain Moore found a better well from which the troops unearthed 800 to 1,000 buckets of potable water—their last for the next two days.[90]

Kearny may have wished for the three well-nourished companies he had left in New Mexico, especially if his emaciated troops and mules had to encounter Mexican forces. But after having crossed nearly 1,000 desolate miles, he must also have seen that having his full detachment would have geometrically worsened his command's decimation by hunger and thirst along the Gila and the barren Mojave Desert.[91]

While Kearny weighed his military assets, the multi-talented Emory wondered whether such parched land might ever support an agrarian economy. Although he himself held slaves, and considerable support for the war came from Southerners desirous of expanding slavery, Emory concluded that the southwestern region about to be conquered was unsuitable for the extension of that peculiar institution.[92] "No one who has ever visited this country and who is acquainted with the character and value of slave labor in the United States would ever think of bringing his slaves with any view to profit, much less would he purchase slaves for any such purpose. Their labor here, if they could be retained as slaves among peons nearly of their own color, would never repay the cost of transportation much less the additional purchase money."[93]

But there was little time for the lieutenant to philosophize, as the effects of this sinister land upon the column's health quickly brought him back to the task at hand. The vicious thorns of sage and chaparral gracing the otherwise sterile land, he observed, "were a great annoyance to our dismounted and wearied men whose legs were now almost bare." Dr. Griffin's prediction of a squadron of men in "Georgia uniforms" was fast becoming a reality.[94]

The severe conditions visited upon Kearny's men since leaving Santa Fe did more than discourage plans for slave plantations. The unusually hard march, fatigue, and lack of adequate food and water brought a steady decline in military discipline. On the twenty-eighth, a furious Quartermaster Swords found that some of the men had slaughtered and eaten one of his best pack mules.[95] Instances of loss and destruction of government property (uniforms, tack, and weapons); neglect, abuse, and mismanagement of riding stock; and the command's subsequent despoliation of civilian property during early December also indicated a growing abandonment of soldierly obedience.

But even with their order and energy flagging, the troops' spirits remained high. Travel over the desert and rocky landscape had reduced clothing to rags and ground down the boots, but the ragged men were ready for a fight. Dr. Griffin observed their threadbare uniforms, admitting that "[t]his is rather a bad picture for men who have a hard campaign before them." Yet with typical overconfidence he concluded, "[B]ut then our powder is dry and guns in good order and if they don't pile an unreasonable number up before us—we will be able to give them a good sound thrashing."[96]

Having arrived in California after a grueling seventy-one-day march through nearly a thousand miles of rugged, untracked desert terrain without the loss of single man, General Kearny took pride in knowing that his detachment had again proven itself capable of covering great distances—albeit much of them on foot. On the thirtieth the command rested, the weary men appearing to former midshipman Benjamin Moore more like survivors of a shipwreck than soldiers. Captain Johnston concurred: "Our men were inspected to-day. Poor fellows! They are well nigh naked— some of them barefoot—a sorry looking set." But he proudly added that they, nonetheless, were ready for whatever battles awaited, and that "in those swarthy, sun-burnt faces, a lover of his country would see no signs of quailing. They will be ready for their hour when it comes."[97]

Knowing they neared their objective, the men reached down to garner a last full measure of joie de vivre. As testament to their rugged spirit, on November 27 and 28 alone they covered fifty-four punishing miles of the Mojave Desert. And despite his own suffering in that wilderness, the intrepid Emory never once entered into his journal the least expression of dissatisfaction—only the breathtaking spectacles of nature he ceaselessly documented. Ascending into a range of hills, the men rejoiced as blistering heat gave way to cool fog, a sea breeze, and potable water—elixirs for the aching, exhausted men and beasts. Dr. Griffin summed up their relief at having survived California's Mojave wasteland: "I have seen the Elephant and I hope I shall never be compelled to cross it again."[98]

CHAPTER 8

The Battle of San Pasqual

A Glass to the Dead Already and Here's to the Next Man to Die

Of all arms, cavalry is the most difficult to handle in the field. It cannot engage the enemy except where the ground is favorable. Officers must bear in mind that, however successful a brave and determined body of horsemen may be, there is a limit to everything. The horses must in time get blown, the men tire out, the squadrons scattered; they are then at the mercy of any body of fresh horsemen.

Capt. Louis Nolan, *Cavalry: Its History and Tactics* (1853)

Two more days of hard traveling followed before the tatterdemalion detachment, riding or leading worn mules and horses, climbed out of the desert on December 3 and onto a wooded plain, announcing their arrival at the thriving Warner cattle ranch. The ranch was nestled at 3,500 feet in the oak-studded San Felipe Valley, some seventy miles from San Diego. A passenger on the Butterfield Stage in 1858 captured the beauty of its setting "in the midst of a beautiful meadow" and surrounded by "some delightful oak groves—a most decided improvement on the desert."[1]

Its proprietor was the Yankee expatriate Jonathan Warner, just then being held by the U.S. Navy in San Diego on charges of being a Mexican sympathizer. In Warner's absence Kearny's starving men helped themselves amply to his food and water. Kearny himself gained something of greater tactical importance: information from the ranch manager that more Californio horses and mules grazed nearby. That evening, Lieutenant Davidson and Kit Carson, accompanied by twenty-five troopers, rode out and seized a herd of one hundred Mexican horses and mules. Dr. Griffin judged some of the mounts as saddle-broken and fine, "but the majority were perfectly useless."[2] But even these untrained mounts bettered the sorry stock that had borne many of the men across the desert.

Davidson's raid probably added a good twenty-five adequate riding animals to those the dragoons acquired from the horse thieves on the Colorado River, yielding, conservatively, a total of seventy-five reasonably well-conditioned, but not well-trained, horses and mules. Thus slightly fewer than half of the command was mounted on restive but healthy stock. Given that about fifty men would later engage in mounted warfare with the Californios, it is fair to assume that most of them were riding fresh, albeit imperfectly obedient, creatures. Even better: before long Kearny would receive badly needed human reinforcements.

The next day the troops moved over luxuriant grassland and past scattered groves of live oaks en route to the Santa Isabel Ranch. The weather had suddenly turned cold and wet, but the soldiers were cheered by a day of rest, warm food, California wine, and shelter graciously provided them by Señor Bill, majordomo of the ranch.[3] Before long, the ranch's owner, Edward Stokes, appeared and Kearny requested that he carry a message to Commo. Robert Stockton in San Diego advising him of the dragoons' arrival.[4] Kearny planned to rest the men and their mounts and, once he established communications with the navy, to attack any nearby force of rebels.[5]

Stokes delivered the message and reinforcements were on the way. On a cold, foggy, and rainy fifth of December the troops continued their march to San Diego. At Rancho Santa Maria they joined with Capt. Archibald Gillespie and his mounted detachment: forty-one marines, sailors, and Bear Flaggers (civilians who supported Yankee control of California). Gillespie's detachment boasted a variety of weapons: Colt revolving rifles, Springfield flint muskets, civilian rifles, and old four-pounder cannon taken from Sutter's Fort. Commodore Stockton, forty miles distant, had sent this force to reinforce and lend intelligence to Kearny. This augmentation gave Kearny around 150 reasonably well-armed men and three cannon—seemingly more than sufficient to deal with any Mexican force then operating in California. With them Kearny felt more confident than ever. But what he then learned from Gillespie would give him some pause—it was reported to him that there were six hundred to seven hundred enemy soldiers in the territory "determined upon opposing the Americans and resisting their authority in the country."[6]

Earlier that year, the free-spirited, mendacious, redheaded marine captain had completed a secret mission, traveling overland to deliver messages from President Polk to Vice Counsel Thomas Larkin and John Frémont in California.[7] Stockton rewarded him with the rank of major in the Bear Flag army and placed him in command of the occupation forces in Los Angeles. But Gillespie infuriated the Californios with his draconian rule; they threw him and his men out of Pueblo de Los Angeles, and soon after defeated Capt. William Mervine's relief force of three hundred, who had attempted to retake Los Angeles. The insurrectionists gained control of the southern half of the state by fully surrounding the Americans in San Diego. Hearing the tale, Kearny was now fully apprised of the Californios' tenacity. Indeed, they had clearly demonstrated a spirit entirely contrary to what Kearny and Carson had experienced in their dealings with the Mexican army. Energized by these recent victories, the Californios could hardly be expected to run away from armed engagements. All the more so if they had, as rumored, seven hundred to eight hundred armed men to fight the invaders.

Gillespie further informed Kearny of a small enemy force bivouacked in the Luiseño tribal village of San Pasqual, nine miles distant and blocking the main road to San Diego, and suggested that Kearny go there and "beat them up."[8] The chance of whipping a small force and gaining more riding stock tempted Kearny. With pilfered horses he could remount his entire command and, along with more reinforcements from Stockton, he was convinced he could recapture California.

Kearny may have been the only general in the Mexican War who did not long to become president. He was, simply, a professional, a soldier's soldier. The purity of his ambition to retake California would enshrine him forever in the nation's military pantheon. But this aspiration, while selfless, made him overlook both the woeful condition of his troops and the mettle of his opponents.[9]

After digesting Gillespie's report, Kearny considered how he might immediately mount his men, surprise and scatter the enemy, and gain their much-needed horses. The problem remained that such an action would require a lengthy ride to San Pasqual. Expecting that the Mexicans (and their mounts) would flee a direct attack, he decided first to move his troops unnoticed to within striking distance at a canyon camp two miles from Rancho Santa Maria.[10]

The enemy force of seventy-five vaqueros under the command of Andrés Pico had entered the village on the fifth of December and commandeered the huts and most foodstuffs. A marine second lieutenant, Henry Watson, later would describe Pico as a "fine, handsome-looking young man, who is represented to be one of the best informed and polite men in California & who was induced to join in this last outbreak by the harsh treatment he received from Lieutenant Gillespie."[11] Possessing few firearms and little ammunition, Pico found himself in a perilous position. He feared that Stockton's larger and better-armed force would march out from San Diego and attack him or at least raid the countryside. So Pico's immediate objectives were to keep an eye on Stockton's movements and simultaneously to position his force so it might retreat into the interior. Hearing rumors of an American force already there—that would be Kearny's—Pico ordered a sizeable detachment of his force to scout the land to the east. There is no evidence that this scouting force ever reported back to Pico.

In an unfamiliar region six miles away, the dragoons idled. According to Lieutenant Emory, "besides the rain a heavy fog obscured the landscape, and little could be seen of the country during the day's journey." Despite three days of comfort at the Warner and Santa Isabel ranches, the men were still spent and many steeds were in worse condition. On the eve of battle, in an instance of honesty rare for the man forced to resign from the Marine Corps in 1854 for pilfering his ship's funds, Gillespie bluntly appraised Kearny's troops as physically and morally depleted. Echoing Dr. Griffin's description of November 30 and Captain Moore's of December 2, Gillespie painted the dragoons as unfit for combat, even against supposedly craven Mexican irregulars. For they were "exhausted by their long and arduous march; indeed the whole force, save the officers, presented an appearance of weariness and fatigue rarely, if ever, met with upon any other service. The men were without any exception sadly in want of clothing; that which they wore was ragged and torn, they were almost without shoes; and although we [as seafarers] were constantly accustomed to much privation and suffering, my own men considered their own condition superior to these way worn Soldiers, whose strength and spirits seemed to be entirely gone."[12]

Misprizing the Enemy

While the men relaxed and the animals grazed, Kearny assembled his officers to mull over options. The combative Gillespie, familiar with the enemy's capabilities, volunteered his well-rested and experienced "mountain men" to scout the enemy position and maybe to steal a few horses. Kearny, reflecting his scorn of civilian soldiers, declined his offer and assigned Gillespie's detachment the inglorious job of guarding the supply train at the column's rear.[13] Captain Moore next stood up to argue against scouting the enemy, which risked alerting them, and pressed instead for a full-scale attack. Trooper George Peace of C Company, present at the meeting as a member of the escort for Kearny, recalled hearing

Moore tell the general that the vaqueros' "discovery of the scouts would result in failure to obtain an advantage, as the enemy was well mounted and the most expert horsemen in the world, while the dragoons were mostly mounted on poor, half-starved, and jaded mules; that it would be far better for the whole of us to move and make the attack at once; that by this course we should more than likely get all the horses of the enemy, and to dismount them was to whip them."[14]

Kearny dismissed out of hand Moore's suggestion for an immediate, massive strike and instead dispatched ten dragoons under Lt. Thomas Hammond to pinpoint Pico's position. Hammond and his patrol rattled their way down the dark road to San Pasqual, returning at about two in the morning to report that, as Moore had feared, the noise they made had drawn the Californios' attention. Hammond also mentioned that one of his men had lost a blanket, possibly further advertising the presence of the U.S. Army in the region. Significantly, nowhere in Kearny's report of Hammond's reconnaissance and the battle is there any disclosure of what Hammond discovered with regard to the strength of the Californio force.

Nobody really thought Pico's men, or Pico himself, could distinguish an army blanket embroidered with "U.S." from similar blankets carried by sailors and marines. But given his anxiety Kearny concluded that the Californios now certainly knew of his presence and, fearing that they would either flee or ambush his force, elected to move quickly lest he lose the chance to appropriate their fine horses.[15]

But on this day the general seemed to have forgotten the strategy he had preached so often to his junior officers: Avoid battle whenever possible; when impossible to avoid a battle, fight with intelligence. Kearny in his heyday would have displayed a redoubtable formation to terrify the foe into retreat or surrender. Or if a battle appeared likely, he would have buttressed his troops with Gillespie's sailors, marines, Bear Flaggers, and artillery in the center, and dragoons at each flank. Once formed, he would have advanced the Bear Flaggers and marines, sending the dragoons to attack Pico's flank and drive the Californios from the field.

As the reader has seen elsewhere in this book, this same strategy had been successfully practiced by a host of dragoon officers: Dodge on his march to the Pawnee villages; Wharton meeting with unruly Pawnees in 1844; Cooke confronting the Snively raiders; Sumner dealing with contentious Sioux. Kearny himself employed the tactic on innumerable occasions on the plains as well as very recently, when his whole Army of the West, in fearsome battle formation with sabers drawn and cannon port fires burning, advanced on Governor Armijo both near Puerta del Padre and in the narrow gap outside Las Vegas. Central to each of these encounters was the threat of crushing force coupled with diplomacy. This simple tactic had worked every time and had made the dragoons an invaluable tool of the government.

Kearny had yet another option available to him: coordinating his advance in an archetypal "hammer and anvil" attack stratagem in conjunction with Commodore Stockton's forces coming up from the south. If Pico ran, his force would have scattered and been easily defeated by the commodore's superior force. If Pico stayed to face Kearny, Stockton would pin him against Kearny and attack. In either instance, Pico must have lost. So in almost any permutation, the day would have been Kearny's. José Alvarado, a Californio participant, later admitted that "if General Kearny had appeared in open daylight in compact force," San Pasqual would have been remembered for a peace treaty rather than a fight.[16]

But uncharacteristically, and in wholesale disregard of the recent lessons Gillespie's experiences had taught of Californio war craft and courage, Kearny held that Pico would not stand and fight. Favoring instead what Carson and others had told him, and assuming his own earlier exploits in New Mexico foretold all future outcomes, Kearny believed the Mexicans would skedaddle at the first shot. Underrating his opponent, Kearny would carelessly discard what had repeatedly worked for his regiment throughout its thirteen years, and would act like an unseasoned, shavetail, brevet second lieutenant fresh from the Military Academy.

Another result of Kearny's misjudgment about his antagonists was his disregard for the dragoons' lack of real combat experience. The regiment had campaigned for half a year but had not once battled an enemy. Certainly Kearny himself had tasted warfare at Queenston Heights in the War of 1812, but aside from a few veterans of the French, German, and English armies and a handful who had clashed with Seminoles in Florida or in the Black Hawk War, no dragoon had ever seen fighting. Even more unaccountably, in a possible display of interservice rivalry, Kearny discounted the fact that many of Gillespie's men had actually skirmished with the Californios already, and went out of his way to consign them to the rear. To top it all, perhaps the general cared too much for his own officers' ambitions. In war, brevet commissions and promotions in the regular army piled up like cordwood, but Kearny's hotspurs-in-waiting—Moore, Hammond, Davidson, Emory, Warner, and Johnston—likely trembled lest the war would end before they gained honors in the field. Kearny wished to reward them.

So the usually cautious Kearny devised and pursued a half-baked plan for an all-out assault: rushing into combat; ignoring dragoons' exhaustion and inexperience; burying Gillespie's rested and seasoned troops at the rear; attacking over unknown terrain; commencing the attack before daylight—all of which flowed from the fundamental error of underestimating the enemy. To borrow a popular phrase often used by soldiers, General Kearny *played the devil on his watch*.[17]

Finally, no analyst of this debacle should underestimate the pervasive power of alcohol. Sources strongly suggest that drunkenness played a role at San Pasqual. In an article for the November 13, 1868, edition of the *California Daily Alta*, correspondent Charles Pickett squarely blamed the defeat at San Pasqual upon the officers' consumption of wine on the eve of battle, and Archibald Gillespie's fiery denial in the next day's paper only fanned the flames of rumor. In his biography of Kearny, Dwight

Clarke casually brushes aside Pickett's accusation on the grounds that Pickett wasn't there and Gillespie was. But the journalist's charge deserves more than Clarke's summary dismissal.

For there was another account concerning intoxicated officers at San Pasqual written by someone actually in the battle. French, the enlisted dragoon serving as Dr. Griffin's aide and later a successful doctor and prospector, observed bluntly that the "officers [were] full of wine." Certainly, officers brought spirits for the trip along the Gila River and consumed them before reaching California. And while at the Rancho Santa Isabel officers and men alike enjoyed a considerable amount of California wine, likely the first they had drunk in several weeks.[18] This liberal imbibing of spirits surely gladdened their hearts, but may well have dissolved their judgment.

An argument overlooked by Gillespie and Clarke is that, if officers and men were truly inebriated on that historic morning, they would not have been able to mount, ride, and guide their animals down the steep mountain trail in pitch black. However, while drink may not have severely impaired the motor skills of most, hard-drinking officers and enlisted men were all too common on the antebellum frontier. An officer on the frontier stated, "the soldier who *will* have whiskey *can* procure it," and Ulysses Grant concurred stating, "soldiers are a class of people who will drink."[19] In 1852, a dragoon in New Mexico tells of heavy quaffing by officers: "The Colonel got pretty drunk; our officers felt their brandy. They refused to obey the Commanding Officer, were put under arrest, threatened to shoot him, but when the effects of liquor were gone, their 'bravado' went with it."[20]

The 1st Dragoons was hardly immune from heavy drinking. Now, there has never been the least indication that Kearny himself overindulged. If anything, he seemed to believe what he preached to the tribes about liquor being the real enemy, and distrusted officers who loved their drink. But this was not the case with his officers and men. Before leaving Leavenworth for Santa Fe in 1846, he intentionally left behind known alcoholics Maj. Pat Trenor and Capt. Philip Thompson to continue their drinking at the fort, and would have discarded any seriously intoxicated officers or men on the approach to San Pasqual.

Court-martial records of the period bulge with cases against drunken soldiers and officers of the regiment. We offer for the reader's perusal four sad tales of Mexican War–era dragoon alcoholics. First is the tale of Maj. Pat Trenor. He had been court-martialed in 1841 for being drunk.[21] Restored to duty, when learning of his promotion in 1846 to the rank of major—based on his seniority, not sobriety—he immediately got seriously intoxicated. Major Trenor was to die due to the affects of his alcoholism on February 16, 1847.[22]

And then there is Pvt. Nelson Archy, whom we have previously met. His father sought to gain the discharge of his underage son. In a series of events quite reminiscent of Thomas Russell's efforts to secure his release from the dragoons due to a recruiting sergeant's misrepresentations in 1834, the recruit's connection with a congressman was brought into play. On January 29, 1848, the senior Archy contacted Congressman William Sawyer and pleaded with him to intercede. The congressman made an inquiry with the War Department and discovered that Nelson Archy was no longer in the service, but had been dishonorably dismissed by reason of a court-martial. According to his court-martial transcript, young Archy had acquired a fond appetite for alcohol, which hampered attending to military duties. On the evening of November 24, 1847, while in a drunken state, he entered into Lt. Patrick Noble's unoccupied quarters and from there removed a couple of horse pistols. Then taking the pistols, his Hall carbine, and a blanket, he deserted to Albuquerque, where young Archy spent the night at the home of a female acquaintance. The court-martial panel included Lt. John Love, the man who recruited the underage Archy in 1845. On December 1, 1847, the panel found him guilty of being utterly worthless as a soldier and dishonorably dismissed him from the service. Deciding, perhaps, to spare him corporal punishment attendant to a finding of desertion, it found Archy not guilty of such.[23]

Then there was Felix Leggit, a member of Company K, 1st Dragoons, who got drunk while on occupation duty in Mexico City in 1847. He walked into a room, cursed, killed (for no apparent reason) a Mexican stable hand, and then passed out. Felix's defense was that he was a kindly fellow, a good soldier, and had, being drunk, no memory of the event. The court-martial panel convicted him and sentenced him to be strung up. Leggit was executed on January 5, 1848, becoming the only regular soldier to be executed for an atrocity committed against a civilian during the war.[24]

Finally, there was an old soldier, 1st Sgt. John Fowler of Company B, 1st Dragoons, who, while conducting an escort of the paymaster in 1849, got wildly drunk one night and conspired with other drunk dragoons to kill the paymaster and to steal his gold. Due to his long service the panel, led by Major Sumner, felt a degree of leniency for Fowler and discharged him from the service.[25]

Indeed, one can hardly turn a page in the journal of Pvt. William Antes, who served in Company A of the First Dragoons from 1854 through 1859, without reading of the abuse of spirits in the army.[26] So it is not surprising that Kearny and Stockton, upon capturing Los Angeles in 1847, ordered that all supplies of brandy and wine be placed under guard.[27]

Likely, a cask or two were brought on the march, loaded on a pack mule, and several men and officers undoubtedly filled their canteens with wine. In sum, enough officers drank enough alcohol soon enough before the battle that it must be considered as a factor in its outcome.[28]

The Country Expects Every Man to Do His Duty

The initial act of that battle would be quick, confused, shrouded in darkness, and lasting no more than fifteen minutes. None of its participants knew what was happening ten yards away, and reports of its first five minutes yield a blurry description. Worse, many accounts proved self-serving, and they often conflict one another. Captains Moore and Johnston, notably reliable sources, were killed early on, and the usually dependable Swords and Griffin were too far behind the fighting to see much of anything and relied on what others told them. Of those in the thick of it, Kearny and Gillespie regularly shaded the truth to suit their purposes and please their superiors, and Kit Carson often told tall tales in his account. Emory, as Kearny's escort, might have produced a credible record, but chose not to besmirch his superior's reputation—nor to endanger his own career by doing so.

For some reason, Gillespie claimed in his report to Commodore Stockton that during the march "[t]he weather had cleared, the moon shone as bright as day almost, but the wind coming from the snow-covered mountains made it so cold, we could scarcely hold our bridle reins." But virtually all other accounts describe a cold rain and thick fog utterly blanketing the dark valley floor below. From these accounts we know that in the pre-dawn hours of December 6 the dragoons marched nine miles through black and narrow canyons and over brush-filled countryside until they came within a mile of the Californio position. Most participants fully recognized that they were traveling over unknown terrain against an alerted enemy of unknown strength. Aside from Gillespie's Bear Flaggers and naval personnel, the men were worn from their nine-hundred-mile march and many rode equally tired mounts or imperfectly saddle-broken stock.[29]

Stopped on a bluff overlooking the valley, the troops eyed the distant Californio campfires. Pvt. William Dunne of Company K recalled that as he peered into the gloom he believed it to be too dark to commence an attack. Although he was no expert on tactics, his common soldier's appraisal mirrored the views expressed by the nineteenth-century Prussian military genius Carl von Clausewitz. The Prussian was especially skeptical of night attacks because of the confusion wrought upon attacker and defender alike. He believed night attacks were, at best, permissible as raids once the aggressor had fully scouted the defender's position, but cautioned commanders to avoid them whenever possible.[30] Historian Arthur Woodward, writing of the battle, commented,

"With all of the knowledge of warfare he must have had, Kearny could not have been so blind as not to foresee the results of such a poorly conceived action. One wonders why he did not take the open or at best poorly guarded road into San Diego via El Cajon, or did not wait until daylight when he could see the terrain and the forces arrayed against him."[31]

Perhaps Kearny believed he would reach San Pasqual at day-light and undetected. He was wrong. Kearny would have been wise to wait even an hour before launching his attack, as a December sunrise in San Diego comes around 6:30 in the morning. When the troops entered the valley before dawn, the sky was only faintly lit and shadows hugged the valley floor and canyons. Drizzle and fog limited visibility even more, to just a few yards. If Kearny expected a night march would cover his approach and find Pico unawares at dawn, his ear-splitting advance guard again scotched any such hope and delivered the men to San Pasqual in utter dark-ness. The approaching column of 160 mounted men, three can-non, and pack animals, with sabers clanking against brass stirrups, carbines, tin cups, and other metal equipage; some four hundred horseshoes striking rock; artillery limbers and cannon creaking and groaning; and mules braying under their heavy loads must have sounded to Pico's men like an approaching carnival. As Gillespie poetically reported, "The clang of the heavy Dragoon Sabres, echoing amongst the hills upon this cold frosty morning, and reverberating from the mountain top back upon the Valley, seemed like so many alarm bells to give notice of our approach." Indeed, while Hammond's nocturnal scouting had awakened them, the noisier advance convinced Pico that an enemy force was near, and his vaqueros were saddled, armed, and ready to fight.[32] In sum, the column would enjoy no advantage of surprise that day. And as a harbinger of disasters to come, the dragoons on weaker mounts steadily fell behind those riding heartier stock and clatter-ing down the otherwise silent canyon, allowing Pico's men to deal piecemeal with the attacking column.

Standing on the bluff, Kearny gathered his men around and, in the heroic language he may have borrowed from Lord Horatio

Nelson's speech prior to the Battle of Trafalgar, told them that the country expected them to do their duty. The general advised them to avoid slashing with their sabers and to recall that one thrust of its point requires less force and results in more injury. Never imagining that his men might stand before highly skilled lancers on expertly maneuvered horses, he failed to mention that a saber thrust also costs the attacker his full ability to parry a counter-thrust.[33]

As the men stood "to horse," sergeants and corporals inspected the mules and horses to ensure that saddle girths were tightened, and checked that weapons were loaded and primed. The troops then mounted, formed a column of twos, and rode off. After nearly fourteen years of nonviolent diplomacy, two companies of the 1st Dragoons were poised to engage in the regiment's first real battle.

At the column's head Captain Johnston smartly trotted with twelve dragoons mounted upon the command's fittest horses. General Kearny, Captain Turner, an escort, and staffers closely shadowed Johnston's vanguard. Behind Kearny came fifty dragoons under Captain Moore and Lieutenant Hammond, many of the men riding mules or unbroken horses filched from the Mexicans. Then followed a detachment of sailors, marines, and Bear Flaggers with the brass four-pounder cannon they had expropriated from John Sutter's fort, in turn backed by Lieutenant Davidson's two mountain howitzers on battered carriages lashed together with ropes and rawhide straps. The remaining staff, a few marines, and the pack train brought up the rear under the command of Capt. Thomas Swords.[34]

"Charge as Foragers!"

Johnston's men rode at a cautious pace down the narrow canyon. As they entered the northern end of the long valley, there suddenly appeared two mounted Californio vedettes who, seemingly true to stereotype, turned and fled. Johnston and his men, their blood stirred, immediately gave spur to their horses to chase them down. However, since their mounts were not trained to maintain formation the "charge was not made," in the words of one participant, "with our whole force, or as much precision as desirable."[35] Capt. Samuel DuPont of the U.S. Navy, after speaking to combatants, gave his account of the initial cavalcade:

> Instead of proceeding as a compact force of riders, Kearny's men lost all cohesion. . . . An advance guard of twelve dragoons under Captain Johnston soon broke away from the men mounted on mules, and with everyone riding madly forward on as unimpressive an array of quadrupeds as ever graced the field of honor, it must have resembled a gold rush rather than a cavalry charge. Behind Johnston— a long way behind, as it transpired—rode Kearny, Lieutenant Emory, and the engineer, William Warner, while behind them, laboring along on mules exhausted by their thousand-mile journey, were a further fifty dragoons. At the back, dragging the guns, came Gillespie with his volunteers.[36]

Johnston's heavily encumbered chargers were no match for the swift horses capably ridden by the Californios, who easily outdistanced them. In the advance party, Kit Carson's horse fell while crossing the dry bed of San Bernardo Creek, throwing him from the saddle and breaking the stock of his plains rifle. Carson hit the ground hard and rolled over to see Kearny's onrushing escort about to trample him. Though stunned, the feline-like scout sprang out of the way, dusted himself off, and instinctively searched for his rifle, which he discovered now ruined. He took off on foot, hoping to catch up to the troopers before the battle ended.[37]

Approaching the village, Captain Johnston and his men thought they saw, off to their right, a shadowy group of vaqueros frantically attempting to assemble. Johnston's dragoons sharply swiveled toward them, drew sabers, and charged up a slope.

Trooper William Dunne, desperately trying to keep up with Johnston, later recalled that the confusion, the dark, and the weakness of the mounts dissolved the onrushing vanguard's formation. The fight quickly became chaotic, with "every man for himself."[38] Although General Kearny could barely see the movement of Johnston's men ahead, he sensed that Johnston was about to engage fleeing vaqueros and ordered his bugler, James McKee, to sound, "Charge as foragers!"

In the murkiness, Captain Johnston could not see Pico's men—clearly warned by their "cowardly" vedettes—perfectly positioned to meet his charge. Out of the shadows a vaquero drew his *escopeta* (carbine) and fired into the dark at Johnston and the approaching dragoons. The ball struck Johnston in the head, instantly killing him. Johnston became the first and the only dragoon, according to Dr. Griffin and Lieutenant Emory, to die by gunfire during the battle. Other Californios now fired but caused no serious injuries. Seeing General Kearny, Captain Moore, and their men steadily advancing, and knowing his ammunition was almost used up, Pico ordered a retreat to about a half-mile down the road to San Diego.[39]

Kearny's Strategies and Arms

Let us stop for a moment—mid-charge—to take stock of the tactics and weapons employed by Kearny. Pvt. George Pearce heard that bugle call to "charge as foragers," which, he clarified in his memoir, ordained that "every one shall, single handed, select and slay as many of the enemy as he can and in his own way." So that each man might target the nearest foe, the call allowed horses more freedom of movement than formed ranks would have, and was an entirely valid stratagem when troopers could kill more of the enemy by individual pursuit than by pursuit as a body.[40] But for Kearny to have ordered "charge as foragers" before ascertaining what was occurring in the obscurity was an incomprehensibly bad idea that proved fatally premature, since the enemy had formed and stood ready to repel the uncoordinated attack. This decision, like so many of the general's that day, courted catastrophe.

Reviewing contemporary military opinion clarifies the extent of Kearny's other miscalculations. Concerning the respective numbers of the combatants, Napoleon taught, "God is on the side of the biggest battalions." Kearny arrived at San Pasqual with twice Pico's eighty combatants, so by Napoleon's dictum Kearny should have had a heavenly advantage. But Napoleon kept in mind the fine point that distribution matters as much as mass. At San Pasqual, the full weight of Kearny's force was spread out over the entire line of attack and never came pointedly to bear against Pico. Captain DuPont observed that the column stretched across more than a mile—and, worse, in disarray, since officers rode swifter mounts than did most of their men—resulting in the loss of all cohesion, organization and effectiveness: "Those which [sic] were passably mounted naturally got ahead and they of course were mostly officers with the best of the dragoons, corporals, and sergeants . . . and very soon this advance guard to the number of about forty got far ahead. . . . [The Californios] began to discover the miserable condition of their foes, some on mules and some on lean and lame horses, men and mules worn out by a long march."[41] The dragoons' scattered arrival compensated the defenders for their smaller numbers, and let them defeat their attackers by virtue of that devilish detail.

Another strategic element at play at San Pasqual concerns weaponry. Pico's men—locals pressed into military service—fought primarily with lances, and throughout the war the Mexican army deployed numerous companies of traditional military lancers.[42] At least two dragoon officers believed Mexican lancers constituted a capable enemy. Col. Albert Brackett of the U.S. Cavalry, and a former 1st Dragoon, penned, "Mexicans were more agile [than dragoons], and could handle their horses as well as any people on earth. With the lance they were greatly our superiors, and used that weapon with great effect at both Buena Vista and at San Pasqual."[43] Lt. Fayette Robinson, another former dragoon, was equally impressed and hoped in the future this "formidable a weapon in the hands of Mexican rancheros and cavalry might not be introduced with propriety into our service."[44]

Nonetheless, with the exception of San Pasqual, in every battle in which lancers fought against U.S. volunteer or regular horsemen using sabers, the lancers came out worse. True enough, the lancers at Buena Vista slew fleeing foot soldiers and disorganized Arkansas mounted riflemen, but later met their match when they engaged the dragoons. Even Robinson stood with most tacticians of the Napoleonic era, who judged the lance effective against disorganized foot soldiers or routed horsemen,[45] but believed a competent dragoon using a saber to fight a lancer usually wins, especially if the lancer remains conveniently stationary.[46] The French officer Baron de Marbot observed, "In a cavalry fight the length of the lances is a drawback when their bearers have lost their order and are pressed closely by adversaries, who are armed with swords which they can handle easily, while the lancers find it difficult to present the points of their poles."

Also, a well-poised saber will likely block a lance. Further, a lance, once parried, is awkward to swing laterally because the horse's head often gets in the way, leaving the lancer vulnerable to a riposte by a saber-wielding dragoon or to an attack at his exposed flank.[47] Worse, even a lancer's successful thrust might invite a host of problems. When driven into a target while the bearer gallops, the lance often transfers the shock of the impact to the lancer, knocking him off his horse. Even successfully impaling one's enemy carries risk. The lance may get stuck deep in a victim's body; should the deceased fall off his horse, his body might pull the lance out of the attacker's hand or make the attacker himself topple. Any attempts to recover a lance wedged in a victim exposed the now-unarmed attacker to the vengeance of his victim's comrades. For all these reasons, post-Napoleonic armies tended to deploy only a limited number of lancer regiments in their mounted brigades. For example, in 1854, when the British brought with them nine cavalry regiments to fight in the Crimea, only one regiment, the 17th Regiment, was armed with lances.

Naturally, armies tried to mitigate these problems. Military lances were lightened and adorned with cloth pennants that would scare an opponent's horse but not remain in an enemy's body. Lances were also given sturdy straps so they might be held onto after the thrust. Yet none of these improvements worked that well in application.[48] Thus in Napoleonic times when all armies used massed formations of mounted troops, most of them deployed their lancers for scouting, guarding the flanks, and disrupting a defeated army rather than as a defensive or aggressive formation.

So it is clear that military wisdom of the period predicted an easy rout of Pico's lance-wielding vaqueros. Trouble was, these were not typical lancers. Most were well-mounted ranch hands from Los Angeles—incomparably skilled riders particularly adept at driving and roping with lance and lariat, their daily tools for herding range cattle. Captain Cooke later described these vaqueros in a letter to the *Missouri Republican* as "the most formidable horsemen in America."[49] Dr. Griffin noted that "they seem to aim their lances as to strike a man near the kidneys." Indeed, the descriptions of wounded dragoons suggest that the vaqueros used their lances expertly to wound and to draw blood, to prod and to control, as would ranchers on the open range, from whom bullfighting picadors learned their tricks. In this manner the Californios inflicted multiple shallow lesions on their victims and avoided the inconveniences of extricating a lance from deep within a body. Only when a dying dragoon fell to the ground from blood loss and pain would the lancer grant him a deadly gash to the heart or lung.[50] And significantly, the lancers were fighting a disorganized enemy that was not well mounted. So much for Napoleonic stratagems.

Elements of Companies C and K Enter into the Fray and are Destroyed Piecemeal

We may now return to Kearny's muddled charge and Pico's clearer tactics in action. Captain Moore, saber held high and cutting edge at tierce point, mounted upon one of the finest horses in the regiment, raced onward. Riding on inferior horses and mules, most dragoons in his company were unable to keep up with him. Moore was followed, however, by a small knot of troopers: Pearce, Dunne, Asa Bowen, and a few others. They crested a small rise and found themselves facing a large group of menacing Californios. Bowen recalled "rounding the point and seeing . . . a million people making for us." Rather than wait for the rest of his detachment to arrive, Moore and his little band foolishly pitched into the enemy.[51]

Moore was immediately lanced and knocked off his horse, but remounted and, saber in hand, resumed fighting.[52] He saw a lancer leaving the field—possibly Andrés Pico—and tried to engage him. Moore charged and was about to slash the man when the latter agilely spun his horse and, with his heavy wooden lance, blocked the blow and shattered the blade of Moore's saber just inches from the handguard. The captain threw away his saber and reached into his pommel holster for his Colt pistol when lances wielded by two vaqueros, Leandro Osuna and Dionisio Alipas, fatally struck him. Seeing Moore in peril, Lieutenant Hammond— Moore's brother-in-law—charged forward to save him, only to receive a series of lance wounds from the same vaqueros who had slain Moore. Hammond managed to retreat and receive medical attention, only to die of his injuries hours later.[53]

Inevitably, the better-mounted officers and noncommissioned officers reached the enemy well before the poorly mounted privates. Ironically, the officers' seeming advantage became their misfortune as they found themselves in the worst of the fray and suffered a disproportionate number of casualties compared to the privates. Ten dragoon officers and seven noncommissioned officers were either killed or wounded, while nine privates, entirely from Moore's Company C, were reported killed, missing or seriously wounded.[54]

Next into the action came the gallant band of noncommissioned officers led by 1st Sgt. Otis Moore of Company K. Once again, these well-mounted men rode far ahead of the privates and paid a price for outpacing their own support: Californio lances soon dispatched Sergeant Moore and five noncommissioned officers.[55] The private troopers of Company K, in contrast, suffered no fatalities. It is unclear whether First Sergeant Moore received any help at all from those privates riding so far behind him. Perhaps their poor mounts could not reach the fight until the first phase of the battle had ended. Or might there have been other reasons?

The dearth of casualties among the lower ranks suggests that on that day many of the private troopers (as well as their mounts) manifested a bad case of the slows. After wrestling mules over mountain after mountain and over unforgiving desert, surviving on reduced rations, watching boots and clothing shred, suffering cold and wet and heat, and enjoying little or no sleep for the whole previous day, their waning enthusiasm for battle should not surprise. Certainly, the officers had endured the same conditions and privations, but they at least might hope to earn fame and brevets in combat, and noncommissioned officers could find favor in the eyes of their company commanders. In contrast, lowly privates stood to gain some glory among their comrades and possible mention in official reports. They knew that displaying too much zeal in battle could get them killed or, at best, grievously wounded, which would consign them to a life as impoverished, crippled pensioners. Being poorly mounted certainly saved many privates from death. And did many of the privates, especially those of Company K, graciously leave the valiant and foolish heroics to those with bars on their shoulders or stripes on their sleeves?

Another unintended favor befalling the men, it turned out, came in the form of their thick woolen U.S. Army coats and blankets, which provided wholly unexpected shields from the lances. Whoever had not tossed, lost, sold, or traded his jacket would wear it gratefully that chilly morning, and may well have blessed his lucky stars that night. The heavy items restricted arm movement and thus saber-play, but also made it difficult for the lancer to see where to thrust. And when he did so, the substantial fabric may have absorbed and deflected some of the shock. Lances struck Captain Turner and Lieutenant Davidson, both clad in overcoats, and neither was seriously hurt. Turner wrote to his wife of the protection his outerwear had afforded: "My wound is nothing at all, barely through the skin on my right side, so slight that I have mentioned it scarcely to any one; the lance passed through my great coat, jacket and shirt, cutting the skin about an inch in length; I have experienced not the slightest inconvenience from it."[56]

Archibald Gillespie: The Beau Sabreur?

Imprudently speeding ahead of his detachment, Captain Gillespie of the marines galloped, sword drawn, and quickly found himself surrounded by several vaqueros—some of whom, he claimed, recognized him as the detested former military ruler of Los Angeles and thus a prized target. Gillespie had long prided himself on his swordsmanship, and longed to show these brash, upstart vaqueros the harm he could inflict. He embroidered the event for posterity:

> As soon as I was seen by the Enemy, they shouted, "Ya está Gillespie. Adventro hombres. Adventro!" (There is Gillespie. Charge, men. Charge!), and I was immediately set upon by seven fellows with long lances and Escopetas and when parrying a lance from the front, coming at full speed, having beaten them off on both sides with good effect, I was struck under the neck from the rear and unhorsed. As I was rising from the ground, a Californian drove his lance at my head, which, striking my mouth on my clenched teeth, only cut my lip and broke a front tooth, throwing me on my back as the fellow leaped his horse over me. Almost at the same instant another one of them dashed his lance into my left breast, making a fearful wound, but striking across the ribs, did not touch the lungs. I was on my feet very quickly, and cut my way to the rear.[57]

Gillespie survived through pure luck. He may have been armed with a short, curved marine officer's sword patterned after the light, thin scimitars carried by Napoleon's Mamluks in Egypt. Such ceremonial swords could wave about quite gracefully but could hardly parry lance thrusts, much less cut one's way through a pack of opponents. Indeed, having traveled through Mexico in disguise in order to get to California, he would not want to be carrying a sword with him. One must certainly discount much of what Gillespie wrote of his role in the fight. In any event, confused from pain and loss of blood, Gillespie wandered along the front lines trying to find Dr. Griffin, and finally escaped to safety at the rear.[58]

The costly opening battle had lasted less than a quarter of an hour and had already rendered Kearny's dragoons *hors de combat.* Within those short moments three dragoon officers and sixteen enlisted men lay dead or dying and another fifteen dragoons were badly wounded—more than half of the force engaged in the initial combat. Among the severely injured was General Kearny himself, having received two lance gashes that rendered him easy prey for a vaquero. In fact, one such was poised to deal Kearny the coup de grâce with a blow in the back, when Lieutenant Emory galloped up and fired at the lancer with his pistol, missing but chasing him off. In great pain, Kearny foolishly ordered a retreat. Confusion now reigned supreme: without effective leadership, all efforts to rally the men to order failed and a hectic backwards dash ensued. Gillespie described the twenty-five to thirty troopers then in the combat zone as "completely panic stricken, the best men in this command having already fallen in unequal combat."[59]

With the wounding of Kearny and the deaths of Johnston, Moore, and Hammond, Captain Turner became the senior functioning line officer on the field. The screams of wounded and terrified troopers, mixed with the cacophony of battle, the jeers of the Californios, and the neighing of panicked horses, sounded to Turner as if all hell had broken loose. But although he had never seen combat, he instinctively appreciated the peril to troops who attempt to flee from lancers: showing one's back to a lancer was an invitation to be speared. Instantaneously, Turner realized that the entire detachment might be slaughtered by retreating. Sitting proudly erect in the saddle, saber drawn, calm face masking an inner sickening fear, he cantered about the frightened men as if on Fort Leavenworth's parade ground, and exhorted, "No, never, men. Never turn your backs on these men, or you will all be cut down. Dismount!"[60]

Although inexperienced, poorly mounted, and disorganized, the dragoons were still better armed than the vaqueros. With Turner's rallying cry, the Americans drew their firearms, smartly formed a skirmish line, and stood their ground. Typical of their spirit that day was the mood of Pvt. John Brown of Company C. Though hardly a model soldier, Brown, with blood streaming from his lacerations, stood and fought alongside Turner. The morning dampness may have hampered reloading his flintlock pistol, but the weapon afforded him at least one shot. Private Bowen and others mentioned in their memoirs that "some of us had pistols" nestled in covered leather pommel holsters, unaffected by the climate. Using these, the dragoons shot at the menacing vaqueros and thereby saved their own lives.[61]

Incorrectly, then, too many historians, such as Kearny biographer Dwight Clarke, conveniently pin the military disaster at San Pasqual on defective Hall carbines. Clarke wrote: "The carbines were well-nigh useless because of the wet weather and sodden ammunition."[62] To be sure, Hall carbines seldom performed perfectly, but their failures were not generally due to wet gunpowder. In fact, in no other campaign—including the protracted war against the Seminoles in Florida's steamy swamps—were these weapons ever reported to have been incapacitated by inclement weather. Unlike flintlock weapons, these carbines were perfectly functional under wet conditions. The double flaps of each dragoon's leather cartridge box, carried on his belt, kept between thirty and forty-four paper-wrapped carbine rounds perfectly protected, and each fresh round from a properly closed box was dry and quite effective.[63] So, contrary to the theories of some, these cartridges could not have been damaged by the cold, fog, and drizzle at San Pasqual or anywhere.

In short, the carbines did play a role on that fateful day. Imagine the difficulty encountered by shivering troopers, mounted on agitated animals, as they tried to carefully place the small cop-per percussion cap upon the weapon's tiny nipple.[64] The fulmi-nate charge of the cap was often too weak to light the gunpowder. Even in the best of weather and even once the cap was placed on the nipple, it sometimes took several trigger pulls to fire the gun.[65] A further problem with the Halls likely manifested itself early in the battle. When marching, troops carried their carbines with muzzles pointed down, so some loose powder and ball inevi-tably bled down from the weapon's breech and out of the barrel as the troops bounced along the trail. In 1840 an army inspector observed the result of this design flaw: "[A]fter a day's march of 25 to 30 [miles] . . . a loss of fire of 2/5 might be expected" from the powder leaking down the muzzle.[66]

But once the sun rose and the men dismounted, their Halls served them well. In fact, the account of on-the-scene weapons expert Kit Carson refutes claims that Hall carbines were useless that day: as noted, the stock of Carson's trusty plains rifle broke in his fall from his horse; Carson picked up a dead trooper's Hall carbine and cartridge box and "joined in the melee,"[67] noting no problems with them anywhere in his autobiography. Other proof of the carbine's utility came but moments later. Upon Turner's command, the troops dismounted, formed a skirmish line, and with their Halls noisily banged away at the vaqueros, who quickly retreated beyond carbine range.[68] If the Hall carbines had not been operative due to the damp and cold, even the small band of vaqueros could have easily overwhelmed Turner's makeshift for-mation. Yet with the dragoons' functional carbines and remaining members rushing to their rescue, Pico elected not to risk more casualties.

As further evidence, the Hall carbines would again prove their efficiency the very next day. Kearny's report states that his dismounted troops charged a strong Mexican force that was shooting at them from Mule Hill. Carbines in hand, the dragoons advanced and, without losing a soldier, drove the Mexicans off the hill. Kearny claimed, though he may have exaggerated, that the enemy lost five men at Mule Hill. Considering that sabers and short-ranged pistols would be insufficient for such a long-range engagement, it is reasonable to assume that the dragoons employed their slightly longer-range Halls to excellent effect.[69]

Big Guns and a Pause in Fighting

By the final moments of the short-lived event of December 6, the battle had disintegrated into a scene of dismounted dragoons firing their Halls at distant mounted vaqueros. Finally, Kearny's slow-moving artillery groaned into action. Two mountain howitzers, each attached by ropes and rawhide straps to jury-rigged prairie limbers and each pulled by a pair of mules, wobbled to the front like a child's homemade toys. The men attempted to turn the guns so their barrels would point at the enemy and not at Turner's dragoons and the rifle-toting Bear Flaggers, sailors, and marines assembled as a defensive shield.

It was at this time the dragoons lost one of their howitzers to the enemy. There are three different accounts of this event. Kearny, in his official report of December 13, 1846, blames the loss upon restive mules: "Our howitzers were now brought into the action but coming to the front at the conflict, before they were turned so as to admit of being fired upon the retreating enemy, the two mules before one of them [mule teams] got alarmed, and freeing themselves from their drivers ran off & among the enemy, & was lost to us."[70]

Dr. Griffin, an otherwise reliable witness to the battle, has a different account. He reported that the howitzer crew of three had been attacked by the vaqueros; one gun's driver was speared while attempting to steer the mules, and the other gunners were slaughtered. But company returns for December 31 listed all the men assigned to either gun detail as unharmed. Given that the doctor was stationed in the rear and received this information by hearsay it must hold, little, if any value.[71]

The self-promoting Gillespie offered a more accurate account in his report to Commodore Stockton. According to Gillespie, the howitzer was lost during a repositioning of the troops. He wrote that Turner chose to have his troops fall back upon the reserves and ordered the two cannon to follow his movement. One of the guns did so and Turner's men rallied around it. But the blown mules struggled to pull the second howitzer to the rear. Unable to speed the mules, and with the vaqueros closing in, its gun crew panicked and raced on foot for the safety of Turner's line, abandoning the weapon.[72]

Gillespie embellished his report by asserting that, though gravely wounded and nearly unconscious, he called upon the retreating men to "save the gun," but that they refused to do so. He recalled his horror at seeing vaqueros ride up and, using a lariat with a lance to prod the flanks of the two mules, moved the gun into Pico's lines. Fortunately for the dragoons, the gun's ammunition chest had been removed earlier. But even knowing that his Californios were too low on gunpowder to use the howitzer, Pico wisely removed it from the field lest it fall back into Kearny's hands.

To say the least, Kearny was furious over the loss of his cannon—a humiliation spared that contemporary personification of military greatness, the Duke of Wellington. (Of course, Gen. Zachary Taylor's loss of two cannon at the Battle of Buena Vista two months later, while a source of pride to the Mexican army, would not tarnish Taylor's great "victory.") With one exception, every officer who survived the battle would receive Kearny's recommendation to Congress for a brevet rank for heroism. That single exception was Lieutenant Davidson, who had abandoned the howitzers under his care and lost one without a struggle. Although Kearny never blamed Davidson explicitly, neglecting to recommend a brevet for him signaled his profound displeasure with the junior officer. As we shall soon see, the loss of the howitzer and the facts under which it was lost would be raised anew by Frémont at his court-martial.

Back on the firing line, the crew wheeled the remaining howitzer into battery position and discovered that it, too, lacked an ammunition chest. In good time the ever-active Emory galloped back to the pack train, secured a chest of artillery ammunition, and raced back to the front with it. Into the surviving howitzer the troops rammed home a charge of gunpowder and a load of grapeshot and took aim. To fire the weapon a crewmember had to hold a smoldering stick called a "port-fire" against the vent hole atop the rear of its barrel. But in the chaos, nobody had bothered even to secure, much less light, a port-fire. In his romanticized account Gillespie claimed to have used a common type of self-lighting or friction-lit match known as a cigar Locofoco to set off the howitzer, before fainting from his wounds. This rousing tale, the subject of a later painting, is unfortunately entirely apocryphal. First, upon ignition the blow-back from the vent hole would have badly burned Gillespie's hand and uniform, neither of which occurred; second, it is unlikely anyone would have allowed a bleeding, half-conscious man close enough to the gun to ignite it; and third, from all credible accounts the howitzer was never actually fired.

The quartermaster, Captain Swords, stationed to the rear, reported hearing only a single cannon discharge—and not from the dragoon howitzer but from the Sutter gun. Its navy crew smartly deployed the antiquated weapon and Midn. James Duncan likely fired a round of grapeshot. Chased briefly by a few Bear Flaggers, the Californios quickly retreated out of range. With this, at eight in the morning, the fighting ended for the day.[73]

After Pico's withdrawal the dragoons sent parties to gather their wounded and bring them to Dr. Griffin. Now eighteen dragoons lay dead and another thirteen were wounded, some of whom would die within hours, staining the forsaken field. The enemy had retreated but still surrounded the dragoons at a safe distance. The dragoons thus found themselves encircled thirty-nine rough miles from the well-armed, well-supplied Pacific Squadron harbored in San Diego Bay.[74]

Assuming command from the wounded Kearny, Captain Turner immediately wrote to Commodore Stockton of the regiment's desperate plight:

We have about eighteen killed and fourteen or fifteen wounded; several so severely that it may be impracticable to move them for several days. I have to suggest to you the propriety of dispatching, without delay, a considerable force to meet us on the route to San Diego, via the Soledad and San Bernardo, or to find us at this place; also, that you will send up carts or some other means of transporting our wounded to San Diego. We are without provisions, and in our present situation find it impracticable to obtain cattle from the ranches in the vicinity.[75]

The messengers snuck past enemy lines and delivered Turner's plea. To his ever-lasting discredit, the commodore took no immediate action to assist Kearny.[76]

Pico reported losing one man, with fourteen seriously hurt. Two weeks after the battle Dr. Griffin offered to treat the enemy wounded, but Pico rejected the favor. A report later reached the doctor that eleven Californios had been killed in a recent fight with the Luiseño tribe near Temecula, but he and others believed they had actually died fighting Kearny's forces.[77]

With the coming of evening, the dragoons buried their fallen in a willow grove near where the battle had commenced. Lieutenant Emory movingly observed the rites: "Thus were put to rest together, and forever, a band of brave and heroic men. The march of 2,000 miles had brought our little command, both officers and men, to know each other well. Community of hardships, dangers, and privations that produced relations of mutual regard which caused their loss to sink deeply in our memories."[78]

The next day failed to bring relief to Kearny's command. Kearny believed that he was on his own. "The morning of the 7th dawned upon the saddest and most dispirited Camp, perhaps, ever known in the American Arms," wrote Captain Gillespie.[79] An exaggeration to be sure, but their casualties and the ferocious bravery of the vaqueros revealed the latter to be anything but cowards, and this realization had deeply shocked the dragoons.

The troopers quickly loaded the wounded onto makeshift travois and headed south with the command. Kearny sent calls for help to Commodore Stockton. The timid commodore, proffering the excuse that he lacked horses and mules, again declined to send a relief force. Meanwhile the Californios occupied the surrounding hills, content to harass the dragoons and plan their next move. The dragoons reached Rancho de San Bernardo at about two in the afternoon. Finding its owner not present, they freely helped themselves to the food they found on the premises and, after a short rest, continued their retreat.[80]

Pico's vaqueros repeatedly intimidated the slow-moving column. Given the discomfort of the injured, the officers thought it advisable to settle atop a nearby knoll—later named Mule Hill—and await relief. As noted, a party of skirmishers drove the vaqueros from the slopes and Kearny took possession of the hill. He placed his remaining howitzer and the Sutter gun on the slopes and had the men move rocks to construct crude defensive positions. Here, the soldiers finally felt secure from enemy attacks until help might arrive. Only then did it dawn on them that they had comfortably entrenched themselves on a hill without any access to water.

The Navy to the Rescue

Realizing that Pico had maneuvered him into an untenable position and no longer contemptuous of assistance from the navy, Kearny again cried for help. That evening he sent Carson, Beale, and a Luiseño named Panto to slip through the lines and somehow secure aid from the erstwhile uncooperative Stockton.[81] They managed to get through, and on the ninth of December Stockton finally dispatched a detachment of 180 sailors and marines to rescue Kearny. On the evening of December 10, a relief force under Lt. Andrew Gray arrived and lifted the siege.

With the road to the harbor now clear, Kearny piled saddles, equipage, and supplies and burned them before resuming his retreat. On the way to San Diego, the ravenous troops fell upon the deserted but well-larded rancho of Señor Francisco Alvarado. Asserting their belief in the rumor that Alvarado was in league with Pico, the men promptly declared his estate forfeit. But hunger would have easily trumped discipline, regardless of the verity of Alvarado's alleged treachery. An appalled Emory spoke for the more civil among the troops when he wrote that the "havoc committed" by the starving dragoons "on the comestibles was immense."[82]

When the column reached its destination in San Diego, their seafaring comrades-in-arms showered them with accolades and, still better, with fresh clothing, medical care, and food. The dragoons did not stand upon ceremony when offered sailor uniforms, even though there were no boots available. Kearny dispatched Captain Swords to the Sandwich Islands to stock up on precious supplies and edibles. Swords left San Diego on December 21 and arrived in Honolulu eighteen days later, but due to their exorbitant prices could purchase only "articles as were indispensable for our operations in California," and returned after twenty-five days at sea.[83]

While the dragoons rested, ate, refitted, and recuperated, Kearny penned his report to the War Department. Not surprisingly, he proclaimed victory over a force of superior strength, inflating enemy numbers to 160. Kearny baldly reasoned that, despite heavy losses, at the end of the battle he held the field and thus had vanquished the enemy. In the account he pinned the loss of the howitzer not on his frightened crew or even on the irresponsible Lieutenant Davidson, but on runaway mules.[84]

Immediate Costs and Rewards of the Battle

Kearny remained well regarded by many of the troops despite the debacle at San Pasqual, and none of his men would publicly criticize him. After the battle a private described him as "the best explication of a republican Soldier possible, rigorously strict almost to severity, when on duty, but affable, just, and kind when off duty."[85] One of his junior officers wrote that Kearny was "a rigid disciplinarian, and known only to the *honest citizen* to be respected and esteemed as a gentleman well qualified for anything in life"[86] (emphasis in original). Second Lieutenant Watson, who was to serve under Kearny after the dragoons reached San Diego, opined:

> Brigadier General Kearny is one of the most polite, gentle-manly and urbane men I have ever known, kind and affa-ble in his conversation, polite in his bearing and in a word he is both as a gentleman and a soldier one of the very first men in the army or this country. . . . [T]here is no detail however minute connected with the army . . . the General did not give his personal attention, studying the comforts of the men, even many times to the neglect of his own. To the Military ability, and the natural fondness which the whole army had for him was the cause for our success.[87]

In contrast, the candid Lieutenant Watson declared Stockton unfit for command as "the most overrated man I have ever met"—an opinion he claimed matched "the sentiment of a great many or most of the men of the squadron." In particular, he found him "pompous, inflated, morose, and not infrequently course and vulgar in his manners, wrapped up in his own importance, he is totally regardless of the feelings of others, vain beyond belief."[88]

At the campaign's end Congress would later award Kearny a brevet rank of major general for his actions in New Mexico and California. If Congress thought San Pasqual a victory, it was cer-tainly a costly one. All told, the dragoons had lost twenty-two sol-diers, a civilian member of the topographical engineers, and a Bear Flagger. In the weeks that followed a number of dragoons received surgeon's certificates declaring them unfit for service due to wounds. These heavy losses forced Kearny on December 28 to issue an order disbanding Company K and transferring its forty-three surviving enlisted men to Company C; that company of elite dragoons, having no sound horses upon which to ride, would now be common foot soldiers.[89]

Over the years much ink has been spilt debating whether San Pasqual counts as a victory or a defeat. Biographer Clarke completely agreed with Kearny's claim that he had triumphed according to military criteria because—like the Duke of Wellington at Waterloo—he had held his ground whereas the enemy ultimately retreated.[90] But war is not a sporting event. However assessed, the event permanently ended the combat effectiveness of the dragoon squadron. Kearny's men endured considerable misery to come to California, only to have their sacrifices, and the lives of many, squandered in a needless battle. Beyond the human suffering, San Pasqual resulted in the significantly reduced effectiveness of the only detachment of regular army troops then stationed in Alta California. Fortunately for the war effort as a whole, the immediate and fortuitous overland arrival of Cooke's Mormon Battalion, and by sea the 3rd Artillery's Company F and the 1st New York Volunteers, would crush the Californio uprising regardless of what had happened at San Pasqual.[91]

Interestingly, most historians have overlooked, perhaps, the most valuable result of Kearny's torturous 1846 march to California: the Emory Report. The thirty-five-year-old Marylander in the Topographical Engineers, who had saved Kearny's life, wrote a masterful account of the trek from Santa Fe to San Diego. Congress immediately recognized its importance and published no fewer than 10,250 copies. Emory's precise, detailed map supplanted all previous ones; it "became a standard reference on the Southwest and guided countless overland parties to the Pacific."[92] Emory had included meticulous accounts of the plants, animals, peoples, geology, climate, and archaeological ruins enriching the region, and in 1854 Secretary of State James Buchanan and James Gadsden gratefully consulted his findings as they negotiated with Mexico to purchase the Gila region of southern Arizona for the transcontinental railroad route.[93]

The Conquest of the Pueblo de Los Angeles

At the conclusion of the battle of San Pasqual the once-proud dragoons were demoted in the military hierarchy. General Kearny, who prior to the battle proudly commanded a mounted force, and although superior in rank to Stockton, now graciously subordinated himself to serve under the commodore as his aide de camp. Captain Turner, commanding the dragoon company, was forced to have them serve as foot soldiers. On December 23 he wrote to Commodore Stockton, "I have the honor to state that, in my opinion, not one of the horses referred to is fit for dragoon service, being too poor and weak for any such purpose; also, that the company of dragoons under my command can do much better service on foot than mounted on those horses."[94]

In preparation for another campaign against the Californios, Kearny oversaw the training of sailors and marines. Drawing on knowledge from his infantry days, he taught them how to march in a column, form into a two-rank firing line, and position themselves as a hollow square to fend off cavalry. By late December they were ready to march. Emory was impressed by the rapid adaptability of the sailors and marines to foot soldiery. On December 28, 1846, as the band from the USS *Congress* played patriotic airs, Stockton began his march from San Diego to the Pueblo de Los Angeles. His force consisted of forty-seven naval artillerists with six pieces of artillery, forty-eight volunteers, fifty-seven dismounted dragoons, 397 sailors and marines, and a supply train. There he expected to meet with Frémont's army moving south from Monterey, and with this combined force they would crush Pico and the Californios.[95]

The combined Yankee detachment marched steadily toward its objective, unhindered by the enemy. But on January 8, Stockton's force found themselves facing General Flores and his five hundred men and artillery on the west bank of the San Gabriel River. Kearny, following the military orthodoxy that artillery is not to cross rivers while under fire, wished to unlimber the artillery on the east bank to give cover to the crossing. Stockton, however, believed the enemy was out of artillery range and ordered that the guns cross the river. Lieutenant Watson observed, "Although this was extremely unmilitary, yet the Gen. [Kearny] to avoid collision consented."[96]

So the American troops, with their unlimbered artillery pulled by sailors, advanced across the river. Turner's dragoons, supported by sailor musketeers, led the advance as skirmishers with sailors on either flank, followed by four 9-pound artillery pieces. The river was about one hundred yards wide, knee-deep, with a quicksand bottom. Despite the quagmire that nearly swallowed his entire battery, and blessed with Flores' ineffective gunfire, Stockton gained the opposite bank within fifteen minutes; his cannon went into battery and opened fire. One sailor had been struck by grapeshot and killed during the crossing.[97]

Stockton's artillery fire immediately devastated the Californios' solitary long-range gun. Kearny formed his sailors and foot soldiers, ordering them to fix bayonets and advance. Relying upon his training as an infantry officer, he twice formed his men into protective hollow squares when threatened by cavalry charges and drove the Californios from the field. In marked contrast to the Battle of San Pasqual, the dragoon regiment suffered but a single casualty when trooper Mark Childs had a spent musket ball lodge in his heel.[98]

On the next day, with their band playing patriotic music, the commodore's troops advanced briskly across the broad La Mesa plain, marching in a large square formation around artillery, baggage train, and cattle. Kearny had given this unique order so the troops, still unskilled in organizing into a hollow square on the march, would already be so formed. As they neared the present town of Vernon, Flores deployed his artillery and fired a few unprofitable rounds. Stockton's artillery response resulted in minor damage to the Californios.

Before long, Flores was out of ammunition and would soon be out of options. But he still had plenty of fight left and ordered a daring charge by his lance-wielding vaqueros, reasoning that what had worked so well at San Pasqual would also work here. However,

Flores was not as valiant as Pico, and Kearny was no longer the blunderer of San Pasqual. Employing tactics he had learned during the War of 1812, Kearny formed his troops into two ranks, had the front rank kneel, and ordered them to hold their fire until the lancers were nearly upon them. Lieutenant Watson breathlessly witnessed the Californios' attack:

> I have never before seen in my life a more beautiful sight than they presented. They were mounted on elegant horses [and] are without exception the best horsemen in the world. They all had broad white bands around their hats, we learned after that this was worn by them as a distinguishing mark, for as they said that they should break our lines, and then in confusion which would ensure they might kill some of their friends, unless there was some mark by which they might be known. . . . They formed in a single file, and charged on us at full speed, we remained firm in our ranks, they came within fifty yards of our left flank, when they received a most galling fire of musketry from our lines.[99]

The effect of the ragged volley was devastating as .69-caliber lead balls, along with a round of grapeshot, tore into the enemy ranks and stopped the charge in its tracks. According to Watson, "We saw a number of vacant saddles, and wounded horses. The Californios retreated in considerable confusion." Flores ordered another charge, this time simultaneously from two directions. Again the steady musketry and a grapeshot round turned back the vaqueros. The Californios retreated north. Hoping to obtain a better deal from the approaching Frémont, they surrendered to him at Rancho Cahuenga, in present-day North Hollywood, on January 13, 1847.[100]

Stockton's force entered the Pueblo de Los Angeles on January 10 and Gillespie, wounded yet again, proudly raised the Stars and Stripes over his old headquarters.[101] The next day Lieutenant Watson reported rumors of "something going on between Gen.

Kearny, Com. Stockton, and Col. Frémont of an unpleasant character, which has not leaked out." He also noted that heavy drinking by sailors and dragoons on the evening of January 19 resulted in one hundred men "almost helpless Drunk, and a good many staggering in their ranks." Watson proudly recorded that, after the flag-raising and victory celebration, his sober marines were able to march the hungover sailors to their ship awaiting them at San Pedro.[102]

Captain Cooke would later note on the Company C muster roll for January–February 1847 that, despite not having been paid in ten months, the men's discipline and accoutrements were good and instruction was improving; but as for their clothing: "[a] mixture of soldier, sailor & citizen; many ragged, some positively naked."[103] Once again, such was a dragoon's lot.

While the dragoons settled into garrison duty in Pueblo de Los Angeles, Kearny bore direct orders from President Polk giving him military command of California. Frémont, however, was unwilling to act under his command. Colonel Frémont, having been appointed military governor by Commodore Stockton and consistently backed by him, refused to relinquish his authority and troops to General Kearny, his superior officer. Luckily, the arrival of Cooke and his 550 Mormons in San Diego on January 29 shifted the balance of military power to Kearny, averting an ugly, possibly armed confrontation between him and Frémont. Colonel Mason, who had set sail from New York bearing dispatches for Kearny, arrived by the supply ship *Erie* in March of 1847. When Mason heard of Frémont's disobedience to a superior officer, he threatened to place the rebellious Pathfinder in irons. Frémont responded and challenged Mason to a duel with shotguns. Cooler heads prevailed.[104]

Capt. Henry Turner, having arrived back in St. Louis, wrote in a personal letter of Frémont's insolent and mutinous conduct toward Kearny, a superior officer. Turner, as did all regular army officers stationed in California, believed that Frémont's contemptuous behavior nearly resulted in a civil war between the Bear Flaggers and the army and, as such, bordered on treason. He believed it was only the departure of Stockton, coupled with the timely arrival of Commodores William Shubrick and James Biddle (who backed Kearny), that forced Frémont to back down.[105]

On May 31, Kearny, Frémont, Emory, Turner, an escort composed of fifteen members of the Mormon Battalion, a few discharged dragoons, and about forty-five others left California for Fort Leavenworth. Cooke, having been promoted to the rank of major in the 2nd Dragoons effective February 16, 1847, resigned his commission with the Mormon Battalion and joined Kearny on his trip east. With Kearny's departure, Colonel Mason became the military governor of the state.[106] Cooke's promotion resulted in the regiment losing one of its most capable and experienced officers.

Aftermath

On August 22 Kearny's party arrived at Leavenworth to a hero's welcome, complete with a thirteen-gun salute. Following the ceremonies, Kearny promptly arrested Frémont, charged him with mutiny, and ordered the brash explorer officer to Washington, D.C., to stand trial before a court-martial panel. Senator Thomas Benton, Frémont's powerful father-in-law, was furious and would attempt to turn the court-martial into an investigation of Kearny's performance at San Pasqual.

There was private grumbling among officers and men over Kearny's leadership at San Pasqual. Lt. John Hollingsworth of Stevenson's 1st New York claimed to have gained the impression from Dr. Griffin that someone, likely Kearny, had blundered: "There was a great mistake made somewhere but who made it is difficult to determine as the officers who were in it generally do not like to talk about it."[107] Explicit criticism of the general would later come from the likes of Commodore Stockton, Captain Gillespie, General Frémont, and Senator Benton. The latter gentleman would be acting as Frémont's counsel at the court-martial.

At the hearing, Frémont attempted to discredit Kearny by adroitly pointing out that Kearny minimized the loss of the gun. He pointed out: "The loss of cannon is a great grief in all armies; the recovery is a subject of exultation. The loss is often without discredit; the recovery is always with honor. They are trophies which one side is proud to take and the other to recover. The loss and recovery of these trophies is a point of honor, independent of the value of the thing, and for which brave men die. The loss is always excused and lamented; the recovery is always reported and celebrated." Benton may have also established that Kearny was retreating when the howitzer was lost. Alas, Frémont was unsuccessful when the court properly declared as irrelevant his questions to Kearny concerning the battle.[108] Generations of historians of the battle have struggled with what really occurred at San Pasqual. Had Frémont not failed in his efforts to embarrass Kearny by forcing him to answer this question, he would have gained evidence concerning what happened that misty December morning at San Pasqual.

On January 31, 1848, the court-martial panel sustained Kearny's charge of mutiny against Frémont and, although the president later reversed this finding, sustained the specification charging Frémont of refusing to follow Kearny's orders. A fuming and chastised Frémont promptly resigned his commission in the Mounted Rifles.[109]

Even though the war neared its conclusion, the army needed the vital services of General Kearny. Although worn and sickly, he traveled to Mexico to act as commander at Vera Cruz and then to Mexico City to become military governor and, with war's end, supervise the removal of Yankee troops from Mexico. Benton, however, was not through with going after Kearny. On August 9, 1848, while the Senate considered crowning Kearny with a major general's brevet, "Old Bullion" Benton rose in opposition. He argued that Kearny had covered up his tactical blunders at San Pasqual, as it was a disastrous defeat by about equal numbers through the mismanagement of the general, and that his report thereof is false, and that he was afterward besieged on the hill of San Bernardo for four days by inferior numbers, and unnecessarily burnt his baggage.

Unable to stop the Senate's confirmation of the promotion, Benton next initiated proceedings in the Senate to have the president authorize a court-martial of Kearny, upon the specification that he attempted to foment civil war in California when he confronted Benton's son-in-law Frémont, and had filed a false report concerning what had really occurred at San Pasqual. This measure passed the Senate and, for the moment, historians were potentially afforded the opportunity to review what had occurred at San Pasqual.[110] But it was not to be. While serving in Mexico, Kearny fell seriously ill with yellow fever and had to return to his home in St. Louis, where he died on October 31, 1848, at the age of fifty-five. With Kearny's untimely passing, Benton's heated call for an inquisition of the general ended.[111]

There was yet another casualty resulting from San Pasqual. On July 21, 1848, Bvt. Maj. Henry Turner, West Point class of 1834, resigned his captaincy, likely tired both of war and of army politics. One of Kearny's most trusted officers; he would go on to become a successful banker in Missouri. With his resignation Turner became the ninth of Kearny's original gifted cast of dragoon commanders lost to death, transfer, or resignation during the Mexican War.

CHAPTER 9

Love's Defeat at
Coon Creeks

And when the bugle sounded, our captain gave command.
"To arms, to arms!" he shouted, "and by your horses stand!"
I saw the smoke ascending, it seemed to reach the sky,
And then the thought it struck me, my time had come to die.

Cowboy Songs and Other Frontier Ballads,
collected by John A. Lomax (1929)

A s the reader will recall, in October 1846 General Kearny, receiving the news from Kit Carson that California had been captured by John Frémont's Bear Flaggers and the navy, broke up Company B, sending it back with Major Sumner to refit and recruit at Fort Leavenworth. During the Mexican-American War, Jefferson Barracks and Fort Leavenworth were beehives of activity. These posts served as major staging areas for supplies and troops heading to the far-flung places where the war was being fought, as well as training facilities where the recruits learned basic drill, companies were organized, and men equipped.

While many officers were gaining glory and brevets on distant battlefields, officers stationed at these posts had the unrewarding task of ordering supplies and instructing recruits in the school of the soldier. Three such officers were 1st Lieutenants Henry Stanton, Eugene McLean, and Leonidas Jenkins.[1] Similar to those other officers left behind, they performed their important duties but wished for the public acclaim and military honors endowed upon brother officers engaged in combat.[2]

Returning from service in New Mexico, Lt. John Love found correspondence from Lieutenant McLean with the news from Fort Leavenworth. Renewing feelings typical of those officers serving back in the States, McLean wrote:

> We are still here doing peace service, while our "brother warriors" are earning for themselves imperishable fame in the field; and we feel this the more deeply as we appear to be the only company so situated in the whole army; sometimes when I sit down and ponder over matters, I can hardly realize that I am here and every body else fighting, or marching to fight with hearts bounding with hopes of glory and distinction before them. All is here so peaceful and calm; the sad and solemn beauty of the scenery so little like war and its noisy accompaniments that I can scarcely bring myself to think that such a thing is going on. But luck is, nevertheless, the fact, and here are we enjoying all the comforts of a soldier's life, while you and every one else are undergoing the hardships, fatigues, and dangers—I cannot last, I feel as if we could not linger out an inglorious existence here while all our friends are in the field.
>
> A few days ago [Lt. Richard] Ewell[3] was here, and tried hard to be ordered out to join you; but it was no use the Lt. Col. could not take the *responsibility.*—He says he feels more disgusted that we *can;* for we have the consolation of knowing that our company has not been ordered, whereas his is in the field, and *he* on recruiting service. He feels quite bad about it, and would give any thing in the world to be with you.[4] (emphasis in original)

McLean reminded Love that due to the war, there were many promotions occurring in the dragoons.[5] At this time the dragoons had already lost some of their most promising officers: Stephen

Kearny, as he had been promoted to the rank of general, Edwin Sumner gained the rank of major in the 2nd Dragoons, Allen had died of illness, and in December of 1846, Johnston, Moore, and Hammond would be killed in action at San Pasqual. McLean supplied Love with news of the war: "Taylor's army is on the march for Monterrey. [General William] Worth is in advance with his divisions where if he has luck he may retrieve his former blunder.[6] They marched from Camargo—all their baggage and so on is taken on pack mules—transportation by wagons being, it is said, impracticable. . . . The health of the regulars is good but there has been much sickness amongst the volunteers and a great deal of mortality.[7]

In the fall of 1846 a detachment under the command of Major Sumner left New Mexico, marching east to Fort Leavenworth. Sumner, now a major in the 2nd Dragoons, and newly promoted 2nd Lt. Bezaleel Armstrong were under orders to proceed to Texas, where they were to rendezvous with their new regiment. Included in this eastbound detachment were Lieutenant Love, Corporal Baker, and the entirety of Company B's noncommissioned officers. The trip was hard on men and animals, as it was late in the season and there was not much grass for their stock to graze upon; fortunately, Love had purchased a supply of corn and fresh mules from villagers before the detachment had left New Mexico, and the trip was completed without serious incident.[8]

After their return to "the states," the two young officers, Lieutenants Love and Armstrong, headed by steamer for St. Louis, where they knocked about, enjoying thoroughly the sights and comforts of this wide-open city. From there, Armstrong proceeded down the Mississippi to New Orleans and thence to Brazos Island, Texas, where he was to take over the temporary command of a group of 2nd Dragoon recruits bound for the war. Love, meanwhile, went up the Mississippi River to the Ohio River thence to Dayton, Ohio, on recruiting duty with directions to build Company B to its wartime complement of eighty enlisted men.

Soon after his arrival in Dayton, Love received word from Armstrong that he had contracted a serious case of dysentery, which plagued him while he was encamped upon Brazos Island.[9] Nevertheless, the lieutenant bravely made his way to the seat of war at Vera Cruz, but there the dysentery worsened. Armstrong, aged twenty-six, was to die of dysentery on February 17, 1849.[10]

In April of 1847, Love received a letter containing remarkably frank complaints from three of his recruits who were undergoing basic training at Newport Barracks, Kentucky.

> We wish to inform you that our condition is very unpleasant on account of the absence of our officers. We are here drilled in the infantry squads, and obliged to do duties that we believe we would be exempted of were you with us and on this account there is some, not inconsiderable, dissatisfaction prevailing in regard to our having no officers of our own company with us. We would inform you that the discord referred to, has already been the cause of the one of the company—deserting—but we do not think that any who came with us, will, on any consideration be guilty of so base an act, but could you favor us with an officer of our own, greater satisfaction would exist, and a greater degree of confidence would be concentrated in you by your men. We consider it right you should know these circumstances and also that is binding on us to inform you of it. [Anthony] Gardner is dead and another one of the Company [are] not expected to recover. We have considered it our duty to write this much.
>   We remain your friends and Obedient soldiers,
>   John W. George
>   Jeptha Powell
>   George W. Gibson[11]

The letter moved the lieutenant. A few weeks after receiving this letter, Love "liberated" his sorrowful recruits and sent them to be trained as dragoons at Jefferson Barracks. While Lieutenant Love busily scoured the countryside of Ohio and Indiana for dragoon recruits, Lieutenant Jenkins had set up a recruiting station in St. Louis and was fast reaching his quota of recruits. The energetic lieutenant took his men down to Jefferson Barracks, where he drilled and equipped them. In the following letter from Lieutenant Jenkins to Lieutenant Love we are given a glimpse of the mindset of a young officer who was performing the valuable task of securing and training recruits, but feels that his chance for fame and brevet rank was fast slipping away while the star of his dear friend was on the rise.

I have just returned from Fort Leavenworth where I have been and left 25 recruits and 24 sorrel horses for your company.[12] A fair lot of men and tollerable [*sic*] horses and the new saddle and equipments.[13] It stormed all the way up and took me 16 days to make the march.[14] I came back by steamboat. . . . I have 13 men and in a few days think I will make it up to 20—as good men as ever enlisted.[15] They get along rapidly in their drill on foot and if I only had a few horses and saddles could have them pretty well instructed by the time that you are ready to receive them. . . . Where do you expect to get your horses? If I had a few here for drill I could advance your men considerably in the school of the trooper mounted. I am disgusted with the duty. Won't you exchange with me? This would be a delightful place for you and you won glory enough last summer.[16]

By spring of 1847, Lieutenants Love and Jenkins had recruited enough men to rebuild Company B to full wartime strength. Love's recruits, having undergone their basic training at Newport Barracks or Jefferson Barracks, were now assembled and formed into Company B at Fort Leavenworth. It was here that they underwent mounted drill.

Corporal Baker, meanwhile, with barely a year in service to proclaim himself a veteran, proudly described for his nephew his daily duties and responsibility of turning the raw recruits into hard-riding dragoons: "Our Company is about full and will be organized either here or at Jefferson Barracks near St. Louis in about three weeks, when we will get orders to proceed either to join Gen. Scott or, once again, to visit Santa Fe, I prefer the latter, on account of the climate for it is the most healthy climate in the world."[17]

Company B into the Breach

On June 7, 1847, Company B of the First Dragoons, many of whom were troopers wearing the company's signature nonregulation blue shirts and black slouch hats, passed in review on the parade ground, took the salutes of Lieutenant Colonel Wharton, and rode out of Fort Leavenworth bound for Santa Fe.[18] Their mission was to escort Paymaster Edward Bodine with a dozen wagons of supplies and $350,000 to pay monies owing the troops in New Mexico. Accompanying the column was Lt. Jack Duer of the U.S. Navy who, like Archibald Gillespie and Edward Beale before him, was carrying dispatches overland to California. Lieutenant Love proudly rode at the head of the column. This was the first time he was allowed to lead an independent command, yet he was no stranger to the Santa Fe Trail, having previously accompanied many expeditions on the trail in peace and in war.

It took considerable time to train the mounted soldier of the nineteenth century. A soldier may be readily taught how to march and fight while on foot, but it is quite another thing to instruct him how to march, attack, and rally when on horseback. Further, in contrast to the foot soldier, the mounted trooper had to learn how to care for, feed, groom, and saddle his mount. He also was required to be taught the proper care of his tack and horse.

The 1841 manual for the training of dragoons, the *Poinsett Cavalry Tactics*, contemplated that the typical recruit was to spend his first six weeks in dismounted drill, the next twelve weeks learning to ride, and five weeks learning to ride in military formation. Due to the immediate need of reinforcements to quell the recent uprising in New Mexico, the 1841 manual was ignored. Most of B

Company's recruits had to learn in fewer than two months' time the skills a dragoon in peacetime usually learned in six.

George Ruxton, a British cavalry officer footloose in the west, described Jenkins's men riding to Fort Leavenworth from St. Louis as "superbly mounted: the horses, uniting plenty of blood with bone, so a great desideration for cavalry, about fifteen hands high, and excellent condition." He was less impressed with the riders, whom he considered to be "soldierlike neither in dress nor appearance."[19]

If B Company was composed primarily of recruits, it also contained a cadre of veteran noncommissioned officers. Amongst this group was bugler Langford Peel, who had been practically born into the army. Sgt. Percival Lowe, who served with Peel from 1849 to1854, described Peel as being "naturally bright, clear headed, cheerful and helpful always . . . a perfect horseman, possessing unlimited courage and endurance, he was a man to be relied on and trusted in every emergency."[20] The other veterans included 1st Sgt. Frederick Muller, German born, who had been a dragoon in B Company since 1834, and Sgt. Ben Bishop, reared in Pennsylvania, who had enlisted in the dragoons in 1834 and was initially assigned to Company I. The most senior enlisted man was Sgt. Joseph Martin, recruited in B Company by Sumner on April 17, 1833. We shall be reading more about Sergeant Martin later on. Among the veterans was Pvt. Thomas Crosby, a twenty-six-year-old British soldier who had enlisted in 1841 and then re-enlisted in the dragoons when the war started.[21]

The expedition traveled at a casual pace of about twenty miles per day. After a week's march, they arrived at Council Grove, a wooded and well-watered site at the junction of the Neosho and Arkansas Rivers. It was here that Indian agent and longtime dragoon guide Thomas Bad Hand Fitzpatrick joined the expedition on his way to his agency at Bent's Fort.

During the march, Love handled a myriad of administrative matters having little or nothing to do with his mission: collecting moneys enlisted men owed to the post sutler; tending to a herd of cattle grazing on the trail whose drovers had abandoned; dealing with news of a deserter from his company who had been captured near Fort Leavenworth and placed in custody; and arranging for the return of personal effects, among which was the slave, of Captain Burgwin, recently killed at Taos.[22]

The year 1847 was to be the bloodiest year yet on the Santa Fe Trail. Comanches freely attacked government supply trains: forty-seven Americans were killed, 330 wagons destroyed, and 6,500 head of stock plundered. The Comanches had been provoked by the effects of government trains carrying supplies to the troops in New Mexico. The heavy traffic resulted in the destruction of natural resources such as game, timber, and grasses; water pollution along the trail; and most tragically the introduction into their territory of a host of the deadly European diseases such as smallpox, cholera, dysentery, and typhoid.[23]

A few of the troops had a foreboding feeling that they might not survive the trip yet were falsely confident that no Plains tribe would be so foolish as to attack a company of dragoons. Corporal Baker's letter to his nephew expresses sentiments typical of the dragoons with Love. He penned that he dreaded that hordes of Comanches and Pawnees were freely raiding along the Santa Fe Trail, but hoped to give the raiders "a severe punishment for they richly deserved it."[24]

To ensure against attacks, wagon trains merged together and happily accepted military escort. Love's party overtook two large, outbound government supply trains and the lieutenant agreed to provide an escort for them. Agent Fitzpatrick wrote that the dragoons and wagon trains "traveled along happily . . . until we arrived at Pawnee Fork, a tributary of the Arkansas River, three hundred miles from Fort Leavenworth."[25]

At Pawnee Fork, on June 23, they came upon the encampment of three government commissary wagon trains: two westbound and one eastbound. High water and steep banks had prevented the trains from crossing the Arkansas. Warriors had attacked the Missouri-bound wagon train two days prior, leaving three men wounded. The train lost most of its oxen to the marauders and was left without the means of hauling several of its wagons any farther. The teamsters burned twenty of their wagons to prevent their contents from falling into the hands of the raiders. Love promised the dejected wagon boss that he would avenge the attack on the train.

Agent Fitzpatrick, a seasoned frontiersman, was critical that these trains failed to take precautionary steps when camped. He jotted, "[B]y imbecility and bad management of the party, over twenty more wagons with their necessary accoutrements, were added to recent losses sustained by the government on that road. And from like causes." Fitzpatrick was to soon witness more bad management and the attendant loss of wagons and supplies.[26]

Now more than ever, the wagon trains traveled together for their mutual protection. Lieutenant Love ordered that henceforth the westbound trains were to travel and encamp with the dragoons for the duration of their trip. Charles Hayden, the twenty-two-year-old captain of one of the outbound government trains, chafed at being told what to do by a shavetail lieutenant. Although this was his first trip on the Santa Fe Trail, Hayden claimed to have received detailed instructions from the quartermaster at Fort Leavenworth to take whatever course of action he thought prudent. Sticking with the dragoons, in his mind, was not prudent.

It took all of the following day for the wagon trains to cross Pawnee Fork. The wagons were slowly lowered by ropes, crossed the swollen and muddy river, and then hauled up the opposite bank by twenty to twenty-five men pulling on ropes. Love once again reminded the wagon bosses to travel and camp together. The next morning, nonetheless, the wagons of Hayden along with two wagons belonging to civilian trader Henry Miller slipped out on the trail at dawn's light. Hayden was determined to travel without interference of a military escort and hoped to beat them with his goods into Santa Fe.[27]

The wagons were anxious to get through Comanche land and traveled along at a brisk pace, making twenty-seven miles that day. They camped that evening on a plain about a mile from the Arkansas River (what is today about nine and one-half miles west of US 56 near Garfield, Kansas). The dragoons made their camp on the north bank of the Arkansas River. The plain was sandy and nearly barren of grasses, yet the river bottoms provided good grazing for the animals. Two washes, known as Little Coon Creek and Big Coon Creek, flowed southward into the Arkansas, bisecting the treeless plain.

The Battle of Coon Creeks

Lieutenant Love was angry that Hayden and Miller, attempting to shake off the army and other wagons, had left early the day before and then made camp about five hundred yards to the west of the dragoon camp. Fitzpatrick later reported Hayden's poor judgment: "[I]f the Indians themselves had made the selection of the ground, they could not have chosen a more favorable position for the accomplishment of their plans." Love and Fitzpatrick knew that in the event of a raid the soldiers, with their short-ranged Hall carbines, could not effectively protect Hayden's wagons and stock placed at a distance. Love planned to speak to Hayden the next day about the need for him to camp within supporting distance of the other wagon trains and troops.[28]

In the pre-dawn hours of June 26, 1847, Lieutenant Love saddled his horse and rode to the top of a slight rise. The sky was clear and the sun beneath the horizon, about to show itself. A slight breeze gently blew up from the south. Experience on the plains had trained him to not allow horses and mules to freely graze until it was safe to do so—that is, after sentries confirmed that no raiders lurked in high grasses or in nearby washes. Accordingly, Love kept the dragoons' horses and mules tethered to the picket lines and under guard. The young officer heard the distant sound of reveille coming from the camp below. He saw his troopers slowly turn out of their blankets, getting dressed and forming in line for the morning roll call and inspection. Looking to the west he noticed the inexperienced Hayden had foolishly turned his oxen out of the corral to graze.

Love opened his spyglass for a better view of the countryside. His jaw dropped as he saw over one hundred mounted Comanches spilling out of the Big Coon Creek wash. Lieutenant Love could see the teamsters frantically grabbing the few weapons they possessed and firing wildly at the raiders. He later wrote, "The herdsmen used every effort to drive the oxen back into the corral; but, unable to do so, placed themselves between the oxen and Indians, hoping to prevent their being driven off. The Indians charged boldly amongst the oxen, frightened them, and drove them into the prairie, wounding in the charge two or three herdsmen." Spurring his horse down the rise, Lieutenant Love galloped back to the dragoon camp and ordered bugler Peel to sound "Boots and Saddles." Noncommissioned officers barked orders to their men, horses were saddled, weapons gathered, and the men were soon smartly standing to horse, under arms, awaiting further orders. Love intended to recapture the oxen and to this end, he ordered his detachment to mount. Just then he saw about 150 Comanches splashing across the Arkansas River with the intent of attacking his camp. Faced with this new danger, Love ordered his men to dismount and fight on foot as skirmishers with their Hall carbines to protect the paymaster's wagons.

Seeing that the warriors displayed little interest in his wagons, but were intent upon raiding the livestock, Love mounted a portion of his company with the intent of attacking the Comanches. In a letter written to his nephew a day after the battle, Corporal Baker provided an enlisted man's firsthand account of what happened next: "About Twenty-one men (only) started off in pursuit of the Indians. . . . Our men (21) headed by a sergeant made a gallant charge on the Indians and they commenced to run off— At this time the Indians on the other side run their horses up the river a few hundred yards—crossed and charged in the rear after our men."[29]

The Comanches had cut off Sgt. Ben Bishop's detail from support. Love, in his official account, wrote what he observed next: "When the sergeant [Bishop] arrived in the vicinity of the oxen, the Indians swarmed in from all directions, and completely surrounded his platoon; he charged fearlessly amongst them, but our horses being wild, and unaccustomed to the yells of the Indians and shaking of blankets (all done to frighten the horses), could not be held by the riders. So great was the number of Indians—supposed to be three hundred on the north side, and two hundred on the south side of the river—that all hope of cutting a way through to the oxen was abandoned."[30]

Sergeant Bishop's account of the battle, published in the *Missouri Republican*, gave details of what he experienced. Within striking distance of the Comanches, Bishop formed his men into an extended mounted line and charged, driving them off. No sooner had he done so than another band of raiders crossed the river, severing Bishop's connections from the dragoon camp. The Comanches "charged us in the rear with great fury, and preventing us from rallying, but had to cut our way through them. About this time I was shot, and charged on by several Indians." He suffered a "very severe wound I received from a [musket] ball in the side, which is lodged backwards and cannot be extracted."[31] Sergeant Bishop claimed he had used his sabre "to drink blood, having killed one and wounded another." Given that the Comanches seem to have endured only a minimum of casualties in the half-hour fray, these figure are likely unrealistic.

Corporal Baker, left in camp to protect the paymaster's wagons, provided his nephew with a solid account of Company B's men as they rode back into camp: "The first man that came in was Segt. [*sic*] Bishop, wounded with a bullet just above the kidneys— He is not as yet thought dangerous, although it is rather doubtful. The next was a young man by the name of [Henry] Vancaster, son of a German Baron, who fell from loss of blood &c off his horse some 200 yds from Camp. Besides being lanced, he had an arrow, still in him, which entered under the right arm and the steel point was sticking out through him just above the heart."[32] Baker gave the badly wounded thirty-year-old Vancaster, recruited three months prior in St. Louis, little chance of living, but he survived these dreadful wounds and was discharged on a surgeon's certificate.

Sergeant Muller called the roll and five men were unaccounted for. He sent Baker out with a patrol to look for five men who did not return to camp.

[T]he first one we found was the dead body of a fine young man of my mess–named Arlidge [Jonathan Arlege]. He was stripped of all clothing, but his scalp wasn't taken. Then on looking around we found the dead bodies of three more [George] Blake—[Moses] Short & [John] Dickhart—all three were horribly butchered. Moses besides being lanced in a dozen places had his throat cut from ear to ear—Dickhart had his ears cut off and mouth mutilated. All of these three had their scalps taken—We buried them all in a single grave with honors of war. The fifth man—Gaskin [George Gaskill]—we did not find until this morning, he was dreadfully mutilated, his scalp was not taken, but half of his hair was pulled out, I suppose the one that killed him had no knife about him.[33]

The battle was over, but the wagon trains and dragoons were forced to remain to await the arrival of sufficient stock to pull the civilian wagons. Corporal Baker concluded his letter: "It may be my fate never more to return; if such should be the case it is my wish that whatever may be due me by government as well as my other property shall become your own—I will write again when I arrive in Santa Fe. An express starts at dark for Fort Leavenworth by which I sent you this letter. . . . I hope it may get through safe."[34]

In his after-action report, Lieutenant Love stated, "With pride, I call your attention to the gallant conduct of this platoon of the company, as shown in the list of killed and wounded. We have no means of telling, as their [Comanche] dead were carried off the field." He lamented that, "[t]he oxen of one train having been driven off, I have encamped both trains together, and shall remain with them until enough trains arrive to take the government property to Santa Fe." Having been defeated by the Comanches, a wiser and chastened Love concluded, "[I]t is nearly as much as a company of dragoons can do to prevent their horses from taking a 'stampede;' that the Indians, thoroughly acquainted with the country, and constantly having everything in their favor; that being the most expert horsemen in the world, they are enabled to make an attack, alarm the animals, and be out of sight in an incredibly short time. You can judge, when from the time they were first seen approaching on the 26th, until they had the oxen over the river and out of sight, was not more than half an hour."[35]

The dragoons remained encamped at Coon Creeks to allow Assistant Surgeon Horace Wirtz the opportunity to tend the serious wounds suffered by six troopers.[36] That no dragoon died of his wounds is testimony to Wirtz's competence.

A train of eight wagons approached from the east. Lieutenant Love and agent Fitzpatrick rode out to meet this train to seek assistance from the wagon boss. Fortunately, this train had a number of spare mules and Henry Miller was able to purchase mules to pull his two wagons. On July 2, 1847, Lieutenant Love deemed it safe to move his wounded. The remaining oxen were redistributed between the two government wagon trains and in this manner Hayden obtained enough oxen to pull thirteen of his wagons.

After being camped for six days, the caravan again began to move. Making five to eight miles a day, the wagons limped their way toward the small government outpost of Fort Mann. Finding the fort to be abandoned, Love finally exercised his rank as the senior line officer present, and ordered Hayden's train to remain at Fort Mann with instructions that it stay there until a relief party arrived. The battered dragoon formation, and its precious cargo of army payroll, reached Santa Fe on August 6, 1847.

When details of the battle reached "the states," newspapers were quick to call the battle "Love's Defeat." Agent Fitzpatrick and Sergeant Bishop submitted positive accounts for the press. In these stories they commended the manner in which Love handled his troops during the battle with the Comanches. Fitzpatrick hastened to fault wagon captain Hayden for not following Love's order to place his camp next to that of the two other wagon trains. He was "very certain that, if Hayden had obeyed the

order of Lieutenant Love, no such misfortune would have happened." Overlooked by Love's supporters was that the lieutenant,
being the highest-ranking line officer present and in overall field
command of the expedition, should have ordered the disobedient
Hayden, a civilian contractor of the Quartermaster Department,
to obey his orders to camp near the troops or face arrest.[37]

CHAPTER 10

The War in Mexico

From Buena Vista's Mountain Chain to the Adobe Walls of Santa Cruz de Rosales

The 1st Dragoons did not fight solely in New Mexico and California. Other elements of the regiment were to fight and die in Mexico. As the war with Mexico progressed, the regiment became broken in pieces and it was to take years for the records of the detached companies to be completed. General Kearny led five companies into New Mexico. He went on to California with Companies C and K, leaving Companies B, G, and I in New Mexico. Companies A and E were ultimately attached to Zachary Taylor's army. Company F was briefly attached to Taylor but was transferred to Winfield Scott's invading force. Company D remained in Indian Territory throughout the war, keeping the peace in that troubled region.[1] This chapter explores the battles fought by those companies not under the field command of General Kearny.

The Battle of Buena Vista

In the summer of 1846, the army assigned a squadron consisting of Companies A and E of the 1st Dragoons, commanded by Capt. Enoch Steen, to Gen. John Wool's Central Division being organized at San Antonio, Texas. The dragoons served alongside Capt. Benjamin Beall's company of 2nd Dragoons, two Illinois infantry regiments, a regular army six-gun field battery, and an Arkansas cavalry regiment.[2]

Into this encampment wandered Sam Chamberlain, a wild and impudent sixteen-year-old Bostonian seeking adventure in the war. On September 8, 1846, Capt. Enoch Steen enlisted Sam Chamberlain into Company E of the 1st Dragoons. It didn't take young Sam long to be immediately impressed with a kindred spirit in the form of Bvt. Maj. Ben "Old Brilliant" Beall. In *My Confessions*, Sam recounted his first meeting with Beall. Sam wanted to attend a fandango in San Antonio and took his pass to be approved by Major Beall, who was soon to be transferred to the 1st Dragoons. The major was described by Sam as a "short, red-faced and nosed man, [who] looked the Major all over, and it was evident that nature intended him for that position and nothing else. He was known in the army as 'Old Brilliant,' and, from his unusual brilliant appearance at this time, I judged that the influence of Old Rye had something to do with it."

The "hail fellow well met" Beall formed a party of dragoons to attend the fandango, where they danced and drank away the night. As the troops approached their camp at dawn, they encountered Col. David Harney of the 2nd Dragoons. Chamberlain recalled, "We expected to be roughed and were not disappointed. Those who knew Harney can appreciate the scene. To all that was said by Harney our major had only one reply, 'Brilliant Fandango, brilliant! By G—d, brilliant Girls, Colonel, brilliant night!' Harney placed him under arrest and we were consigned to the quarters of 'Company Q' [jail] for 24 hours."[3]

Once General Wool's division was formed, it entered northern Mexico and reinforced Taylor's victorious army. Fearing the presidential ambitions of Gen. Zack Taylor, a Whig, President Polk, a Democrat, created a new division and placed it under the command of Gen. Winfield "Fuss and Feathers" Scott, also a Whig. The new plan was to have Scott "conquer a peace" by landing his troops at Vera Cruz and marching inland to capture the Mexican capital, thus ending the war on Polk's terms. Scott's division took away most of Taylor's best-trained regiments, including Beall's company of 2nd Dragoons. Taylor was left primarily with volunteers, along with a handful of regular artillery, two companies of the 2nd Dragoons, and two companies of 1st Dragoons.[4]

Despite having the size of his army reduced and losing most of his best troops to Scott, Taylor was not about to remain inactive. In early February of 1847 Taylor's reduced force of 4,600 men (406 of whom were regular dragoons and artillerymen) moved south to Agua Nueva, Mexico. General Santa Anna received news of Taylor's reduced and exposed army. He saw an opportunity for a quick victory that would swing momentum back to Mexico. Santa Anna assembled an army of 21,000 men and marched it north from Mexico City through the rugged and dry terrain of central Mexico, to defeat Taylor's division. It was Santa Anna's sole offensive operation in the war. After the expected defeat of Taylor, the Napoleon of the New World planned to rush his victorious army south to defend against Scott's invasion.[5]

With Taylor's reduced army, serving as the commander of a dragoon company and a member of Taylor's staff, was Lt. James H. Carleton, the formerly court-martialed lieutenant who ably described the dragoon expeditions of 1844 and 1845. Keeping pen and paper handy during the engagement, Carleton was about to add to his literary credits with his eyewitness account of the Battle of Buena Vista, published in 1848.[6]

Beginning on February 10, the dragoons and other mounted units, acting as the eyes of Taylor's force, scouted to the south for evidence of the anticipated approach of Santa Anna's army. On February 20, Carleton, along with four hundred men under black-bearded Bvt. Col. Charles May, advanced to the hacienda at Potosi. Here they observed in the distance large clouds of dust indicative of a large army on the march. When two scouts failed to return and distant shots were heard, Colonel May was convinced of the proximity of Santa Anna's army and ordered a hasty retreat back to Taylor's camp. After traveling sixty miles in the space of twenty-one hours, May's detachment reunited with Taylor. May's report caused Taylor to retreat to the better defensive positions, one carefully selected by General Wool, in the Buena Vista mountain pass.[7]

The pass at Buena Vista was located in the chain of the Sierra Madre Mountains. The high valley it sits upon varies in width from one to four miles. In 1847, much of the land was under cultivation. A road running south from Saltillo to Agua Nueva runs through the valley. One and one half miles south of Buena Vista, the terrain narrows at a place called La Angostura. Here the road crosses a series of deep ravines that emanate diagonally from a range of mountains lying to the west. To the east of the road is a high, rocky plateau that, if gained, would permit the rapid movement of troops. This narrow pass constituted a "formidable obstacle to any species of troops whatever; being upwards of twenty feet in depth, with sides so precipitous as to prevent their being ascended." It was at La Angostura that Taylor and Wool were to place the bulk of their troops in a line, anchored on either side by rock walls.[8]

Santa Anna believed Taylor to be unaware of his movements and ordered a night march so that he might surprise Taylor on the morning of February 22 at Agua Nueva. Finding that Taylor had withdrawn, Santa Anna again furiously whipped his tired and famished troops forward, hoping to overtake Taylor's retreating forces as they were strung out on the line of retreat. When he finally reached Taylor's army, Santa Anna was disappointed to discover an enemy army forming its artillery in battery, banners flying, bands playing, men cheering, situated on a good defensive ground, digging in but not yet ready to engage in battle. In the view of historian Justin Smith, had Santa Anna attacked immediately, he may have whipped Taylor then and there.[9] Realistically speaking, Santa Anna's force was spent by the night march and was in no condition to attack immediately.

Nonetheless, Santa Anna was confident of his chances of overwhelming Taylor's pint-sized army. He promptly sent a messenger carrying a dispatch pointing out the disproportionate advantage the Mexicans enjoyed in terms of troop strength, and demanded Taylor's surrender. Taylor refused to concede the possibility of defeat. He and General Wool felt confident in the strength of their position and were not about to surrender or retreat. To a classically educated soldier such as General Wool, however, "like Spartans of old, [we] were defending Thermopylae."[10] Taylor's little army was, in his words, "occupying a line of remarkable strength. The road at this point becomes a narrow defile, the valley on its right being impracticable for artillery by a succession of deep and impassable gullies, and on the left by a succession of rugged ridges and precipitous ravines extend[ing] back towards the mountain which bounds the valley."[11]

At three o'clock, Mexican artillery opened fire on Taylor's left, placing the Arkansas and Kentucky Cavalry Regiments directly in harm's way, "under a most galling fire from the infantry in front, a cross fire of grape and canister." Following the barrage, Gen. Pedro de Ampudia advanced his light infantry on Taylor's left flank, where they were met by withering musket fire from the 2nd Indiana. Fighting in this sector continued all afternoon, with the Mexicans gradually turning Taylor's left flank, when evening's darkness brought a halt to the fighting. Fearing that the Mexicans were moving under cover of night to attack his supply depot at Saltillo, an overly cautious Taylor led a portion of his army, including the two 1st Dragoon companies, to the rear.[12]

The morning of February 23 dawned cold, bright, and clear as the U.S. forces awaited the next attack. Due to Taylor's partial withdrawal, the strength of the American force was reduced to about 3,300 men. As a distraction intended to draw down Wool's forces, Ampudia's division renewed its probing assault on the left flank and drove back the advanced pickets. Wool didn't go for the diversion. He knew he had a strong defensive position and was not about to move his troops. Within a few hours, Santa Anna assembled his men and prepared to launch a series of heavy attacks against Wool's center and right flank. Carleton was duly impressed with the approach of this impressive force, describing it as follows: "The men were all in full dress, the horses were gaily caparisoned, and the arms of both cavalry and infantry shone bright as silver. Every regiment, corps, and squadron had its standards, colors, and guidons unfurled; and, while the infantry marched steadily onward with a most perfectly marked and cadenced step, the cavalry moved with the regularity and precision it would have observed in an ordinary field review."[13]

At about nine in the morning, three thousand Mexican infantry crashed into the center of the plateau held by Wool's 2nd Indiana and 2nd Illinois, supported by regular artillery. These volunteer troops calmly stopped the first onslaught, but when hit by a renewed assault the frightened Col. William Bissell of the 2nd Indiana Regiment panicked and precipitously ordered a retreat down the road to Saltillo. Wrote a soldier, "This led to the disorderly flight and some few of the men could not be induced again to join the troops and continue to fight."[14]

Capt. Enoch Steen, commanding the squadron of 1st Dragoons, was stationed immediately behind the 2nd Indiana, and when they routed, he rode forward in a failed attempt to rally them and was seriously wounded. Command of the 1st Dragoons devolved to Lt. Daniel Rucker.[15]

The sudden retreat of the 2nd Indiana left a hole in the American line, held precariously by Lt. John O'Brien's three pieces of artillery and six companies of the 2nd Illinois. These troops became the subject of the entire weight of the Mexican force as it attacked the center. O'Brien and the Illinois regiment eventually were compelled to retreat, leaving behind an artillery piece captured by Santa Anna, who later sent it back as a precious trophy to display in Mexico City.[16]

Santa Anna, to exploit his achievement by drawing off Wool's reserve troops, dispatched troops to turn the flanks of the defenders. A trooper of the 2nd Arkansas observed, "The enemy was now pouring masses of cavalry and infantry along the foot of the mountain, which made matters rather serious." These troops reached the plateau, threatening to cut off retreating troops from their bases at Buena Vista and Saltillo. With these maneuvers, momentum had decidedly shifted to Santa Anna.[17]

It was only the timely appearance of General Taylor at 9:00 A.M. that saved the Yanqui army. Returning from Saltillo, bringing with him dragoons, artillery, and the Mississippi Rifles, he threw his force into the fray. Into the opening in the line marched the regular artillery and the 3rd Indiana Regiment of Infantry, and these troops stabilized the defense. Riding with careless abandon along the front lines Taylor directed the steady fire from his men. At one critical moment, Taylor ordered Capt. Braxton Bragg to "double-shot your guns and give them hell, Bragg." The artillery proceeded to render "sad havoc among the enemy." The musketry of the 3rd Indiana and the 1st Mississippi, along with grapeshot fired by O'Brien's, Bragg's, and Tom Sherman's massed batteries, stopped the Mexican assault cold in its tracks, caused it to pause, and to retreat.[18] For the time being, Taylor had staved off the attack to the center and his line had held. Now it was time to protect his flanks.[19]

Thus far, the dragoons had fired but few shots, had not participated in any significant engagement, and their casualties were light. It was now their turn to engage in the heavy fighting. Santa Anna had placed three cannon on the heights, from where their gunfire could effectively enfilade the left flank of Taylor's battered army. The San Patricios, a battalion containing mainly Irish-born deserters from the United States Army, manned these cannon and were peppering the gringos with accurate shot. Taylor wanted to seize this battery and called upon Lt. Daniel Rucker and his dragoons to capture it.[20] Off at a trot in a column of twos the dragoons gallantly went, sabers drawn, looking forward to gaining a measure of glory by capturing the Mexican cannon. They emerged from a gully and found themselves facing the barrels of Mexican cannon. The combined effects of cannonade coupled with a sudden rainstorm caused the dragoons to lose their élan and quickly retreat into a ravine.[21] While hunkered down in the ravine, they joined forces with Colonel May's squadron of 2nd Dragoons, safely positioned in a deep gulch. Private Chamberlain observed the faint-hearted behavior of the multi-honored Colonel May:

> May, in seeing that the girths were all right, remained a long time under the lea of his steed. "Jot McClure," a chum of mine, remarked, "Jack, it is of no use for you and me to keep the saddle when colonel has taken cover." So

we slipped off, others done the same, and soon the whole
command was dismounted and examining Saddle girths!
After a half hour of patient investigation, finding our saddles all secure, and that there was a lull in the fighting,
the "Heroic"[colonel] gave orders to mount, "Fours right
about wheel" and we marched out of the ravine without
loss.[22]

In an effort to regain lost momentum, Santa Anna now
deployed his elite lancers in an attack on the rear of the Yanqui line. While the fighting on the plateau was going on, a brigade of Mexican lancers under Gen. Anastacio Torrejon slipped
around the left flank, easily brushed aside disorganized Arkansas
and Kentucky horsemen attempting to stop them, and rushed on
to threaten Taylor's supply depot at the Buena Vista hacienda.
The troops guarding the supplies took shelter in the hacienda's
buildings.

In stark contrast to the Battle of San Pasqual, lances are
useless when deployed against determined infantry, especially
when they are stationed in buildings. In the ensuing battle the
defenders' musketry caused the lancers to retreat. Failing to capture and destroy the supplies, the fifteen hundred resplendently
dressed lancers regrouped and advanced slowly to attack the fast-
approaching Hoosiers and Mississippians. Two well-directed volleys were fired at eighty yards by the steady 3rd Indiana and Col.
Jefferson Davis's red-shirted, straw-hatted, rifle-toting Mississippians, grape and canister belched forth from a howitzer, and these
were followed by the deadly roll of continuous rifle fire by file.
All this quickly decapitated the compact mass of lancers, sending
them reeling.[23]

There was no question that the Mississippians and the artillery played a major role in saving the day. Often overlooked in
history are the contributions of determined soldiers who stood
their ground, such as those in the 3rd Indiana. In a letter home an
overly proud Hoosier boasted of his regiment's accomplishment:
"The Third Regiment Indiana Volunteers, you may rely on it,

saved the pass. Had we given way before the charge of lancers and infantry all was [*sic*] lost. Our loss is severe in officers and men."[24]

It wasn't long before the 1st Dragoons were back in action. Lieutenant Rucker had received belated word that the Buena Vista depot was under attack by lancers and, with sabers again drawn, raced to defend the depot. As he approached, Rucker's column was exposed to musketry and his guidon-bearer and several men were wounded.[25]

When they arrived, the Mexican horsemen were in a disorganized retreat following defeat by a mixed force consisting of Mississippians, Hoosiers, artillery, quartermasters, and various troops who had retreated to the rear. Rucker's dragoons, with elements of the Kentucky and Arkansas Cavalry regiments, slammed into the retreating lancers on their flank. They swept through the disorganized troops, routing them further. In the brief skirmish, dragoon casualties were two wounded.[26]

Checked by the defenders, Santa Anna continued to sense that victory remained close at hand and renewed his assault on the center of Taylor's line. In the eyes of those who held this ground it was the "hottest and most critical part of the action."[27] Heavy and confused fighting continued throughout the afternoon but Taylor's line somehow held—barely. With the coming of darkness, the shooting came to an end. For all practical purposes, contrary to the words of the old sea chantey "Santy Anno," though Santa Anna had gained the day, General Taylor was not about to run away. He was defeated and bloodied, but prepared to grimly stand his ground to fight on the next day.[28]

Taylor, Wool, and their men spent the chilly night tending their wounded and burying the dead. An Arkansas trooper recalled how the men "bivouacked without fires and suffered not a little from the cold." They had lost, in terms of killed, wounded, and missing, 666 men in the battle—14 percent of the army. Generals Taylor and Wool spent the night preparing the survivors for an anticipated assault the next day. Given that they were greatly outnumbered by Santa Anna's army, Generals Wool and Taylor expected their tough little band was on the brink of defeat. If there was going to be a retreat on the next day, the dragoon companies knew that they would be ordered to cover the withdrawal and expected to suffer casualties in doing so.[29]

Unknown to the Yankee troops, Santa Anna had suffered even more serious losses in the battle; he needed time to reorganize and feed his army and ordered a nighttime retreat of ten miles back to his supply base at Agua Nueva. Santa Anna was ready to again fight Taylor, hoping that the latter would attempt to attack him. When this did not happen, the Napoleon of the West took a second look at the poor condition of his army: in addition to the killed and wounded, nearly a ninth of his men were already ill with dysentery. Deciding that with the captured cannon and flags he could proclaim victory in Mexico City, he retreated.[30]

With the breaking of dawn, Taylor's battered army looked around and discovered that it was Santa Anna who had vacated the field with his army. What was the Napoleon of the New World up to? Riders went out and discovered that Santa Anna had retreated. General Taylor was standing before a fire when informed. When he heard the news, "he began rubbing his hands, which he continued to do for some seconds, and then said, 'Boys, give us three cheers.'" Then came a "prolonged and thrilling shout from all around: VICTORY! VICTORY! VICTORY! THE ENEMY HAS FLED! THE FIELD IS OURS!" The battle was over. Santa Anna had lost his nerve, leaving Taylor's worn and battered force in control of the field.[31]

Taylor ordered his cavalry to pursue Santa Anna's forces. An Arkansas cavalryman described the battlefield: "The ground was literally covered with men wounded, dead, and dying, and the heart-rending and piteous moans sent up by those still alive were sufficient to cause the stoutest hearts to shudder and the most bluntest [sic] feelings to sympathize." The cavalry rode to the outskirts of Agua Nueva, where it found Santa Anna's camp. It was here that Lieutenant Rucker rashly sought permission to charge the entire Mexican army, but fortunately changed his mind. The exhausted dragoons went into camp at Buena Vista, where they drank cups of coffee and ate fresh meat for the first time in forty-eight hours.[32]

With his remarkable victory at Buena Vista, "Rough and Ready" Taylor immediately became a national hero who, a year later, would ride his battlefield triumph to the White House. A young songwriter named Stephen Foster captured the mood of the nation with his catchy song "A Little More Grape, Captain Bragg."[33] On a more pedestrian level, dragoon Sam Chamberlain wrote of a homespun piece sung by his drunken companions shortly after the battle and just before an inevitable brawl with the local citizenry:

> It was on the 22d, the day being clear,
> We espied the advancing Army of Mexican Lancers,
> At two o'clk [*sic*] they fired a shot when we returned
>   the same.
> "Damn ye eyes," old Zack cries, for now commence
>   the game.
> (Chorus)
> So cheer up my lively lads, for it never will be said,
> That the First Dragoons was ever yet afraid.[34]

Companies A and E of the 1st Dragoons participated in the battle, but were fortunate—just nine of their members were among the wounded and they did not suffer a single fatality. Carleton received a major's brevet for his role in the battle and gathered a wealth of material for his book. During the remaining year of the war, there would be no further major battles fought by this squadron, and they joined General Wool for garrison duty in northern Mexico. Chamberlain was to remain with the regiment throughout and after the war, and would write his account of his service in a book that was not published until many years after his death.

Phil Kearny's Charge at Churubusco

> The first object [of cavalry] is to break through and disorder the enemy's array, then make use of the sword to complete his discomfiture.

When a charge has once begun, carry it out whatever may be the odds that suddenly present themselves against you.

An officer in command of cavalry must know what he intends doing; this he must carry out with energy and resolution, for under vacillating commanders, no cavalry, however brave, will do good in the field.

Cavalry must act independently once it starts for the charge: the fire of infantry and artillery may pave the way before, or even during the attack, but there must be no hesitation when the cavalry advances to the attack: kept back to the right moment, when it breaks forth, let it be to *fight*.

Louis Nolan, Cavalry (1854)

"Thank God we are all young. I may have another chance yet."

Phil Kearny

Phil. Kearny

[to the tune of "Rosin the Bow"]
Oh, have you not heard of Phil. Kearny?
He's a man among men in the army!
To his country is given, the arm that is riven—
Long life to what's left of Phil. Kearny!
When Phil had resigned from the army,
War came—yet let this not alarm ye!
For never could Phil rest idle and still,
When duty cried "Come out! Phil. Kearny!"
Before Mexico's walls now are swarming
Armed hosts, as her works we are storming,
And the dust-biters feel, there's weight in the steel
That's sway'd by the arm of Phil. Kearny.
Then fill, and fill full to Phil. Kearny!
This man among men in the army,
For his country he'll part with the blood of his heart,
Long life to what's left of Phil. Kearny!

St. Louis Reveille, April 8, 1848, from the New York Spirit[35]

The above doggerel hardly matched the lasting quality and eloquence of Alfred Lord Tennyson's classic "Charge of the Light

Brigade" (1855). In terms of military heroism, however, Phil Kearny's charge at Churubusco was in many ways nearly as glorious and doomed as was the fabled charge of the Light Brigade, which occurred seven years later. And yet, unlike the dauntless charge of Lord Cardigan, the glory of Kearny's assault immediately faded from public acclamation.

The War with Mexico is replete with heroic mounted actions by combatants of both sides: Capt. Charles May's heroic charge, which captured, then lost, a Mexican battery at Resaca de Palma; Andrés Pico's vaqueros and their courageous stand against Gen. Stephen Kearny's dragoons at San Pasqual; or Gen. Pedro de Ampudia's brave charges at Buena Vista. Lost to history is the most glorious North American cavalry charge of the war: Phil Kearny's charge during the Battle of Churubusco. The gallantry of the assault inspired not only the above poem, but also war correspondent George Kendall of the *New Orleans Picayune* to comment, "The charge of Kearny's dragoons upon the flying masses of the Mexicans in the battle of Churubusco is one of the most brilliant and decisive feats which has occurred in the war. . . . In every narration of the events of Churubusco we have seen this charge and pursuit of KEARNY's dragoons commemorated and applauded, but it appears to have impressed the Mexicans far more than the popular mind of our own countrymen. In various letters which we have seen written by them from their capital, they speak of the audacity of the dragoons as terrible and almost supernatural."[36] Not to be outdone by the *Picayune*, the editor of the New Orleans *L'Abeille de la Nouvelles-Orléans* wrote on September 10, 1847: "The impetuous and gallant manner in which the charge was executed is a theme of universal admiration. Officers and men seemed to view with one another who should be foremost in the pursuit."

It is true that Kearny's charge came nowhere near matching, in terms of magnificence and casualties, the celebrated 1854 charge of the British Light Brigade at Balaclava. Nor was there a great poet willing to compose elegant prose describing the gallantry of the failed charge. Rather, a public that was weary of a war that had lasted a year and a half, with no end in sight, took little notice of this or any other heroic exploit by the military. Like many other heroes and battles in an unpopular war, this attack quickly found itself relegated to the dustbin of history . . . until now.

Phil Kearny's wealthy family had wanted him to pursue a career in law or the family business, and he secured a law degree from Columbia College in 1833. But Phil Kearny wanted to be a soldier like his uncle. In 1837 the very rich, vainglorious, and impetuous nephew of Col. Stephen W. Kearny used his family and political connections to secure a lieutenancy in the regiment. Due to family influence, his first years with the army were spent acting as an aide de camp for Gens. Alexander Macomb and Winfield Scott. As previously noted, Kearny attended military college in Saumur, France. It was during this time that he observed French cavalry fighting in Algeria and became imbued with the French strategy of "*Attaque, attaque, toujours l'attaque!*" (Attack, attack, always the attack!) It was this teaching that was to remain with Phil Kearny his entire life.[37]

Field duty took him west with his uncle on his 1845 expedition to the Rocky Mountains. Hoping to gain a promotion, he resigned his dragoon commission in April of 1846, so that he might gain an appointment to a higher rank in the newly created Regiment of Mounted Rifles. When no appointment was forthcoming, and war with Mexico declared, Kearny withdrew his resignation and was restored to duty.[38] War! An excited Kearny wrote to his friend Lt. John Love, mentioning that he was able to rescind his resignation and be reappointed in his old regiment: "Thank God, some feeling of pride in my regiment, if none for my country. I [would] gladly go through the strife [and] most willingly pledge my life for its glory."[39]

It wasn't long before Kearny gained a chance for field command. Capt. Phil Thompson was, when sober, a reasonably gifted officer who commanded Company F, 1st Dragoons; his addiction to alcohol, however, was troubling to Colonel Kearny and he was left behind at Fort Leavenworth when the colonel assembled his mission to conquer New Mexico. Lt. Phil Kearny, in spite of his youth, perhaps as a result of nepotism, obtained the wartime field command of Company F. The colonel decided to break up F Company, sending most of its enlisted men to other companies, and ordered Lts. Kearny and Ewell to recruit the company to full wartime strength. Kearny advertised in St. Louis newspapers, including an advertisement placed in the German-language St. Louis *Deutsche Tribüne,* for July 18, 1846, and then traveled to Indiana seeking more recruits.[40] Ewell, meanwhile, headed for Ohio where he recruited twenty-seven men for the company. By August 22, 1846, Kearny and Ewell had recruited more than one hundred men—more than enough to fill the ranks of Company F.[41]

Young Kearny used his own funds to purchase horses, tack, and equipage for the company. He and Ewell trained the men at Jefferson Barracks and did a respectable job in doing so.[42] Lt. Eugene McLean, 1st Infantry, described Phil Kearny's troops as "a fine company of young men raised principally by Kearny, who exerted himself in every way to fill the company."[43]

Following Gen. Zachary Taylor's capture of Monterrey, President James Polk believed that the war with Mexico would soon end. He was wrong. The proud Mexican government refused to negotiate for surrender. Thus, the U.S. military planned "to conquer a peace" by an invasion that had as its objective the capture of Vera Cruz and Mexico City. Under this plan General Taylor was required to transfer most of the regular soldiers in his army to the invasion force fashioned by Gen. Winfield Scott, being assembled at Palo Alto Landing, Texas.

Dragoons, as did other mounted troops, often served as couriers and escorts used for the delivery of orders. Thus in January of 1847 a detachment of ten men of F Company, escorted by Lt. John Richey, 6th Infantry, left Palo Alto Landing, Texas, carrying important papers from General Scott to General Taylor. These dispatches contained not only information regarding Scott's planned expedition to Vera Cruz, but hinted at the depleted condition of Taylor's army. On January 13, 1847, at the pueblo of Villa Gran in the Mexican state of Sonora, Richey foolishly left behind his escort and entered the town, allegedly to purchase food supplies for his men. He was set upon by Mexican guerillas and murdered.[44] The assailants may have stolen the military dispatches and attempted to deliver them to Gen. Antonio Lopez de Santa Anna. General Taylor believed that the dispatches "were doubtless forwarded" to the Mexican army headquarters. It really mattered not as Santa Anna already knew of the depleted condition of Taylor's army and had already begun his march north to defeat Taylor.[45]

On January 27, 1847, from his camp near Monterrey, Taylor wrote to Scott about Richey's death and the loss of the orders.

> I respectfully report my arrival at this place on the 24th instant. After I had left my camp, near Victoria, I received Major General Scott's letter, of December 20, and was advised, at the same time, of the murder of Lieutenant Richey, 6th infantry [*sic*], and the loss of dispatches conveyed by that officer.
>
> It seems that on reaching the town of Villa Gran, on the 13th instant, Lieutenant Richey separated himself from his escort, for the purpose of purchasing provisions and forage; that he was assaulted by a gang of desperadoes, lassoed and brutally put to death. He had been dispatched to my head-quarters by Major General Butler, with some communications, the most important being General Scott's original instructions to me, of January 3d. Those instructions, with other dispatches found on Lieutenant Richey's person, were doubtless forwarded to San Luis. Every effort was made, by the offer of rewards, &c, to recover the dispatches and apprehend the murderers, but, it is feared, without success. I have, however, in custody a Mexican, who is unquestionably criminated in the affair.[46]

Taylor, who was in desperate need of replacements, must have had thoughts of placing the ten F Company dragoons, formerly escorting Lieutenant Richey, into his command. Lieutenant Kearny, having personally recruited nearly half of the fifty-eight privates in his company and used his own funds with which to smartly mount the company, had a keen interest in getting these ten men and their horses returned. He feared that Taylor would press the men into service with his understrength army; in short, the loss of his ten men represented about one-sixth of his troop, which was in his mind tragic. He wrote to his friend and mentor General Scott on February 6, 1847, requesting that his men be sent back to his command.

> The fear of losing a single instant must be my excuse for addressing you, even on a military subject so directly. Although I feel that from this <u>injury</u> that may be done my Company that it is almost equally a private wrong. The detachment of 10 Dragoons, that accompanied Lt. Ritchie [*sic*], have been attached to Col. May's Company. This I trust is merely contemplated as temporary, and yet, if it happens that they do not join my Company in time I fear that this will be assumed as the grounds for a Transfer. I now solicit, that you may be pleased to issue instructions, for said men of this Company ('F,' 1st Drs) to join as quickly as possible—and wherever the Company may have proceeded, if embarked before their arrival at the Brazos.[47] (emphasis in original)

By the end of February, Taylor returned Kearny's missing dragoons.[48]

Kearny had no sooner recouped his ten men when he had to deal with complaints coming from an unexpected quarter. A significant number of dragoons suffered from disease and this caused the army's medical examiner to single out the company and complain to headquarters. Kearny, who prided himself on caring for the well-being of his men, objected to the would-be whistleblower. On April 23, 1847, he wrote this letter to L. Scott, aide-de-camp to the commanding general.

> I am informed through Dr. Barnes that a report of the "Neglect of the Sick of my Company" has been made to the

Surgeon General. As such a report did not originate with myself, and, as I know that no grounds exist for the same, and that if said neglect occurred through me, or had been passed over in silence by me, that I am the responsible person. I have the honor to request, with as little delay as practicable, to be furnished with a copy of the said report.

Nothing further came of this criticism as the medical examiner undoubtedly came to realize that the problem was manifest in Scott's entire army—as bad or even worse in those other military formations fighting in Mexico. Historians have come to realize that the Mexican War was the deadliest of our wars with respect to the proportion of deaths due to disease when compared to deaths due to combat.[49]

Beginning at Puebla, Company F served as General Scott's bodyguard. On August 8 it took part in minor skirmishes with Mexican cavalry. In one skirmish, on August 13, a patrol from Company F attacked a superior force of Mexican cavalry and routed it at Mil Flores. In this skirmish Lt. Lorimer Graham, recently transferred to the 1st Dragoons from the 10th Infantry, gained a brevet for heroism.

The American army entered into the Valley of Mexico with the objective of capturing Mexico City. Strong Mexican lines blocked the advance and Scott sought a path around the enemy's lines. On August 18 the company served as an escort for Capt. Robert E. Lee and Lt. Pierre Beauregard of the engineers, who were seeking to locate a route for Scott's army through the lava fields known as the Pedregal to Mexico City. On this mission Mexican irregulars attempted to attack Lee but were driven off by the dragoons.[50] Lieutenant Ewell, writing to his brother, was very impressed with the topographical skills of Captain Lee, concluding he is "one of the most talented men connected with the army." And sure enough, Lee found a way for the troops to slip through the Pedregal.[51]

Following Lee's trail through the Pedregal, Scott flanked Santa Anna's forces and advanced to the outer defenses of Mexico

City. On August 20, 1847, however, Mexican infantry and artillery stopped Gen, Winfield Scott's overconfident columns in their tracks at the Battle of Churubusco. Scott rallied his men and eventually overwhelmed the Mexican positions. It was "[n]ot one of Scott's best battles," remarked historian K. Jack Bauer. "[T]he American success resulted from the élan of the individual soldier, who simply refused to believe he could be beaten." It was only after both sides suffered heavy losses that Mexican defenses were breached and the defenders sent reeling back to Mexico City. Scott's bloodied troops chased the defeated army for about two miles.[52]

As the Mexican defenders fled down the highway and poured onto a narrow, three-quarter-mile-long causeway leading back into the city, Col. William Harney, in command of Scott's cavalry, ordered elements of the 1st, 2nd, and 3rd Dragoons, and the Mounted Rifles to pursue the fugitives. An abandoned and burning Mexican ammunition train initially blocked the entrance to the causeway. Fearing a great explosion, the troopers could not continue with the chase until the wagons were cleared. A handful of brave soldiers dismounted, climbed into the wagons, and tossed the ammunition chests into the water. The road to Mexico City was now clear and pursuit renewed.[53]

It was a moment that nearly every cavalryman wished for: a broken army running away from the field of battle. "Attack, attack, always attack!" Then, as he spurred his charger, came Kearny's verbal order, "Draw sabres, troop forward at the trot, charge!" With Phil Kearny's Company F in the lead—about seventy of its men brandishing their bright sabers, riding boot to boot on grey horses in a column of fours—the cavalry wildly galloped down the half-mile-long causeway. Kearny, his saber raised high and cutting edge at tierce point, and mounted upon one of the finest horses in the regiment, raced onward, riding down and slashing those fugitives who did not jump out of his way off the causeway into Lake Texcoco. So far, the charge resembled a foxhunt more than a battle. Behind Company F rode a troop of Third Dragoons under the command of Capt. Andrew McReynolds, a troop of Mounted

Rifles commanded by Lt. Julian May, and Company B of the 2nd Dragoons under Capt. Croghan Ker.[54]

Wrote a soldier-witness to the charge: "Oh, what a glorious sight" to see the dragoons slaughter the defenseless fugitives on the causeway.[55] The *New Orleans Picayune* contained this eyewitness account by George Kendall, its war correspondent:

> Kearny's dragoons rushed upon the yielding masses of Mexicans with an impetuosity and fury which made amends for the scantiness of their numbers, and bore them back in confusion upon the town. . . . The audacity of the onset of Kearny's troops struck dismay to the hosts which fled before them. The retreat became a confused rout, and the causeway was blocked by the entangled masses of the enemy. But even through this obstacle the triumphant dragoons forced their way, trampling down those who escaped their relentless sabres. Scattering the foe before them, the dragoons came at last within reach of the formidable batteries which defended the gates of the city, and a murderous fire was opened upon them, which was even more terrible to the fugitive Mexicans than the dragoons.[56]

Colonel Harney did not participate in the charge that he had set into motion. Rather, he casually observed it from a comfortable distance to the rear. In antebellum times the place for a commander of a charging cavalry regiment was at its forefront. As Lieutenant Ewell, who participated in the charge, wrote to his brother, "Col. Harn[e]y had refused to lead the charge & of course should not have interfered as it was out of his power to control once we had passed him." For doing what he was about to do, Harney, as commander of the 2nd Dragoons, he ought to have known better.[57]

Because of his refusal to lead the charge, Harney was unable to gain a clear perspective of what Kearny was facing. Since he knew that there were only a handful of mounted troops attached to Scott's army, it made no sense for them to risk any further casualties. As the charge ventured ever closer to the city's fortified walls he became fearful that his men would suffer significant casualties. Harney suddenly ordered his bugler to sound "recall."

Stopping a mounted charge midstream over any terrain has never been an easy task. A cavalry assault, once initiated, cannot be shutdown as simply as a light is extinguished when one flips a switch. Thus, a charge, for better or worse, will most often continue until it reaches its objective. In short, Harney, once he ordered a charge, was powerless to recall it.

Mounted charges should take place only upon a firm and broad plain, allowing ease of lateral movements by both man and horse. Ideally, cavalry charges in a line formation. This is because it is easier to maneuver while in line than in mounted column. Even worse, it is nearly impossible to recall a charge by a column of cavalry that is taking place upon a restricted path over gravelly ground. This is because the lead element of the charge cannot quickly stop or turn on the slippery ground, lest the fast-moving column of fours behind slam into those horses stopping ahead and a wrecked formation result.

In short, the narrow and cluttered causeway over which Kearny and his men were riding forced his troops to ride in a compact formation, giving them no room to maneuver and making them an ideal target for the Mexican artillery, which the troops were fast approaching. Kearny later wrote of "[t]he ordeal of [re-]calling a squadron of ho[rse] on a hard gravelled [*sic*] avenue [with?] cries, in the [turn] around & confusion to boot!!!"[58]

Long before the war with Mexico and long afterward, generals typically communicated their orders to units in four ways: mounted couriers, signal flags, drums, and bugles. Signal flags are unlikely to be seen by charging horsemen. A message sent by way of a galloper to charging cavalry was of no use as it traveled only as fast as a horse can run. Drums are used to signal infantry. Thus Harney had to depend solely upon the bugle as a means to recall Kearny's charge.

A portion of the troops to the rear of the column heard the bugle and were able to retreat. Kearny's force of Company F of the 1st Dragoons and Company G of the 3rd Dragoons, dashing excitedly at a full gallop, was not about to stop because the din of battle made it impossible for the vanguard of the charge to hear the distant call for retreat. Kearny's men thundered onward.[59]

Quite possibly, Kearny might have been able to hear Harney's retreat call had his formation contained a bugler stationed to the rear. A typical company of dragoons was allotted two buglers. They were usually mounted upon white horses so that the officers could easily identify them. One bugler was to ride at the head of the column near the company commander, the second bugler at the tail end of the company. The latter's role was to relay orders sent to the company from a distant commander stationed in the rear. Unfortunately, on that day Company F had no bugler (one of its buglers deserted in 1846 and Edward Smith, the remaining bugler, was discharged due to illness in May of 1847).[60] Thus it is not surprising that neither Kearny nor his men heard Harney's bugler sounding recall and they proceeded, unreinforced, with the doomed charge.

Lieutenant Ewell described what happened next: "We approached the gate . . . & then I saw a piece of artillery frowning over the works." Kearny's eyes opened wide as he got close to the city's gates and saw a double line of defense with infantry and cannon placed at the end of the causeway. Capturing even a single cannon, however, was the ultimate honor for any glory-hunting cavalryman and Kearny was a glory hunter. Kearny quickly sized up the tactical situation facing him: the potential prize of a captured cannon, an open gate with fleeing and disorganized defenders on the causeway blocking the gunners' line of sight. He recognized that, if reinforced by the full weight of the attacking column, the troops could breach the entrance. Or as *Picayune* reporter Kendall later penned, if Kearny had "been supported by a hundred resolute men, the garita [gate] of San Antonio Abad might have been held. A single infantry regiment, supported by a light battery, might even have entered the capital and taken possession of the grand plaza and National Palace, for Santa Anna could not have rallied a formation sufficiently strong to resist such a force."[61]

The Mexican musketry and cannon fire had ceased due to confusion caused by the mass of fleeing humanity on the causeway, blocking their field of fire. Kearny, who was "determined, when opportunity offered, to win distinction for ourselves," quickly realized that the fugitives shielded the dragoons from hostile fire and he was going to take advantage of this. Attack! Attack! Attack!

To make their way safely through the thick, packed, confused mass of retreating *soldados* on the causeway, Kearny yelled for his men to dismount and fight on foot, ordering them to move on foot around the flanks of terror-stricken runaways. About a dozen enlisted men, weapons in hand, obediently followed Kearny and breached the first defense line. Approaching the second line, Kearny did not notice that the supporting dragoons to the rear of the column had dropped back as they heard the bugle call to retreat. Lt. Richard Ewell heard Kearny's order to dismount and capture the piece. But when the lieutenant "looked around, to my horror, I found the Dragoons retiring some distance in the rear. . . . As it took some time for the information to get to the head of the column, they had not being [*sic*] able to hear in all the noise and confusion, we were engaged while the rear was retreating."[62]

All but one man in Kearny's remaining column dismounted to fight on foot. Maj. Frederick Mills of the Fifteenth Infantry, who joined the charge for glory, riding on a wild mount, raced past the garita into the city, becoming the only U.S. soldier to do so on that day. The major was promptly slain.

With most of the mob of fugitives safely within the walls of the city, the field of fire from the garita was clear; cannon and musketry could now readily fire at the exposed dragoons. It was time to retreat. Kearny grabbed a horse whose owner had been killed and turned to flee upon it. A cannon bellowed loudly nearby, Kearny recoiled as several small balls of grape shot struck him in the left arm and shoulder. Falling from the saddle, bleeding profusely, Kearny collapsed and was carried away to safety by four of his men bearing him on a blanket. He later suffered the amputation of his left arm.

The resurgent defense began to take its toll on the aggressors. Ewell, seeing Kearny fall, assumed command, mounted, and his horse was promptly killed by a musket shot. He seized a second mount, which was struck by canister shot; although badly wounded the gallant horse carried Ewell to safety. Lieutenant Graham, the hero of Mil Flores, suffered a serious wound while escaping down the causeway. At the end of the fighting, Kearny's squadron lost six men killed and four wounded.

General Scott had lost an opportunity to enter the Mexican capital. It was widely reported that had "this movement been supported, or the *Dragoons embodied*, the city would have been entered the same evening, and our flag would now be flying from the highest point of the Palace of the Montezumas!"[63] (emphasis in original). In fact, Scott did not wish to have his troops enter into Mexico City on that bloody day: he was content to drive Santa Anna's forces into the city, and feared that it would be difficult for him to maintain discipline over his exhausted and hungry troops if they gained possession of the city.

Scott was thoughtful of President Polk's intention to "Conquer a Peace"—negotiate the purchase of California and New Mexico—not to take over an entire nation. Scott and State Department envoy Nicholas Trist were hopeful of securing a treaty with the Mexican government. Capturing Mexico City would cause members of the government to flee in all directions, making it impossible to negotiate with it. Writing to Secretary of War William Marcy, Scott stated he wished "to leave something to the republic—of no value to us—on which to rest her pride, and to recover her pride, and to recover temper—I halted our victorious corps at the gates of the city."[64]

Unfortunately, nobody mentioned Trist's and Scott's intentions to Kearny and the men before he led on them on their charge. Negotiations broke down and more fighting was to follow. On September 8, Scott captured Molino del Rey and on the twelfth he entered Mexico City. Riding with Scott when he entered the city was his escort—the survivors of Company F.[65]

Phil Kearny did not vent his rage against Scott, his mentor. Rather, Kearny privately placed the blame squarely on Harney for squandering the lives of his men and causing him the loss of an arm. He wrote to Lt. John Love on November 4, 1848:

> I understand that there are whispered rumors of rashness on my part to detract from what our troop did at Churubusco. My answer is, that those who investigate the matter will find far sooner cowardice (of, at least, a moral nature), and stupid doltish incapacity on the part of Col. Harney, who interfered with our columns which he was too far in the rear to comprehend the position of. I hold Harney, who took the command out of my hands, responsible for sounding the "Recall" at all, or too late [as when the head of it being committed, the foremost were left in the lurch]. From the first moment of seeing the "El Pinon," and understanding the enemy's double line of defences, I had determined, when opportunity offered, to win distinction for ourselves, by [charging?] into the second line of defences, protected by their own fugitives. It was on the eve of accomplishing this, when I found the rear part of the column had been withdrawn. The ordeal of [re-]calling a squadron of ho[rse] on a hard gravelled [*sic*] avenue [with?] cries, in the [turn] around & confusion to boot!!! Lt. [Julian] May recalled the men from his rear. Neither Ewell nor myself, nor Sergt. Reid ever saw or heard him. Thank God we are all young. I may have another chance yet. You would be surprised to find how little the loss of an arm incommodes me."[66]

Weeks after the battle, Kearny was able to rise from his sickbed, gain a major's brevet, and ride as an escort for Gen. Winfield Scott as he victoriously entered Mexico City. Wounded or not, Kearny became one of the first members of the Aztec Club.[67]

Membership in this club, which was formed in Mexico City in 1847, was dependent upon descent, direct or dependent, of a regular or volunteer commissioned officer who had participated in the war against Mexico. Initially it was a gentlemen's social club for the occupying army; the original membership consisted of 160 individuals. The members included most of the major participants in the war, many of whom would play a major role in the American Civil War.

After the war Kearny took leave and went home to tend to his wounds. Unwilling to remain long a casualty of war, Kearny returned to field command, running a recruiting depot in New York City. He learned to ride with one arm and it wasn't long before he again yearned for glory. He then went west to take command of Company A of the 1st Dragoons. The one-armed Captain got to engage in another mounted charge near the Rogue River in Oregon Territory in 1851. Attack! Attack! Always Attack! The army accommodated its young hero, ordering him to sail to Benicia, California, and thence to Sonoma Barracks to take over command of Company A. There he occasioned "a great deal of military parade, guard mounting . . . dress foot parade at retreat, with trumpets sounding, sometimes with full band . . . from day break until nine at night tattoo."[68]

Due to the failure of his marriage and his frustration with the unimaginative bureaucracy commanding the army, the hyperactive Kearny resigned his commission in October of 1851 and sailed around the world, visiting Hawaii, China, Ceylon, and France. While in Paris, Kearny fell in love with Agnes Maxwell, but was unable to marry her because Diana, his first wife, would not grant him a divorce. In 1854, Kearny was injured when the horse upon which he was riding fell through a rotten bridge. Agnes Maxwell moved into his home to take care of him. His continued close relationship with Agnes became a high-society scandal. Because of the scandal, Agnes and Kearny left New York City and moved into Kearny's new mansion at Bellegrove, New Jersey.

In 1858, Diana agreed to grant him a divorce. Kearny and Agnes Maxwell moved to Paris, where they were married. In 1859,

Kearny joined his beloved Chasseurs d'Afrique, who were at the time fighting against Austrian forces in Italy, and he fought in another cavalry charge at the Battle of Solferino. For this charge he was awarded the French Légion d'honneur.

Kearny returned to the United States at the start of the Civil War and was appointed a brigadier general of New Jersey volunteers. He eventually rose to the rank of major general and was placed in command of the 3rd Division of the III Corps in Gen. George McClellan's Peninsula Campaign. After the Battle of Malvern Hill, McClellan ordered a withdrawal, and Kearny angrily wrote: "I, Philip Kearny, an old soldier, enter my solemn protest against this order for retreat. We ought instead of retreating should follow up the enemy and take Richmond. And in full view of all responsible for such declaration, I say to you all, such an order can only be prompted by cowardice or treason."[69]

Kearny is credited with devising the first cloth insignia issued by the U.S. Army. In the summer of 1862, he issued an order that his officers should wear a patch of red cloth on the front of their caps to identify themselves as members of his brigade. The enlisted men, with whom Kearny was quite popular, quickly followed suit voluntarily. Members of other units picked up on the idea, devising their own insignia, and these evolved over the years into the modern shoulder patch.

On September 1, 1862, following the Union defeat at Second Bull Run, Virginia, Major General Kearny, covering the retreat at Chantilly, suddenly came upon Rebel skirmishers. Ignoring a demand for his surrender, he tried to escape on horseback, when muskets were fired. Kearny was struck with a rifle ball that killed him instantly. Kearny's courage earned him the respect of his soldiers and fellow officers alike, including Winfield Scott who called him "the bravest and most perfect soldier" that he had ever known. We shall never know what might have been had he lived. Maybe his greatest acclaim would have come from President Abraham Lincoln, who was about to sack the ever-cautious McClellan and replace him with "Kearny the Magnificent." "*Attaque, attaque, toujours l'attaque!*"[70]

The Battle of Santa Cruz de Rosales

Once Lieutenant Love's Company B had reached Santa Fe and rested after its trip and harrowing battle with the Comanches at Coon Creeks, the army announced it was going to convert the dragoon company into an artillery battery. The army was in need of field artillery to fend off feared Mexican efforts to recapture New Mexico. On August 16, 1847, Love drew six cannon from military stores in Santa Fe: two powerful 24-pounder howitzers, one 12-pounder mountain howitzer, and three captured Mexican artillery pieces. One of the Mexican guns was a 6-pounder seized by Mexican troops from an ill-fated expedition of the Republic of Texas, which had sought to conquer Santa Fe. The gun was then recaptured by General Kearny's forces when they took possession of Santa Fe in 1846.[71]

On September 7, 1847, departmental headquarters ordered Company B to go to Albuquerque, where it encamped with veteran dragoon Companies G and I. While their horses and mules grazed peacefully under stands of cottonwood and willow trees along the grassy banks of the meandering Rio Grande, the men of B Company drilled as artillerists.

Although this book is about the mounted arm, some observations about Mexican War–era field artillery are in order. The terms "24-pounder" and "6-pounder" refer to the weight of solid shot fired from the cannon. In addition to solid round shot, cannon of this period could also fire explosive spherical case shot: a hollow ball filled with small pellets, a bursting charge, and timing fuse. For firing at enemy troops at under four hundred yards, the guns fired canister: a tin can filled with iron balls when fired, which turned the weapon into a massive shotgun. Howitzers were designed to lob projectiles at an arc into enemy positions. In order to improve their maneuverability in the field, these pieces employed barrels that were shorter and lighter than those of other kinds of cannon.[72]

Compared to the training of an infantryman or cavalryman, the training of an artilleryman was the most difficult. Each gun employed a crew of eight men. Whether designated a driver or a cannoneer, each member of the crew was trained to load, estimate distances, aim, and fire the piece, cut fuses of explosive shells, mount and dismount the gun and limber, harness and drive a team, and replace a damaged wheel. Over and over, day in and day out, Love's men practiced these tasks until they became part of a well-oiled machine.

Once these multifaceted skills had been learned, the crew of the mule or horse-drawn cannon and its accompanying ammunition limber drilled to act as part of a section of two guns, and then as a light artillery battery of six cannon, six limbers, traveling forge, and ammunition wagon.[73] A battery of light artillery— pulled by eighty-four horses or mules, with the crew riding on horses (usually not upon the limbers), moving at a fast trot across the plain, and swinging into action—was a sight to behold and required well-choreographed and disciplined movement of artillery, limbers, men, and horse.

On the plains outside Albuquerque a powerful unit of the Army of the West was taking shape. Slowly but surely, the recruits of Company B were learning to become a competent battery of light artillery. By December of 1847, Love's artillery was ready for combat. The war was fast coming to an end, but it was not long before this galvanized artillery would be put to the test of combat.

A Cease-Fire Is Declared but the Fighting Continues
in the State of Chihuahua

On March 16, 1848, the shooting was officially over, a cease-fire having been signed at Guadalupe Hidalgo, Mexico, on February 2. But owing to poor communications, Gen. Sterling Price, the overly ambitious general commanding the Army of the West, was unaware of the war's end. This was because in 1848 word of the cease-fire traveled slowly: 255 miles by horseback from Mexico City to the harbor at Vera Cruz, by steamer to New Orleans, and thence by telegraph to Washington, D.C., and from there back to St. Louis by telegram and then to Santa Fe by courier.

The Battle of Santa Cruz de Rosales would last for an entire day. During the fight the Mexican force lost over a quarter of its strength. Occurring after war ended and in a remote part of Mexico, the battle resolved nothing in President James Polk's grand plan to conquer and gain Mexican land. As was the case with Phil Kearny's failed—but brave—charge at Churubusco, the American public was fast losing interest in a war that appeared to have no end. In the same manner, the Battle of Santa Cruz de Rosales received little, if any, mention in newspapers and books about the Mexican War. That volunteer troops from Missouri and Santa Fe may have slaughtered several dozen surrendered Mexican soldiers received virtually no mention at all.

Six months prior to the Battle of Santa Cruz de Rosales, on September 14, 1847, Gen. Winfield Scott captured Mexico City.[74] Afterward, the war wound down to a few scattered skirmishes while diplomats attempted to find a way to end hostilities. In the fall of 1847, however, rumors were reaching Santa Fe that a Mexican army of 3,000 men was marching north from Chihuahua to recapture the region.[75] These reports proved to be wildly inaccurate, but General Price, having returned from Missouri to Santa Fe in December of 1847 with a promotion to the rank of general, and sensing a chance for glory in battle, had other ideas.[76]

In March of 1847, Missouri troops under the command of Col. Alexander Doniphan brushed aside significant Mexican forces at Brazito and Sacramento. He briefly occupied the city of Chihuahua, met General Wool in Saltillo, and then marched north to Texas. The campaign accomplished little, if anything, militarily, but made Doniphan a national hero.[77] Less than a year later, the Mexican state of Chihuahua was purportedly alive with military activity. In reality, the opposite was true: the inhabitants of that state viewed with apprehension the steady buildup of American forces in El Paso. No matter; in an obvious effort for personal glory, General Price was about to replicate Doniphan's actions for his personal gain.[78]

The *St. Louis Republican* of March 18, 1848, quoted the January 19, 1848, edition of the *Faro*, a Chihuahua newspaper, reassuring the populace that the Yanquis lacked sufficient supplies and provisions to invade Mexico. The *Faro* also mentioned that Ignacio Roquillo, a rancher in El Paso, had complained of Price's men taking seven hundred of his sheep without compensation. The *Faro* was wrong about troop movements.

General Price decided to move the greater part of his forces down the Rio Grande Valley to El Paso where they would be nearer the approaching enemy.[79] Arriving with his troops in El Paso, General Price immediately discovered the accounts of a gathering Mexican army to be false. He received orders from Adj. Gen. Roger Jones directing him to stay put in El Paso and, if possible, to send five to six hundred of his mounted troops west to reinforce the weak garrison occupying California. General Price disregarded Jones's instructions, since he was bent on topping, if not bettering, Colonel Doniphan's campaign of February–March 1847, and was determined to march to and capture Chihuahua.[80]

A former Democratic member of Congress from the state of Missouri, Price resigned his seat when the war with Mexico broke out and helped to raise the 2nd Regiment of Missouri Mounted Volunteers. The army sent him to command a backwater garrison of the war, with orders that he was simply to occupy and hold New Mexico.[81] With the war about to end but with current rumors flying around, here was the last chance for the politician-turned-general, soon to return to politics, to garner laurels on the field of battle.

The bulk of the general's troops were composed of the 3rd Missouri Volunteer Regiment and the Santa Fe Battalion—both formations containing a number of unruly racists. Also under his command were three companies of dragoons from the regular army, many of whom were immigrants and took pride in their professionalism. Stationed at Albuquerque, Companies G and I of the 1st Dragoons had been with the Army of the West during Gen. Stephen W. Kearny's conquest of Santa Fe in 1846. These men remained in New Mexico after Kearny headed to California, saw action against Navajo and Comanche raiders, and had aided in the suppression of insurgents during the 1847 Taos uprising.

Joining them was Company B, composed in large part of men recently recruited in Ohio, Indiana, and Missouri.

On February 26, General Price ordered Maj. Robert Walker's three companies of the Santa Fe Battalion to ride ninety miles south and to occupy the desert town of Carrizal. Price believed that from this location Major Walker could command the passes on the roads to Chihuahua and observe the operations of any approaching force. Major Walker dutifully occupied the town, sent out patrols ranging far and wide into the Chihuahuan Desert, and rounded up a few Mexican army stragglers, but he found no evidence of any organized Mexican force in the field.[82]

Ignoring the intelligence gathered by Walker, as well as orders from the adjutant general to remain in El Paso, General Price headed across the wilderness of the Chihuahuan Desert, following the well-worn Mexican commercial road known as El Camino Real de Tierra Adentro. As he neared the scene of Alexander Doniphan's 1847 victory at the Rio Sacramento, a Mexican patrol approached under a flag of truce. The commander gave General Price a note from Governor-General Angel Trias, which contained surprising news: a treaty had been signed on February 2 at Guadalupe Hidalgo, and the combatants had declared a cease-fire.[83]

Having received no official word of a peace treaty from army headquarters in Washington and doubting Trias's representations of a cease-fire, General Price continued with his advance. It is true that Price was at a distance from reliable sources of intelligence, but he had reason to believe Trias: Price knew that Mexico City had been taken five months prior, his scouts had proven false the rumor of a large Mexican army marching north, and he was in receipt of explicit orders from the adjutant general to hold his forces at El Paso.[84]

Governor-General Angel Trias was thirty-nine years of age at the time of the invasion. After being educated in Europe, he had returned to his native state of Chihuahua to serve in the Mexican army. Trias became head of the committee of defense and then was named as interior minister for Chihuahua. Following his participation in the battles of Sacramento and Cerro Gordo, Santa

Anna made him governor-general of the state of Chihuahua. Trias would prove to be an honorable and competent opponent.[85]

Seeking to avoid bloodshed and having inadequate forces at his disposal to defend his capitol, the governor-general abandoned Chihuahua and, with four hundred soldiers and eight cannon, retreated south toward Durango. Price's troops entered defense-less Chihuahua on March 7. The ambitious General Price, not content with the bloodless capture of his objective, now planned the destruction of Trias's army before it could be reinforced and while it was strung out on the march. He ordered two companies of Maj. Benjamin Beall's dragoons to ride overland and to inter-cept Trias. The dragoons, attempting a difficult night march over unfamiliar mountainous terrain, became lost and were unable to block Trias's avenue of retreat.[86]

Price Lays Siege to Santa Cruz de Rosales

After a rapid march of sixty miles in twelve hours, down the high-way to Durango, Price caught up with General Trias on March 9. By this time Trias had gained a small number of reinforcements and, hearing of Price's location, entrenched his troops within sheltered, thick mud-walls of the small village of Santa Cruz de Rosales. The governor-general once more insisted to Price that a peace treaty had been signed. He requested an armistice so that a messenger might bring a copy of the document from Mexico City. General Price, realizing that he lacked sufficient troops and artil-lery to carry the town, agreed not to take any action for five days.[87]

Both sides honored the five-day armistice and both generals called for reinforcements. During the wait, Price's forces camped in the woods a mile east of the town. In the meantime, more than one hundred Mexican troops under the command of Col. Cay-etano Justiniani slipped through the Yanqui lines and entered Rosales on March 10. A few nights later, two hundred additional troops of the 2nd Battalion of the Mexican National Guard entered the town. With these reinforcements Trias's force swelled to over eight hundred men.[88]

Lieutenant Love's battery was initially encamped 210 miles north of Santa Cruz de Rosales, awaiting further orders. On March 12, Love received Price's command to support him at Rosales. Mounting some of his newly trained artillerists on fast-traveling sorrels and others on mules, accompanied by three companies of the Third Missouri Horse, he raced to the scene of the siege—covering the distance in three and one-half days, sixty miles in the final twenty-four hours. This feat was made all the more remarkable in that he had to travel over desert and mountainous terrain with guns not designed for rapid movement.[89]

Santa Cruz de Rosales hardly appeared to be an appropriate site for a bloody siege and massacre. Situated at an elevation of 3,900 feet, the town sat adjacent to the Rio San Pedro, a clear mountain stream that courses through the plain on its northeastern pathway down to the Rio Grande. Surrounded by freshly plowed fields watered by irrigation ditches, the town sat astride the dusty road from Chihuahua to Durango to Mexico City. Franciscan missionaries founded the town in 1714 to minister to nearby tribes such as the Mescaleros and Utes. Spring had arrived early in March 1848. Philip Gooch Ferguson, a Missouri Volunteer, noted in his journal, "The cottonwoods were in full leaf; and the grass quite green; peas and other vegetables in full blossom."[90]

The town was but a way station on the road between Chihuahua and Durango. In 1848, Santa Cruz de Rosales extended for about three-quarters of a mile along the road in a northeast/southwest axis. It was about a quarter mile at its widest point. In the town's center was a two-hundred-yard-long plaza that contained a corral for cattle. On the west side of the plaza sat an imposing and elegant cathedral. Most buildings in the town were low, mud-walled structures with flat roofs.[91]

General Trias's defending force was a mixed lot, consisting of elements of the 2nd Battalion of National Guard along with some *permanente* (regular) artillerymen and cavalry. Included in the defense force were numerous *campesinos* (farm workers) pressed into duty, many against their will. The infantry was mainly armed with British war surplus Brown Bess muskets—flintlock relics of the Napoleonic-era weapons, inaccurate and with an effective range of about seventy-yards. Many of these weapons were in poor condition. There was also a small detachment of *presidial* lancers commanded by Lt. Col. Vicente Sanchez. Inadequately equipped even as a police force, the black-hatted, blue-jacketed lancers guarded and protected Mexico's northern frontier. And as was the case during the war, Mexican gunpowder was of a decidedly inferior quality.[92]

To protect most of his troops from exposure to artillery fire, General Trias, knowing the *resilience* of thick adobe walls to cannon shot, placed most of his men inside buildings, within the town's interior. He ringed the town plaza with entrenchments, barricades, wall cannon, and fortifications. The bulk of Mexican artillery was placed securely behind nearby fortifications, with a clear field of fire down the broad boulevards that led to the plaza. The flat roofs of the buildings adjacent to the plaza and cathedral bristled with infantry and small-caliber wall cannon. As at Taos and Monterrey, these positions were designed to expose an attacking force to deadly enfilade fire. What Trias did not bank on when he placed his cannon was Price's plan to avoid attacking down the streets and to use shrapnel shells to kill rooftop snipers.

By mutual agreement, noncombatants were afforded the opportunity to leave the town before the start of the battle. As these terrified citizens streamed out of the town, Love's six-gun battery galloped across the cultivated plain toward positions to the west of Rosales. The lively strains of a bugle sounded and the detachment halted five hundred yards to the northwest of the town plaza. Then came the command, "Fire to the rear—caissons, pass your pieces, trot-march—in battery." In seeming confusion, cannon, caissons, limbers, horses, and men moved in every direction. Within a few minutes, however, the guns were unlimbered in line and the cannoneers stood at their proper posts, limbers and ammunition caissons properly aligned behind each piece.

Lt. Col. Richard Lane's squadron of the 3rd Missouri, meanwhile, rode out from the east woods to take positions north of Rosales. Stationed behind Love's battery were four dismounted companies of Col. John Ralls's 3rd Missouri. Maj. Robert Walker's Santa Fe Battalion and two mountain howitzers covered the southern approach to the town. Major Beall's two companies of 1st Dragoons and Capt. W. L. F. McNall's company of 3rd Missouri remained mounted in reserve to the east of the town.[93]

The Mud Bricks Begin to Fly

With the troops in position it was time to start the battle. At 10:30 A.M. on March 16, 1848, General Price ordered his artillery to open fire. Love gave the command to fire and each of six gunners touched their smoldering portfires to the vents of their cannon. Smoke and flame belched forth as six cannonballs arched across the clear morning sky. An American merchant named James Glasgow was doing business in Chihuahua, Mexico. He rode south to observe the battle that was taking place at the sleepy village of Santa Cruz de Rosales. He wrote of the shots striking the adobe buildings, "making the mud bricks fly about pretty lively and so continued for the greater part of the day."[94] For more than a deadly hour the American and Mexican cannon dueled at short range and before long, two Mexican cannon were silenced.

Upon General Price's orders, a section of the battery, consisting of a 24-pound howitzer and a 6-pounder, under the command of Ordinance Lt. Alexander Dyer, were shifted seven hundred yards south to the town cemetery and began to bang away at a Mexican 9-pounder located in the plaza. The remainder of Love's battery in next to no time joined Dyer's guns, positioned at a distance of less than four hundred yards from the town. Despite intense counter-battery fire by Yankee cannon, the Mexican gun in the plaza continued its fire. Most of its shots, however, flew high and did little damage to Love's battery. Some of the overshot cannonballs, however, landed amongst Colonel Ralls's dismounted troops, killing Cpl. T. Ely, wounding another trooper, and killing six horses.[95]

Mexican artillery, in time, began to take effect on Love's battery. He later observed that during the close-range artillery duel,

Mexican grapeshot "fell like hail among the men striking the cannon, limbers, and caissons." Enemy fire struck Pvt. George Meyers, a recruit from St. Louis, and he lost his right arm. The Irish luck of Pvt. John Vance, an old soldier from County Tyrone, ran out when pieces of a shot hit him in the face. Private Vance survived his wounds, but lost his right eye. Old hand Thomas Crosby was also seriously injured by counter-battery fire. Four other B Company Dragoons were slightly wounded during the intense artillery exchange.[96]

At midday, the fortunes of battle appeared to shift to the Mexicans. American scouts reported a column of nine hundred lancers fast approaching from the south. Fearing an attack in his rear by reinforcements, Price ordered Lieutenant Love to change the battery's position in order to protect the American encampment and his ammunition train. As the battery rapidly changed positions, the defenders believed they had driven off the enemy; rousing cheers and loud shouts of "Venceremos!" "Viva Mexico!" and "Santiago" could be heard from the village.[97]

Price sent men from the Santa Fe Battalion to engage the reinforcements. When these troops got close they discovered the supposed reinforcements to be nothing more than a few horsemen and unarmed campesinos from neighboring towns. These individuals, hearing the distant rumble of artillery like trader Glasgow, had come to witness the battle, but fled when they saw the approach of the company of horsemen.

During a lull in the fighting Glasgow briefly napped in a field near the battle, only to be awakened by the screams of a wounded man whose leg was being sawed off by an army surgeon. A short distance away he saw hospital attendants "dressing the stump of another's which had just been cut off." Glasgow wrote that he "didn't feel sleepy again for some time" and concluded, "War is an ugly business and I could not help thinking when it was all over, that this thing of people's killing each other is the greatest nonsense extant."[98]

General Price decided that the lengthy artillery bombardment had not shaken the resolve of the well-entrenched defenders and that his troops needed to enter the town. At three o'clock in the afternoon, he ordered Lieutenant Love's cannon back to the cemetery with orders that it provide covering fire for the impending attack. Love's artillery, under fire from two Mexican artillery pieces, trotted forward and once more swung into position.[99]

Upon the resumption of firing by Love's guns, Colonel Ralls's four companies of Missourians advanced on foot at the double-quick from the southwest quarter. With their pent-up rage unleashed after withstanding Mexican cannon shot all morning, the Missourians charged over the open plain and into the village. Colonel Ralls's detachment of 190 men, shouting "Huzza!" three times, and moved cautiously along the streets that led to the plaza. A participant wrote, "The Charge of Col. Ralls's column was a splendid affair. It moved like a thunder-bolt, precisely in the direction it was sent, spreading dismay, death, and destruction."[100]

From their position high atop the church and the roof of a neighboring two-story building, Capt. Juan Talamantes and a company of infantry guardsmen took up exposed positions on the rooftop to meet the attack. Unfortunately, his movement attracted the attention of the Yanqui gunners. Well-aimed exploding case shots rained down shrapnel from above, killing Captain Talamantes and most of the men in his detachment.[101]

Lieutenant Colonel Lane's three companies of Missourians dismounted and advanced swiftly from the north along the road to Chihuahua. Meeting little resistance, Lane's detachment cut through several walls and came to within a hundred yards of the plaza. Protecting the plaza were a couple of artillery pieces, masked by secure fortifications and commanded by Col. Vicente Sanchez and Capt. Francisco Montes de Oca. Sanchez ordered his troops to open fire. A fusillade of bullets and grapeshot felled Lt. George Hepburn of Company D and Privates Beckman and Scharfenburg of Company B. The fire from the plaza increased and five or six of the attackers lay wounded. Lane's men, finding their exposed position perilous, beat a retreat back to their original position. General Price rode up and ordered Lane to mount his force and reinforce Colonel Ralls at the southwestern side of the town.[102]

Ralls later described the Mexican positions he encountered: "Every house and wall, from the point of our entrance into town to the steeple of the church was filled with infantry, protected by barricades or parapets, and, in fact, the outlines of the walls and houses bristled with musketry, which continued to pour in the direction of our party, added to which were hand grenades (likely lighted artillery projectiles), which the enemy was constantly throwing into our midst."[103]

The resistance confronting Ralls stiffened the closer he got to the plaza. To his front stood a formation of forty-three National Guard skirmishers commanded by Lt. José Escobar. The skirmishers swiftly parted, unmasking a barricade in which was placed a 24-pound howitzer. The weapon belched forth a deadly round of grapeshot into Ralls's formation and sent it reeling. Rather than risk a suicidal charge, he ordered his men to fall back and take cover in the adjacent buildings. Using crowbars, picks, rifle butts, and shovels, this detachment slowly bashed, clawed, cursed, and dug their way through the thick interior adobe walls of buildings. In time they came within fifty yards of the plaza defenses and, peering through the dense white gun smoke, opened fire.[104]

From their fortified position in the plaza, the defenders had successfully withstood artillery bombardments and repelled attacks coming from the north and western fronts. Mingled with wreckage and burning material, the dead and unattended wounded were lying all over the ground. Visibility was severely limited as the sky was filled with gun smoke and grimy smoke from the burning interiors of buildings. More attacks would come.

At about five o'clock in the afternoon, Major Walker's detachment of Santa Fe volunteers and Missouri Horse began their approach from the southwest. Sergeant Drescher observed that the Mexican grapeshot "fell as thick as hail around us," but owing to defective gun powder, "we minded it no more than straw."[105] Brushing aside skirmishers, Walker's men steadily advanced toward the plaza and soon came upon a strong position under the command of Col. Cayetano Justiniani. Walker's men cleared the position by poking holes into the walls of fortified houses and then tossing lighted howitzer shells into the rooms. Walker brought up a 12-pound mountain howitzer and, firing canister and shell, gunned down more than a few Mexican rooftop snipers. Angry grunts, yells, curses, screams, and cries could be heard as the attackers poured volley after deadly volley into the plaza.[106]

The Mexican forces had endured more than six hours of bombardment and fighting. They were now being attacked on two sides and the casualties were mounting. At twenty minutes after six and with darkness fast approaching, General Trias ordered a cease-fire and surrendered. The final assault upon Rosales had taken about an hour and ahalf.[107] Price's losses for the battle were four killed and nineteen wounded. Mexican losses were significantly greater.

After the Shooting Finally Stops: Casualties and Fallout

Philip Gooch Ferguson of the 3rd Missouri wrote that as soon as the battle ended it had become dark and he bedded down in the church. "The next morning the sight that had met the eye was shocking to behold. Piles of dead Mexicans, both soldiers and civilians, were seen in various quarters, many of them most horribly mangled." Acting Assistant Surgeon E. S. Gale of the 3rd Missouri surveyed the south side of town after the battle and counted 182 dead Mexican soldiers. Lieutenant Dyer estimated that 230 Mexican soldiers had been killed.[108] Sergeant Drescher, Hassendeubel's Light Artillery Company A, initially wrote, "I cannot state with certainty [the Mexican casualties]; it is supposed 70 or 80." He later observed additional casualties, possibly civilians, were found in the houses and concluded the number of Mexicans killed exceeded two hundred.[109]

Price's official report lists Mexican deaths at two officers and 236 enlisted men. In contrast, General Trias reported two officers and thirty privates as having died in the battle. The Mexican command structure, disorganized in the course of the retreat from

Chihuahua, ceased to exist at the end of battle. Most likely, Mexican officers, all of whom were made prisoners, hastily computed the number of dead.[110] Adding to the confusion over casualties was the fact that the Mexican troops defending Rosales were a mix of federal, national guard, and civilians. In brief, accurate troop rosters and Mexican casualties were, and remain, nonexistent.

Price didn't wish to remain in the bloodstained village. On the following day, General Price and the bulk of his command marched back to better quarters in Chihuahua. Not until July 24, 1848, did the United States' forces depart from Chihuahua for Santa Fe.[111]

After the war, Secretary of War William Marcy wrote to General Price, remarking that the general's unilateral decision to invade Chihuahua was jeopardizing the fragile peace by creating "great uncertainty as to what will be our future relations with Mexico." The secretary of war also expressed anger that Price had not, contrary to his instructions, sent any of his men westward to reinforce the army in California. Sensing the all-too-common hostility of volunteers to the Mexican populace, he urged the general to take "great pains . . . to prevent all irregular or disorderly conduct in our troops."[112] No matter. The war was over, General Price got the victory he wanted, and the secretary of war was essentially powerless to hurt a war hero who was about to leave the army.

After temporarily turning control of the territory over to Major Beall, Sterling Price and his volunteers returned to Missouri that fall, where they were hailed as conquering heroes. A local newspaper wrote that Price was "beloved by his soldiers, respected by his fellow citizens, and laurels encircled around his brow that will perpetually bloom in the affections of his countrymen." In 1852, Price was elected governor of Missouri.[113]

With the coming of the Civil War, Sterling "Old Pap" Price cast his lot with the secessionists and became a general in the Confederate Army. Forsaking surrender in 1865, Old Pap again crossed the Rio Grande River and entered Mexico with a group of unreconstructed Rebels. Vowing his support for Emperor Maximilian, he attempted to establish a safe haven for Rebels in the French-occupied state of Vera Cruz. With the fall of Emperor Maximilian in 1867, Price took flight to St. Louis, where he died on September 29, 1867.

In six of the major battles fought in the war the percentage of casualties (killed and wounded) suffered by the United States when compared to Mexican losses ranges between a low of 23 percent (Palo Alto and Churubusco) to a high of 133 percent (Monterrey).[114] The total loss of United States soldiers in these representative battles averages out to roughly 34 percent of Mexican losses. At Santa Cruz de Rosales, Price's losses were a mere 1.6 percent of reported Mexican casualties. These figures are especially remarkable considering that Price was attacking entrenched defenders who had forted up inside a village. An army attacking prepared defenses can expect to take heavy losses.[115]

Was There a Massacre of Mexican Prisoners?

The loss of just two Mexican officers out of over two hundred casualties also raises suspicion that the slaughter may have occurred after the officers were separated from their men. Either that or it may mean that most of the officers hid from hostile fire, At first blush, the disproportionate casualties at Santa Cruz de Rosales may be attributed to the combination of wildly inaccurate Mexican marksmanship and the reckless exposure of Mexican troops to artillery fire. These factors may be responsible for a portion of the significantly disparate figures, but there may be a darker reason for the unusually high toll of Mexican enlisted casualties: many of the Mexican soldiers might have been ruthlessly shot by volunteers after they had surrendered.

While true that the press sometimes reported personal accounts of atrocities, not all atrocities were publicized. "It was extremely rare for an individual volunteer to break ranks with his fellows and unashamedly declare that his comrades were out-and-out murderers. . . . [T]he closed mouths and closed ranks of the volunteers made it difficult to achieve corroboration of those stories."[116] And there was silence amongst those volunteers who fought at Santa Cruz de Rosales on that sixteenth day of March. But there are clues that, if viewed in the aggregate, make a strong case for calling this a historical abomination.

Historians agree there was widespread racism during the Mexican American War.[117] Justin Smith summarized this phenomenon: "Conquering soldiers in a foreign land, especially when the enemy is deemed cowardly, treacherous, and cruel, are not likely to be angels; and we may count upon meeting here with disagreeable as well as complimentary facts."[118] Writing about atrocities committed by volunteers eighty-three years after the publication of Smith's work, Paul Foos was more blunt: "Their proclivity [of the volunteers] for racist, religious, or nationalist rationales for their crimes took up the language of manifest destiny, suffusing their criminal activity with heroism and comradeship implicit in their cause."[119]

Two weeks after the battle, local merchant James Glasgow wrote to his sister from Chihuahua that Mexicans are "cowardly in the extreme" having "perhaps fewer redeeming traits of character than any other nation; not excepting Comanches nor the wild Arabs."[120] This attitude was hardly unique. Indeed, we have previously seen how widespread prejudice against Mexicans was a major factor in Kearny's defeat at San Pasqual.

In marked contrast with volunteers, most soldiers of the regular army were proud of their efforts to refrain from racist and anti-Catholic behavior. Letters and reports by regular-army soldiers chronicled some of the outrages by volunteers. After seeing a volunteer officer murder a Mexican in cold blood, First Artillery Lt. D. H. Hill, later a Confederate general, decried, "How can the Army have any tone or character when such wretches hold commissions in it?" A private in a regular army regiment wrote to his father in 1847, "The majority of the Volunteers sent here are a disgrace to the nation; think of one of them shooting a woman while [she was] washing on the bank of a river—merely to *test* his rifle."[121] This is not to suggest that regulars were not entirely immune from aberrant behavior. As noted, Sam Chamberlain recalled that in 1846, Major Beall led a band of dragoons who burst into a Mexican shop in Parras, and he allowed the men to loot the establishment of liquor and tobacco.

Journalist Phillip Ferguson frequently reported of the contempt the Missourians had for Mexicans. On October 21, 1847, the men of a troop of 3rd Missouri Volunteers ransacked the town of San Pedro, confiscated property, took prisoners, shot a Mexican, and looted a church.[122] Single incidents of racism do not necessarily prove the existence of a massacre, though the conduct of Sgt. William C. Holbrook of Company E of the 3rd Missouri Regiment might shed further light upon the character of a number of volunteers from Missouri and Santa Fe. After the battle at Rosales, the sergeant faced a general court-martial—which is the military equivalent of a felony proceeding—for having attempted to enter, while intoxicated, the home of a resident of the city of Chihuahua. The court-martial tribunal found him not guilty of the forcible entry, but guilty of the charge of intoxication. Because of Holbrook's prior service to the country at the battles of Palo Alto, Resaca, Monterey, and Vera Cruz, in the regular army, General Price annulled the charge.[123]

Holbrook remained in New Mexico at war's end, enlisted in Company I of the 1st Dragoons, and became first sergeant. In 1850, while stationed at Rayado, New Mexico Territory, he led a patrol that reportedly killed and scalped five Jicarilla Apache horse thieves. On March 30, 1854, Sergeant Holbrook, still serving with Company I, died in a battle with the Jicarilla Apache in northern New Mexico Territory.[124]

In Col. John Ralls's March 17, 1848, official account of the Battle of Santa Cruz de Rosales, he candidly reveals that, after his troops had gained a position near the plaza, they observed a white flag of surrender floating overhead and Ralls's order for his men was to "cease firing." Colonel Ralls wrote, "[S]o intent were the men, and so determined was their enthusiasm to occupy the church (from which so much mischief had been done) and the plaza before night, that the officers (including myself) *had much difficulty in restraining* [the troops], and to get them once more into ranks"[125] (emphasis in original). The meaning of Ralls's report is plain: several volunteers disobeyed commands to cease firing and ruthlessly gunned down Mexican soldiers who were attempting to surrender.

For many years thereafter, residents of the region would recall with horror the murders and other atrocities committed by Price's troops. In 1849, a regular army officer reported to Congress that all throughout northern Mexico, "The smiling villages which welcomed our troops on their upward march are now black and smoldering ruins, their gardens and orange groves destroyed, and the inhabitants who administered to their necessities have fled to the mountains. The march of Attila was not more withering and destructive."[126] The many courts-martial proceedings of the Army of the West held in May of 1848 chronicle the wide scope of misconduct of United States troops during the weeks following the Battle of Santa Cruz de Rosales.[127] Decades later, Francisco Montes de Oca, the captain of artillery at Rosales whose cannon stopped Lane's advance in its tracks, related how, following the battle, the invaders ransacked the town.[128]

Without consulting with General Price, Colonel Ralls allowed uncensored accounts of the battle to be printed on a broken-down press that had been found by his soldiers in Santa Cruz de Rosales.[129] The newspaper, entitled the *Santa Cruz Banner*, was circulated among the troops. Two weeks later, Colonel Ralls, worried about the battle having been fought after the rumored cease-fire, bypassed General Price, sending a copy of his report and a letter to General Wool, the commanding officer of Center Division army headquarters in Saltillo, Mexico: "Feeling a strong desire to have news from the United States and Mexico, I have thought it proper to send this communication to you, with the request that it may be laid before the General Commanding, in order that I may have returned to me the latest and most authentic intelligence. There was a rumor at this place, and it was so reported to General Price before his capture of this town, which took place on the 16th Inst, [heard?] there was an armistice, but no facts could be furnished bearing evidence sufficient to convince the General that there existed such an armistice."[130]

General Price was furious when he learned that Colonel Ralls had communicated directly with military headquarters in Saltillo and, worse, he had allowed copies of uncensored accounts of the battle to be printed without Price's knowledge and placed into the hands of his troops. He ordered Colonel Ralls to report immediately to his headquarters in Chihuahua and upon Ralls's arrival, Price placed him under house arrest.[131]

On April 4, 1848, Colonel Ralls responded to Price's charges. He acknowledged that the newspaper had been printed with his knowledge but took umbrage at Price's assertion that this behavior somehow violated a sense of military protocol: "The document [the *Banner*] referred to was not printed by my order. Nor does it contain my official report—however, in justice to those who executed the printing, it was done by my consent in the hour of excitement after the achievement of victory over our enemies. The printing was permitted without any mischievous intent on the part of myself or any others—believing as I did at the time that any accusation of such notoriety of the Battle of Santa Cruz could be printed without being [injurious?] to the public service. . . , The facts published were generally known in this Country and being communicated in every direction by each party engaged in the Conflict."[132]

On April 5, 1848, Price wrote to General Wool that he had "made every effort to suppress circulation of this [unofficial printed] Report, and at once ordered Colonel Ralls to report to me in person: his corroboration of these facts led at once to his arrest." The next day, Price released Ralls from confinement.[133] Despite all efforts by Price to suppress circulation of the *Banner,* its contents were reprinted in the April 22, 1848, edition of the *Santa Fe Republican.*[134]

Some veterans of the Battle of Santa Cruz de Rosales later intimated that there was a massacre of Mexican troops following surrender to Price's men. On May 22, 1848, Lt. Cave Couts wrote to Lt. John Love from army headquarters at Saltillo, Mexico.[135] "We are delighted to hear from Capt. [William] Grier that you had nothing to do with the "Cowpen Slaughter" at Santa Cruz. Something had been heard of it previous to the arrival of the Capt., which agreed with his version of the affair, viz: you penned up a number of Mexican regular greasers, and slaughtered them by file. We are all proud, and feel happy in learning that you gave countenance to no such inhumanity."

These two paragraphs, standing alone, may not prove that mass murder occurred. Lieutenant Couts was not at the battle and his knowledge of acts of violence was obtained from secondhand sources. Captain Grier, however, was at the battle and was likely a reliable declarant.

Couts's letter is not, perhaps, proof of the atrocity, but there's another letter to Lieutenant Love that adds fuel to the fire. On March 6, 1854, Maj. Benjamin Beall, Love's commanding officer at Rosales, wrote to him to inquire about opportunities in the private sector for a retired officer. In this letter Major Beall, making a passing reference to the incident at Santa Cruz de Rosales, asked whether "a poor devil like me [could] make any money in this business? Or must I go back to [the State of] Chihuahua and meet such fellows as you, [Adrian?] Terry, Folger, [John] Adams, [Langdon] Easton, [Rev John?] McCarty, & a lot of others who congregated in that *abominable Corral*"[136] (emphasis added).

While there is no direct proof of a slaughter of surrendered troops, there is a wealth of circumstantial evidence establishing such: there was a significantly disproportionate number of dead Mexican enlisted soldiers; the likely racial animosity of volunteers toward Mexicans; the report of Colonel Ralls that he had difficulty getting his troops to stop shooting; the reference by Lieutenant Couts to the "Cowpen Slaughter" of "greasers;" the characterization by Colonel Beall of the affair as being "abominable;" and lastly, the overreaction of the politically ambitious General Price in which he suppressed the distribution of the *Santa Cruz Banner.* Price certainly feared that if word of the massacre reached the wrong ears or came to the attention of anti-war Whigs, he might be prosecuted in a military tribunal and this would frustrate his chance to become governor. Indeed, all the more so should his political ambitions be frustrated if it were revealed that the general recklessly disobeyed orders and attacked after a cease-fire had been agreed to by General Scott, U.S. diplomat Nicholas Trist, and Mexican politicians.

After the War

Hostilities with Mexico were finally spent, and scattered dragoon companies sailed or marched from Mexico to answer the shortage of troops in the newly conquered territories of California and New Mexico. Only Companies C and G remained where they had been stationed during the war, in California and New Mexico, respectively. Among those units rushing overland from Monterrey, Mexico, to occupy California were the men of Company A of the 1st Dragoons, under the command of Lt. Cave Couts. Lieutenant Couts, nephew of Postmaster General Cave Johnson in the Polk administration, received word of the peace. This was not good news. In his view, he had missed out on the glory, excitement, and career opportunities that attended a good battle. Worse, on August 26 came orders to march his troop of dragoons 1,057 miles to California. Couts joined an expedition of Companies A and E of the 1st Dragoons, Companies I, K, and L of the 2nd Dragoons, and a battery from Third Artillery. Lt. Col. John Washington commanded the force.[137]

Sam Chamberlain, a veteran of the Battle of Buena Vista, described the departure of the troops from the outskirts of Monterrey: "The bugles sounded loud and clear, 'to horse' and then 'forward,' and the finest appearing column of United States Troops that was ever seen debouched from the woods of San Domingo and wound its way past the 'Black Fort' towards Monterrey. The entire column was dressed in [nonregulation] bright flannel shirts and black broad brim felt hats, this with their white belts, burnished arms, gay banners, with dashing [local] horsewomen, galloping along the flanks, all combined to make up an effect seldom witnessed in the dull routine of Uncle Sam's service."[138]

But soon after the glorious departure, rations and forage began to fail. Couts observed, "A quarrel with Quartermaster from time of arrival in camp until night has been the almost imperative duty of every dragoon Company commander since the commencement of our march."[139] Despite shortages of food and provender, the hardships of the march, and attendant thievery by the soldiers, Couts and Chamberlain were buoyed by the kindness of the locals. The campesinos' friendliness surprised them since, for the previous two years, conquering armies of Generals Alexander Doniphan and Sterling Price had brutalized them and plundered their property.[140] When they reached the city of Chihuahua, Governor Trias, who had been defeated and captured at the Battle of Santa Cruz de Rosales, showed his appreciation of their departure from his state by graciously bidding the detachment farewell with a military review, dinner, and a grand ball.[141]

The 1st Dragoons would have little luck with leaders or men. Near the site of the 1847 Battle of Sacramento, they separated from Col. John Washington's Santa Fe-bound column. Now under the command of Bvt. Maj. Lawrence Graham, the dragoons roughly followed the trail blazed in late 1846 by Captain Cooke and the Mormon Battalion: westward into the state of Sonora, through the Guadalupe Pass, and along the San Pedro River.[142] Observing Graham's intoxicated condition, Sam Chamberlain found him unfit for command, and began to wonder if "there was too much whiskey at [headquarters] for the expedition to be a success." Couts confirmed this impression: "Our commanding officer drunk nearly all the while, and interfering with everyone's business, giving the men whiskey by the bucketful, from 7 o'clock until encamping." Chamberlain wrote that he became disgusted with Major Graham's inebriated and often vindictive behavior and quit en route. He may well have become frustrated over the major's behavior, but despite his book, he did not desert on the trip west. Finishing the hard trip across the California desert, Couts and Chamberlain arrived in Los Angeles just in time for the March 1849 Gold Rush to draw twenty-nine of Graham's men, including Chamberlain and Darwin French, off to the gold fields, leaving Couts but thirty-six troops.[143]

Epilogue

They weren't supposed to shoot. But by October 29, 1849, much had changed since Dodge's first peace councils with the Pawnees. Prowling through high grass, willows, and grape vines on the Platte River, former blacksmith Jacob Martin led a detachment of dragoons scouring an island for the Pawnee warriors rumored to be hiding there.

Some in the company scoffed at the cautious orders from their commander, Capt. Robert Chilton. Chilton wanted prisoners: to intimidate but not kill the Pawnees, and so to bring them to a peace council, as Colonel Dodge had done in 1834 when Martin had come this way in a time of diplomacy and trust. Now reduced to starvation and desperation, the Pawnees were characterized in local newspapers as "pestiferous banditti." In the press's view, the occasional crimes of young Pawnees posed an existential menace to western-bound covered wagon traffic, which was exploding right when the Pawnees had been forced by circumstances into its path. In the period of Martin's earlier expedition under Dodge, few whites braved this plains region south of the Platte. But this year, instead of a few scouts, 20,000 settlers were passing through, with three times as many hungry animals. The whites thinned herds of buffalo and antelope, allowed their horses to eat the corn crops the Pawnee women planted, and not infrequently shot Indians on sight.

In the year of gold fever the Pawnees were homeless, cholera-stricken, and often set upon by their mortal enemies the Sioux, whose raiders that summer had recently burned down a Pawnee village. There also lingered a sense of betrayal at the hands of white missionaries and government authorities, who promised much but whose efforts often drove them into the clutches of the Sioux. One aborted effort to Christianize the children of the Pawnees and to settle the tribe at Loup Fork, Nebraska, ended abruptly in 1846 when Sioux attacks sent white schoolmasters scattering.

Meanwhile white traders at Fort Laramie continued to sell weapons to their enemies, while rivals thwarted promises of U.S.-supplied ammunition, and twelve years of protection ran out as a treaty was allowed to expire. The Pawnees questioned the sincerity of a Great White Father whose professed love came with an expiration date. "From their untutored way of looking at it," writes historian George Hyde, "such a friendship, measured with a stick and cut off at a certain point, was a sham."[1]

Sgt. Jacob Martin, an old soldier like S. W. Kearny, his late commanding officer, had served in the dragoons long enough to expect that the recent troubles with Pawnees harassing travelers needed to be dealt with in the old way, Kearny's way: to demonstrate just enough force to resume peace.[2] The orders, recalled Percival Lowe, a trooper in the company, were "empathetic" and "not to shoot—he wanted to make [the warriors] prisoners."

Unfortunately, Martin did not appreciate the mindset of the men under his command, strangers to the old peace-keeping methods forged in the regiment by Dodge and Kearny. The prevailing new mindset was expressed by a soldier in Company H who—frustrated at being assigned peace-keeping duty at Fort Gibson rather than being allowed to join in the invasion of Mexico—had written home two years earlier with this counsel to a young relative: "Tell Cyrus that I should like to see him with his little gun on his shoulder marching after the Birds. But tell him to Learn to Shoot well and Then mabe [sic] he may Become a Soilder [sic] and Kill The Indians[.]"[3]

When the troops came upon the Pawnees, who fled rather than surrender, the other men ignored the captain's orders. They promptly opened fire with their Hall carbines, killing three of the Pawnee warriors.

A lone Pawnee remained. Martin cornered him, moving fast with his fellow soldier Langford "Farmer" Peel, a bright, quick-thinking bugler and Englishman. But according to Peel, the Pawnee "gave his final war-whoop and dropped the muzzle of his gun" to aim at Martin. The warrior pulled the trigger and Martin fell dead. Peel fired at the same moment, killing the Pawnee. The captain rode up and was furious over his men's disobedience to orders. Private Lowe, a fresh recruit, ridiculed what he saw as Chilton's naïve plan to avert violence. Martin, he said, was a victim of his captain's order.[4] In 1849 the peacemaking tactics that Kearny and Dodge had pioneered were seen by the new generation of soldiers as absurd.

Many Missions

As the reader may recall, former Lieutenant Schaumburg had been trying for years to regain his commission and be promoted to captain. In 1848, writing to Lewis Cass, now chair of the Senate Military Committee, about the Schaumburg debate, Henry Turner recalled the first fifteen years of the dragoons' history: "I believe more Officers of this Reg't have fallen in battle than any other Reg't of the service. . . . My interest in it is that Officers of the Reg't may not suffer the injustice and humiliation of having Mr. S placed over them in the Reg't he resigned near 12 years ago while they have served, without other reward for faithful services, than such promotions as survivors have attained from the death of those in service or fallen in battle."[5]

The next year, Lieutenant Colonel Sumner wrote to Secretary of War George Crawford on the same dispute. In this letter he reminded the secretary of the terrible price paid in the late war and of how unjust it would be to deprive the survivors of that conflict their promotions. "The officers have been struggling on for years through difficulty, and danger, to attain their present ranks, and now, at the close of the war, to find themselves thru cut backs has such a withering influence upon the regiment, that it is utterly [unintelligible] for the field officers of the regiment to counteract it. His Excellency the President will perceive this at a glance."[6] It was not solely the regiment's performance in war that made it extraordinary. Lt. Fayette Robinson opined that the 1st Dragoon Regiment "had done more duty and marched farther than any other body of men that have ever existed." Although Robinson had overlooked the exploits of Genghis Khan, Napoleon, Alexander, and the like, his appraisal was not altogether undeserved. Dodge's and Kearny's regiment had "gone thrice to the [Rocky] mountains, and a part of it has visited the shores of the Pacific. The men have been almost to the head of the Mississippi, and have been far to the northwest along the Canada line; from Texas to the extreme point of the western frontier this regiment has marched, always sustaining every expedition formed of it."[7]

In 1848, former secretary of war and current Democratic candidate for president Lewis Cass had to be pleased with the multifaceted achievements of the 1st Dragoons. As Cass had hoped, the dragoons successfully kept the numerous removed tribes to the west of the Mississippi and of that other great waterway, the Missouri. Moreover, for thirteen years Dodge's and Kearny's dragoons had protected burgeoning trade on the Santa Fe Trail and had kept peace on the Great Plains. Far beyond Cass's wildest expectations, the dragoons became Polk's vanguard for so-called Manifest Destiny: conquering and opening the West for trade and white habitation from "sea to shining sea." Once the original dwellers of the region (i.e., the tribes) were subdued, two-thirds of this country's landmass was open for (white) settlement. In 1848 westward conquest had only begun to impinge on Native American life. But to the dismay of the peoples residing in its path, what has been vaguely referred to as Manifest Destiny would gain in strength, destroying tribe after tribe, eradicating traditional cultures, and leaving the survivors traumatized and impoverished. Within the space of forty-two years (1848–90) the tribes of the West were to be wholly subjugated.

The Price Paid

With the Mexican War now ended, the regiment resumed constabulary services in the expanded West—the future states of California, New Mexico, Missouri, Oregon, Washington, and Minnesota. But its muster contained a host of new faces among officers and ranks, in many instances vastly inferior to those whom they succeeded.

While its losses were ever so slight and cannot be compared to those thus far suffered by Native peoples, the regiment paid dearly for its accomplishments. The 1846–48 war with Mexico brought death, illness, injury, transfer, and resignation of many of the regiment's best officers and enlisted men. As Fayette Robinson observed, "[no] regiment of the army has paid so heavy a quota to the war with Mexico as has the 1st dragoons."[8] The butcher's bill was indeed significant. Captains Johnston, Moore, and Burgwin, and Lieutenant Hammond had perished leading their troops in combat. In Mexico, Lieutenants Leonidas Jenkins and Bezaleel Armstrong died of disease, respectively in 1847 and 1849. Philip Cooke, a promising officer, was lost through promotion and transfer to the 2nd Dragoons in 1846. Heavy drinking hastened the death of the bright, roundly beloved Captain Allen in 1846 and that of the talented, roundly reviled Major Trenor the following year. Lt. Col. Clifton Wharton died July 17, 1847, at Fort Leavenworth.

Key losses continued during the years immediately following the war. Cholera claimed Colonel Mason in 1849. Lts. Thomas Castor and George Evans became mortally ill while serving in Mexico; Castor died in 1855, Evans in 1859. Clarendon Wilson died of disease while serving in New Mexico in 1853. The army cashiered Capt. Philip Thompson, severely hampered by his longstanding addiction to alcohol, in 1855. Capt. Enoch Steen and Lts. Richard Ewell and Phil Kearny remained in the 1st Dragoons but had been crippled by wounds suffered in the war. Within three years after war's end, promising officers such as Cave Couts, Henry Turner, and John Love became fed up with military politics and, each of the trio having married into wealth, resigned to secure their futures in civilian enterprises.

But the biggest single loss to the regiment began when, after the California campaign, Brig. Gen. Stephen Watts Kearny headed east to bring court-martial charges against the insubordinate John Frémont. We have seen that Frémont's powerful father-in-law, Senator Thomas Hart Benton, failed to turn the court-martial proceedings into an inquisition of Kearny's performance in California. Still, he did manage to drag Kearny through a congressional investigation, and those ordeals no doubt battered Kearny's spirit. Already in failing health, Kearny died in 1848, before the nation could properly recognize him for all that he had won for it.

The shuffling and loss of seasoned officers, along with the increased territory the dragoons now had to police, strained the regiment during the decade of the 1850s and began the decline of the once-elite corps. Nowhere was this more apparent than in New Mexico where Col. Thomas T. Fauntleroy succeeded Colonel Mason as commander of the 1st Dragoons.[9] In stark contrast to Kearny's pre-war regiment, Fauntleroy's dragoons would become embroiled in a series of deadly wars with the tribes, and needless battles such as at Cieneguilla, New Mexico Territory, Hungry Hill, Oregon Territory, and Tohotonimme, Washington Territory, would cause ever greater losses of key personnel.[10]

In August 1861, purely for the sake of bureaucratic efficiency in a reorganized federal army, Abraham Lincoln's War Department changed the names of the dragoons and mounted rifles regiments to "cavalry," to fight the Confederacy. The 1st Dragoons thus disappeared, renamed the 1st Cavalry, but the regiment deserves particular attention for the disproportionate number of Civil War generals and brevet generals it produced.[11] Gen. John Buford had served only briefly with the 1st Dragoons but perfected their tactics and used them to delay Gen. Robert E. Lee's advance at the Battle of Gettysburg.[12] The 1st Cavalry served throughout the Civil War in the Army of the Potomac and left its mark on North and South. For though the dragoons passed from the scene in America as in Europe, the strategies of mounted warfare they developed to possess and protect the West were copied not only by the new 1st Cavalry but by hundreds of volunteer cavalry regiments on both sides of the Civil War.

Then, as the postwar United States expanded, the army added four new cavalry regiments to the six created for the Civil War. Through new leaders and campaigns, these regiments would complete the conquest of the West, and the model of warfare invented by the 1st Dragoons would become even more deeply ensconced in national history and legend.

Eternal Echoes

The United States Cavalry comes whooping to the rescue not once but twice—and beautifully. Yet for any one who has the slightest regard for the spirit—not to mention the facts—of American history, it will prove exceedingly annoying.

New York Times film critic Bosley Crowther
on *The Santa Fe Trail* (1940)

The greatest part of the general public's knowledge of the Indian Wars derives from movies in which Native people are depicted as an impediment to progress, and in need of removal from the path of civilization by mounted forces. Although the dragoons are rarely depicted in film (*Kit Carson* (1940), *Distant Drums* (1951), *Centennial* (1978) and, tangentially, *Jeremiah Johnson* (1972) are the few that come to mind), for a generation of citizens raised on Saturday matinees, the United States Cavalry played the role of champions of the American Way in the deserts of the West. When director John Ford's *Stagecoach* premiered in New York in 1939, it established John Wayne as a star, set off the first tsunami of grade-A Westerns, painted Indians as dangerous impediments to civilization, and imprinted onto a whole generation the image of the horse soldier as the rescuer after all other hope is lost.[13]

The setting: the American Southwest of the post-dragoon era (as in all of Ford's cavalry movies). Wayne, as the outlaw Ringo

Kid, travels by stage, joined by fellow passengers, each from a different walk of life, each on a different quest—the cavalry wife, the prostitute, the salesman, and the doctor ride into an Arizona the movie poster warns is "the last frontier of wickedness." Wreaking most of this wickedness is no less a figure than Geronimo, the Apache leader who rampages at will in his wild domain: "It was one of those years in the territory," begins the original *Collier's* magazine story adapted for *Stagecoach*, "when Apache smoke signals spiraled up from the stony mountain summits and many a ranch cabin lay as a square of blackened ashes on the ground."[14]

In a climax whose images came to symbolize all cavalry fighting out west, Geronimo and the Apaches attack the wayfarers just when they believe themselves out of harm's way. (In real life, they probably would have been as Geronimo couldn't have chosen a worse place for an ambush than the dry lakebed they were traversing.) Right when the ammo has run out, wounds have been suffered, and a pistol has been put to the head of the cavalry wife to save her from ravishment, we hear the cavalry bugle and know that the tables have turned. The cavalry courses across the lake bed, abreast with sabers held high and the red-and-white swallow-tailed guidon fluttering proudly, to make short work of the Apaches. The iconic scene was so successful that Ford recycled it in *Fort Apache*, part of a trilogy that deepened the legend and portrayed the cavalry as a microcosm of American democracy, where rollicking Irish-immigrant drill sergeants mixed with former Confederate officers and smart-aleck city kids.

In the real West, of course, horse soldiers rarely charged to rescue whites and conditions were harsh instead of heroic. But cavalry legend still defines how Americans see themselves. It appears in the story of George Custer, whose 1876 defeat at Little Big Horn made him the singular emblem of the many tragedies of the Indian Wars. Paratroopers jumping out of planes cried, "Geronimo!" and during the Vietnam War some soldiers wore black cavalry slouch hats and called Viet Cong territory "Indian Country." The myth even found its way into the 2011 raid on the headquarters of Osama bin Laden: code-named Geronimo, it cast

Pakistan as Monument Valley's "last frontier of wickedness," where the cavalry alone could preserve honor.

The flesh-and-blood mounted arm remained for just 108 years, but the tactics and organization developed by the 1st Dragoons lived on in all U.S. mounted units well into the twenty-first century. The strategies they developed were used as machine-gun platoons replaced Hall Carbines and sabers, and until the last cavalry horses gave way to tanks in 1940. Even today, the 1st Cavalry Regiment survives as the 1st squadron of the 1st Cavalry Division, known as the Blackhawks, part of the 2nd Brigade Combat Team, 1st Armored Division, a heavily armored division of 19,000 soldiers stationed at Fort Bliss, Texas. This is near the site where Benjamin Beall's dragoon squadron camped in 1848 on its way to Santa Cruz de Rosales. Perhaps more significant, the myth of the cavalry riding to the rescue remains one of the most abiding.

Notes

Prologue

1. Aurora Hunt, *James Henry Carleton, 1814–1873, Western Frontier Dragoon*, Frontier Military Series, no. 2 (Glendale, Calif.: Arthur H. Clark Co., 1958), 30; Will and John Gorenfeld, "Punishing the Paiutes," *Wild West* (December 2001); Hampton Sides, *Blood and Thunder* (New York: Anchor, 2007).

2. Adam Kane, "James Carleton," in *Soldiers West: Biographies from the Military Frontier*, ed. Paul Hutton and Durwood Ball, 2nd ed. (Norman: University of Oklahoma Press, 2001), 59.

3. Hunt, *Carleton*, 71, 76.

4. George Catlin, *Letters and Notes on the Manners, Customs, and Condition of the North American Indians*, vol. 2, *1841* (London: published by the author, 1841).

5. Kane, "Carleton," 137.

6. President Andrew Jackson's Message to Congress, "On Indian Removal," December 6, 1830, Records of the United States Senate, 1789–1990, Record Group 46, National Archives and Records Administration (NARA);National Parks Service, http://www.nps.gov/museum/tmc/MANZ/handouts/Andrew_Jackson_Annual_Message.pdf,last accessed October 20, 2014.

7. See Sam Watson, *Peacekeepers and Conquerors: The Army Officer Corps on the American Frontier, 1821–1846* (Lawrence: University Press of Kansas, 2013), 105 ff.

8. Robert Utley, *The Indian Frontier, 1846–1890* (Albuquerque: University of New Mexico Press, 1984), 35.

9. James Mooney, *History, Myth, and Sacred Formulas of the Cherokee* (Asheville, N.C.: Bright Mountain, 1992), 98–99.

10. William H. Goetzmann, *Exploration and Empire: The Explorers and Scientists in the Winning of the American West* (New York: Knopf, 1966), 105.

11. Robert Wooster, *The American Military Frontiers: The United States Army in the West, 1783–1900* (Albuquerque: University of New Mexico Press, 2009), 83.

12. Francis Heitman, *Historical Register of the United States Army, from its Organization, September 29, 1789, to March 2, 1903* (Washington, D.C.: Government Printing Office, 1903), 2:394–396; Watson, *Peacekeepers*.

13. V. Vuksic and Z. Grbasic, *Cavalry: The History of a Fighting Elite, 650 BC–AD1914* (London: Cassell, 1993), 25–26, 100; Louis Nolan, *Cavalry: Its History and Tactics* (1854; repr., Yardley, Pa.: Westholme, 2007).

14. Nolan, *Cavalry*, 38. The American army later added a light howitzer to the dragoon's arsenal, allowing this versatile corps to encompass all three combat arms: horse, foot, and artillery. John Elting, *A Dictionary of Soldier Talk* (New York: Scribner Press, 1984), 90.

15. Curt Johnson, "The Decline of the Knight," in *The Cavalry*, ed. James Lawford (London: Roxby Press, 1976), 74.

16. Nolan, *Cavalry*, 39; Peter Schmidt, *Hall's Military Breechloaders* (Lincoln, Nebr.: Andrew Mowbray, 1996), 57; Theophilus Rodenbough, *From Everglade to Canyon with the Second United States Cavalry* (Norman: University of Oklahoma Press, 2000), 8.

17. Nolan, *Cavalry*, 39.

18. Vuksic, *Cavalry*, 174; Gregory Urwin, *The United States Cavalry: An Illustrated History* (Dorset, UK: Blandford Press, 1984), 29.

19. Urwin, *United States Cavalry*, 21, 23.

20. Ibid., 49.

21. Randy Steffen, *The Horse Soldier, 1776–1943: The United States Cavalryman: His Uniforms, Arms, Accoutrements, and Equipments*, vol. 1, *The Revolution, the War of 1812, and the Early Frontier, 1776–1850* (Norman: University of Oklahoma Press, 1977), 84, 88.

Chapter 1

1. Col. Henry Dodge, United States Dragoons, to Gen. Roger Jones, April 4, 5, 1834, "Letters Received by the Office of the Adjutant General (Main Series)" (hereinafter LRAG), 1822–1860, M619, NARA, Washington, D.C.

2. Jefferson Barracks stood near the edge of civilization, on the west bank of the Mississippi River. Its primary function in 1833 was to train, supply, and concentrate troops as well as to provide supplies for frontier outposts. George Croghan, *Army Life on the Western Frontier: Selections from the Official Reports Between 1826 and 1845 by Colonel George Croghan*, ed. Francis Prucha (Norman: University of Oklahoma Press, 1958), xxxiii.

3. Thomas Russell to Hon. John Blair, Fort Gibson, Indian Territory, December 2, 1833, LRAG, 1822–1860; Jones to Dodge, 1834, LRAG, M569, 1834.

4. Kearny to Jones, Jefferson Barracks, February 10, 1834. "Sept. Treadway was a Recruit of 1832 & by your letter of April 17, 1833, was assigned to the Drag[oon]s. He deserted in October last from a Steam Boat, in the Ohio River being on his way from Louisville to this Post. The fact was not reported to you, because I didn't bear him on my Returns, he having been enlisted in the Dept. He was neither Sergeant Major, Major nor Col. of the Drags. each of which (I

have ascertained) he occasionally thought proper to assume. I have no doubt, he has told many a falsehood, & deceived many recruits!" Contained in LRAG, 1822–1860, Jones to Dodge, 1834, M569, D47–1834.

5. James Hildreth, *Dragoon Campaigns to the Rocky Mountains: Being a History of the Enlistment, Organization, and First Campaigns of the Regiment of United States Dragoons; together with incidents of a Soldier's Life, and sketches of scenery and Indian Character* (New York: Wiley & Lane, 1836), 47.

6. Monthly Returns, September 1833–December 1833, Regiment of Dragoons, Regimental Returns, United States Army, War Department, M744, R1,NARA.

7. Philip St. George Cooke, *Scenes and Adventures in the Army or, Romance of Military Life* (Philadelphia: Lindsay & Blakiston, 1859), 224.

8. Dodge to Jones, April 4, 5, 1834, LRAG 1882–1860, M619, NARA.

9. Contained in Dodge to Jones, LRAG, M569, 1834.

10. Hildreth, *Dragoon Campaigns*, 14; Joseph Thoburn, "The Dragoon Campaigns to the Rocky Mountains," *Chronicles of Oklahoma* 8, no. 1 (March 1930): 35.

11. Hildreth, *Dragoon Campaigns*, 79.

12. John Flynn, "Reminiscences of Some Incidents in the Career of an United States Dragoon Between the Years 1839 and 1844," *Texas Quarterly* 9, no. 3 (Autumn 1966): 8.

13. *Army and Navy Chronicle* 8, no. 24 (June 13, 1839): 382.

14. Flynn, "Reminiscences of Some Incidents," 29.

15. The known and identified published works by dragoon enlistees, to name a few, include a work by Pvt. James Hildreth, who was in the original Company B and described its first year, 1833–34, in *Dragoon Campaigns to the Rocky Mountains.* Sgt. Percival Green Lowe described his enlistment during 1849–54 in *Five Years a Dragoon ('49 to '54)* (Kansas City, Mo.: F. Hudson Publishing Co., 1906). Pvt. (later Bvt. Brig. Gen.) Samuel E. Chamberlain told the truth (mostly) while penning a rollicking, exaggerated story of his Mexican War adventures in Company E in *My Confession: The Recollections of a Rogue* (New York: Harper & Brothers, 1956). Sgt. Maj. Frank Clarke became regimental sergeant major of the First Dragoons; he also served in Company F in New Mexico; his letters have been collected and edited by Darlis Miller as *Above a Common Soldier: Frank and Mary Clarke in the American West and Civil War, 1847–1872* (Albuquerque: University of New Mexico Press, 1997). Pvt. (sometimes Sgt.) James A. Bennett (who enlisted and served as James Bronson) served in New Mexico variously with Companies I, G, and B; his occasionally truth-stretching diary of two 1st Dragoon enlistments and a desertion was edited by Clinton E. Brooks and Frank D. Reeve, as *Forts and Forays: A Dragoon in New Mexico, 1850–1856* (Albuquerque: University of New Mexico Press: 1996). The memoir, "Personal Recollections—A Trumpeter's Notes ('52–'58)," of bugler (later chief bugler) William Drown, which includes his time in Company H, 1st Dragoons, also in New Mexico, is contained

in Rodenbough's *From Everglade to Canyon with the Second United States Cavalry.* James Parrott was a sergeant in Company I of the 1st Dragoons, 1833–36, and became a Civil War general of volunteers; Mary Whitcomb, "Reminiscences of Gen. James C. Parrott," *Annals of Iowa* 3, nos. 5–6 (April, 1897): 369–70. Unpublished enlisted journals include manuscripts by William Antes, at the Beinecke Library, and James Stevenson, at the Gettysburg College Library.

16. Hildreth, *Dragoon Campaigns* and *Recollections of the United States Army: A Series of Thrilling Tales and Sketches by an American Soldier Written During a Period in "The Service," since 1830* (Boston: James Munroe & Co. 1845). While the latter book was published by an anonymous author, a copy of the book in the authors' possession contains an inscription, "by the author," whose handwriting matches that of James Hildreth as it appears in his recruitment document.

17. Whitcomb, "Reminiscences of Gen. James C. Parrott," 70.

18. Catlin, *Letters and Notes on the Manners*, 2:37.

19. Charles Latrobe, *The Rambler in North America: 1832–1833* (New York: Harper & Bros., 1835), 2:231.

20. Francis Prucha, *The Sword of the Republic: The United States Army on the Frontier, 1783–1846* (London and New York: Macmillan, 1969), 254; Felix Cohen, *Handbook of Federal Indian Law* (Albuquerque: University of New Mexico Press, 1958), 54.

21. Kerry Trask, *Black Hawk: The Battle for the Heart of America* (New York: Henry Holt, 1996), 91.

22. Watson, *Peace Keepers*, 79.

23. Cohen, *Indian Law*, 54.

24. "Report to the President of the United States," February 16, 1832, Indian Office Letterbook, box 2, NARA.

25. Watson, *Peace Keepers*, 79, 105.

26. *Missouri Republican* cited in *Niles' Weekly Register* 47, no. 2 (October 4, 1834): 76.

27. Cohen, *Indian Law*, 54. The headwaters of the Missouri, the longest river in North America, begin high in the Rocky Mountains. From there the great river courses across the plains, gathers strength and current from many tributaries, and reaches a junction with the Mississippi River at St. Louis, 2,341 miles downstream. Beyond lies the Mississippi Valley, one of the most fertile regions in the nation. Crossing back across either of these great rivers can be difficult— nearly impossible without the aid of a raft or boat. In the 1830s they became ideal barriers to stop the vanquished tribes from returning home.

Boatmen and fur traders who plied the rivers of the eastern woodlands in the early part of the nineteenth century were the first to sing "Shenandoah," a lilting American folk tune whose white man's romantic fantasy of Indian displacement echoed, in riparian geography if not in catastrophic scale, the more substantially catastrophic loss suffered by Indians forced west. In time soldiers and settlers adopted variants and then the song went to sea as a shanty. A rendering known as the "Wide Missouri" evoked the forced relocation of Indian tribes to the far west: a fair maiden living with her tribe west of the Missouri River is courted by a white trader, who tricks her father and takes her to the eastern side of the river, in former Indian homelands wherein he is now forbidden to travel.

28. Prucha, *Sword of the Republic*, 234.

29. Ibid., 236; Otis Young, *The West of Philip St. George Cooke, 1809–1895* (Glendale, Calif.: Arthur H. Clark, 1955), 37.

30. Albert G. Brackett, *History of the United States Cavalry, from the Formation of the Federal Government to the 1st of June, 1863* (New York: Harper, 1865), 34.

31. William Skelton, *An American Profession of Arms: The Army Officer Corps, 1784–1861* (Lawrence: University Press of Kansas, 1992), 13.

32. Brackett, *United States Cavalry*, 34; Prucha, *Sword of the Republic*, 241.

33. Washington Irving, *A Tour on the Prairies*, ed. John McDermott (Norman: University of Oklahoma Press, 1956), 59.

34. Prucha, *Sword of the Republic*, 242; Louis Pelzer, *Henry Dodge* (Iowa City: State Historical Society of Iowa, 1911), 77.

35. Wooster, *Military Frontiers*, 81.

36. Pelzer, *Dodge*, 78.

37. The government's cost-benefit analysis overlooked the cost of supplying horse and tack for the new regiment—the rangers, as mentioned, were required to provide their own clothing, weapons, tack, and horses. Report of Lewis Cass, Secretary of War, Dept. of War, November 25, 1832, reported in *Niles' Weekly Register* 43 (January 26, 1833): 364; see also Prucha, *Sword of Empire*, 242; Young, *Cooke*, 67.

38. Report of Lewis Cass, November 25, 1832. Secretary Cass also wrote:

> I have caused a comparative view to be appended to this report, showing the difference of cost between the maintenance of this corps of rangers, and of a regiment of dragoons. It will be perceived, that the former exceeds the latter by one hundred and fifty-three thousand nine hundred and thirty-two dollars. The rangers costing annually two hundred and ninety-seven thousand five hundred and thirty dollars, and the dragoons one hundred and forty-three thousand five hundred and ninety-eight dollars; an excess of expenditure well worthy of consideration unless there are circumstances connected with the nature of the duties of these corps, which give to the rangers, as at present organized, a decided preference over the dragoons. It is my conviction, that there are no such circumstances, and that a regiment of dragoons would be more efficient as well as more economical. From the constitution of the corps of rangers, and from the short periods of their service, their organization is but little superior to that of the ordinary militia. Every year

there must be a great loss of time in the reconstruction of the corps, and in the acquisition of the necessary experience and knowledge. And its constitution is so dissimilar from that of any other branch of the army, that a perfect union of sentiment and action between them can scarcely be expected. The want of these must frequently be injurious to the public service.

39. Secretary of War Cass's report accompanying the *Message from the President of the United States to the Two Houses of Congress, at the Commencement of the First Session of the Twenty-Third Congress, December 3, 1833* (Washington: Duff Green, 1833), 18; Prucha, *Sword of the Republic*, 240.

40. Report of Secretary of War Lewis Cass, dated November 29, 1833, accompanying the *Message from the President to Congress, December 3, 1833*, 18.

41. Pelzer, *Dodge*; Watson, *Peacekeepers*, 54.

42. Pelzer, *Dodge*, 16 ff.

43. William Salter, "Henry Dodge in the Black Hawk War," *Iowa Historical Record* 5–6 (1890): 360.

44. Trask, *Black Hawk*; Watson, *Peace Keepers*, 58; Pelzer, *Dodge*, 49.

45. Pelzer, *Dodge*, 45.

46. Robert Nesbit, *Wisconsin: A History* (Madison: University of Wisconsin Press, 1930), 96.

47. Trask, *Black Hawk*, 282.

48. Perry A. Armstrong, *The Sauks and the Black Hawk War* (Springfield, Ill.: H. W. Rokker, 1887), 470–78; Trask, *Black Hawk*, 286.

49. Trask, *Black Hawk*, 292.

50. Prucha, *Sword of the Republic*, 229.

51. Dwight Clarke, *Stephen Watts Kearny, Soldier of the West* (Norman: University of Oklahoma Press, 1961), 12.

52. Alan Taylor, *The Civil War of 1812: American Citizens, British Subjects, Irish Rebels* (New York: Random House, 2011), 187.

53. Ibid., 281.

54. Clarke, *Kearny*, 31.

55. Paul Andrew Hutton and Durwood Ball, "Stephen Kearny," in *Soldiers West*, 123.

56. Clarke, *Kearny*, 30; Sides, *Blood and Thunder*.

57. Clarke, *Kearny*, 23.

58. Dodge to Adj. Gen. Roger Jones, August 28, 1833, LRAG, M567, roll 82, Record Group 94.

59. Skelton, *Profession of Arms*, 143.

60. George Cullum, "Ethan Allen Hitchcock," in *Biographical Register of the Officers and Graduates of the U.S. Military Academy at West Point, N.Y., from its Establishment March 16, 1802, to the Army Re-organization of 1866–67* (New York: D. Van Nostrand, 1868), 82; Richard Grippaldi, "The Politics of Appointment in the

Jacksonian Army: The (Non) Transfer of Ethan Allen Hitchcock to the Regiment of Dragoons 1833," *U.S. Army History* 27(Winter 2009).

61. Hitchcock to brother, March 31, 1834, box 1, Hitchcock Papers, Library of Congress, Washington, D.C.

62. Grippaldi, "The Politics of Appointment in the Jacksonian Army," 26; Kearny to Jones, April 30, 1833, LRAG, 1822–1860, M619; Benjamin Homans, *Military and Naval Magazine of the United States* 1 (April 1833):118.

63. Kearny's efforts to convince Adjutant General Jones to limit the appointment of dragoon officers to graduates of the Military Academy is found in "'The Best Possible Appointments Should Be Made': The Officers of the U.S. Regiment of Dragoons and Military Professionalism," unpublished doctoral dissertation delivered by Richard N. Grippaldi at Temple University and the United States Army Historical Center, Carlisle, Pennsylvania, 2006.

The regiment's lieutenancy included a mix of former rangers and graduates from the Military Academy, among whom were: Thomas Swords, Philip St. George Cooke, Jefferson Davis, William Eustis, T. B. Wheelock, B. A. Terrett, Benjamin Moore, Daniel Rucker, James Allen, James Schaumburg, and J. H. Burgwin. Rodenbough, *The Army of the United States*, 154.

64. Jefferson Davis, "Autobiography of Jefferson Davis," in *The Papers of Jefferson Davis*, vol. 1, *1808–1840*, ed. Haskell Monroe, Jr., and James McIntosh (Baton Rouge: Louisiana State University Press, 1991); John Doran to Davis, June 11, 1886, cited in *The Papers of Jefferson Davis*, 1:285.

65. Davis, *Papers of Jefferson Davis*, 1:liii; Cullum, *Register of the Officers and Graduates*, "Jefferson Davis," 148.

66. Davis, *Papers of Jefferson Davis*, 1:267, 289.

67. Heitman, *Register*, "James Schaumburg," 2:863.

68. August Kautz, *Customs of Service for Non-Commissioned Officers and Soldiers as Derived from Law and Regulations and Practised in the Army of the United States, Being a Hand-book for the Rank and Files of the Army, Showing What Are the Rights and Duties, How to Obtain the Former and Perform the Latter, and Thereby Enabling Them to Seek Promotion and Distinction in the Service of their Country* (Philadelphia: J. B. Lippincott & Co., 1864), 73.

69. Kautz, *Customs of Service*, 73.

70. National Archives and Records Administration, Washington, D.C., Microfilm Publication, U.S. Department of War, United States Army, Regimental Returns, Regiment of Dragoons, Monthly Returns, M744, Roll 1, 101.

71. In a letter to Gen. Alexander Macomb, dated June 11, 1835, Lt. Philip Cooke belatedly complained that during the Pawnee Expedition of 1834 Company C was composed of recruits who were too ill trained "for an extraordinary march . . . over a desert." Young, *Cooke*, 79.

72. Skelton, *Profession of Arms*, 147; Heitman, "William Bowman," *Register*, 1:235.

73. Heitman, "William Gamble," *Register*, 1:444.

74. Regimental Returns, July 1845, M744, Roll 2, 34, NARA.

75. General Order Number 17, Headquarters, Fort Leavenworth, Missouri Territory, First Dragoons, June 16, 1846.

76. Orders No. 34 (Oct. 6, 1846) and 35 (Oct. 16, 1846), Army of the West, Microfilm Publication, T1115 Roll 1, NARA; William Gorenfeld and Tim Kimball, "Such is a Dragoon's Life: Corporal Mathias Baker, Company B, First Dragoons, 1845–1849," *Missouri Historical Review* 105, no, 4 (July 2011): 218.

77. *Missouri Republican,* July 23, 1847.

78. Lt. Col. Thomas Staniford, 8th Infantry, commanding the Department at Jefferson Barracks. Heitman, "Thomas Staniford," *Register,* 2: 915.

79. Captain Haley went on to gain honors while serving with the 3rd Missouri. "I have the honor to submit a report of my operations, from the period of adopting the intentions expressed in my communication to the War Department, dated 6th February, 1848, to the present instant. . . . I also mention with pleasure the services of Captain Haley, Missouri horse, acting brigade inspector of my command, who voluntarily led his company at the storming of the town, under the immediate command of Colonel Ralls." General Sterling Price to Adjutant General Roger Jones, Report of the Battle of Santa Cruz de Rosales, Headquarters of the Army of the West, Chihuahua, March 31, 1848, attached to Report of the Secretary of War, following the *Message from the President of the United States,* House Ex. Doc. No. 1, 30th Cong., 2nd Sess., 1848, pp. 114–19.

80. Post Return for October 1847, *[Fort] Leavenworth, KS; Aug. 1827–Dec.1850,* M617, Roll 610, RG94, Records of the Adjutant General's Office, 1780s–1917, Record Group 94 (Washington, D. C: National Archives, 1968).

81. Rodenbough, *The Army of the United States,* 153; Fayette Robinson, who briefly served as a lieutenant in the 1st Dragoons, erroneously observed in 1848: "[I]t is believed there is not an officer living who has ever seen a dragoon corps leave the saddle to fight on foot." Fayette Robinson, *An Account of the Organization of the Army of the United States, with Biographies of Distinguished Officers of all Grades* (Philadelphia: Butler & Co., 1848), 2:151.

82. Robinson, *Organization of the Army,* 2:156.

83. Richard Winders, *Polk's Army: The American Experience in the Mexican War* (College Station: Texas A&M University Press, 1997), 50.

84. Ibid., 64.

85. *Army and Navy Chronicle,* no. 38 (Sept. 17, 1835): 304. Five days after this notice appeared, Captain Sumner penned a letter to the *Chronicle* protesting that the letter was written by one of his sergeants, without his knowledge, and the description in the letter, published on the 17th, was, in Sumner's words, "substantially correct; right in most details, but not in all."

86. *Buffalo Journal,* quoted in *Niles' Weekly Register,* August 24, 1833, 318.

87. Sgt. James Parrott, who served in Company I of the dragoons, stated that Nathan Boone "much resembled his father in taste and habit. He was at that time past middle life . . . one of the most celebrated woodsmen on the frontier, though

a rather ordinary looking man, small of stature, and with little of the military about him. He was much loved by his men to whom he was friend and father. When horses were lost it was always Captain Boone who attended to the details of finding them." Whitcomb, "Reminiscences of Gen. James C. Parrott," 369–70.

88. Cooke, *Scenes and Adventures*, 201.

89. *New York Evening Post*, November 18, 1833.

90. Louis Pelzer, *Marches of the Dragoons in the Mississippi Valley: An Account of Marches and Activities of the First Regiment United States Dragoons in the Mississippi Valley between the Years 1833 and 1850* (Iowa City: State Historical Society of Iowa, 1917), 17.

91. Hildreth, *Dragoon Campaigns*, 28.

92. Cooke, *Scenes and Adventures*, 219; Hildreth, *Dragoon Campaigns*, 38.

93. Letter quoted in Pelzer, *Marches of the Dragoons*, 19.

94. Whitcomb, "Gen. James C. Parrott," 366. Davis ceased being adjutant on February 5, 1834, and was placed with Capt. David Perkins's Company E. Heitman, "Jefferson Davis," *Register*, 1:358.

95. Robinson, *Organization of the Army*, 2:157.

96. The first books available to the dragoons on mounted tactics were: Colonel Harries's *Instructions for a Volunteer Corps of Cavalry* (1811), Adj. Gen. William Dunne's *Handbook for Cavalry* (1814), and Winfield Scott's *A System of Tactics: Rules for the Exercises and Maneuvers of the Cavalry and Light Infantry and Riflemen of the United States*, translated from French books on cavalry tactics (1826). Alonzo Gray, *Cavalry Tactics Illustrated by the War of Rebellion, Together with Many Interesting Facts Important for Cavalry to Know (Part 1)*, (Leavenworth, Kan.: U.S. Cavalry Association, 1910), 8. See also Robinson, *Organization of the Army*, 2:157. See also Theodore Rodenbough, *The Army of the United States: Historical Sketches of Staff and Line with Portraits of the Generals-in-Chief* (first published in 1896; republished New York: Argonaut Press, 1966), 153.

97. Hildreth, *Dragoon Campaigns*, 119.

98. Letter from Jefferson Barracks, March 18, 1834, in *A Winter in the Far West*, vol. 2, by Charles Hoffman (London: Richard Bentley, 1835), 96.

99. Hildreth, *Dragoon Campaigns*, 119; Kearny to Adj. Gen. Roger Jones, Camp Jackson, June 18, 1834, Letters Received, Adjutant General.

100. Pelzer, *Marches of the Dragoons*, 22.

101. Prucha, *Army Life*, 61.

102. The portion of the secretary of war's report accompanying the *Message from the President to the 23rd Congress*, November 29, 1833, is found in War Department, "Fort Des Moines (No.1), Iowa," *Annals of Iowa* 7, no. 3 (1897): 351.

103. Hildreth, *Dragoon Campaigns*, 63.

104. Bud Hannings, *Forts of the United States: A Historical Dictionary, 16th through 19th Centuries* (Jefferson, N.C.: McFarland & Company, 2006), 385.

105. "The records of the hospital of Fort Gibson will show (they have been examined for the purpose of ascertaining the fact) that in the last *ten years* there

have been about *five hundred deaths* at the post." (Emphasis in original.) Anonymous letter from Fort Gibson, dated October 8, 1835 and printed in *Army and Navy Chronicle* 1, no. 46 (November 12, 1835): 361.

106. Cooke, *Scenes and Adventures*, 224.

107. Camp Jackson, Arkansas Territory, December 25, 1833, and February 15, 1834, Col. Dodge to Col. Roger Jones, Adjutant General, Washington, D.C.; John Newman, "Henry Dodge: Colonel, U.S. Dragoons 1833–36," *Iowa Historical Review* 7, no. 3 (January 1891): 101.

108. Hildreth, *Dragoon Campaigns*, 78.

109. Cooke, *Scenes and Adventures*, 220.

110. Dodge to Jones, April 4, 5, 1834, LRAG, 1822–1860, M619.

111. Hildreth, *Dragoon Campaigns*, 85.

112. Cooke, *Scenes and Adventures*, 225.

113. Newman, "Dodge" Dodge to Jones, 103.

114. Hildreth, *Dragoon Campaigns*, 85.

115. Dodge to Roger Jones, April 18, 1834, private letter reported in "Letters of Henry Dodge to Gen. George W. Jones," ed. Dr. William Salter, *Annals of Iowa* 3, no. 3 (Third Series): 211–22; also reported in Pelzer, *Marches of the Dragoons*, 28.

116. Kearny to Gen. Samuel Cooper, April 2, 1839, Record Group 391: Records of the United States Regular Army Mobile Units, 1821–1942, Entry 612, Letters Sent, 1833–1906. 9W2: 29/9/3, vol. 1, *Letters Sent*, First Dragoons, July 24, 1833–December 13, 1839, Dragoon Letter Book (hereinafter "Letter Book"), p. 428.

117. Hildreth, *Dragoon Campaigns*, 43; Kearny to Macomb, September 19, 1836, Letter Book, 143.

118. Headquarters, Left Wing, U.S. Army, Fort Gibson, reported in Hildreth, *Dragoon Marches*, 108.

119. Hildreth, *Dragoon Campaigns*, 109; NARA, Regimental Returns, Regiment of Dragoons, Monthly Returns, May 1834–June 1834, M744, R1. Muster rolls for 1834 reveal that many of the dragoons were issued rifles, and carried, hatchets on their first expedition.

120. Edward Coffman, *The Old Army: A Portrait of the American Army in Peacetime, 1784–1898* (New York: Oxford University Press, 1986), 202; James McCaffrey, *The Army in Transformation, 1790–1860* (Westport, Conn.: Greenwood Press, 2006). 112; William Gorenfeld, "The Taos Mutiny of 1855," *New Mexico Historical Review* 88, no. 3 (Summer 2013): 303.

At the 1842 court-martial of Lt. James Carleton, Lt. Col. Richard Mason of the First Dragoons was asked whether he had stated to friends that, when serving on a court-martial panel, he "would never vote to break an officer upon the testimony of a soldier?" Mason answered, "I know I have frequently spoken upon the little credibility that I have frequently given to a soldier's evidence, but whether I have used the words there stated I cannot say, perhaps In conversing about matters and things of this sort, I may have used them." Court-Martial of Lt. James Carleton, First Dragoons, Fort Gibson, Cherokee Nation, December 19, 1842, convened pursuant to Orders No. 21, December 5, 1842, Headquarters, 2nd Military Department, in Adjutant General Order No. 24, March 20, 1843, Records of the Office of the Judge Advocate General [Army] Proceedings of U.S. Army, Court-Martial of James Carleton, case number DD213, 1843, NARA. (Hereafter referred to as Carleton Court-Martial.)

121. For example, see Courts-Martial, CC-445, 1838, NARA; Court-Martial of Pvt. William Lewis, Company C, First Dragoons.

122. For example, see Court-Martial of Pvt. George Roy, May 14, 1855, HH 518.

123. Hildreth, *Recollections*, 89.

124. Hildreth, *Dragoon Campaigns*, 42; Captain Sumner, on April 30, 1834, wrote that the weapons and accoutrements of his company were "not good." With the arrival of the Halls, Sumner's appraisal of arms was "good." Semiannual Muster Rolls, April 30, and October 31, 1834, Regiment of Dragoons, RG94, NARA.

125. Schmidt, *Hall's Military*, 57.

126. Cooke, *Scenes and Adventures*, 225.

127. See Robert Reilly, *United States Military Small Arms, 1816–1865: The Firearms of the Civil War* (Highland Park, N.J.: Gun Room Press, 1970), 108; Steffen, *Horse Soldier*, 1:131. Kearny wrote to Maj. Rufus Baker, Ordnance Dept., West Point, on June 19, 1837, stating that the Hall carbine be modified to include a "small iron . . . secured over and along the chamber to be used for ramming the cartridge, instead of the little finger, which cannot force it down sufficiently tighter." Letter Book, 252. This modification was adapted in some later versions of the carbine.

128. *The Ordnance Manual for the Use of the Officers of the United States Army* (Washington, D.C.: Gideon & Co., 1850), 162; Steffen, *Horse Soldier*, 1:136.

129. Schmidt, *Hall's Military*, 59. "The carbine is of a peculiar description; it is on the principle of Hall's rifles, it loads in the breech, and the part containing the charge is so constructed as to separate from the barrel by means of a spring. This part may be called the chamber, and is about six inches long; when loaded, it is easily returned to its position, and then, if the percussion cap is put on the touch-hole, the piece is ready for firing; it requires no ramrod, yet it is furnished with one, which answers the purpose of a wiper, and, when drawn out, makes a bayonet equal in length in the barrel of the piece, and is a *very* formidable weapon. The whole piece weighs seven pounds and a half, and carries balls twenty-four to the pound." *Niles' Weekly Register* 89 (August 2, 1834): 389.

130. Kearny to Commanding General Alexander Macomb, Washington, D.C.,1st Dragoon Letter Book, 143, September 19, 1836.

131. William Pickerall, *History of the Third Indiana Cavalry* (Indianapolis: Aetna Printing Co., 1906), 12. In later pages the reader will conclude, due to reports of accidental, self-inflicted wounds, that the ungainly horse pistol was deadly at close range.

132. Croghan, *Army Life*; Steffen, *Horse Soldier*, 1:121. George Croghan of Kentucky had fought in the War of 1812 with various infantry regiments, resigning in 1817. In 1825, he was appointed as a colonel and inspector general of the army. Heitman, "George Croghan," *Register*, 1:339.

133. Steffen, *Horse Soldier*, 1:88 ff; Don Troiani, Earl Coates, and James Kochan, *Soldiers in America, 1754–1865* (Mechanicsburg, Pa.: Stackpole Books, 1998), 112; Stephen Starr, *The Union Cavalry in the Civil War*, 3 vols. (Baton Rouge: Louisiana State University Press, 1979), 1:121, 127.

Chapter 2

1. Dodge to Jones, Camp Jackson, February 15, 1834, Newman, "Henry Dodge," 105–06.

2. Stephen Hyslop, *Bound for Santa Fe: The Road to New Mexico and the American Conquest* (Norman: University of Oklahoma Press, 2002), 175; Leo Oliva, *Soldiers on the Santa Fe Trail* (Norman: University of Oklahoma Press, 1967), 38.

3. Robinson, *Organization of the Army*, 2:158.

4. Fred Perrine, "Military Escorts on the Santa Fe Trail," *New Mexico Historical Review* 2, nos. 2 and 3 (April 1927): 273.

5. Robinson, *Organization of the Army*, 2:159.

6. Hyslop, *Bound for Santa Fe*, 175.

7. Robinson, Organization of the *Army*, 2:277.

8. Robinson, *Organization of the Army*, 2:280.

9. *Niles' Weekly Register* 47 (September 30, 1834): 38.

10. Prucha, *Sword of the Republic*, 370, makes no mention of Gregg's subsequent rejection of a military escort. Gregg states that, aside from an accidental meeting with Bowman's company of dragoons, there were to be no further escorts of caravans by dragoons on the Santa Fe Trail until 1843. Josiah Gregg, *Commerce of the Prairies, or, The Journal of a Santa Fe Trader, 1831–1839* (New York: Langley, 1844), 1:183.

11. Carolyn Thomas Foreman, "Nathan Boone: Trapper, Manufacturer, Surveyor, Militiaman, Legislator, Ranger, and Dragoon," *Chronicles of Oklahoma* 19, no. 4 (December 1941): 324.

12. Catlin, *Letters and Notes on the Manners*, 2:464.

13. Perrine, "Military Escorts on the Santa Fe Trail," 2:269; Hildreth, *Dragoon Campaigns*, 118; Catlin, *Letters and Notes on the Manners* 2:40; John Swanton, *The Indian Tribes of North America* (Washington, D.C.: Smithsonian Institution Press, 1952), 271.

14. Hildreth, *Dragoon Campaigns*, 118; Fred Perrine, ed., "The Journal of Hugh Evans, Covering the First and Second Campaigns of the United States Dragoon Regiment in 1834 and 1835. Campaign of 1834," *Chronicles of Oklahoma* 3, no. 3 (September 1925): 175, 181. Sergeant Evans was born in Clark County, Indiana, in 1811, enlisting in the dragoons on October 16, 1833. The army assigned him to Company G, under the command of Capt. Lemuel Ford. Evans was the first sergeant of the company during its first two expeditions. On August 8, 1836, he drowned while attempting to cross the Missouri River. Fred Perrine, ed., "Hugh Evans' Journal of Colonel Henry Dodge's Expedition to the Rocky Mountains in 1835," *Mississippi Valley Historical Review* 14 (Sept. 1927): 192.

15. Louis Pelzer, ed., "A Journal of Marches by the First United States Dragoons 1834–1835," *Iowa Journal of History and Politics* 7, no. 3 (July 1909), 332–33. Historian Louis Pelzer was unable to determine the authorship and believes this journal could not have been written without access to an official account, such as the journal kept by Lt. Albert Lea of Company I. The authors believe that Sgt. James Parrott (later a general) prepared the journal. Parrott was first sergeant of Company I and a close friend of Lt. Miller Lea.

16. Hildreth, *Dragoon Campaigns*, 119.

17. Bi-annual Muster Roll for August 31, 1834, Company B, First Dragoons, NARA.

18. Hildreth, *Dragoon Campaigns*.

19. Ibid., 119.

20. Young, *The West of Philip St. George Cooke*, 79.

21. Ibid.; Cooke, *Scenes and Adventures*, 225.

22. George Shirk, "Peace on the Plains," *Chronicles of Oklahoma* 28, no. 1 (Spring 1950): 8, contains the journal of Lt. Thompson Wheelock, the official chronicler of the expedition.

23. *Message from the President of the United States to the Two Houses of Congress, at the Commencement of the Second Session of the Twenty-Third Congress, December 2, 1834* (Washington, D.C.: Duff Green, 1834), Serial 266; Thompson Wheelock, "Journal of Colonel Dodge's Expedition from Fort Gibson to the Pawnee Pict Village," reprinted in *News of the Plains and Rockies, 1803–1865*, by David White (Spokane, Wash.: Arthur H. Clark, 1998), 4:24; Perrine, "The Journal of Hugh Evans, 1834," 181.

24. *Niles' Weekly Register* 89 (August 2, 1834): 389.

25. Shirk, "Peace on the Plains," 10.

26. Shirk, "Peace on the Plains," 11; Hildreth, *Dragoon Marches*, 187.

27. Catlin, *Letters and Notes*, 84.

28. Shirk, "Peace on the Plains," 12.

29. Ibid.

30. Catlin, *Letters and Notes*, 2:51.

31. Shirk, "Peace on the Plains," 13.

32. Catlin, *Letters and Notes*, 2:47.

33. Pelzer, *Dodge*, 95.

34. Catlin, *Letters and Notes*, 2:47.

35. Shirk, "Peace on the Plains," 15; Perrine, "The Journal of Hugh Evans, 1834," 186.

36. Shirk, "Peace on the Plains," 15; Perrine, "The Journal of Hugh Evans, 1834," 186.

37. Hildreth, *Dragoon Campaigns*, 141–45; Shirk, "Peace on the Plains," 38.

38. Gregg, *Commerce of the Prairies*, 2:200.

39. *Reports of Explorations and Surveys to Ascertain the Most Practical and Economic Route for a Railroad from the Mississippi River to the Pacific Ocean, 1853–6, According to Acts of Congress of March 3, 1853, May 31, 1854, and August 5, 1854* (Washington, D.C.: Beverley Tucker, 1855), 11:37.

40. Perrine, "The Journal of Hugh Evans, 1834," 186–87. Sgt. Evans described this region as containing "thick undergrowth or Mushy thickets . . . with some steep riveens [*sic*]."

41. Gregg, *Commerce of the Prairies*, 2:201.

42. Hildreth, *Dragoon Campaigns*, 147.

43. Samuel Stambaugh, "Expedition of the Dragoons to the West," *Arkansas Gazette*, September 9, 1834; Anonymous, "Journal of Marches," 348.

44. Catlin, *Letters and Notes*, 2:55.

45. Perrine, "The Journal of Hugh Evans, 1834," 188; Shirk, "Peace on the Plains," 40.

46. Hildreth, *Dragoon Campaigns*, 154; Catlin, *Letters and Notes*, 56.

47. Perrine, "The Journal of Hugh Evans, 1834," 189.

48. Hildreth, *Dragoon Campaigns*, 153–159; Perrine, "The Journal of Hugh Evans, 1834," 188. Thirty more soldiers were too ill to proceed beyond this location and, on July 19, Colonel Dodge left them behind under a guard of thirty healthy men. Perrine, "The Journal of Hugh Evans, 1834," 189.

49. Shirk, "Peace on the Plains," 44; Stambaugh, "Expedition of the Dragoons."

50. *Niles' Weekly Register* 48, no. 1 (August 8, 1835) reprinted in "A Fragment of History," *Chronicles of Oklahoma* 13, no. 4 (December 1935): 481–82. The unidentified writer is possibly Sgt. Hugh Evans.

51. Dodge did not learn of the general's death until August 5. Hildreth, *Dragoon Campaigns*, 180.

52. *Niles' Weekly Register* 48, no. 1 (August 8, 1835): 482; see also Pelzer, *Dodge*, 100.

53. Stambaugh, "Expedition of the Dragoons;" Anonymous, "Journal of Marches," 354.

54. *Niles' Weekly Register* 48, no. 1 (August 8, 1835): 482. Officers and noncommissioned officers wore pantaloons with yellow cloth stripes attached. Evans was a sergeant. Perrine, "The Journal of Hugh Evans, 1834," 192.

55. Perrine, "The Journal of Hugh Evans, 1834," 193.

56. Pelzer, *Dodge*, 101.

57. Anonymous, "Letter from a dragoon officer at Fort Gibson to Colonel [and, in 1837, vice president] Richard Johnson," dated August 29, 1834, published in the *Ohio (Canton) Repository*, October 17, 1834.

58. Hildreth, *Dragoon Campaigns*, 162. Sergeant Evans wrote, "The boy whom we recovered yesterday is the son of Judge Martin before mentioned, who was killed some weeks since by a party of those Indians. The boy was with his Father on a hunting excursion 2q [*sic*] and being parted from him. (This death however he did not witness and is now in ignorance of it.) The boy relates that after being parted from his Father the Indians who had taken him were disposed save one to kill him. This one shielded him and took care of him in sickness, adopted him into his family as a member thereof protecting him from angry insults." Perrine, "The Journal of Hugh Evans, 1834," 200.

59. Shirk, "Peace on the Plains," 51.

60. Anonymous, "Letter from a dragoon officer at Fort Gibson to Colonel Richard Johnson," *Ohio Repository*, October 17, 1834; Pelzer, *Dodge*, 103.

61. Anonymous, "Letter from a dragoon officer at Fort Gibson to Colonel Richard Johnson," *Ohio Repository*, October 17, 1834; Pelzer, *Dodge*, 205. Sergeant Evans came to realize that the original route, over which they had been guided by a Pawnee guide, was "the worst country ever passed over by any troop."

62. Hildreth, *Dragoon Campaigns*, 178.

63. Shirk, "Peace on the Plains," 54; Pelzer, *Dodge*, 110.

64. Shirk, "Peace on the Plains," 34.

65. Perrine, "The Journal of Hugh Evans, 1834," 208.

66. Catlin, *Letters and Notes*, 2:76.

67. Catlin, *Letters and Notes*, 2:76.

68. Shirk, "Peace on the Plains," 57.

69. Shirk, "Peace on the Plains," 35–36.

70. Wheelock, *Journal*, 92; Shirk, "Peace on the Plains," 36.

71. Dodge to Kearny, Letter Book, 44.

72. Shirk, "Peace on the Plains," 37.

73. Pelzer, *Dodge*, 110.

74. Perrine, "The Journal of Hugh Evans, 1834," 212.

75. Hildreth, *Dragoon Marches*, 187.

76. Catlin, *Letters and Notes*, 2:80.

77. Ibid.

78. Mason to Maj. General Jessup. NARA, RG 92, Records of the Office of the Quartermaster General Consolidated Correspondence File, Fort Gibson, M206, 1834.

79. Perrine, "The Journal of Hugh Evans, 1834," 214.

80. Cooke, *Scenes and Adventures*, 227.

81. Anonymous, "Journal of Marches," 361; Perrine, "The Journal of Hugh Evans, 1834," 215.

82. "Anonymous, "Journal of Marches," 364.

83. Dodge to George W. Jones, Fort Gibson, October 1, 1834, found in Pelzer, *Marches of the Dragoons*, 47.

84. *Niles' Weekly Register* 48, no. 1 (February 7, 1835): 403.

85. Ibid.

86. Colonel Dodge to George Jones, October 1, 1834. Quoted in Anonymous, "Journal of Marches," 360.

87. Alterations and Causalities Incident to the Dragoons during the Year 1834, M744, R1, NARA.

88. Cooke, *Scenes and Adventures*, 225.

89. Catlin, *Letters and Notes*, 2:82.

90. Anonymous, "Letter from a dragoon officer at Fort Gibson to Colonel Richard Johnson, *Ohio Repository*, October 17, 1834. Not mentioned was the captive slave released to Dodge for return to the Martin family.

91. *American State Papers, Military Affairs*, 5:358, cited in Pelzer, *Marches of the Dragoons*, 248.

92. Carolyn Thomas Foreman, "General Richard Barnes Mason," *Chronicles of Oklahoma* 19, no. 1 (March 1941): 14, 17.

93. Grant Foreman, *Pioneer Days in the Early Southwest* (Cleveland: Arthur H. Clark, 1926), 154.

94. Catlin, *Letters and Notes*, 83.

95. See, for example, Francis Prucha, *Great Father: The United States and the American Indians* (Lincoln: University of Nebraska Press. 1995), 528.

96. Perrine, "The Journal of Hugh Evans, 1834," 192, 193.

97. Hildreth, *Dragoon Campaigns*, 43.

98. Monroe and McIntosh, eds., "Proceedings of a Court of Inquiry," *The Papers of Jefferson Davis*, vol. 1, *1808–1840*, 418.

99. James Carleton, *Prairie Logbooks: Dragoon Campaigns to the Pawnee Villages in 1844, and to the Rocky Mountains in 1845*, ed. Louis Pelzer (Chicago: Claxton Club 1943), 57.

100. Monroe and McIntosh, *Jefferson Davis*, 1:367.

101. Monroe and McIntosh, "Proceedings of a General Court Martial," *Jefferson Davis*, 1:356; Foreman, "General Mason," 17.

102. Sarah Davis died of malaria on September 15, 1835. Jefferson Davis soon entered into politics, but was not through with military life. He returned to the army as a volunteer colonel in the Mexican War and then as secretary of war under President Franklin Pierce, 1853–57. Zachary Taylor had served in the army since 1808. In 1837, he obtained a brevet general's commission for his service in the Seminole War. During the War with Mexico, Taylor commanded American forces at the Battles of Palo Alto, Resaca de la Palma, Monterrey, and Buena Vista. Heitman, "Zachary Taylor," *Register*, 1:949.

103. Prucha, *Sword of the Republic*, 373; Pelzer, *Marches of the Dragoons*, 64.

104. Foreman, "Richard Barnes Mason," 18.

105. Jones to Dodge, Adjutant General's Office, Washington, March 9, 1835, Order no. 12, in *Army & Navy Chronicle* 1, no. 12 (March 19, 1835): 96.

106. Ibid.

107. Pelzer, *Marches of the Dragoons*, 64.

108. Ibid., 194.

109. Captain Gantt served on the frontier with the 6th Infantry. Following a court-martial, he was dismissed from the service in 1829. Thereafter, he became a respected mountain man, guide, and trader. Heitman, "John Gantt," *Register*, 1:444.

110. Quoted in *Semi-Centennial History of the State of Colorado*, by Jerome Smiley (Chicago: Lewis Publishing Co., 1913), 1:136.

111. *Army and Navy Chronicle* 2, no. 18 (May 5, 1836): 277.

112. Dodge to Jones, LRAG, 1835, Dodge D198, p.7; Perrine, "Evans's 1835 Journal," 195.

113. Perrine, "Evans's 1835 Journal," 199; Pelzer, *Dodge*, 118.

114. Perrine, "Evans's 1835 Journal," 200; Pelzer, *Dodge*, 200.

115. Journal of Lt. Gaines Kingsbury quoted in Pelzer, *Marches of the Dragoons*, 69.

116. Perrine, "Evans's 1835 Journal," 203.

117. Pelzer, *Dodge*, 121.

118. Perrine, "Evans's 1835 Journal," 207.

119. Ibid., 205.

120. Ibid., 206.

121. Cullum, "Lancaster Lupton," *Register of the Officers and Graduates*, 1:435.

122. Perrine, "Evans's 1835 Journal," 212.

123. Pelzer, *Dodge*, 234n181.

124. Perrine, "Evans's 1835 Journal," 213; Pelzer, *Dodge*, 125.

125. Dodge to Jones, LRAG, 1835, D198, p. 62, 74, NARA, M744, R1, Regimental Returns, September 1835.

126. Pelzer, *Marches of the Dragoons*, 75.

127. Dodge to Jones, LRAG, 1835, D198, p.63.

128. Pelzer, *Marches of the Dragoons*, 75.

129. Thomas Hall, *Medicine of the Santa Fe Trail* (Dayton: Morningside Books, 1971), 85.

130. Anonymous, "Journal of Marches," 365.

131. Ibid., 372.

132. Ibid., 368.

133. Ibid., 374.

134. Ibid., 376.

135. Douglas Hunt, *Nathan Boone and the American Frontier* (Columbia: University of Missouri Press, 1998), 179.

136. Anonymous, "Journal of Marches," 378.

137. Lea's Journal, see note 142.

138. Foreman, "General Mason," 18.

139. Pekka Hamalainen, *Comanche Empire* (New Haven: Yale University Press, 2008). 294; Kevin Sweeney, "Thirsting for War, Hungering for Peace: Drought, Bison Migrations, and Native Peoples on the Southern Plains, 1845–1859," *Journal of the West* 41, no. 3 (Summer 2002): 71.

140. Pelzer, *Dodge*, 128.

141. Rodenbough, *The Army of the United States*, 154. The post was abandoned on June 1, 1836, and its squadron marched to Fort Leavenworth. Foreman, "General Mason," 20.

142. Watson, *Peacekeepers*, 351.

143. Ibid.

Chapter 3

1. The typical former Mounted Rangers officer resigned within months of Dodge's departure from the regiment in 1836. The one exception was Capt. Nathan Boone who served until 1853. See gen., Richard Grippaldi, "Best Possible Appointments."

2. Rodenbough, *The Army*, 155.

3. Hannings, *Forts*, 123; Rodney Gilsan, *Journal of Army Life* (San Francisco: A. L. Bancroft, 1874), 17, 21.

4. *Kansas (Leavenworth) Weekly Herald*, October 8 and November 24, 1854, quoted in Louise Barry, *The Beginning of the West: Annals of the Kansas Gateway to the American West, 1540–1854* (Topeka: Kansas Historical Society, 1972), 1223.

5. Cooke, *Scenes and Adventures*, 93.

6. Kearny to Atkinson, July 12, 1836, Letter Book, 117.

7. C. M. Conrad, "Report of the Secretary of War, Washington City, November 30, 1850," in *Message from the President of the United States to the Two Houses of Congress at The Commencement of the Thirty-First Congress, December 2, 1850* (Washington, D.C.: Printed for the Senate, 1850), Part 2, 3.

8. Kearny to Adjutant General Jones, July 29, 1836, Letter Book, 117.

9. Regimental Returns, First Dragoons, RG 391, M744, R 1. The regiment's monthly returns for the first six months of 1836 reveal the following:

Month	Discharged	Deserted
January	3	4
February	19	3
March	11	10
April	79	2
May	8	1
June	0	3

10. Kearny to Adjutant General Jones, June 16, 1837, Letter Book, 251; Kearny to Colonel Cutler, Recruiting Service, New York, February 1, 1837, Letter Book, 198.

11. Kearny to Ford, January 12, 1837, Letter Book, 191; Kearny to Col. Enos Cutler, Superintendent Recruiting Services, January 12, 1837, Letter Book, 192.

12. Croghan, *Army Life*, 156; *Army and Navy Chronicle* 2 (1836): 313, and 6 (1838): 8.

13. Political unrest and widespread poverty in the German states of the 1830s and 1840s resulted in a significant wave of immigrants from that troubled land to the United States. Eager to show their patriotism for their new homeland and desperate for employment, these men rallied to the colors when war was declared against Mexico. The muster roll and recruitment records for Company B of the 1st Dragoons in 1847 reveals that, at the time this rebuilt company left Fort Leavenworth the second time for Santa Fe, over one-quarter of its privates were of German extraction. Croghan, *Army Life*, 128.

14. Kearny to Jones, October 22, 1839, Dragoon Letter Book, 444; Baker to Martin, September 11, 1846, Gorenfeld and Kimball, "Such is a Dragoon's Life," 213, 221. The term "Dutch" was a corruption of the German word for their homeland "Deutsch"—it was an appellation that was not especially well liked by Germans.

15. Dictation from Erasmus French, Poway, California, July 7, 1887, H. H. Bancroft Library Collection.

16. Robinson, *Organization of the Army*, 156. Army companies stationed on the frontier maintained their own libraries; some wore distinctive fatigue clothing and possessed their own dinnerware. Each dragoon company rode matched horses of the same color: black, grey, sorrel, etc. On many occasions, companies ventured out alone on long campaigns. Although line officers were usually promoted to different companies, a promotion to a noncommissioned rank tended to be reserved for company personnel. Thus, most soldiers, observed military historian Don Rickey, took pride in their company and tended "to look on the company as their home and family, a feeling especially important to younger, homeless men, and to the old professional privates who re-enlisted in the same units time after time." Don Rickey, Jr., *Forty Miles a Day on Beans and Hay: The Enlisted Soldier Fighting the Indian Wars* (Norman: University of Oklahoma Press, 1963), 79.

17. Regimental Returns of the First Dragoons for December 1837, NARA, RG 397, M 744, R 1; Kearny to Col. George Bomford, December 26, 1838, Letter Book, 397.

18. Coffman, *The Old Army*, 231.

19. Kearny to Lewis Cass, Secretary of War, August 31, 1836, Letter Book, 132. The four Military Academy cadets from the Class of 1836, their class standing, and who the selected 1st Dragoons were:

Name	Class standing	Cadet career history
Richard Stockton	44	Resigned Apr. 30, 1837, became a physician
Lloyd Tilghman	46	Resigned Sept. 30, 1836, became civil engineer and later a Confederate general
Thomas McCrate	47	Served with the Dragoons until his death on Sept. 18, 1845
Henry Moorhead	48	Resigned Sept. 30, 1846, became an attorney

Source: Cullum, *Register of the Officers and Graduates*, 212.

20. Historian Richard Grippaldi studied the length of enlistments of dragoon officers and discovered that nine of the fifteen former rangers were gone from the dragoons in less than five years. The typical West Point educated officer served over eight years in the dragoons. "The Best Possible Appointments," 33.

21. With regard to the second-class status extended by graduates of the military to enlisted men promoted from the ranks, see Skelton, *An American Profession of Arms*, 149; Swords to Johnston, November 10, 1844, Fort Scott, Iowa Territory, in *From the Crack Post of the Frontier: Letters of Thomas and Charlotte Swords*, by Harry Myers (Fort Scott, Kans.: Sekam Publications, 1982), 19. Bowman died October 8, 1844. Swords suspected his death was a suicide. Myers, *From the Crack Post of the Frontier*, 22.

22. Kearny to Jones, June 11, 1836, Letter Book, 98.

23. Turner to Cass, Washington, January 31, 1848, LRAG, M567, T488.

24. Sumner to Crawford, April 3, 1849, LRAG.

25. Schaumberg to Jones, Philadelphia, November 3, 1848, LRAG, M567, S1045.

26. "The President [Taylor] says he will never nominate Schaumburg so the vacancy may remain open, at least until another occurs among the Captaincies or First Lieutenancies, as if S. not placed on the Register as a 1st Lt." Swords to Love, Washington City, March 8, 1850, Love Collection; Ewell to Love, Baltimore, December 30, 1849, Love Collection; *New York Times*, February 4, 1853.

27. *Raleigh Observer*, January 9, 1878.

28. Cullum, "Richard Ewell," *Register of the Officers and Graduates* 2:40; Percy Hamlin, ed., *The Making of a Soldier: Letters of General R. S. Ewell* (Richmond, Va.: Whittet & Shepperson, 1935), 30.

29. George Cullum, "Leonidas Jenkins" and "John Love," in *Register of the Officers and Graduates*, 2:79.

30. Newton to Love, John Love Collection, Indiana Historical Society, Indianapolis, Indiana.

31. Cullum, "John Newton," *Register of the Officers and Graduates*, 2:38.

32. Ulysses Grant, *Personal Memoirs* (New York: Charles L. Webster & Company, 1885–86), 1:34.

33. Cullum, "Ulysses Grant," *Register of the Officers and Graduates*, 2:85; Grant, *Personal Memoirs*, 1:34; *Cavalry Journal* 21, no. 126 (Washington, D.C.: United Cavalry Association, Jan. 1922): 310.

34. Cullum, "Joseph Whittlesey," *Register of the Officers and Graduates*, 2:100; Cullum, "Alfred Pleasonton," *Register of the Officers and Graduates*, 2:103.

35. Cullum, "Clarendon Wilson," *Register of the Officers and Graduates*, 2:146.

36. Heitman, *Register*, "John Pegram," 1:780.

37. Croghan, *Army Life*, 98.

38. Steffen, *Horse Soldier*, 1:122.

39. Grant Foreman, *A Traveler in Indian Territory: The Journal of Ethan Allen Hitchcock, late Major-General in the United States Army*, (Norman: University of Oklahoma Press, 1996), 31.

40. See also Croghan, *Army Life*, 97: "ignition [is] doubtful even though the cap should explode." Garry James, former editor and writer for *Guns & Ammo Magazine*, read Inspector General Croghan's criticism and found it to have merit.

41. Kearny to Talcott, June 30, 1843, Letter Book, 199.

42. Steffen, *Horse Soldier*, 1:97–98; Kearny to Col. George Bromford, Ordnance Dept., Washington, D.C., December 26, 1838, Letter Book, 397. Officers of the antebellum era were often critical of breech loading (broken-back) carbines and rifles. See for example, William Hallahan, *Misfire: The Story of How America's Small Arms have Failed our Military* (New York: Charles Scribner's Sons, 1994), 74; see also Kearny to Maj. Rufus Baker, Ordnance Dept., West Point, June 19, 1837, Letter Book, 252.

43. Kearny to Macomb, September 19, 1836, Letter Book, 143; Kearny to Maj. R. Baker, Ordnance Dept, West Point, June 19, 1837, Letter Book, 252. Kearny also believed the Halls were too long to be used effectively while a dragoon was mounted. He called upon the Ordnance Department to slice six inches off the barrel, to provide the dragoons with a shorter version, with a shorter chamber, a rammer to be used to better seat the powder and ball, and a saddle ring moved from the rear of the stock to nearer to the trigger. Kearny to Colonel Bromford, Ordnance Dept., April 3, 1837, Letter Book, 228; Stephen Kearny, *Carbine Manual or Rules for the Exercise and Manoeuvres for the United States Dragoons* (Washington, D.C.: Government Printing Office, 1837).

44. Kearny to Adjutant General Atkinson, September 11, 1839, Letter Book 474; Records of the Judge Advocate General, Proceedings of U.S. Army Courts-Martial, 1809–1890, CC-445; National Archives, Court Martial of George Allen; Registration of Enlistments, vol. 41, 1837.

45. Kearny to Maj. Rufus Baker, Ordnance Dept., West Point, June 19, 1837, Letter Book, 252; *Niles' National Intelligencer*, April 5, 1845.

46. *Niles' Weekly Register* 9, no. 24 (August 9, 1834): 408.

47. Anonymous, "The Dragoons in the Iowa Territory, 1845," ed. Robert Rutland, *Iowa Journal of History* 31, no. 1 (April 1953): 156, 164; Cooke, "Journal,"

78; Heitman, "Burdette Terrett," *Register*,1:951; John Griffin, *A Doctor Comes to California: The Diary of John S. Griffin, Assistant Surgeon with Kearny's Dragoons 1846–1847* (San Francisco: California Historical Society, 1943), 60.

48. Steffen, *Horse Soldier*, 1:152.

49. Sumner to Asst. Adj. Gen. Samuel Cooper, Carlisle Barracks, January 13, 1842, Letter Book.

50. Foreman, *A Traveler in Indian Territory*, 31; Kearny to Maj. Clifton Wharton, Fort Gibson, February 14, 1837, Letter Book, 203.

51. Steffen, *Horse Soldier*, 1:156.

52. Kearny to Maj. Gen. Thomas Jessup, St. Louis, October 4, 1844, Letter Book, 247; Steffen, *Horse Soldier*, 1:166; William Gorenfeld, "Jefferson Barracks: 'I am Disgusted with the Duty,'" *Military Collector & Historian* 55, no. 4 (Winter 2003/2004): 211.

53. Kearny to Col. E. Cutler, New York, September 8, 1836, Letter Book, 138.

54. Kearny to Adjutant General Jones, January 29, 1839, Letter Book, 410.

55. U.S. Army, Enlistment Records for 1846, 45:101.

56. John Mahon, *History of the Second Seminole War, 1835–1842* (Gainesville: University of Florida Press, 1985), 326.

57. Prucha, *Sword of the Republic*, 274.

58. *An Act authorizing the President of the United States to accept the service of Volunteers and to raise an additional regiment of Dragoons or Mounted Riflemen*, Chap. 80—Approved May 23, 1836—Vol. 5, p. 32. See also Rodenbough, *From Everglade*, 18.

59. Rodenbough, *From Everglade*, 19.

60. Ibid., 22. First Dragoon lieutenants Wheelock (Military Academy Class of 1822) and James Izard (Class of 1828) died in 1836 while on detached service in the Florida War. Heitman, "James Izard," 1:566, and "Thompson Wheelock," 1:1025, *Army Dictionary*. See also Rodenbough, *The Army of the United States*, 154.

61. Mahon, *History of the Second Seminole War*, 321. "[Davy] Twiggs, [William] Harney, [Phillip] Cooke, and 'Old Ben' Beall, for example, shaped the 2nd Dragoons to fit Professor [Dennis] Mahan's definition of the Hussar as 'that epitome of military impudence'—an image quite in contrast to that of the more dignified and methodical 1st Dragoons of [Stephen] Kearny and [Richard] Mason." Robert Utley, *Frontiersmen in Blue: The United States Army and the Indian, 1848–1865*, (New York: Macmillan, 1967), 23.

62. Worth to Captain John Sprague, *New York Times*, July 16, 1916.

63. Report of Maj. Gen. Alexander Macomb, attached to the *Message from the President to the 24th Congress*, 2d sess., no. 1, Senate Executive Document #2, (Washington, D.C.: Blair & Rives, 1836), 133.

64. The authors are unable to determine whether the recently independent nation of Texas asked for U.S. assistance or whether Mexico, who claimed ownership of the territory, filed a diplomatic protest.

65. It has been estimated that in 1836 as many as 575 U.S. soldiers deserted from those regiments stationed along or near the Texas border and joined the revolution. Watson, *Peacekeepers*, 550.

66. Jan Onofrio, "James Perry," *Texas Biographical Dictionary* (New York: Somerset, 1996), 113; John Brown, *History of Texas, 1685–1892* (St. Louis: Becktold & Co., 1893), 2:47; William F. Gray, *The Diary of William Fairfax Gray, from Virginia to Texas, 1835–1837* (Dallas: William P. Clements Center for Southwest Studies, Southern Methodist University, 1997), 142; Thomas Cutrer, "Algernon P. Thompson," *Handbook of Texas Online* (Texas State Historical Association, 2010), http://www.tshaonline.org/handbook/online/articles/fth15.

67. Annual Report of the Commissioner of Indian Affairs for the Year 1848 (Washington, D.C.: Wendell and Van Benthuysen, 1849) [not published as congressional document].

68. Ibid.

69. Kearny to Terrett, July 31, 1836, Letter Book, 119.

70. Watson, *Peacekeepers*, 66.

71. Kearny to Atkinson, July 14, 1836, Letter Book, 111; Watson, *Peacekeepers*, 67; Roger Launius, *Alexander William Doniphan: Portrait of a Missouri Moderate* (Columbia: University of Missouri Press, 1997), 11.

72. Kearny to Steen, September 11, 1836, Letter Book, 139; see also: Annual Return of the First United States Dragoons for the Year 1836, RG 393, M744, R1, NARA.

73. Kearny to Terrett, July 31, 1836, Letter Book, 119; see also Kearny to John Doherty, Indian Agent, Fort Leavenworth, August 31, 1836, Letter Book, 132. On August 8, while on this expedition to the Yankton Sioux, Sgt. Hugh Evans, the thoughtful journalist of the 1834 and 1835 expeditions, attempted to cross the Upper Platte River but was swept away by its current and drowned.

74. Pelzer, *Marches of the Dragoons*, 62.

75. Kearny to Thompson, July 28, 1836, Letter Book, 116 and 139; see also: Annual Return of the First United States Dragoons for the Year 1836, RG 393, M744, R1.

76. Regimental Returns for 1st Dragoons, June 1837, 1st Dragoons, NARA, M744, R1; Kearny to General Atkinson, St. Louis, October 15, 1837, Letter Book, 287.

77. Kearny to Atkinson, December 11, 1837, Letter Book, 302.

78. Kearny to Atkinson, November 17, 1837, December 11, 1837, and December 27, 1838, Letter Book, 296, 302, and 399; Regimental Return, January 1839, M744, R1; K. Jack Bauer, *The Mexican War 1846–1848* (New York: Macmillan, 1974), 196.

79. Regimental Returns for 1st Dragoons, 1837, 1st Dragoons, NARA, M744, R1; White, *News of the Plains and Rockies*, 4:17.

80. Letter Book, 312. But as nothing could dissuade Kearny from his long-standing wish to recast the dragoons as an elite European-style regiment, he proceeded with plans to establish a training site at Carlisle Barracks. Notwithstanding Gaines's and Mason's alarm over the chance of war in Cherokee Territory, Kearny believed the situation peaceful enough to allow his projected encampment, and approved Commanding General Henry Atkinson's formal order detaching Captain Sumner to begin a training program at Carlisle in 1838. Envious of French mounted regiments trained at the Saumur cavalry school, whose bands often included a pair of kettledrums, on April 13 Sumner wrote the general commanding the Commissary Department seeking authorization for such, but no record suggests the drums were ever delivered. Capt. Edwin Sumner, Carlisle Barracks, April 14, 1839, to Commissary General Callendar Irvine.

81. Robinson, *Army of the United States*, 2:157; J. Watts De Peyster, *Personal and Military History of Philip Kearny* (New York: Rice and Gage, 1969), 52.

82. Pelzer, *Marches of the Dragoons*, 79; Hannings, *Forts*, 116.

83. Prucha, *Great Father*, 248.

84. Captain Sumner to Governor Boggs, Fort Leavenworth, March 31, 1838, Letter Book, 323.

85. Major Wharton to Lieutenant Alexander, Jefferson Barracks, March 14, 1838, Letter Book, 318; Rodenbough, *The Army*, 155.

86. *Army and Navy Chronicle* 6, no. 21 (May 24, 1838): 334: "General Atkinson, who proceeded some three weeks since to the frontier, in consequence of the recent Osage disturbances, returned from Fort Leavenworth two days since. We learn through him, that Col. Kearny, who marched into the Osage country with 200 dragoons, immediately on the occurrence of the difficulties, had succeeded in amicably adjusting matters with the Osage nation, and that several of the offenders in the late depredations on the property of the whites, and in the conflict that resulted in the death of one white man and two Indians (who were captured by Col. Kearny on his march), had been punished with stripes by the nation, in presence of the troops. It is, however, thought necessary to keep a mounted force on the Osage frontier, during the summer, to range upon the line between the whites and Indians, and orders to this effect have been given. See also Kearny to Governor Lilburn Boggs, Jefferson City, April 11, 1838, Letter Book, 323.

87. Watson, *Peacekeepers*, 141; Prucha, *Sword of the Republic*, 249; Swanton, *Indian Tribes*, 222.

88. "IMPORTANT FROM THE WESTERN FRONTIER—INDIAN TROUBLES," *St. Louis Republican*, August 14, 1838; "ANTICIPATED INDIAN HOSTILITIES," *Nashville Banner*, August 22, 1838.

89. Rodenbough, *The Army*, 155. Military historian Sam Watson wrote that General Gaines's excitability "at the first rumor of Indian unrest" led to his being "sidelined from operational command for the last decade of his career." Watson, *Peacekeepers*, 42.

90. Hitchcock, *A Traveler in Indian Territory*, 77.

91. Donald Pfanz, *Richard S. Ewell: A Soldier's Life* (Chapel Hill: University of North Carolina Press, 1998), 33.

92. Pfanz, *Ewell*, 31; Hannings, *Forts of the United States*, 387.

93. The *Little Rock Gazette* reported on May 15, 1838: "About the 1st inst., a caravan with 40 men and 18 wagons, besides a number of mules, left Van Buren, in this State [Arkansas Territory], fitted out by Messrs. Pickett & Gregg, of that place, bound on the land voyage to Chihuahua, in the republic of Mexico, with an assorted stock of merchandise, principally dry goods. About 40 U. S. dragoons, under command of Lieut. BOWMAN, were to meet them at Camp Holmes, on the Canadian, 150 miles west of Fort Gibson, to escort the caravan a portion of its journey through the country of the wild Indians." See also: *Army and Navy Chronicle* 8, no. 24 (June 13, 1839): 383; *St. Louis Republican*, November 30, 1839.

94. Howard Van Zandt, "The History of Camp Holmes and Chouteau's Trading Post," *Chronicles of Oklahoma* 13, no. 3 (September, 1935): 323; Gregg, *Commerce of the Prairies*, 2:39

95. *Army and Navy Chronicle*, vol. 9, no. 18(October 31, 1839): 285.

96. Ibid. In 1845, a book was published by an anonymous author, established by the authors to be former Private James Hildreth of Company B, First Dragoons, entitled, *Recollections of the United States Army: A Series of Thrilling Tales and Sketches by an American Soldier Written During a Period in "The Service," since 1830* (Boston: James Munroe & Co. 1845). The book was published anonymously. The authors, however, managed to obtain an original edition of this work and it contains the handwritten inscription, "Presented to Mrs. F. Andrews with the Respect of the Author, Boston, Jan 1st 1846." The handwritten inscription matches the signature of James Hildreth on his enlistment document dated, August 7, 1833. NARA, U.S. Army, Register of Enlistments, 1833, vol. 40, p. 86.

On pages 132–33 of this book is a fictionalized account of a dragoon patrol on the Platte River coming across the skeleton of a drown dragoon and his gear "in an obscure place on the river's bank" and how his remains were carefully "collected and deposited in a large chest, and buried with honors of war."

97. Hildreth, *Recollections*, 131.

98. *Army and Navy Chronicle* 9, no. 18 (October 31, 1839): 286.

99. Ibid.; Kearny to Gen. Henry Atkinson, September 27, 1839, Letter Book, 475; Watson, *Peacekeepers*, 67.

100. Kearny to Gen. Henry Atkinson, September 27, 1839, Letter Book, 475; see also Kearny to Cooper, June 23, 1843, Letter Book, 197.

101. *Army and Navy Chronicle* 9, no. 18 (October 31, 1839): 286.

102. Kearny to General Jones, October 22, 1839, Letter Book, 484.

103. *St. Louis Republican*, August 14, 1839; *Nashville Banner*, August 22, 1839.

104. Kearny to General Arbuckle, Dragoon Camp, Fort Wayne, November 11, 1839, Letter Book, 486.

105. Ibid.

106. Douglas Hurt, *Nathan Boone and the American Frontier* (Columbia: University of Missouri Press, 1998), 194.

107. Kearny to Jones, LRAG, 1840, K 60, Gen. M. Brooke to Gen. H. Atkinson, Fort Crawford, Wis. Terr., June 21, 1840; First Regiment of Dragoons, Annual Report, 1840, RG 391, M744, R1, p. 296.

108. Young, *The West of Philip St. George Cooke*, 99.

109. Barry, *The Beginning of the West*, 417; Young, *The West of Philip St. George Cooke*, 99.

110. Barry, *The Beginning of the West*, 423; *Arkansas Gazette*, April 7, 1841.

111. Pelzer, *Marches of the Dragoons*, 89; Young, *The West of Philip St. George Cooke*, 102.

112. Foreman, *A Traveler in Indian Territory*, 245.

113. Leo Oliva, *Fort Scott: Courage and Conflict on the Border* (Topeka: Kansas Historical Society, 2008), 8.

114. Barry, *The Beginning of the West*, 445; Oliva, *Fort Scott*, 14, 19.

115. Oliva, *Fort Scott*, 34.

116. Young, *The West of Philip St. George Cooke*, 103.

117. Ibid., 104.

118. Cooke, *Scenes and Adventures*, 380.

119. Ibid., 381.

120. Ibid., 382.

121. Barry, *The Beginning of the West*, 456.

122. *St. Louis Republican*, November 30, 1839.

Chapter 4

1. Watson, *Peacekeepers*, 355.

2. *Galveston Civilian & Galveston City Gazette*, May 17, 1843.

3. H. Bailey Carroll, "Stewart Miller and the Snively Expedition of 1843," *Southwestern Historical Quarterly* 54, no. 3 (January 1951): 267.

4. *Galveston Civilian & Galveston City Gazette*, May 17, 1843.

5. Ibid.; *Boon's Lick Times* (Fayette, Missouri), August 5, 1843.

6. U.S. Army, Office of the Judge Advocate, Proceedings of a Court of Inquiry of Captain Philip St. George Cooke, held at Fort Leavenworth, pursuant to General Orders no. 6, February 28, 1844, NARA, DD405 (hereafter referred to as Cooke COI), testimony of Lt. John Love, April 2, 1844, p. 37.

7. Bauer, *The Mexican War*, 13.

8. United States Department of State, Daniel Webster to Gen. Juan Almonte, April 29, 1843, appended as an exhibit in War Department, Cooke COI.

9. Harry Myers, "Banditti on the Santa Fe Trail," *Kansas History* 19, no. 4 (Winter 1996): 284–85; Marc Simmons, *Murder on the Santa Fe Trail: An International Incident 1843* (El Paso: Texas Western Press, University of Texas, 1987), 18, 27, 52.

10. Simmons, *Murder on the Santa Fe Trail*, 18, 27, 52.

11. Simmons, *Murder on the Santa Fe Trail*, 49.

12. Gen. Roger Jones to Col. S.W. Kearny, United States Army, Adjutant General's Office, Washington, D.C., March 29, 1843. (Cooke COI, 8.) United States Army, Headquarters, 3d Military Dist., Order no. 11, April 10, 1843. See also Prucha, *The Sword of the Republic*, 376; Watson, *Peacekeepers*, 357.

13. John Flynn, "Reminiscences of Some Incidents in the Career of a United States Dragoon between the Years 1839 and 1844," *Texas Quarterly* 9 (Autumn 1966): 7–20.

14. Pelzer, *Marches of the Dragoons*, 181; W. Julian Fessler, "Captain Boone's Journal," *Chronicles of Oklahoma* 7, no. 1 (March 1929); Flynn, "Reminiscences," 8.

15. Simmons, *Murder*, 49.

16. Philip St. George Cooke graduated from the Military Academy in 1827. Upon graduation he became a second lieutenant in the Sixth Infantry. Cooke made his first trip on the Santa Fe Trail in 1829, when four companies of the 6th Infantry escorted a caravan of merchant goods heading for Santa Fe. With the formation of the First Dragoons, Cooke became a first lieutenant and on May 31, 1835, was promoted to the rank of captain. Cooke, *Scenes and Adventures*, 41; Cullum, "Philip Cooke," *Register of the Officers and Graduates*, 143.

The other officers in the expedition included Benjamin Moore, who previously had served as a midshipman and as a first lieutenant in the Mounted Rangers. He transferred to the dragoons in 1833 and gained the rank of captain on June 15, 1837. Captain Moore led his company with General Kearny to California and was killed at the Battle of San Pasqual in December of 1846. Heitman, "Benjamin Moore," *Register*, 1:721.

A veteran of the War of 1812, William Bowman later served as an enlisted man in the 1st Dragoons, eventually gaining the rank of sergeant major. In 1837, he gained an appointment as a second lieutenant in the dragoons. On June 27, 1842, he secured the rank of first lieutenant. Heitman, "William Bowman," *Register*, 1:235.

In 1837, Daniel H. Rucker of Michigan gained a presidential appointment to the rank of second lieutenant in the First Dragoons. Heitman, "Daniel Rucker," *Register*, 1:849.

George Mason graduated from the Military Academy in 1842, gaining a brevet second lieutenancy in the Second Dragoons on July 1, 1842. The son of Richard Mason, lieutenant colonel of the 1st Dragoons, Mason was transferred to that regiment shortly prior to Captain Cooke's 1843 expedition on the Santa Fe Trail. He was killed in the initial skirmish of the Mexican War at La Rosalia, Texas, on April 26, 1846. Cullum, "George Mason," *Register of the Officers and Graduates*, 2:64.

Assistant Surgeon Richard Simpson gained his appointment in August of 1840. He served at western outposts prior to and during the Mexican War. He participated in the capture of Santa Cruz de Rosales on March 17, 1848, and was commended by Gen. Sterling Price in his battle report: "The attention and ability displayed by Assistant Surgeon Simpson to our wounded on the field as well as to those of the enemy after the action has won for him admiration and esteem from both armies." Dr. Simpson continued to act as a medical officer until his death from disease at Key West Barracks, Florida on July 4, 1861. Guy Henry, "Richard Simpson," *Military Record of Army and Civilian Appointments in the United States Army* (New York: D. Van Nostrand, 1873), 2:188; Official Account of Forces which were Engaged in the Action at the Town of Rosales against the American Forces, 17 March 1848, Price to Adj. Gen. Jones, ff. 234–42, r. 388, *Letters Received by the Office of the Adjutant General (Main Series), 1822–1860*, Microcopy 567A (Washington, D.C.: National Archives and Records Administration, 1995), Records of the Adjutant General's Office, 1780–1917, Record Group 94, National Archives.

Assistant Surgeon Simpson started out with Capt. Nathan Boone's column at Fort Gibson, and then transferred to Cooke's detachment. Pelzer, *Marches of the Dragoons*, 183.

17. Kearny to Adj. Gen. Roger Jones, Jefferson Barracks, August 22, 1843, Letter Book.

18. Kearny to Jones, August 22, 1843, Letter Book.

19. Durwood Ball, *Army Regulars on the Western Frontier, 1848–1861* (Norman: University of Oklahoma Press, 2001), 67.

20. Young, *The West of Philip St. George Cooke*, 93, 354.

21. Capt. Henry Turner to Maj. Wharton, St. Louis, 25 October 1844, Dragoon Letter Book, p. 250.

22. Stephen Vincent Benet, *A Treatise on Military Law and the Practice of Courts-Martial* (New York: D. Van Nostrand, 1868), 391, 399.

23. Love to Major General Roger Jones, Washington, D.C., 14 November 1851, L194, Letters of the Adjutant General, RG 94, NARA.

24. Brev. Maj. Oscar F. Winship, Acting Assistant Adjutant General, Eastern Division, to Captain Cooke, 22 September 1851, John Love Papers, 1837–1886, Indiana Historical Society, Indianapolis, Indiana.

25. Born in Culpepper County, Virginia, and raised in Tennessee, Love was the son of Richard H. Love and Eliza Matilda Lee. She was the granddaughter of Richard Henry Lee, a signer of the Declaration of Independence and father of Gen. Robert E. Lee. Sister Cecilia Lee Love married Lewis Armistead, later a Confederate general who died in Pickett's Charge at Gettysburg. Educated at the United States Military Academy, John Love accepted a brevet lieutenant's commission in the 1st Dragoons after graduating in the class of 1841. A skilled horseman, in 1841–42 he was initially stationed at the cavalry school at Carlisle, Pennsylvania, next assigned to serve with Company A, stationed at Fort Gibson in Indian Territory, and then to Forts Scott and Leavenworth in Missouri. Cullum, "John Love," *Register of the Officers and Graduates*, 2:13.

26. The 1843 John Love Journal may be found in the John Love Collection of letters and documents (M 0653, OM 0320) at the Indiana Historical Society, Indianapolis, Indiana. Grammatical and spelling errors have not been corrected.

27. Captain Cooke reported that the heavy rain caused the troops to require a second set of boots and the commanding officer, hearing of the plight of the troops, sent out an additional pair for each man. Philip St. George Cooke, "A Journal of the Santa Fe Trail," ed. William Connelley, *Mississippi Valley Historical Quarterly* 21, no. 1 (1925): 72, 74.

28. Cooke reported how, at this stage of expedition, the combined effects of mud and untrained mules slowed the movement of wagons accompanying the expedition as "required much labor of men to start them." Ibid., 75. Even without the rain, the encampment of a mounted force on the march, even in peace time, required soldiers, although weary from travel, to tend to horses, unload wagons, pitch tents, cook, and gather firewood and water. Cooke, *Scenes and Adventures*, 245. In hostile territory it was necessary to post pickets and sentries as well as guard the horses and mules.

29. Cooke, *Scenes and Adventures*, 245; Love, Journal.

30. Love, Journal.

31. Flynn, "Reminiscences," 13.

32. Love, Journal.

33. That night the column camped at Elm Grove, the famous camping site that was described by Peter Burnett, a civilian traveler and later California's first governor, as being located on "a wide, gently undulating prairie. . . . There are only two trees . . . both elms. . . . The small elm was most beautiful . . . and the large one had been so, but its branches [had] been cut off for fuel." Barry, *The Beginning of the West*, 476.

34. Love, Journal.

35. Ibid.

36. Ibid.

37. Ibid.

38. The fact of the matter is that most American travelers on the Santa Fe Trail were equally unattractive. Explorer George Ruxton wrote in 1847 of army-retained teamsters at Bent's Fort: due to their "want of fresh provisions and neglect of personal cleanliness, together with the effects of rigorous climate, and the intemperance and indolent habits of the men, rendered them proper subjects" to disease. George Ruxton, *Wild Life in the Rocky Mountains* (New York: Macmillan, 1924), 239. Later, while approaching Fort Leavenworth, Ruxton espied a departing troop of dragoons, commanded by Lieutenant Love, and described them as "soldier-like neither in dress nor appearance." Ruxton, *Wild Life in the Rocky Mountains*, 268.

39. Flynn, "Reminiscences," 4.

40. Love, Journal.

41. Ibid.

42. Ibid.

43. Ibid.

44. Fessler, "Captain Boone's Journal," 81, 102; Flynn, "Reminiscences," 11.

45. Flynn, "Reminiscences," 18.

46. Love, Journal.

47. Josiah Gregg, *Commerce of the Plains*, 2:169.

48. Daniel Howe, *What Hath God Wrought: The Transformation of America, 1815–1848* (New York: Oxford Press 2007), 109.

49. Harry C. Myers, ed., "The Journal of Captain Philip St. George Cooke, First U.S. Dragoons, on an Escort of Santa Fe Traders in the Year of 1843," in *Confrontation on the Santa Fe Trail: Selected Papers from Santa Fe Trail Association Symposia at La Junta, Colorado, 1993, and at Larned and Great Bend, Kansas, 1995*, ed. Leo E. Oliva (Woodston, Kans.: Santa Fe Trail Association Publications, 1996), 41–75; see also Hyslop, *Bound for Santa Fe*, 159.

50. Myers, "The Journal of Captain Philip St. George Cooke," 227.

51. Ibid., 228.

52. Ibid., 229.

53. Testimony of Lieutenant Love, Cooke COI, 37.

54. Myers, "The Journal of Captain Philip St. George Cooke," 229.

55. Ibid., 227–29; Young, *The West of Philip St. George Cooke*, 117; Testimony of Lieutenant Love, Cooke COI, 36.

56. *The Description and Value of the Arms taken from a Party of Texans, within the Territory of the United States, by Capt. Cooke, 1st Regt Dragoons, June 30, 1843, and deposited at Fort Leavenworth, Mo., January 8, 1846*, Senate Document 43, 1846, 29th Congress, 1st Session, submitted, and ordered to be printed, to accompany bill S. No. 37.

57. Myers, "The Journal of Captain Philip St. George Cooke," 232; Gregory Michno and Susan Michno, *Forgotten Fights: Little Known Raids and Skirmishes on the Frontier, 1823 to 1890* (Missoula, Mont.: Mountain Press, 2008), 64.

58. Flynn, "Reminiscences," 28; Fessler, "Captain Boone's Journal," 90.

59. Cooke, *Scenes and Adventures*, 249–50.

60. Ibid., 255–56; Pelzer, *Marches of the Dragoons*, 106.

61. Reprinted in the October 21, 1843, edition of the *Galveston Civilian and Galveston City Gazette*.

62. *New Orleans Times-Picayune*, May 6, 1843. The bias expressed in the article is obvious. In 1835, George Kendall founded the *Picayune*. Six years later he accompanied Mirabeau Lamar's invasion of New Mexico. It turned out to be a military disaster and Kendall was taken prisoner. American and British diplomats arranged for the release of the Texican prisoners and he was returned to New Orleans. Kendall and his paper were active supporters of the annexation of Texas and later served as a war correspondent. George W. Kendall, *Dispatches from the Mexican War*, edited and with an introduction by Lawrence Delbert Cress (Norman: University of Oklahoma Press, 1999), 13.

63. Flynn, "Reminiscences," 32.

64. J. W. Abert, *Western America in 1846–1847: The Original Diary of Lieutenant J. W. Abert, who Mapped New Mexico for the United States Army*, edited by John Galvin (San Francisco: John Howell Books, 1966), 15.

65. Young, *The West of Philip St. George Cooke*, 253; Cooke, *Scenes and Adventures*, 202.

66. H. Bailey Carroll, "Snively, Jacob," *Handbook of Texas Online*, Texas State Historical Association, http://www.tshaonline.org/handbook/online/articles/fsn07; R. Michael Wilson, *Tragic Jack: The True Story of John William Swilling* (Las Vegas: Stagecoach Books, 2001), 84.

Chapter 5

1. Bruce Mahan, *Old Fort Crawford and the Frontier* (Iowa City: The State Historical Society of Iowa, 1926), 224; "The American Occupation of Iowa 1833–1860," *Iowa Journal of History & Politics* 17, no. 1 (Jan. 1919):83, 89.

2. Mahan, *Fort Crawford*, 223.

3. Hannings, *Forts of the United States*, 115.

4. Skelton, *Profession of Arms*, 314.

5. "The fate of the Winnebago Indians, who were moved from place to place unconscionably, was particularly sad. Once having claimed a large area in what is southwestern and south central Wisconsin, they, like the other tribes were dispossessed to make room for miners and farmers." Prucha, *Great Father*, 259; see also Watson, *Peacekeepers*, 71; "The American Occupation of Iowa 1833–1860."

6. Swanton, *Indian Tribes*, 258.

7. Prucha, *Sword of the Republic*, 164; Prucha, *Great Father*, 259.

8. Prucha, *Sword of the Republic*, 165.

9. Prucha, *Great Father*, 259.

10. Erasmus Keyes, *Fifty Years' Observation of Men and Events: Civil and Military* (New York: Scribner's Sons, 1884), 470.

11. Hamlin, *The Making of a Soldier*, 60; Thomas Clairborne, "Reminiscences," folder 15, Clairborne Papers, Southern History Historical Collection, University of North Carolina, Chapel Hill; Sumner to Adj. Gen. Roger Jones, Fort Atkinson, March 2, 1844, LR Adj. Gen.; see also Russel Beatie, *The Army of the Potomac: McClellan's First Command, March 1862–May 1862* (Havertown, Pa.: Casemate, 2014), 3:204.

12. Ball, *Army Regulars*, 66.

13. Mahan, *Fort Crawford*, 224.

14. Ibid., 225.

15. *The History of Fayette County, Iowa: A History of the County, Its Cities, Towns, & Etc.* (Chicago: Western Historical Society, 1878), 322.

16. Sumner to Bvt. Col. Henry Wilson, Fort Atkinson, April 3, 1843, letter in a private collection.

17. Ibid.

18. *The History of Fayette County, Iowa*, 325.

19. Sumner to Jones, November 9, 1843, Fort Atkinson, LRAG, NARA.

20. Sumner to Maj. Henry Cooper, Assistant Adjutant General, 3rd Military Department, December 31, 1843, Fort Atkinson, LRAG, NARA.

21. Sumner to Cooper, Fort Atkinson, March 2, 1844, LR Adj. Gen.

22. Mahan, *Fort Crawford*, 226.

23. Sumner to Jones, Fort Atkinson, March 2, 1844, S52, LRAG, NARA.

24. Ibid.

25. Jenkins to Sumner, Fort Atkinson, August 5, 1844, enclosure in Sumner to Jones, Fort Atkinson, August 10, 1844, LR Adj. Gen., S184.

26. Johnson Brigham, *Iowa—Its History and Its Foremost Citizens* (Chicago: S. J. Clarke Publishing Company, 1918), 106.

27. Jacob Van der Zee, "Captain James Allen's Dragoon Expedition from Fort Des Moines, Territory of Iowa, in 1844," *Iowa Journal of History and Politics* 11:71.

28. *St. Louis Republican*, August 31, 1846.

29. Cullum, "James Allen," *Register of the Officers and Graduates*, 156.

30. Pelzer, *Marches of the Dragoons*, 108.

31. Rutland, "The Dragoons in the Iowa Territory, 1845," 57, 61. The journalist lists that by August 15 "some of the Horses backs getting sore." On September 16 he wrote that "[h]orses beginning to fail considerably." Sore backs on horses tend to result when the heavy woolen saddle blanket is improperly folded and then placed on the horse and the saddle is not securely cinched. An improperly placed saddle blanket or loose saddle will chafe and rub raw the horse's back. A horse in this condition will not allow itself to be ridden. These observations, along with the mention of several thrown horsemen, indicate that many soldiers in the command were badly trained recruits. (Rutland, "The Dragoons in the Iowa Territory, 1845," 63,73.) Regimental returns for July of 1844, show that Company I received nine recruits from the Recruit Depot that month.

32. Rutland, "The Dragoons in the Iowa Territory, 1845," 65.

33. "Capt. Allen's Journal of the March into the Indian Country in the Northern Part of Iowa Territory in 1844, by Company I, 1st Regiment of Dragoons," Allen to Kearny, August 21, 1844.

34. Allen, "Journal."

35. Rutland, "The Dragoons in the Iowa Territory, 1845," 72.

36. W. L. Marcy, *Letter from the Secretary of War transmitting the report, and map of Captain J. Allen, of the First Regiment of Dragoons, of his expedition of the heads of the Rivers Des Moines, Blue Earth & etc., in the Northwest, in compliance with a resolution of the House of Representatives of the 29th of January of 1845*, Doc. No. 168 (Washington, D.C.: Government Printing Office, 1846). See also C. Stanley Stevenson, "Expeditions into Dakota" *South Dakota Historical Collections* 9 (1916): 343, 356.

37. Pelzer, *Marches of the Dragoons*, 112.

38. Allen, "Journal," September 13, 1844; Stevenson, "Allen's Expedition in 1844," 9:363.

39. Willis Hughes, "The First Dragoons on the Western Frontier, 1834–1846," *Arizona and the West* 12, no. 2 (1970); Post Returns for Fort Atkinson, October, 1844, 115, 133.

40. Allen, "Journal," September 27, 1844.

41. Allen, "Journal," September 30, 1844.

42. Rutland, "The Dragoons in the Iowa Territory," 78.

43. Marcy, *Letter from the Secretary of War*.

44. During the years 1844–60, the years of the great migrations of the California Gold Rush and settlers bound for Oregon, 90 percent of the emigrants who were killed while on the Oregon Trail were murdered in country lying to the west of South Pass. This was a region beyond the limits of the dragoon expeditions. John Unruh, *The Plains Across: The Overland Emigrants and the Trans-Mississippi West, 1840–60* (Chicago: University of Illinois Press, 1993), 185; Howe, *What Hath God Wrought*, 715.

45. Allan Reed Millett and Jack Shulimson, eds., *Commandants of the Marine Corps* (Annapolis: Naval Institute Press, 2004), 36–44.

46. Pelzer, *Dodge*, 128.

47. Rodenbough, *The Army of the United States*, 154. The post was abandoned on June 1, 1836, and its squadron marched to Fort Leavenworth. Foreman, "General Mason," 20.

48. Robinson, *Organization of the Army*, 2:158.

49. *Niles' Weekly Register* 47 (September 30, 1834): 38.

50. Clifton Wharton, "The Expedition of Major Clifton Wharton in 1844," *Kansas Historical Collections* 16 (1925): 272.

51. Heitman, "Clifton Wharton," *Register*, 2:1022.

52. E. A. Dolph, *Sound Off: Soldier Songs from Yankee Doodle to Parley Voo* (New York: Cosmopolitan Book Corporation, 1929), 421.

53. Wharton to Jones, Letter Book, 351.

54. Carleton, *Prairie Logbooks*, 3.

55. Wharton, "Expedition," 274; Young, *The West of Philip St. George Cooke*, 141.

56. Wharton, "Expedition," 274.

57. Carleton, *Prairie Logbooks*, 77.

58. Wharton, "Expedition," 286.

59. Carleton, *Prairie Logbooks*, 92.

60. Ronald Becher, *Massacre along the Medicine Road: A Social History of the Indian War of 1864 in Nebraska Territory* (Lincoln: University of Nebraska Press, 1999), 224.

61. Wharton, "Expedition," 288.

62. Ibid., 290.

63. Kearny to Asst. Adj. Gen. Samuel Cooper, 3rd Military Department, St. Louis, June 28, 1843, Letter Book, 197.

64. Wharton, "Expedition," 293; Carleton, *Prairie Logbooks*, 123.

65. Wharton, "Expedition," 295.

66. Ibid.

67. Carleton, *Prairie Logbooks*, 128.

68. Wharton, "Expedition," 299.

69. Carleton, *Prairie Logbooks*, 131.

70. John Swanton, *Indian Tribes*, 249

71. Wharton, "Expedition," 304.

72. Carleton, *Prairie Logbook*, 149.

73. Carleton, *Prairie Logbooks*, 131, 152, 162.

74. Kane, "James Carleton," 123.

75. Swords to Capt. Abraham Johnston, Fort Scott, Iowa Territory, August 18, 1845; Myers, *From the Crack Post of the Frontier*, 28.

76. Carleton accused Mowry of being a traitor, had him arrested, and confiscated his prosperous mine. Mowry was imprisoned in a dungeon cell for six months at Fort Yuma and then ordered to leave the territory. After the war, Mowry unsuccessfully attempted to resume mining operations; he died in London, England, on October 17, 1871. He had gone there for medical treatment and to seek capital for his mining operations. Mowry was thirty-eight years of age. William Keleher, *Turmoil in New Mexico 1846–1868* (Albuquerque: University of New Mexico, 1982), 246; Lynn Bailey, "Lt. Sylvester Mowry's Report on his March in 1855 from Salt Lake City to Fort Tejon," *Arizona Quarterly of History* 7, no. 4 (1965): 335.

77. Lynn Bailey, *The Long Walk: A History of the Navajo Wars, 1846–1868* (Tucson: Westernlore Press, 1988), 150; Keleher, *Turmoil in New Mexico*, 287.

78. Foreman, *A Traveler in Indian Territory*, 88.

79. Ibid.

80. Testimony of Arnold Harris, Proceedings of a General Court Martial—Trial of James Carleton, War Department, Head Quarters of the 2nd Military District, Ft. Smith, December 5, 1842, Orders No. 21, National Archives and Records Administration, Records of the Judge Advocate General, Court Martial Records DD213, 34.

81. Foreman, *A Traveler in Indian Territory*, 89.

82. Ibid.

83. Ibid., 97.

84. Testimony of Lt. Col. Mason, ibid., 14. Charles Wickliffe graduated from the Military Academy in 1839 and was made a second lieutenant in the 1st Dragoons on July 1, 1839. He was dropped from the regiment on April 12, 1842. During the Mexican War, Charles Wickliffe received a temporary (for the war)

captain's commission in the 16th Infantry and then a temporary major's commission in the 14th Infantry. During the Civil War, Wickliffe was a colonel of the 7th Kentucky Infantry (Confederate States) and died on April 27, 1862, from wounds received at the Battle of Shiloh. Heitman, "Charles Wickliffe," *Historical Register*, 1:1033.

85. War Department, Head Quarters of the Army, Adjutant General's Office, March 20, 1843, General Orders No. 24.

86. Wharton, "Expedition," 272.

87. Carleton, *Prairie Logbooks*, 7.

88. Ibid., 213.

89. Ibid., 10.

90. Ibid., 17.

91. Ibid., 55.

92. Young, *The West of Philip St. George Cooke*, 141.

93. Hutton and Ball, *Soldiers West*, 126, 136; see also Gorenfeld, "Punishing the Paiutes."

94. Howe, *What Hath God Wrought*, 699.

95. Ibid., 717.

Chapter 6

1. Kearny to Jones, LRAG, September 15, 1845, St. Louis, Report of Henry Turner, NARA RG 94, M567, K-113 (hereafter Turner Report).

2. Pelzer, *Marches of the Dragoons*, 120; Carleton, *Prairie Logbooks*, 161; LeRoy Hafen and, W. J. Ghent, *Broken Hand: The Life Story of Thomas Fitzpatrick, Chief of the Mountain Men* (Denver: Old West Publishing Co., 1931; repr. University of Nebraska Press, 1973); Kearny, "Report of a Summer Campaign," Secretary of War delivered to the 29th Congress, in serial set 480, document 2, no. 1 (Washington: 1845), 210–14.

3. Carleton, *Prairie Logbooks*, 172.

4. Turner Report.

5. Turner Report; Carleton, *Prairie Logbooks*, 175.

6. Cooke, *Scenes and Adventures*, 284.

7. Prucha, *The Sword of the Republic*, 389.

8. Pelzer, *Marches of the Dragoons*, 121.

9. Turner Report.

10. Turner Report; Prucha, *The Sword of the Republic*, 389; Carleton, *Prairie Logbooks*, 153–71.

11. Frank Schubert, ed., *March to South Pass: Lieutenant William B. Franklin's Journal of the Kearny Expedition in 1845* (Washington, D.C.: Army Corps of Engineers, 1979), 4. (Hereafter, Schubert, *South Pass*.) Franklin had graduated number one in his Military Academy Class of 1843, and received an appointment with

the Topographical Engineers. Heitman, "William Franklin," *Historical Register,* 1:434. Col. John Abert ordered the twenty-two-year-old Franklin to accompany the Kearny expedition to South Pass. Arriving at Fort Leavenworth on May 22, four days after the expedition had departed, Franklin and his escort did not catch up with the fast-moving dragoon column until May 31. Franklin to Abert, November 5, 1845, Letters Received, Topographical Engineers, NARA, RG 77, LR 150.

12. Cooke, *Scenes and Adventures,* 291.

13. Turner Report, 12.

14. Ibid., 17, 22.

15. Schubert, *South Pass,* 8.

16. Ibid., 9.

17. Turner Report, 23.

18. Carleton, *Prairie Logbooks,* 238, Turner Report, 25; Schubert, *South Pass,* 11.

19. Hannings, *Forts of the United States,* 623.

20. Schubert, *South Pass,* 12.

21. Turner Report, 28.

22. Carleton, *Prairie Logbooks,* 246; Cooke, *Scenes and Adventures,* 338; Turner Report, 42.

23. Kearny to Jones, Letters Received Adjutant General, September 15, 1845.

24. Schubert, *South Pass,* 16; Turner to Capt. William Eustis, Camp on the Platte River, June 18, 1845, Letter Book 1845, 270; Francis Parkman, *The Oregon Trail: Sketches of Prairie and Rocky Mountain Life* (New York: Library of America, 1991), 255; Turner Report, 34.

25. Turner Report, 39

26. Schubert, *South Pass,* 18.

27. Turner Report, 45.

28. Ibid., 47.

29. Kearny, "Report of a Summer Campaign," 259.

30. Schubert, *South Pass,* 22.

31. Cooke, *Scenes and Adventures,* 370.

32. Turner Report, 49.

33. Schubert, *South Pass,* 22.

34. Turner Report, 51.

35. Ibid., 55.

36. Cooke, *Scenes and Adventures,* 393.

37. Ibid., 397; Turner Report, 59.

38. Turner Report, 63.

39. Ibid., 68.

40. Schubert, *South Pass,* 29.

41. Ibid.

42. DeWitt Peters, *Kit Carson's Life and Adventures, From Facts Narrated by Himself Embracing Events in the Life-Time of America's Greatest Hunter, Trapper, Scout, and Guide* (Hartford, Conn.: Dustin Gilman & Co., 1874), 167.

43. Cooke, *Scenes and Adventures*, 402, 418.

44. Turner Report, 71; Kearny to Jones, St Louis, September 15, 1845, Letter Book, 474. Kearny begged General Scott to have martial law declared in order to have whiskey merchants illegally selling their wares to the tribes to be tried by a military court. Watson, *Peacekeepers*, 44.

45. Clarke, *Kearny*, 97; Cooke, *Scenes and Adventures*, 415.

46. Clarke, *Kearny*, 98; Pelzer, *Marches of the Dragoons*, 135.

47. Cooke, *Scenes and Adventures*, 415.

48. Turner Report, 75. Franklin wrote a glowing tribute to Fitzpatrick: "By his modest and gentlemanly manner he had endeared himself to all the Officers of the command. He showed himself to be a perfect master of woodcraft and in his knowledge of the prairies I suppose cannot be equaled. In his responsible and difficult situation (that of a guide) he never failed to universal satisfaction." Schubert, *South Pass*, 30.

49. Kearny's 1845 Report; Clarke, *Kearny*, 98; Turner Report, 80.

50. Turner Report, 76.

51. Turner Report, 77; Schubert, *South Pass*, 31.

52. Cooke, *Scenes and Adventures*, 431; Kearny, "Report of a Summer Campaign."

53. *Niles' Weekly Register* 19, no. 19 (January 10, 1846): 303; Schubert, *South Pass*, 35.

54. Ibid.

55. Clarke, *Kearny*, 98.

56. Grant Foreman, *Advancing the Frontier* (Norman: University of Oklahoma Press, 1933), 223–24.

57. Flynn, "Reminiscences of Some Incidents in the Career," 8.

58. Rutland, "The Dragoons in the Iowa Territory, 1845," 156, 161.

59. Edwin Sumner, "Report of 1845 Expedition to Iowa Territory," reported in "Expeditions into Dakota" by Stanley Stevenson, *South Dakota Historical Collections* 9 (1918): 268; Pelzer, *Marches of the Dragoons*, 116.

60. Pelzer, *Marches of the Dragoons*, 116; Sumner, "Report of 1845 Expedition to Iowa Territory," 376.

61. Sumner, "Report of 1845 Expedition to Iowa Territory."

62. Rutland, "The Dragoons in Iowa Territory," 166.

63. Kearny to Jones, Letters Received Adjutant General, September 15, 1845, St. Louis, Report of Edwin Sumner, NARA RG 94, M567, K-113 (hereafter Sumner Report).

64. Sumner Report, 170.

65. Sumner Report, 173; Sumner, "Report of 1845 Expedition to Iowa Territory," 373; Pelzer, *Marches of the Dragoons*, 118; Watson, *Peacekeepers*, 75.

66. Rutland, "The Dragoons in the Iowa Territory, 1845," 174.

67. Adolphus Berry was one of a levy of nine recruits who reached Company I a few weeks before the company departed on its mission. Berry's wound resulted in the amputation of his leg. The complications from the operation led to his death. Sumner, "Report of 1845 Expedition to Iowa Territory," 379.

68. Rutland, "Dragoons in Iowa," 174; Pelzer, *Marches of the Dragoons*, 119.

69. On August 25, Lt. Leonidas Jenkins returned to Fort Atkinson with nine men detached to escort prisoners to Fort Snelling. Fort Atkinson Post Returns, August 1845.

70. Rutland, "The Dragoons in the Iowa Territory, 1845," 178.

71. Ibid., 182.

72. Fort Atkinson Post Returns, December 1845.

73. Hughes, "The First Dragoons on the Western Frontier: 1834–1846," 115.

74. Howe, *What Hath God Wrought*, 702.

75. Kearny to Capt. Abraham Johnston, March 31, 1846; Hans von Alterburg, *Winning the West: General Stephen Watts Kearny's Letter Book 1846–1847* (Boonville, Mo.: Petitanoui Publications, 1998), 280.

Chapter 7

1. Kearny to Brant, St. Louis, February 16, 1837, Letter Book, 206.

2. Mahan, *Fort Crawford*, 228.

3. Roy L. Swift, "CHIHUAHUA EXPEDITION," *Handbook of Texas Online*, http://www.tshaonline.org/handbook/online/articles/upc01.

4. Dragoon Letter Book, 1846, 303.

5. Watson, *Peacekeepers*, 382.

6. Cooke to Love, Cincinnati, April 16, 1846, John Love Collection.

7. Bauer, *The Mexican War*, 46.

8. Sumner to Brooke, Atkinson, Iowa Territory, May 18, 1848, LRAG.

9. Cooke to Brooke, Fort Crawford, Iowa Territory, May 20, 1846, LRAG.

10. Parkman, *The Oregon Trail*, 26.

11. *Liberty (Missouri) Weekly Tribune*, June 13, 1846.

12. Turner to Major Wharton, May 26, 1846, Letter Book, 1846, 314.

13. Oliva, *Soldiers on the Santa Fe Trail*, 57.

14. Kearny to Howard, Letter Book, June 4, 1846; Oliva, *Soldiers on the Santa Fe Trail*, 64; Barry, *The Beginning of the West*, 587.

15. Kearny to Jones, Letter Book, May 28, 1846, 317; Kearny to Moore, June 5, 1846, Letter Book.

16. Oliva, *Soldiers on the Santa Fe Trail*, 65; Capt. Henry Turner to Love, April 9, 1846, John Love Collection; Barry, *The Beginning of the West*, 591; Letter from Benjamin Moore, *Weekly St. Louis Republican*, July 10, 1846.

17. Kearny to Jones, June 4, 1846, Letter Book, 1846, 917.

18. First Dragoons, Annual Return, 1846, RG394, M744, r1; Francis Baylies, *A Narrative of Major General Wool's Campaign in Mexico in the Years 1846, 1847 & 1848* (Albany, N.Y.: Little & Co., 1851), 11.

19. Wilson to Mott, *Cavalry Journal* 30, no. 126 (Jan. 1922), 300.

20. Barry, *The Beginning of the West*, 623.

21. Ibid., 598.

22. Clarke, *Kearny*, 117.

23. W. H. Emory, *Notes of a Military Reconnaissance from Fort Leavenworth, in Missouri, to San Diego, California, including part of the Arkansas, Del Norte, and Gila Rivers*, 30th Congress, 1st sess., Ex. Doc. No. 41 (Washington, D.C.: Wendell and Van Benthuysen Printers, 1848), 17.

24. Clarke, *Kearny*, 124.

25. Emory, *Notes*, 15.

26. Ibid., 20.

27. Clarke, *Kearny*, 133.

28. Emory, *Notes*, 21.

29. Ibid., 25.

30. Ibid., 26.

31. Ibid., 26.

32. Ibid., 27.

33. Ibid., 28.

34. Oliva, *Soldiers on the Santa Fe Trail*, 62.

35. Justin Smith, *The War with Mexico* (New York: Macmillan, 1919), 1:516, n13.

36. Howe, *What Hath God Wrought*, 759.

37. Bauer, *The Mexican War*, 134.

38. Emory, *Notes*, 29.

39. Baker to Mrs. Hugh Martin, September 13, 1846, WA MSS S-502, Beinecke Library. The text of this letter appears in *Chronicles of the Gringos: The U.S. Army in the Mexican War, 1846–1848: Accounts of Eyewitnesses and Combatants*, by George Winston Smith and Charles Judah (Albuquerque: University of New Mexico Press, 1968), 123–24, in which Corporal Baker is incorrectly identified as "a traveler *en route* to Mexico."

40. Letter from Benjamin Moore, *Jefferson (Missouri) Inquirer*, October 6, 1846.

41. Smith, *The War With Mexico*, 1:293.

42. Emory, *Notes*, 32.

43. Kearny to the Adjutant General, August 24, September 1, and September 16, 1846, printed in Executive Documents, 30th Cong., 1st sess., vol. viii, no. 60, pp. 169–74. Kearny's Code of Laws 1846 is contained in *Laws of the Territory of New Mexico* (Santa Fe, 1851), a Bill of Rights and Code of Laws established prior to the United States' official organization of New Mexico as a territory. Not being

schooled in constitutional law, Kearny was unaware that only Congress had the authority to prescribe laws for New Mexico. (Bauer, *The Mexican War*, 135.) On the other hand, knowing that it would take several months for Congress to act, Kearny found it necessary to immediately put into law an assurance to the Catholic populace of New Mexico that he would not disturb their religious freedom.

44. Emory, *Notes*, 32; Smith, *The War with Mexico*, 1:296.

45. The Mathias Baker Letters of September 13, 1846, Santa Fe, December 13, 1846, Fort Leavenworth, and April 28, 1847, Fort Leavenworth, were found as photocopies of originals in the Beinecke Rare Book and Manuscript Library, Yale University, WA MSS S-502, B175. Extracts of these same letters were found, with two additional complete letters (June 14, 1847, Council Grove; June 27, 1847, Pawnee Fork), all in typescript form, in the Missouri Historical Society Archives, Mexican War Collection 1846–1940, Mathias Baker Folder, RSN: 01/A1037. Subsequent references to these five letters will be as Baker Letters, referring to the earlier three from the Beinecke and the latter dated two from the Missouri Historical Society. A detailed account of Corporal Baker's experiences as a dragoon is found in "Such is a Dragoon's Life," by Gorenfeld and Kimball, 213.

46. Kearny's proposed expedition would be matched by Colonel Doniphan's capture of Chihuahua and Colonel Price's capture of Santa Cruz de Rosales. However difficult and praiseworthy the latter two marches were, neither Doniphan nor Price would be required to course anything as rough and unforgiving as would be faced by Kearny.

47. Griffin, *A Doctor Comes to California*, 17; Clarke, *Kearny*, 165; Report of Capt. Thomas Swords (hereinafter Swords Report), *Message from the President of the United States to the Two Houses of Congress, at the Commencement of the Second Session of the Thirtieth Congress, December 5, 1848*, 229.

48. Order number 33, Army of the West, October 2, 1846, LSAG, 1846, K185; Young, *The West of Philip St. George Cooke*, 184.

49. *Garden City* (Colorado) *Western Mountaineer*, June 28, 1860.

50. Kearny to Roger Jones, October 6 and 11, 1846, K191, K209; Order number 34, Army of the West, LRAG, RG 94, M567, R319; unsigned letter from the "commander of companies C and K [Capt. Benjamin Moore] to a "relative," October 6, 1846, from "Camp on the Rio Grande del Norte," published in *Jefferson City Inquirer*, December 1, 1846; Clarke, *Kearny*, 166.

51. Turner to Love, October 11, 1846, Love Collection.

52. Emory, *Notes*, 27; Kearny to Brigadier General Jones October 6 and 11, 1846; Kearny to Sumner, October 9, 1846, LRAG, M567, R319, RG94; Moore to "relative," October 6, 1846.

53. Griffin, *A Doctor Comes to California*, 20.

54. Ibid.; Emory, *Notes*, 53; Abraham Johnston, "Journal of Captain A. R. Johnston," in Emory, *Notes*, 572; Brig. Gen. S. W. Kearny to Adj. Gen. Robert Jones, Head Quarters, Army of the West, Camp on the Del Norte Camp [*sic*]

below Fray Christobal [*sic*], October 13, 1846, General Orders No. 95, Clarke, *Kearny*, 167.

55. Order no. 35, October 10, 1846, in Orders, Army of the West, NARA, T1115, r1; Emory, *Notes*, 55–56.

56. Turner to Love, October 9, 1846, Love Collection; Emory, *Notes*, 55; Swords Report, 330.

57. Emory, *Notes*, 56; Johnston, "Journal of Capt. A. R. Johnston," in Emory, *Notes*, 574.

58. Griffin, *A Doctor Comes to California*, 22. A "Georgia uniform" is period slang for a person wearing nothing but a shirt collar and spurs. *New Orleans Times-Picayune*, September 24, 1852.

59. Lt. J. W. Abert, November 12, 1846, in Emory, *Notes*, 497–98. See also Lt. Henry Stanton's letter in the *Missouri Republican*, December 29, 1846.

60. United States Army, Office of the Adjutant General, Washington, D.C., Acting Adj. Gen. William Freeman to John Archy, A145, misfiled as Nelson Archer.

61. *Carolina Watchman* (Salisbury, N.C.), January 22, 1847.

62. *Niles' Weekly Register*, April 17, 1847, 112; Goodrich, "Revolt at Mora, 1847," *New Mexico Historical Review* 47, no. 1 (1972): 49–60.

63. Bauer, *The Mexican War*, 139; Carlos Herrera, *The Contested Homeland: A Chicano History of New Mexico* (Albuquerque: University of New Mexico Press, 2000), 40.

64. Capt. I. R. Hendley to Col. Sterling Price, January 23, 1847, in *Message from the President* (1848), 531; James Madison Cutts, *The Conquest of California and New Mexico, by Forces of the United States in the Years 1846 and 1847* (Albuquerque: Horn & Wallace, 1965), 233.

65. Colonel Price's Report, Santa Fe, February 15, 1847, in *Message from the President* (1848), 520; Price to Jones, February 15, 1847, LRAG, p. 150.

66. Price to Jones, February 15, 1847, LRAG, p. 150.

67. Ibid.

68. Ibid.

69. *St. Louis Deutsche Tribune*, April 10, 1847 (translated by Tim Kimball).

70. Ibid.

71. The dead dragoon privates were Frederick Schneikder, Michael Seviey, Nelson Bebee, Jacob Hunsaker, and Isaac Truax. Fourteen more dragoon enlisted men were wounded. "Extract of a Letter of a Member of the late Capt. J. H. K. Burgwin's Company to a member of the same Company, February 13, 1847," printed in the *Missouri Republican*, March 9, 1847.

72. Ibid.

73. *St. Louis Deutsche Tribune*, April 10, 1847; *Missouri Republican*, March 9, 1847.

74. *Missouri Republican*, March 9, 1847; Price Report, 525.

75. "Extract of a Letter," *Missouri Republican*, March 9, 1847.

76. Price Report, 525.

77. Emory, *Notes*, 58.

78. Young, *The West of Philip St. George Cooke*, 222; Emory, *Notes*, 63.

79. Griffin, *A Doctor Comes to California*, 25.

80. Emory, *Notes*, 63.

81. Emory, *Notes*, 81; Griffin, *A Doctor Comes to California*, 25.

82. Emory, *Notes*, 70.

83. Ibid., 76–77.

84. Swords Report, 230; Asa Bowen, Manuscript C-D 202, p. 28, Bancroft Library, University of California, Berkeley, California; Emory, *Notes*, 86.

85. Swords Report, 231; Emory, *Notes*, 89; Griffin, *A Doctor Comes to California*, 34.

86. Clarke, *Kearny*, 188; Emory, *Notes*, 94.

87. Emory, *Notes*, 96; Griffin, *A Doctor Comes to California*, 37; Clarke, *Kearny*, 188.

88. Emory, *Notes*, 95; Johnston, "Journal," in Emory, *Notes*, 609.

89. Swords Report, 232.

90. Johnston, "Journal," in Emory, *Notes*, 610; Emory, *Notes*, 99.

91. Clarke, *Kearny*, 188.

92. Howe, *What Hath God Wrought*, 767.

93. Emory, *Notes*, 99.

94. Griffin, *A Doctor Comes to California*, 22.

95. Emory, *Notes*, 103. Trooper Asa Bowen took a different view of the loss of the prized mule. He and his comrades were famished. Many years later, he admitted to having killed this particular mule and eaten a portion of the beast.

96. Griffin, *A Doctor Comes to California*, 37.

97. Johnston, "Journal," in Emory, *Notes*, 612.

98. Griffin, *A Doctor Comes to California*, 39; Johnston, "Journal," in Emory, *Notes*, 612.

Chapter 8

1. Waterman L. Ormsby, *The Butterfield Overland Mail*, ed. Lyle Wright and Josephine Bynum (San Marino, Calif.: Huntington Library, 1942), 111; see also Emory, *Notes*, 105.

2. Griffin, *A Doctor Comes to California*, 44.

3. Johnston, "Journal," in Emory, *Notes*, 105; Griffin, *A Doctor Comes to California*, 44.

4. Griffin, *A Doctor Comes to California*, 44.

5. Clarke, *Kearny*, 190.

6. Kearny to Jones, LRAG, reprinted in Cutts, *The Conquest of California and New Mexico*, 196.

7. In 1854, Gillespie resigned from the service when charged with pilfering funds from the officers' mess.

8. Clarke, *Kearny*, 19

9. Hutton and Ball, *Soldiers West*, 61.

10. Gillespie, Report of the Battle of San Pasqual, December 25, 1846, made to Commo. R. F. Stockton, Commander in Chief in the Pacific and in California, by Capt. A. H. Gillespie U.S. Marine Corps Commanding Volunteers, Military Commandant of Southern Dept. of California.

11. Henry Watson, *The Journals of Marine Second Lieutenant Henry Bulls Watson, 1845–1848*, ed. Charles Smith (Washington, D.C.: History and Museums Division, Headquarters, U.S. Marine Corps), 284.

12. Gillespie to Stockton, Report of the Battle of San Pasqual.

13. Emory, *Notes*, 107; Gillespie to Stockton, "Report of the Battle of San Pasqual."

14. J. P. Munroe-Fraser, *History of Sonoma County* (San Francisco: Alley, Bowen & Co., 1880), 581. Peace enlisted at Louisville, Kentucky, three years before and was now detached as an escort for Kearny.

15. Munroe-Fraser, *Sonoma County*, 582.

16. Arthur Woodward, *Lances at San Pascual* (San Francisco: California Historical Society, 1948), 79.

17. For example, see Cave J. Couts, *Hepah, California!* (Tucson: Arizona Historical Society, 1961), 20.

18. Woodward, *Lances*, 35.

19. McCaffrey, *The Army in Transformation*, 64; see also Gorenfeld, "The Taos Mutiny of 1855," 287, for a detailed account of the hard drinking habits of 1st Dragoon Company F in 1853–55.

20. Bennett, *Forts & Forays*, 13. Lt. Philip Thompson graduated from the Military Academy in 1835 and gained laurels and a major's brevet for his role at the Battle of Sacramento in 1847. After the war, Thompson resumed command of the company until his excessive addiction to alcohol caused him to be dismissed from the service in 1855. Cullum, "Philip Thomson," *Register of the Officers and Graduates*, 200. Maj. Eustace Trenor graduated from the Military Academy in 1822. After service in the 4th Infantry, he obtained a captain's commission in the newly formed 1st Dragoons. Pat Trenor had an addiction to alcohol and was found guilty of several counts of conduct unbecoming to an officer. He was sentenced to suspension from rank and pay for eighteen months and to be confined to the limits of dragoon posts. War Department, United States Army, General Order No. 5, February 26, 1844, RG 94, NARA; Myers, *From the Crack Post of the Frontier*, 16. This was not Trenor's first offense for drinking: Stephen Benet, *A Treatise on Military Law and the Practice of Courts-Martial* (New York: D. Van Nostrand, 1868), 68. On June 30, 1846, Trenor gained the rank of major, and celebrated it in a drunken spree. He became ill soon thereafter and died in New

York City on February 16, 1847. Cullum, "Eustace Trenor," *Register of the Officers and Graduates*, 110.

21. Court-martial of Capt. Eustace Trenor, pursuant to General Order No. 72, convened at St. Louis on November 19, 1841, and found guilty thereof. Department of War, General Order No. 4, January 4, 1842.

22. Cullum, "Eustace Trenor," *Register of the Officers and Graduates*, 1:287.

23. Court-martial of Nelson Archy, General Order No. 282, November 27, 1847, United States Army, Advocate General, RG 153, Records of the Judge Advocate General's Office, Entry 15, Court-Martial Files 1809–94, Court-Martial Case File GG-76.

24. Court-martial of Felix Legitt, United States Army, Advocate General, November 2, 1847, RG 153, Records of the Judge Advocate General's Office, Entry 15, Court-Martial Files 1809–94, Court-Martial Case File EE-614.

25. Court-martial of John Fowler, November 27, 1849, United States Army, Advocate General, RG 153, Records of the Judge Advocate General's Office, Entry 15, Court-Martial Files 1809–94, Court-Martial Case Files GG-76 and GG-94.

26. Journal of William Antes, Beinecke Rare Book & Manuscript Library, Yale University.

27. Griffin, *A Doctor Comes to California*, 64.

28. Utley, *Frontiersmen in Blue*, 30; Dr. E. Darwin French, July 7, 1887, oral history transcript, H. H. Bancroft Collection, Bancroft Library, University of California at Berkeley.

29. Emory, *Notes*, 108; Gillespie to Stockton, "Report of the Battle of San Pasqual."

30. William H. Dunne, "Notes on San Pasqual," MS C-D 202, H. H. Bancroft Collection, Bancroft Library, University of California at Berkeley, 1878, p. 64; Carl von Clausewitz, *On War*, translated and introduced by Michael Howard and Peter Paret (London: Everyman's Library, 1991), 325. Dunne, of Company K, had enlisted in St. Louis in July 1844.

31. Woodward, *Lances*, 46.

32. Gillespie to Stockton, "Report of the Battle of San Pasqual."

33. Joel Poinsett, *Cavalry Tactics, Part One* (Washington, D.C.: J. and G. S. Gideon and Co., 1841), 133.

34. Kearny to Adj. Gen. Roger Jones, San Diego, December 13, 1846, in *Message from the President* (1848), 516.

35. Christopher Carson, *Kit Carson's Autobiography*, ed. Milo Quaife (Lincoln: University of Nebraska Press, 1966), 111; letter written by John Mix Stanley, an artist attached to the expedition, on January 19, 1847, in *Chronicles of the Gringos*, ed. Smith and Judah, 157.

36. Samuel DuPont, Port of San Diego, January 2, 1847, in *Extracts from Private Journal-Letters of Captain S.F. DuPont, While in Command of the Cyane, During the War with Mexico, 1846–1848* (Wilmington, Del.: Ferris Bros., 1885), 101.

37. DuPont, *Extracts*; Carson, *Autobiography*, 111.

38. Dunne, "Notes on San Pasqual."

39. Turner, *Original Journals*, 145; Emory, *Notes*, 108.

40. Munroe-Fraser, *History of Sonoma*, 582. See also Poinsett, *Cavalry Tactics, Part Two*, 265: "To execute *the charge as foragers*, all the troopers of the squadron disperse, and direct themselves each upon the point he wishes to attack, observing not to lose sight of their officers, who charge with them. The squadron being in line, the first captain orders the sabres to be drawn, and the platoons to charge one after another, commencing by the right. For this purpose the first Captain advances 240 paces to the front, taking a trumpeter with him; and when he wishes the movement to commence, he causes a signal to be given. The platoon moves forward at the command of its chief, as prescribed. . . . It passes successively from the walk to the trot, and from the trot to the gallop, and from the gallop to the charge." [Emphasis in original.]

41. DuPont, *Extracts*.

42. Brent Nosworthy, *With Musket, Cannon, and Sword: Battle Tactics of Napoleon and His Enemies* (New York: Da Capo, 1996), 303. For a brief account of battles between United States mounted forces and Mexican lancers, see, for example, accounts of Buena Vista, Brazito, and Sacramento, in Bauer, *The Mexican War*, 215, 152, 156.

43. Brackett, *United States Cavalry*, 88.

44. Robinson, *Organization of the Army*, 173.

45. Alessandro Barbero, *The Battle: A New History of Waterloo* (New York: Walker & Co., 2003), 163.

46. Nosworthy, *With Musket*, 300.

47. Mark Adkin, *The Waterloo Companion: The Complete Guide to History's Most Famous Battle* (Mechanicsburg, Pa.: Stackpole Books, 2001), 247.

48. Nosworthy, *With Musket*, 301.

49. *Missouri Republican*, June 14, 1847.

50. Doctor Griffin reported many of the wounded and dying as having suffered multiple lance wounds: for example, Private Streeter having eight wounds on one side, one in the neck, five in the chest, and one on each hip; Private Kennedy was pierced through the arm and suffered five lance stabs in the left side of his head. Griffin, *A Doctor Comes to California*, 49.

51. Asa Bowen, "Notes on San Pasqual," C-D202, Bancroft Library, 1878, p. 2.

52. M. J. Moore, "Sketch of Capt. Benjamin Davies Moore," *Publications of the Historical Society of Southern California* 6(1903–1904): 10.

53. Moore, "Sketch."

54. Jean Roemer, *Cavalry: Its History, Management, and Uses in War* (New York: D. Van Nostrand, 1863), 143.

55. Pvt. Hugh McKaffray of Company K was reported as missing in action and presumed dead.

56. Captain Turner to his wife, December 21, 1846, in *The Original Journals of Henry Smith Turner with Stephen Watts Kearny to New Mexico and California 1846–1847*, edited and with introduction by Dwight L. Clarke (Norman: University of Oklahoma Press, 1966),148.

57. Gillespie to Stockton, "Report of the Battle of San Pasqual."

58. Ibid.

59. Ibid.

60. Munroe-Fraser, *History of Sonoma*, 582.

61. Asa M. Bowen, "Notes," p. 2; William H. Dunne, "Notes on San Pasqual," MS C-D 202, Bancroft Library, 1878, p. 64. Brown had been in the army for less than a year and had already been court-martialed, losing half his pay for twelve months. But now he realized, as had Dr. Griffin, that the act of pointing an unloaded weapon might scare away an attacker. Griffin, *Doctor Comes to California*, 46.

62. Clarke, *Kearny*, 204; see also Gillespie to Stockton, wherein he reports: "[T]he carbines of the Dragoons (Hall's breech-loading) had become utterly useless from the rain of the night previous." Pulitzer Prize winner Bernard DeVoto wrote, "The night of rain had made the carbines all but useless." Bernard DeVoto, *The Year of Decision 1846* (New York: St. Martin's Press, 2000), 369.

63. See Riley, *United States Military Small Arms, 1816–1865*, 108. Kearny wrote to Maj. Rufus Baker, Ordnance Dept., West Point, on June 19, 1837, stating that the Hall carbine should be modified to include a, "small iron . . . secured over and along the chamber to be used for ramming the cartridge, instead of the little finger, which cannot force it down sufficiently tighter." Dragoon Letter Book, 252.

64. Clarke, *Kearny*, 204; Woodward, *Lances*, 30.

65. When the Ordnance Department later attempted to address this problem with the newer version of the Hall a different problem occurred. An ordnance officer reported to his superiors, "The nipples of the new pattern [1843 Hall] carbine are rather too large for the caps, which never explode until after the second or third blow of the cock." Lt. A. B. Dyer to Lt. Col. George Talcott, Santa Fe, August 11, 1847, Record Group 156, Records of the Chief of Ordnance, Letters Received by the Chief of Ordnance, D-170–1847.

66. Croghan, *Army Life*, 99.

67. Carson, *Autobiography*, 112.

68. Munroe-Fraser, *History of Sonoma*, 582.

69. Clarke, *Kearny*, 222.

70. Kearny to Adj. Gen. Roger Jones, San Diego, December 13, 1846, Ex. Doc. 8, in *Message from the President of the United States* (1848), 516.

71. The soldiers assigned to the Company K howitzer were Privates Andrews, Chambers, Cutler, and Wilbur. Corporal Wilson, Privates Grady, Mauser, Pinkerton, and White were assigned to the Company C howitzer. As possible evidence

of their lack of devotion to the cause and their unwillingness to protect federal property, both howitzer drivers, troopers White and Wilbur, while stationed in Los Angeles, deserted from the dragoons on April 25, 1847. NARA, M744, R2 and 3, Returns and Muster Rolls of Companies C and K for October, 1846; Griffin, *A Doctor Comes to California*, 46; Carson, *Autobiography*, 113.

72. Gillespie to Stockton, "Report on the Battle of San Pasqual;"*Message of the President of the United States Communicating the Proceedings of a Court Martial in the Trial of Lt. Col. Fremont, April 7, 1848*, 30th Cong., 1st Sess., Ex. Doc. No. 33, 1848, 46.

73. Clarke, *Kearny*, 213.

74. Emory, *Notes*, 108. In 1847, E. D. French, an assistant to Dr. Griffin, penned the following poem about the battle (French papers, Bancroft Library):

> Twenty new graves must be made today;
> Twenty cold bodies to be laid away.
> Or bury them down in one single bed;
> In one single tomb let them rest with the dead.
> At the lone midnight hour they were carried along,
> No salute could be fired—no funeral song;
> For our battle had been in the land of the foe,
> And now in dark silence to the tomb they must go:
> We kindred were there to embalm with a tear,
> The last dying moments to friendship so dear;
> Nor even to weep on that desolate night;
> As their loved ones were buried forever from sight.
> Long had we marched through the heat and the rain;
> Crossed the great rivers that swept through the plain;
> Encountered the mountains that stood in our way,
> And passed through the forest without fear or delay.
> We came to the border—the Mexican land;
> To mountains of granite, and rivers of sand,
> Marched through deep passes and narrow defiles,
> 'Till we came to the valley of sun light and smiles,—
> Here our flag we raised high for the breezes were free,
> As we came to the city of Santa Fe.
> Now echo of cannon pealed loud through the air,,
> The American troops in full conquest were there:
> And we marched through the streets of that time honored place,
> And seized the domain of the Mexican race.
> Nor yet was our halting, for onward we pressed;
> To reach the Pacific; the shore of the west:—

The great rocky mountains we passed in our glee,
Intent to embrace the white waves of the Sea.
California was reached, and her vales of renown,
Were spread in their beauty like gems in a crown.
The journey to us was like a parade
Or some pleasure seeking, holiday made.
But here just at dawn when all nature was still,
The foe we attacked at the base of the hill,
And e're in our triumph the conquest could gain;
In the tide of the fight our companions were slain.
So down in the willows beneath the dark cloud,
Which rolled in the sky like a burial shroud;
We laid the brave men that so suddenly died;
E're they marched o'er the land they had barely espied.
Then peaceful their sleep in the lone grave shall be,
They shall feel no more wounds—no more battle shall see.
No foe with their chargers and lances draw nigh—
No grief e're their zephyr' soft sigh.
Farewell; we have left thee; companions in arms;
Our lives may be joyful, or filled with alarms—
Whatever our joy or sorrow may be,
We'll remember the graves by the one willow tree.

75. Turner to Stockton, San Pasqual, December 6, 1846, Sen. Ex. Doc. 33, 30 Cong., 1st Sess., 190.

76. Commenting on Stockton's refusal to act, DeVoto writes, "Just why he [Stockton] thought he could not [send relief] has not been made clear." DeVoto, *Year of Decision*, 369.

77. Griffin, *A Doctor Comes to California*, 52.

78. Emory, *Notes*, 109.

79. Gillespie to Stockton, "Report on the Battle of San Pasqual."

80. Ibid.; Emory, *Notes*, 110.

81. Dunne, "Notes on San Pasqual", 62; Woodward, *Lances*, 41.

82. Emory, *Notes*, 112.

83. Swords Report, 233; Clarke, *Kearny*, 235.

84. Kearny to Adj. Gen. Roger Jones, San Diego, December 13, 1846, in Ex. Doc. 8, *Message from the President* (1848), 516.

85. Flynn, "Reminiscences," 7.

86. Couts, *Hepah, California!*, 20; Ball and Hutton, *Soldiers West*, 60.

87. Watson, *Journals*, 261.

88. Ibid., 263.

89. Killed:
  1. Capt. Benjamin D. Moore, 1st Dragoons.
  2. Capt. Abraham R. Johnston, 1st Dragoons.
  3. 2nd Lt. Thomas C. Hammond, 1st Dragoons.
  4. Sgt. Otis T. Moore, Co. C, 1st Dragoons.
  5. Sgt. William Whitness, Co. C, 1st Dragoons.
  6. Cpl. William H. Fiel, Co. C, 1st Dragoons.
  7. Cpl. William C. Gohlston, Co. C, 1st Dragoons.
  8. Cpl. Robert S. Gregory, Co. C, 1st Dragoons.
  9. Cpl. David W. Johnson, Co. C, 1st Dragoons.
  10. Cpl. George Ramsdale, Co. C, 1st Dragoons.
  11. Cpl. William C. West, Co. K, 1st Dragoons.
  12. Pvt. George Ashmead, Co. K, 1st Dragoons.
  13. Pvt. Joseph T. Campbell, Co. K, 1st Dragoons.
  14. Pvt. William Dalton, Co. K, 1st Dragoons.
  15. Pvt. John Dunlap, Co. K, 1st Dragoons.
  16. Pvt. William C. Lecke, Co. K, 1st Dragoons.
  17. Pvt. Samuel T. Repose, Co. K, 1st Dragoons.
  18. Francois Ménard, Topographical Engineers.
  19. A volunteer, name unknown.
Missing:
  Pvt. Hugh McKaffray, Co. C, 1st Dragoons.
Wounded:
  1. Brig. Gen. Stephen W. Kearney, Commander, Army of the West.
  2. Capt. Archibald H. Gillespie, U.S. Marine Corps.
  3. Capt. Samuel Gibson, California Battalion.
  4. 1st Lt. William H. Warner, Topographical Engineers.
  5. Sgt. John Cox, Co. K, 1st Dragoons. (Died Dec. 10, 1846 at San Bernardo.)
  6. Pvt. Joseph B. Kennedy, Co. K, 1st Dragoons. (Died Dec. 19, 1846 at San Diego.)
  7. Antoine Robideaux, a guide.
  8. Pvt. Jeremiah Crab, Co. C, 1st Dragoons.
  9. Pvt. John Brown, Co. C., 1st Dragoons.
Sources: Kearny to Adj. Gen. Roger Jones, San Diego, December 13, 1846, in Ex. Doc. 8, *Message from the President* (1848), 516; Muster Rolls of Companies C and K, First Dragoons, 31 December 31, 1846, NARA; Dwight Clarke, "The Final Roster of the Army of the West, 1846–1847" *California Historical Society Quarterly* 43, no. 1 (March 1964): 37; Griffin, *A Doctor Comes to California*, 47–52; see also Edwin Bryant, *What I Saw in California* (New York: D. Appleton & Co., 1848); Steven R. Butler, ed., *A Complete Roster of Mexican War Officers, 1846–1848*

(Richardson, Tex.: Descendants of Mexican War Veterans, 1994); Woodward, *Lances*. Kearny's brevet and the other brevets awarded by congress are reported in *Niles' Weekly Register* 74, no. 1912 (September 20, 1848): 178.

90. Clarke, *Kearny*, 232.

91. Clarke, *Kearny*, 230, 252; Woodward, *Lances*, 46; Bauer, *The Mexican War*, 188.

92. Goetzmann, *Exploration and Empire*, 255.

93. Ibid.

94. Samuel Bayard, *A Sketch of the Life of Commodore Robert F. Stockton* (New York: Derby & Jackson, 1856), appendix B, 31.

95. Clarke, *Kearny*, 242.

96. Watson, *Journals*, 270.

97. Kearny to Jones, Ciudad de Los Angeles, January 12, 1847, cited in Cutts, *The Conquest of California and New Mexico*, 201; Watson, *Journals*, 268; Griffin, *A Doctor Comes to California*, 61.

98. Emory, *Notes*, 119; Clarke, *Kearny*, 248.

99. Watson, *Journals*, 280.

100. Emory, *Notes*, 120; Watson, *Journals*, 280; Clarke, *Kearny*, 249.

101. Griffin, *A Doctor Comes to California*, 61; Emory, *Notes*, 115; Kearny to Jones, January 27, 1847, *Message from the President* (1848), 516; Smith, *The War with Mexico*, 1:343.

102. Watson, *Journals*, 284.

103. Muster Roll, 1st Dragoons, Company C, February, 1847, NARA.

104. Andrew Rolle, *John Charles Frémont: Character as Destiny* (Norman: University of Oklahoma Press, 1999), 97.

105. Turner to Love, September 9, 1847, Love Collection.

106. Heitman, "Philip St. George Cooke," *Historical Register*, 1:325; Young, *The West of Philip St. George Cooke*, 234. A small escort of dragoons and Mormon Battalion volunteers accompanied Kearny, Cooke, and Frémont on their way back to the States. While the party was out on the plains nearing Ash Hollow on the Platte River, bugler Robert Quigley shot himself with his Hall carbine. His arm amputated, he was unable to travel. As he did while ascending South Pass, Kearny left the wounded man behind with a small escort, and continued with his trip. Daniel Tyler, *A Concise History of the Mormon Battalion in the Mexican War, 1846–1847* (Salt Lake City: 1881), 302. The authors wish to thank Tim Kimball for his sharing of this information.

107. "Journal of John McHenry Hollingsworth," introduction by Robert Cowan, *California Historical Quarterly* 1 (Jan. 1923): 240; see also Woodward, *Lances*, 33.

108. Message of the President of the United States communicating the proceedings of the court-martial in the trial of Lt. Col. Frémont, April 7, 1848, Washington, D.C, 30th Congress, 1st. Session, Senate Ex. Doc. No. 33, 204.

109. Hutton and Ball, *Soldiers West*, William Winthrop, *Military Law and Precedents* (Washington, D.C.: Government Printing Office, 1920), 578; Foreman, "Gen. Mason," 31; see also Barry, *The Beginning of the West*, 711–12.

110. *St. Louis Republican*, November 3, 1848; Journal of the Executive Proceedings of the Senate, from December 1, 1845 to August 14, 1848, Inclusive (Washington, D.C.: Government Printing Office, 1887), 472–74.

111. Perhaps, someday in the future historians will discover new documents on the battle and, when coupled with battlefield archaeology, they will help to ascertain the truth. Ronald Wetherington and Francis Levine, eds., *Battles and Massacres on the Southwestern Frontier: Historical and Archaeological Perspectives* (Norman: University of Oklahoma Press, 2014).

Chapter 9

1. 1st Lt. Leonidas Jenkins graduated from the Military Academy in 1841. After two years of service on the Great Plains with the 1st Dragoons, he was assigned to recruiting service in 1845. Cullum, "Leonidas Jenkins," *Register of the Officers and Graduates*, 2:13.

2. Leonidas Jenkins ultimately got his wish and travelled to Mexico before the end of the war. On October 18, 1847, he died of sickness at Vera Cruz, aged twenty-eight. Cullum, "Leonidas Jenkins," *Register of the Officers and Graduates*, 2:145. Henry Stanton, West Point Class of 1842, did not get his opportunity for combat until after the war. Sent west, he was killed while on patrol in New Mexico Territory. Cullum, "Henry Stanton," *Register of the Officers and Graduates*, 1:65. Eugene McLean, West Point Class of 1842, gained a commission in the 1st Infantry. He was sent to northern Mexico, where he performed garrison duty. Cullum, "Eugene McLean," *Register of the Officers and Graduates*, 2:146.

3. Lt. Richard Ewell graduated from the Military Academy in 1840 and, at the time, was serving with the First Dragoons. Soon to be assigned to Company F, he served with Gen. Winfield Scott's forces in the capture of Mexico City. Cullum, "Richard Ewell," *Register of the Officers and Graduates*, 234.

4. McLean to Love, November 26, 1846, Love Collection.

5. Ibid.

6. This episode, once again, illustrates the pettiness that officers of the regular army manifested both in peace and war. William Worth had fought in the War of 1812. He steadily moved up in rank until, in 1842, he became a brevet brigadier general for his efforts in the Seminole War. (Heitman, "William Worth," *Historical Register*, 1:1061.) At a review of the troops, prior to the battles of Palo Alto and Resaca de Palma, Worth claimed that, because of his general's brevet, he outranked Col. David Twiggs and later protested to the commanding general (Scott). After Scott ruled in Worth's favor, the secretary of war appealed to the president. Taylor, meanwhile, ordered a review of the troops and placed Twiggs

in command of the review. Taylor cancelled the review and the president ruled in Twiggs's favor. Rather than sulking in his tent, Worth resigned from the army. He soon changed his mind and withdrew his resignation. Before Worth could rejoin the army, the Battles of Palo Alto and Resaca had been fought. Bauer, *The Mexican War*, 35.

7. During the Mexican War, 711 volunteers were killed in action or died of wounds, and 6,256 volunteers died of disease. In contrast, 1,010 regulars died in battle or soon afterward, and 4,899 regulars died of disease. Heitman, *Historical Register*, 2:281.

8. Returns from U.S. Military Posts, 1800–1916, [Fort] Leavenworth, KS, Aug. 1827–Dec.1850, Microfilm Publication M617, Roll 610, Records of the Adjutant General's Office, 1780s–1917, Record Group 94 (Washington, D.C: National Archives, 1968), December 1846; Gorenfeld and Kimball, "Such is a Dragoon's Life," 218.

9. Armstrong to Love, January 15, 1847, John Love Collection.

10. William Brooks to John Love, February 21, 1849. Authors' collection.

11. John Love Collection.

12. Company B, 1st Dragoons, was typically mounted on sorrel-colored mounts. Lowe, *Five Years a Dragoon*, 83.

13. For most of the war, the standard-issue saddle was the Ringgold. Randy Steffen: *United States Military Saddles 1812–1943* (Norman: University of Oklahoma Press, 1973), 38. In 1844, the army began to experiment with the use of a lighter saddle and horse equipment designed and manufactured by Thornton Grimsley of St. Louis. (Steffen, *Military Saddles*, 38–42.) Lieutenant Jenkins procured these new saddles and issued them to the B Company recruits in March of 1847.

14. Lieutenant Jenkins's detachment arrived at Fort Leavenworth on February 17, 1847. (Company B returns, Records of the Cavalry, 1833–1941, RG 391.3, NARA.) The distance between Jefferson Barracks to Fort Leavenworth is about three hundred miles; the fierce winter weather slowed the pace of Jenkins's mounted column to less than twenty miles a day.

15. During the 1840s, Irishmen made up a substantial portion of the ranks of the regular army. Coffman, *The Old Army*, 141. Yet there is not one Irish surname to be found among the twenty-five men recruited by Lieutenant Jenkins in St. Louis. Was this a case of "No Irish need apply?" See "Catholics and the Regular Army," in Paul Foos, *A Short, Offhand, Killing Affair* (Chapel Hill: University of North Carolina Press, 2002), 25–29; Company returns, First Dragoons, Company B, October 1846,Microfilm M744, R2, NARA. In the 1840s there was also considerable discrimination against Germans. Political unrest and widespread poverty in the German states resulted in a significant wave of immigrants. Many of the immigrants headed west and settled in St. Louis, Ohio, and Indiana. Eager to

show their patriotism for their new homeland, these men rallied to the colors when war was declared against Mexico.

16. Original letter in possession of authors.

17. Baker to Mathias Martin, December 15, 1846, WA MSS S-502, B-175, Beinecke Library, Yale University.

18. Ruxton, *Wild Life in the Rocky Mountains*, 268. Percival Lowe mentions that the traditional garb of B Company men was nonregulation black slouch hats and blue shirts. Lowe, *Five Years a Dragoon*, 83. See also an invoice, dated November 21, 1846, sent to Cpl. Jonathan Nickerson seeking payment due to Hiram Rich, the Fort Leavenworth sutler for a "black hat." Corporal Nickerson also owed Rich an unpaid tab for the recent purchase of wine. Rich to Love, John Love Collection. Although Nickerson had re-enlisted on November 1, 1846, this broken-down soldier stayed behind when Company B left for New Mexico in 1847. He received a surgeon's discharge on February 6, 1848. Company B Muster Roll.

19. Ruxton, *Wild Life in the Rocky Mountains*, 268.

20. Lowe, *Five Years a Dragoon*, 114.

21. Crosby was the soldier who was recognized by George Ruxton at Fort Leavenworth. He had deserted from Ruxton's regiment in Canada. Ruxton, *Wild Life in the Rocky Mountains*, 272.

22. John Daugherty to Love, June 11, 1847 (requesting Love gather his cattle until Daugherty can send additional drovers); Capt. Henry Turner to Love, September 9, 1847 (asking that the remains of Capt. John Burgwin, recently killed in action at Taos, New Mexico, be sent the United States); Sutler Hiram Rich to Love, August 28, 1847 (accounts due for Sgt. Frederick Muller and Cpl. Jonathan Nickerson); all in John Love Collection. Trooper Philip Welsh ran up a sizable bill with the Fort Scott post sutler, who then asked Welsh's company commander, Captain Burgwin, to extract payment.

> "It is necessary for us to call on some friend to serve us, and as our acquaintance with you gives us claim on you, we respectfully ask this favor of you to learn from Philip Welch [sic] in some way if you can, if he ever paid a note to us for $66.28 dated about the 20th March 1844. Which note was given to Capt. Burgwin the same year some time to collect. He was so kind as to receive it and said it should be paid, to enable him to collect it he regulated his trade with Mr. Rice to $3.00 Per Month. We are of the opinion that the Captain collected the amount and hope you can learn from Welch if he has or has not paid the amount &c. Soldiers like he may plead payment had you not first said you have the note and want him to pay it and in this way he will say what has been done or what amount he has paid. You will

please do the best you can and write us so we can send a copy of your letter to his [*sic*] Capt. Burgwin's Father. Private Charles Lynch, late of Company A 1st Dragoons, deserted from this post under the command of Capt. Burbank and gave himself up at Fort Leavenworth and was not tried for desertion and afterwards sent to Santa Fee [*sic*]. We certified it for Lieut. Wallace on the Council of Administration. This account was all created before and previous to his desertion which was the 7th May 1847, owing us Ninety Six dollars and Thirty Seven cents, ($96.37) and forwarded to Col. Wharton, and the Col. cannot Say but that he has forwarded it to Santa Fe &c. This is a tricky man, if you do not know him, please collect it for us. William Bushnell of the same company left here owing us Fifteen dollars ($15.00) and has, we learn, also gone to Santa Fee. He is a good man and believe he will pay if he has not already done so—you will certainly serve us much by giving us your kind ade [*sic*] and assistance in these bothersome matters. We shall enclose this letter to Col. C. Wharton and call his attention of the certificate. Whether he has in his recollection or not forwarded to Santa Fe. For this and all of your kindness we shall ever be thankful, and should you be able to give the wanted information as in the case of Welch please [indecipherable].

And if you should be able to make the collection, pay yourself and send us the balance to us in some shape through Col. Wharton. . . .

We have the honor to be your very
Sincere and obt Servts
Respectfully
Wilson & Bugg

23. William Y. Chalfant, *Dangerous Passage: The Santa Fe Trail and the Mexican War* (Norman: University of Oklahoma Press, 1994), 165–85. For a good discussion of the effects of drought and hunting upon the availability of buffalo on the plains, see Sweeney, "Thirsting for War, Hungering for Peace," 71.

24. Gorenfeld and Kimball, "Such Is a Dragoon's Life," 213.

25. Report of Thomas Fitzpatrick, September 18, 1847, in *Annual Report of the Commissioner of Indian Affairs for the Year 1847* (Washington, D.C.: Wendell and Van Benthuysen, 1848), 121. (Hereinafter: Fitzpatrick Report.)

26. Ibid.

27. Ibid.

28. Ibid.

29. Baker correspondence, to Mathias Martin, June 14, 1847.

30. Love to Adj. Gen. Roger Jones, Camp on the Arkansas, June 27, 1847, reprinted in *Niles' Weekly Register* 72 (July 31, 1847): 343.

31. Sergeant Bishop's account of the battle appears in Cutts, *The Conquest of California and New Mexico*, 240.

32. Baker correspondence, to Mathias Martin, June 14, 1847.

33. Troopers Jonathon Arledge, John Dickhart, Moses Short, George Gaskill, and Henry Blake were killed in the battle. (Gaskill, having enlisted at Edinburgh, Indiana, on April 17, 1847, had been in the army for slightly over two months.) Five other troopers—Benjamin Bishop, Henry Vancaster, John Lovelace, Thomas Ward, James Bush, and Willis Wilson—although badly wounded, were able to cheat death and escape. Fourteen Dragoons in Bishop's detachment somehow managed to reach the camp without suffering any serious wounds.

34. Baker correspondence, June 27, 1847.

35. Love to Adjutant General Jones, June 27, 1847, LRAG.

36. Henry, "Henry Wirtz," *Military Record of Civilian Appointments in the United States Army*, 1:126.

37. J. R. Poinsett, Secretary of War, Article III, Paragraph 12, *General Regulations for the Army of the United States* (Washington, D.C.: J. and G.S. Gideon, 1841).

Chapter 10

1. Annual Report, 1st Dragoons, 1848, M744, R3, F68, NARA.

2. Baylies, *General Wool*, 12.

3. Chamberlain, *My Confession.*

4. Bauer, *The Mexican War*, 202.

5. Ibid., 208.

6. James Carleton, *The Battle of Buena Vista: With the Operations of the Army of Occupation, for One Month* (New York: Harper and Brothers, 1848).

7. Maj. Gen. Zackary Taylor to Secretary of War William Marcy, Agua Nueva, March 6, 1847, (Taylor's Report) in *Message from the President* (1848), 97, 132; Carleton, *Buena Vista*, 20.

8. Carleton, *Buena Vista*, 7; Baylies, *General Wool*, 27.

9. Smith, *The War with Mexico*, 1:384.

10. Carleton, *Buena Vista*, 30.

11. Taylor's Report, "Buena Vista"; Smith, *The War with Mexico*, 385.

12. Jonathan Buhoup, *Narrative of the Central Division* (Pittsburgh: M.P. Morse, 1847), 120; Smith, *The War with Mexico*, 388.

13. Carleton, *Buena Vista*, 56; Buhoup, *Narrative*, 121.

14. "Letter from a Soldier of the Second Regiment," March 13, 1847, Buena Vista, Mexico, *Indiana Sentinel*, May 9, 1847;

15. Lt. Daniel Rucker to Lt. Irvin McDowell, acting assistant adjutant general, *Message from the President* (1848), Ex Doc. No. 8, 162.

16. Baylies, *General Wool*, 32.

17. Carleton, *Buena Vista*, 70; Buhoup, *Narrative*, 121.

18. Bauer, *The Mexican War*, 216; Buhoup, *Narrative*, 122.

19. Smith, *The War with Mexico*, 1:391.

20. Chamberlain, *My Confession*, 159.

21. Bvt. Col. Charles May to Maj. William Bliss, *Message from the President* (1848), 198; Buhoup, *Narrative*, 123.

22. Chamberlain, *My Confession*, 162. For his heroism at Buena Vista, May was awarded a colonel's brevet.

23. Carleton, *Buena Vista*, 98.

24. Baylies, *General Wool*, 34; Carleton, *Buena Vista*, 78; "A Soldier's Account of the Battle of Buena Vista," *Madison Courier*, April 10, 1847.

25. Rucker to McDowell, *Message from the President* (1848), 162.

26. Chamberlain, *My Confession*, 159; Taylor, "Buena Vista;" Buhoup, *Narrative*, 123.

27. Buhoup, *Narrative*, 126.

28. Smith, *The War with Mexico*, 1:395.

29. Ibid., 1:397; Buhoup, *Narrative*, 127.

30. Smith, *The War with* Mexico, 1:398.

31. Carleton, *Buena Vista*, 128; Buhoup, *Narrative*, 128.

32. Buhoup, *Narrative*, 128.

33. Vera Lawrence, *Music for Patriots, Politicians, and Presidents: Harmonies and Discords of the First Hundred Years* (New York: Macmillan, 1975), 316.

34. Chamberlain, *My Confession*, 285. The tune to this song appears to be from the British folk song, "The Fourteenth of July/The Little Fighting Chance," the chorus of which is: "So cheer up, my lively lads, for it never shall be said/That the sons of old Britannia shall ever be afraid."

35. Material supplied by Tim Kimball, Albuquerque, New Mexico.

36. *New Orleans Times-Picayune*, November 21, 1847.

37. De Peyster, *Philip Kearny*, 52.

38. P. Kearny to Adjutant General Jones, New York, April 15, 1846, K54, LRAG, 1846.

39. Phil Kearny to Love, letter in private collection; Heitman, "Philip Kearny," *Historical Register*, 1:586.

40. The October 31, 1847, muster roll for Company F includes ten to fourteen names of men who may have been immigrants from Germany. Twenty-five men on the Company F muster roll hailed from Indiana. The authors are grateful to Tim Kimball for his finding of the advertisement in German for dragoon recruits.

41. P. Kearny to Adjutant General Jones, Terre Haute, August 22, 1846, K137, LRAG, 1846.

42. Pfanz, *Ewell*, 49.

43. Mclean to Love, Fort Leavenworth, September 21, 1846, John Love Col lection; De Peyster, *Philip Kearny*, 124.

44. Cullum, "John Richey," *Register of the Officers and Graduates*, "born & appt'd from Ohio, 18th in USMA class 1845; Bvt 2nd Lt 5th Infy, at Palo Alto, Resaca de la Palma, 2nd Lt 4th Infy, 29 June 1846; killed Jan 13, 1846, while carrying dispatches, at Vila Gran [*sic*]."

45. "Correspondence between the Secretary of War and Generals Scott and Taylor, and between General Scott and Mr. Trist," *Message from the President of the United States Transmitting Reports from the Secretary of State and Secretary of War with Resolution of the House of Representatives of the 7th of February 1848*, Ex. Doc. No. 60 (Washington, D.C.: Wendell & Van Benthuysen, 1848), 890.

46. Ibid.

47. P. Kearny to Scott, letter in authors' collection.

48. The names of the ten Company F Privates—Bakon, Bullard, Dellahay, Frankenberg, Hart, Hoffman, Prather, Lee, John W. Smith, and Whitener—were listed on the regimental bimonthly return as "absent on detached service" and as leaving Saltillo for Monterrey on January 8, 1847. During the ensuing campaign the company participated in the battle of Churubusco wherein Private Prather was wounded and taken prisoner, on August 20, 1847, and exchanged on September 3. Pvt. George Dellahay was also wounded in that battle, captured, and died in a hospital in Mexico City on October 3, 1847. In that battle Kearny lost his left arm and Lt. Richard Ewell was severally wounded. Pvt. Philip Frankenberg remained absent, on detached service; Pvts. Pliny Bakon and Robert C. Whitener, absent on detached service, were left at Mier (Mexico) February 7, 1847. Bakon transferred to Company C, 4th Infantry, Puebla, on August 21, 1847; Whitener was later reported dead at Perote, date unknown, December 1847 returns. Frankenberg apparently returned in June 1847, but was no longer carried on the muster roll as he was on detached service. Company F Returns, 1847, Returns from Regular Army Cavalry Regiments, 1833–1916, First Cavalry, 1845–47, Microcopy 744, Roll 2, frames 349–372, NARA, Washington, D.C.

49. "Nearly 13 percent of the entire U.S. force perished from disease. Of the total 12,535 war deaths, 10,986 (88 percent) were due to infectious diseases (overwhelmingly dysentery, both bacterial and amoebic); seven men died from disease for every man killed by Mexican musket balls. Camp pollution was the greatest error committed by U.S. troops in the Mexican War. The indifference of line officers and recruits to the need for proper sanitation and military hygiene fueled the dysentery outbreaks, and the poor conditions in military hospitals contributed further to the spread of disease. This defect in military culture undermined the health of the army and led to medical disaster." Medline (Summer 2009), National Institutes of Health, www.ncbi.nlm.nih.gov/pubmed/19684375.

50. Heitman, "Lorimer Graham," *Historical Register*, 1:468; Regimental Returns, First Dragoons, 1847.

51. Pfanz, *Ewell*, 54.

52. Bauer, *The Mexican War*, 301.

53. DePeyster, *Philip Kearny*, 141.

54. Irish-born Andrew McReynolds became a captain in the 3rd Dragoons on March 9, 1847. Wounded at Churubusco, he received a brevet for gallantry. He was discharged at the end of the war and settled in Michigan. At the beginning of the Civil War, Phil Kearny recommended McReynolds to command the 1st New York Cavalry and he was appointed colonel of that regiment. Heitman, "Andrew McReynolds," *Historical Register*, 2:683. Julian May of Washington, D.C., gained an appointment in the Regiment of Mounted Rifles on July 1, 1847. He was to receive a brevet for gallantry at the Battles of Contreras and Churubusco. After the war, May served as the regiment's quartermaster until his death on November 22, 1859. Heitman, "Julian May," *Historical Register*, 2:699.

55. Smith, *The War with Mexico*, 2:118.

56. *New Orleans Times-Picayune*, November 21, 1847; Kendall, *Dispatches from the Mexican War*, 723.

57. Pfanz, *Ewell*, 56.

58. Kearny to Lt. John Love, November 4, 1848, letter in private collection.

59. On August 24, 1847, a badly wounded Phil Kearny gamely filed the following report of the battle:

> Sir: As I was not wounded until the last of the action of the 20th, I have the honor to report of the movements of my squadron (F troop of the 1st, and K of the 3d regiments, dragoons). Twenty-five men under Lieutenant Ewell, myself attending, accompanied the general-in-chief to the redoubt at Contreras, captured a short time previously. At Cayoacan, coming up to the head of our pursuing column, I was sent with my dragoons and some twenty riflemen under Lieutenant Gibbs, mounted on horses taken from the enemy, to cover Captain Lee, of the engineers, on a reconnaissance towards San Antonio. This place was found to be in possession of General Worth and, his columns rapidly following up the victory.
>
> Returning without delay to the general-in-chief, I was joined by the rest of the squadron, which had been rapidly and efficiently brought up by Captain McReynolds of the 3d dragoons, and received orders to report to General Pillow, and to join in the attack going on the right; the ground immediately in front was found to be impracticable for cavalry action. During the carrying of the village and redoubt of Churubusco, I moved to the right, hoping to make a diversion and get on the road to the rear, but, finding this impossible, returned to my former position.

After the enemy's works were carried, I was ordered to charge down the road towards the city, after the retreating enemy. On the route I was joined by Colonel Harney with several companies of the 2d dragoons; he assumed command, and directed me with my three troops of dragoons, to place myself and command at the head of the cavalry column; the Mexicans were overtaken soon after we entered on the causeway, about three-fourths of a mile from the city, and suffered a severe slaughter up to the very gates.

Understanding that a battery was on the end of the causeway next [to] the town, I communicated through Lieutenant [William] Steele, A.A.A. General, to Colonel Harney my firm intention to charge it, trusting to their panic to enter with the fugitives. Myself, Lieutenant Steele, and Lieutenant Ewell, together with some dragoons whose horses were over excited, were considerably ahead of the main body, coming full on the redoubt, when the enemy opened a fire of grape upon us, amongst the fugitives, and I gave the command to the men around me to dismount and carry it, presuming that the movement would be observed and followed by the rest of the column. This movement not being understood by our men, and the recall which had been sounded and imperfectly heard from the rear, caused them to halt and retire, but in creditable order.

On having been sent to combine with the attack on the right, I was joined by Captain [Alphonse] Duperu, with his company of the 3d dragoons, who accompanied me throughout the rest of day, and behaved very handsomely under such fire as we had passed through.

Company F, of the 1st dragoons, was the leading one on the causeway, and which explains its severe loss.

I have particularly to mention the gallant conduct of Lieutenant Steele, who was constantly at the head of the column, and of Lieutenant Ewell, who had two horses shot under him, immediately at the barricade, and whose conduct in our previous affair of the squadron on the 18th instant, was most conspicuous; also Lieutenant L. Graham, who was wounded, deserves my thanks for his efficiency on this day, as well as the handsome manner of heading a detachment of the company against superior odds on the 12th instant.

Captain McReynolds, acting as second captain of the squadron, was throughout the day every way active, and suffered by a severe wound in his arm.

But it is to the noncommissioned officers and privates that credit is more particularly due for their conduct here and elsewhere.

Statement of loss on the 20th instant.

Killed

1. Pvt. Patrick Mart, Co. F, 1st Dragoons.
2. Pvt. McBrophy, Co. F, 1st Dragoons.
3. Pvt. James McDonald, Co. F, 1st Dragoons.
4. Pvt. John Ritter, Co. F, 1st Dragoons.
5. Capt. Seth B. Thornton, Co. F, 2d Dragoons.
6. Pvt. Edward Curtis, Co. G, 3d Dragoons.
7. Pvt. Augustus Delsol, Co. G, 3d Dragoons.
8. Pvt. George DeDuve, Co. G, 3d Dragoons.

Wounded

1. Capt. Philip Kearny, Co. F, 1st Dragoons, severely, lost left arm.
2. Lieut. Lorimer Graham, 10th Infantry attached to 1st Dragoons, severely.
3. Capt. A. T. McReynolds, Co. K, 3d Dragoons, severely.
4. Private Cowden, Co. K, 3d Dragoons.

60. The movement of Company F to San Antonio, Texas, and the replacement of the easy-going Capt. Philip Thompson with Lieutenant Kearny, resulted, on September 14, 1846, in Henneburg's second desertion. Regimental returns of the 1st Dragoons for April of 1847 also show that bugler Edward Smith was among the seven men who were ill and unavailable for duty. NARA, M744, r2, 355–56.

61. *New Orleans Times-Picayune*, November 21, 1847; Kendall, *Dispatches from the Mexican War*, 723.

62. Hamlin, *The Making of a Soldier*, 72.

63. *L'Abeille de la Nouvelle-Orléans*, September 10, 1847.

64. Bauer, *The Mexican War*, 301.

65. De Peyster, *Phil Kearny*, 148.

66. Kearny to Love, November 4, 1848, letter in private collection.

67. Richard Breithaupt, *Aztec Club of 1847: Military Society of the Mexican War* (Universal City, Calif.: Walika, 1998), 1.

68. De Peyster, *Personal and Military History of Phil Kearny*, 159.

69. De Peyster, Philip Kearny, 352.

70. "Kearny at Seven Pines" by Edmund Clarence Stedman

> So that soldierly legend is still on its journey,—
> That story of Kearny who knew not to yield!
> 'Twas the day when with Jameson, fierce Berry, and Birney,
> Against twenty thousand he rallied the field.
> Where the red volleys poured, where the clamor rose highest,
> Where the dead lay in clumps through the dwarf oak and pine,
> Where the aim from the thicket was surest and nighest,—
> No charge like Phil Kearny's along the whole line.

When the battle went ill, and the bravest were solemn,
Near the dark Seven Pines, where we still held our ground,
He rode down the length of the withering column,
And his heart at our war cry leapt up with a bound;
He snuffed, like his charger, the wind of the powder,—
His sword waved us on and we answered the sign;
Loud our cheer as we rushed, but his laugh rang the louder,
"There's the devil's own fun, boys, along the whole line!"

How he strode his brown steed! How we saw his blade brighten
In the one hand still left,—and the reins in his teeth!
He laughed like a boy when the holidays heighten,
But a soldier's glance shot from his visor beneath.
Up came the reserves to the melee infernal,
Asking where to go in—through the clearing or pine?
"O, anywhere! Forward! 'Tis all the same, Colonel:
You'll find lovely fighting along the whole line!"

O, evil the black shroud of night at Chantilly,
That hid him from sight of his brave men and tried!
Foul, foul sped the bullet that clipped the white lily,
The flower of our knighthood, the whole army's pride!
Yet we dream that he still,—in that shadowy region
Where the dead form their ranks at the wan drummer's sign,—
Rides on, as of old, down the length of his legion,
And the word is still Forward! along the whole line.

71. Original in John Love Collection, Indiana Historical Society.

72. Lester R. Dillon, *American Artillery in the Mexican War, 1846–1847* (Austin, Tex.: Presidial Press, 1976), 11–19; Richard B. Winders, *Polk's Army* (College Station: Texas A&M Press, 1997), 89–92.

73. Dillon, *American Artillery*, 55.

74. Smith, *The War with Mexico*, 2:163.

75. *Santa Fe Republican*, October 9, 1847.

76. Robert G. Shalhope, *Sterling Price* (Columbia: University of Missouri Press, 1971), 67.

77. Bauer, *The Mexican War*, 157. Dragoon Capt. Philip Thompson served as a military advisor for Doniphan and received a major's brevet for his services at the Battle of Sacramento. Heitman, "Philip Thompson," *Historical Register*, 1:957.

78. The *Richmond Enquirer* for February 22, 1848, reported: "The Mexicans in that part of the country are making every effort to oppose their march with a strong force. At first they did not intend making any resistance whatever; but, emboldened by the long delay of our troops at El Paso, they set to work in good

earnest, and have now a considerable numerical force and twelve pieces of cannon. Should our troops continue on their march, they will probably have a second edition of the battle of Sacramento."

79. Ralph P. Bieber, ed., *Marching with the Army of the West, 1846–1848* (Glendale, Calif.: Arthur H. Clark, 1936), 63. In March of 1847, troops under the command of Col. Alexander Doniphan marched from New Mexico, brushed aside a significant Mexican force at Sacramento, and then easily conquered Chihuahua. The campaign accomplish little, if anything, militarily, but made Colonel Doniphan a hero back in his home state of Missouri and humiliated the Mexican defenders.

80. Smith, *The War with Mexico*, 2:166; Shalhope, *Sterling Price*, 71.

81. Shalhope, *Sterling Price*, 69.

82. Price to Jones, March 31, 1848, in U.S. Congress, House, *Message from the President* (1848) 113; *American Star* (Mexico City), March 25, 1848, p. 3. The *American Star* was a newspaper started by a group of Yankee journalists in 1847 that followed General Scott's army from Vera Cruz to Mexico City. Smith, *The War with Mexico*, 2:227.

83. Bieber, *Army of the West*, 353; Price to Jones, March 31, 1848, in U.S. Congress, House, *Message from the President* (1848), 114; Francisco R. Almada, *Perfiles Biográficos del General Angel Trías* (Chihuahua: Ediciones del Gobierno del Estado de Chihuahua, 1981), 29.

84. Shalhope, *Sterling Price*, 72–73.

85. S. J. Joaquin Marquez, *Hombres Célebres de Chihuahua* (Mexico: Editorial Jus, 1953), 273, 275. Five months after the battle of Santa Cruz de Rosales, Cave Couts, a lieutenant with the 1st Dragoons, described Governor-General Trias as showing "himself more of a man than I thought possible to be in the frame of a Mexican, and in private intercourse *a perfect gentleman*, good and sociable companion, loves a frolic and always ready for one." (Emphasis in original.) Couts, *Hepah, California!* 29. Lieutenant Couts reported that at dinner General Trias toasted the Yankee troops: "The Americans as enemies you whip us, as friends you *slay us*." (Emphasis in original.) Couts, *Hepah, California!*, 30. Unable to obtain weapons from Mexico City, General Trias had the eight cannon fabricated in foundries located in Chihuahua. Smith, *The War with Mexico*, 2:419.

86. Beall to Price, March 22, 1848, *Message of the President* (1848), 120–21.

87. *Santa Fe Republic*, April 22, 1848; Price to Jones, 114–15.

88. Bieber, *Army of the West*, 356. During the siege Major Walker reported that members of his Santa Fe Battalion had wounded and captured two Mexican soldiers who were attempting to escape through the lines. Walker to Price, March 22, 1848, *Message of the President* (1848), 132; *American Star* (Mexico City), April 25, 1848.

89. Lt. Alexander Dyer to Maj. Jubal Early, April 5, 1848, in *Chronicles of the Gringos*, ed. Smith and Judah, 143; Love to Beall, March 22, 1848, *Message of the President* (1848), 124.

90. Bieber, *Army of the West*, 356; see gen., Eduardo Esparanza Terrazas, *Santa Cruz, Antigua region de los tapacolmes: Historia del la Villa de Rosales* (Chihuahua: Solar, 2004).

91. Ralls to Price, March 17, 1848, *Message from the President* (1848), 128.

92. William DePalo, *The Mexican National Army, 1822–1852* (College Station: Texas A&M Press, 1994), 50, 74.

93. Price to Jones, *Message from the President* (1848), 116.

94. Mark L. Gardner, ed., *Edward James Glasgow and William Henry* Glasgow, *Brothers on the Santa Fe and Chihuahua Trails* (Niwot: University of Colorado Press, 1993), 135.

95. Love to Beall, March 22, 1848, *Message from the President* (1848), 124–125.

96. Beall to Price, March 23, 1848, *Message from the President* (1848), 124.

97. Price to Jones, March 31, 1848, and Walker to Jones, March 22, 1848, *Message from the President* (1848), 117, 132.

98. Glasgow, *Brothers on the Santa Fe and Chihuahua Trails*, 135–37.

99. Love to Beall, 12, March 22, 1848, *Message from the President* (1848) Ex. Doc. No. 1, 124–125.

100. *Santa Fe Republic*, April 22, 1848.

101. Ibid. The Battle of Santa Cruz de Rosales is remarkable in that, after his surrender, Colonel Justiniani provided General Price with a detailed report indicating the disposition of his troops and cannon prior to the attack. "Official Account of Forces which were Engaged in the Action at the Town of Rosales against the American Forces, Mar. 17, 1848," LRAG, M567, R388, 234–38.

102. Bieber, *Army of the West*, 357. After the battle, the Missouri troops came across the body of Lieutenant Hepburn and "found [it] completely stripped of clothing."

103. Ralls to Price, March 17, 1848, *Message of the President* (1848), 128.

104. Ibid.; Walker to Price, March 22, 1848, *Message of the President* (1848), 132.

105. *Missouri (Palmyra) Whig*.

106. Walker to Price, March 22, 1848, *Message of the President* (1848), 132; *Missouri (Palmyra) Whig*, June 1, 1848. The authors are indebted to Tim Kimball for finding and transcribing a letter from William B. Drescher, of Capt. Francis Hassendeubel's Light Artillery Company A, to his brother, which appeared in the *Whig*.

107. Almada, *Perfiles Biográficos*, 30; Price to Jones, March 31, 1848, *Message from the President* (1848), 118.

108. Bieber, *Army of the West*, 358; Gale to Price, 25 March 1848, f. 282, M567, r.388, RG 94, NA; Alexander Dyer, Mexican War Journal, 1847–1848, Fray Angelico Chavez History Library, New Mexico History Museum, Santa Fe, 102.

109. *Missouri (Palmyra) Whig*, June 1, 1848.

110. *American Star* (Mexico City), April 25, 1848. Elsewhere, Mexican losses are reported by the archives of the Secretaria de la Defensa National to be twenty-six killed. Francisco R. Almada, *Resumen de Historia del Estado de Chihua-hua* (Chihuahua: Centro Libero La Prensa, 1955), 229. The day after the battle, Fray Juan José Perez counted 24 dead bodies in the plaza. Eduardo Esparza Terrazas, *Santa Cruz, Antigua*, 116–17. Historian George Rives noted that Price's reported figure of Mexican dead was "obviously impossible, unless it is meant to include the prisoners, besides the killed and wounded." George Rives, *The United States and Mexico* (New York: Scribner, 1918), 2:581n1. Rives was obviously unaware of the figure reported by Surgeon Gale. See also Bauer, *The Mexican War*, 159.

111. "The Official Register of Durango contains a communication from the Minister of War to Trias, late Governor and *commandante general* of Chihuahua, stating that he is at liberty [the reader will remember that General Price sent him to Chihuahua from Rosales after the battle]. He says the Provisional President, the moment it was known the American troops were advancing up [on Chihuahua], determined that reparation should be made in case of disaster. It was therefore agreed with the American commander in chief that if any Mexicans should be captured, they should not be held as prisoners, nor warlike stores and munitions be considered as lawful prize. Sen. Trias is therefore set at liberty, the trains, &c., are to be restored, and as the editor of the Register remarks, 'there is only the loss that will be felt, that of the brave men who fell at Rosales.'" *American Star*, April 26, 1848.

112. Marcy to Price, *California and New Mexico: Message of the President* (1849–1850), Ex. Doc. No. 17, 31st Cong., 1st Session, 256–57.

113. Shalhope, *Sterling Price*, 75.

114. Bauer, *The Mexican War*, 57, 62, 100, 217, 301, and 311.

Battle	U.S. killed & wounded	Mexican killed & wounded	Percentage
Palo Alto	53	23	123
Resaca de Palma	122	359	34
Monterrey	488	367	133
Buena Vista	659	1,639	40
Churubusco	998	4,297	23
Molina del Rey	706	2,000	35
Total	3,026	8,893	34

115. At Monterrey, the Mexicans were defending their position from behind walls and fortified buildings. The United States forces, in assaulting these positions, suffered greater casualties than did the Mexicans. Likewise, at the 1847 Battle of Molina del Rey, where a portion of the Mexican defense was anchored

to some buildings, the United States' losses were 35 percent of the Mexican losses.

At the Battle of Sacramento, Doniphan lost nine men killed and wounded, and he reported Mexican losses to be in excess of three hundred. Bauer, *The Mexican War*, 156. There has never been any suggestion of a massacre. The disproportionate losses at Sacramento, however, may be attributed to the reckless and uncoordinated Mexican cavalry charges that ran into rifle and howitzer fire. One participant in the battle wrote that Mexican losses at Sacramento were closer to around twenty-five dead. William Glasgow's "Morandums" quoted in Gardner, *Brothers*, 170.

116. Foos, *Killing Affair*, 116.

117. Bauer, *The Mexican War*, 101. The *Niles' Weekly Register* of January 28, 1848, for example, pointed out that "the aborigines of this country have not attempted and cannot attempt, to exist independently alongside of us. Providence has so ordained it; and it is folly not to recognize the fact. The Mexicans are aboriginal Indians, and they must share the destiny of their race. The destiny of the race of *aboriginal Indians* along side of us has been extinction—rapid extinction—not subjection, as we all know." (Emphasis in original.)

118. Smith, *The War with Mexico*, 2:210

119. Foos, *Killing Affair*, 113.

120. Gardner, *Brothers*, 137.

121. Foos, *Killing Affair*, 116.

122. Bieber, *Army of the West*, 333.

123. Letters Received by the Office of the Adjutant General, NARA, microfilm roll 5, T-1115, roll 1, May 10 and May 22, 1848.

124. Holbrook to McLaws, April 7, 1850, Letters Received, 9th Military District, M-1102, roll 2, RG 393, NARA; Munroe to Jones, April 15, 1850, M269/1850, Letters Received, AGO, RG 94, NARA; Carson, *Autobiography*, 136–37. The report sent along to the War Department included a note from Sergeant Holbrook's commanding officer Capt. William Grier, another veteran of Santa Cruz de Rosales, who stated that the scalping was performed by Mexican civilians who had accompanied the expedition. *Message from the President of the United States to the Two Houses of Congress at the Commencement of the 31st Congress, December 2, 1850,* Ex. Doc. no. 1, Senate version, Report of the Secretary of War, 70–71; Bennett, foreword to *Forts and Forays*, xxiii.

125. Ralls to Price, Ex. Doc. 1, 128. In Trias's official report of the battle, he mentions that the American troops did not stop shooting notwithstanding a bugle calling for cease-fire. *American Star* (Mexico City), April 25, 1848. See also Ramon Alcaraz, *Apuntes para la historia de la Guerra entre México y los Estados Unidos* (Mexico City: D. F., Tipografia de Manuel Payno, 1848), 51. This would not be remarkable in that the men of the 3rd Missouri often refused to follow orders and did not respect their officers. Bieber, *Army of the West*, 331–32.

126. Almada, *Resumen de Historia*, 230; Report of the Secretary of War, 31st Cong, 1st sess., Ex. Doc. No. 32, 43–44, as reported in Foos, *Killing Affair*, 120.

127. Army of the West dockets of courts martial, NARA, microfilm roll 5, T-1115.

128. José Maria Ponce de Leon, *Resanas Historicas del Estado Chihuahua* (1913), quoted in EsparzaTerrazas, *Santa Cruz, Antigua*, 116.

129. John Gooch Ferguson, a newspaper reporter in civilian life, penned that "[a] day or two after the battle I found an old press and types, and issued one number of a paper called the *Santa Cruz Banner*, containing Colonel Ralls's and Colonel Lane's reports and an account of the battle." (Beiber, *Army of the West*, 358.) The *Banner*'s article on the Battle of Santa Cruz de Rosales, appears in the April 22, 1848, issue of the *Santa Fe Republican*. It was found and generously provided to the authors by Tim Kimball. The reader will note that the *Banner* article lavishly praises Colonel Ralls and his gallant charge, but barely mentions General Price.

130. Ralls to Commanding Officer, Saltillo, Mexico, March 24, 1848, f344, r388, M567, RG 94, NARA. On April 2, 1848, Col. John Hamtramck, commanding officer at Saltillo, wrote to a friend of having received Ralls's correspondence: "I have but a moment to say that I have just received an express from Gen. Price's column, announcing the pleasing intelligence that Gen. Trias, with all his forces, has surrendered to our arms. Gen. Price entered Chihuahua on the 9th of March, and immediately gave pursuit to the enemy, whom he overtook at Santa Cruz de Rosalio, a strongly situated town some sixty miles South of Chihuahua, on the 16th. The place was invested, and after fighting all day, the plaza and church were nearly attained by burrowing through the houses, when the enemy surrendered. Our loss was one Lieutenant, two noncommissioned officers, and 12 privates—the enemy's loss is 300 and odd killed and 72 wounded, his whole force [800,] all his artillery [12 pieces], 2,000 stand of arms, some 800,000 dollars worth of public property, many field officers, and General Trias at their head. Col. Ralls's command on one side, and Col. Lane's on the other, acted most heroically, and took the place." *Richmond Enquirer*, May 5, 1848.

131. In his journal for April 2, Private Gooch wrote: "This morning Colonel Ralls left for Chihuahua. There is a rumor that he has been arrested by General Price for printing his report of the battle. There is also a report of an armistice [that] has been agreed upon which terminates in May next. Many rumors of peace are also afloat." Bieber, *Army of the West*, 359.

132. Ralls to Price, M-567, R388, NARA. The text of the entire letter is:

"While in arrest without written information as to the nature of the charges it is intended to prefer against me for insubordination given by you on yesterday when you placed me in arrest, I am led to the conclusion that you have done so relative to the printing of what purported to

be my official report of the action taken by the forces under my com
mand at the Battle of Santa Cruz Rosales, on the 16th of March in connection with the letter forwarded by me from that place to the officer
in command of the United States forces stationed at Saltillo from which
you seem to infer that I am disposed to assume a command which you
think belongs only to yourself."

133. Bieber, *Army of the West*, 359; General Orders, Army of the West, April
5, and April 6, 1848; Price to Wool, 338–39, r388, M567, RG 94, NARA; Special
Order no. 18, Headquarters Army of the West, Chihuahua, 16 April 1848, f170,
r1, Orders Issued by Gen. Stephen W. Kearny and Gen. Sterling Price to the
Army of the West, 1846–1848, T1115, RG 94, NARA.

134. With special thanks and appreciation to Tim Kimball, an indefatigable
researcher, who found this story taken from the *Banner*:

CAPTURE OF SANTA CRUZ

We copy the following from the *Santa Cruz Banner*, a small sheet published at that place by P. G. Ferguson:

On the first of March Gen. Price set out from El Paso with four
companies of the Missouri regiment of horse under command of Colonel Ralls, two companies of U. S. Dragoons under command of Major
Beall, and two mounted howitzers with an artillery detachment under
command of Capt. Hasseduebel [*sic*] for a forced march upon the city
of Chihuahua, 300 miles distant, south from El Paso, at Carasel [*sic*,
Carrizal], 100 miles upon the road. The Santa Fe battalion, Major Walker's, joined us, making in all nine companies, with which we marched
on to Chihuahua, in the unprecedented time of six days; reached the
city with the nine companies, but the enemy under Gen. Trias, with
his forces some eight hundred strong, with principally Cavalry, had
left some 12 hours before with all the public property, including a
[blurred] of newer artillery for the South. A few hours after our arrival
at Chihuahua, we were put en route to overtake the enemy. Our forced
march upon the city exhausted a great many of our horses and men
and we set out for the South with skeletons of nine companies, number-
ing in all about 300; with this force, we kept our march in pursuit—we
made sixty miles march in about 12 hours, and approached Santa Cruz
at about sunrise, where the enemy had already fortified himself, his
batteries fixed, and full and efficient disposition made for defense of
the place, he having reinforced himself to the number of about 1,200
in all behind his barriers, also occupying the church itself, a perfect fortification. As we moved our column around the west of the city, a nine
pounder was discharged by the enemy, passing our centre, when several

of the companies of his infantry filed through the balcony, ranging in order upon the church, a person supposed to be a priest, harangued them, and the surrounding populace, a part of which was heard and distinctly understood, was replied to by loud cheers by the soldiery, and the people with many "vivas" and "vevar Republicano Mexicano." An express was sent back to hurry on the pieces, and the place was put under siege. We permitted no communication with the place, allowed women and children and non-combatants two days to leave the city with their effects, when our pickets were closed upon them. The siege last[ed] from the 9th to the 16th. Many attempts were made by parties of the enemy during the siege to leave the town, but few succeeded— now and then, a fleet horse would outrun our pickets and get to the mountains. The third day of the siege, the commander of one of the pickets sent word to the general that a number were escaping, which he could not prevent, his picket was too small. On the morning of the 16th, Lieut. Col. Lane, arrived with artillery &c., and we received the enemy's invitation to come on. Our forces are referred to the reports of Col. Ralls and to Lt. Col. Lane in this number, which detail their part of the affair. The reports of Major Walker and Beall would make this account complete. Maj. Walker's command distinguished itself by storming the South of the town while the dragoons acted well the part assigned them, and Capt. Hassandeuebel [*sic*] and Lieut. Love, gallantly managed their batteries the whole day, with great science and skill. The charge of Col. Ralls's column was a splendid affair. It moved like a thunder-bolt, precisely in the direction it was sent, spreading dismay, death, and destruction, and it was over this column that Col. Sanchez extended the flag of surrender. It was a proud day for all, but for those leading and directing this column, it was particularly so, and Col. Ralls in his report has but rendered justice to his officers and men, and that report does that commander distinguished honor for the virtue of his head and heart. An entire park of artillery was captured with about 2,000 stand of arms and munitions, with other public property to the value of seven to eight hundred thousand dollars. We captured the whole force, including thirty commissioned officers, Gov. Maj. General Trias at their head. After the day had nearly expired we learned that the place could only be carried by storming. The order to charge was given, and in one hour's time the city surrendered, our arms as ever, victorious, adding another trophy to the Fame of the great Republic we serve.

LIST OF THE KILLED—2d Lieut. George O. Hepburn of Co. D, privates Schafenberg and Bockman, Co. B. WOUNDED.—Private Ripper, Greff and Dedrich, Co. B, Jackson, Kearnes, Williams and Gillam, Co. D. We also understand by a private letter that a young man by the name of Maston, commissary sergeant, start[ed] out from Santa Cruz to meet Love's command and has never since been found or heard from; he is supposed to have been killed.

135. First Lieutenant Cave J. Couts, also from Tennessee, was the son of the postmaster general and graduated from the Military Academy in 1843. Cullum, "Cave Couts," *Register of the Officers and Graduates*, 259. The original of this letter is in the John Love Collection.

136. The original of this letter is also found in the John Love Collection. In the parlance of the nineteenth century, the word "abominable" has a special meaning: inhuman or beastly. Joseph Worchester, *A Dictionary of the English Language* (Boston: Brewer and Tileston, 1864), 6.

137. Couts, *Hepah, California!*, 12; Chamberlain, *My Confession*, 309.

138. Chamberlain, *My Confession*, 277. Chamberlain wrote that he had resigned from the army and served as a wagonmaster during the trip west. He is mistaken. Army records have him reported as a private who deserted from Company A in Los Angeles. Company A Returns, January and March 1849, NARA, RG 93, M744, R3.

139. Couts, *Hepah, California!*, 14.

140. Ibid., 16; Chamberlain, *My Confession*, 280.

141. Couts, *Hepah, California!*, 29.

142. Ibid., 32.

143. Ibid., 50; Chamberlain, *My Confession*, 281; Company A Returns, January and March 1849, NARA, RG 93, M744, R3.

Epilogue

1. George E. Hyde, *The Pawnee Indians* (Norman: University of Oklahoma Press, 1988), 210–31.

2. Martin enlisted in the Dragoons in 1833 and served with Dodge's 1834 expedition to visit the Pawnee villages. He re-enlisted in Company B at Fort Crawford in 1839 and then at Fort Atkinson on April 6, 1846, and gained the rank of sergeant, participating in General Kearny's invasion of New Mexico. He remained with Company B after it was broken up and sent back to Fort Leavenworth. After the company was supplied with recruits, Martin accompanied it under Lieutenant Love as it escorted the paymaster to Santa Fe. It was on this trip that he first tasted combat, battling the Comanches at the Coon Creeks. In 1848, Martin and his company supported Gen. Sterling Price on his invasion of Chihuahua, and he served as an artilleryman at the Battle of Santa Cruz de Rosales. First Dragoons, Register of Enlistments 1833, 1841, and 1846 (p. 167). His commanding officer, Robert Chilton, of Virginia, graduated 48th in his class of 1837, and gained a second lieutenancy in the 1st Dragoons. On February 21,

1842, Chilton was promoted to first lieutenant and became the regiment's assistant quartermaster. In the Mexican War Chilton served as a captain on Zachary Taylor's staff at the Battle of Buena Vista and gained a major's brevet for gallant conduct. Cullum, "Robert Chilton," *Register of Officers and Graduates*, 1:220.

3. Daniel Koller to Daniel Litzel and Sarah Litzel, December 14, 1847, letter in private collection.

4. Lowe, *Five Years a Dragoon*, 31. Born in Liverpool, England, in 1831, Peel had immigrated to America with his step-father, Private Lyons. The private, who had joined Capt. Sumner's B Company, enlisted his step-son, at age twelve, to become an army bugler. (Turner to Sumner, St. Louis, February 6, 1845, Dragoon Letter Book, p. 259.) Langford, who grew to 5-foot-9 and 160 pounds, served in the Mexican War and claimed to have killed three Plains Indians. See Will Gorenfeld and George Stammerjohan, "Dragoons vs. Comanches," *Wild West* (June 2004); Lowe, *Five Years a Dragoon*, 90. These killings only whetted his appetite for violence, and Peel left the army, his wife, and infant son to become a notorious gunfighter and gambler. William and John Gorenfeld, "John Bull Shot Down His Gambling Pal, Soldier-turned-Gunfighter Langford Peel," *Wild West* (April 2011).

5. William Gorenfeld, "Get a look at the mighty Pacific: Lt. Col. Thomas Swords in Antebellum San Francisco," in *Bugler, Sound the Charge: The 1st Dragoons Out West, 1833–1860* (October 9, 2007), http://www.chargeofthedragoons.com/2007/08/31/get-a-look-at-the-mighty-pacific-thomas-swords-dragoon-quarter master/.

6. Sumner to Jones, 3 April 1849, HQ, First Dragoons, Fort Leavenworth, S215, Letters Received, Adjutant General's Office, roll 415, M567, RG 94, NARA. The authors would like to thank Dr. Durwood Ball for finding this letter and sharing it with us.

7. Robinson, *Organization of the Army*, 2:157.

8. Ibid., 2:162.

9. Gorenfeld, "The Taos Mutiny of 1855."

10. See Utley, *Frontiersmen in Blue*, 201; Wetherington and Levine, *Battles and Massacres*, 12.

11. By the end of the Civil War, the 1st Dragoons had contributed the following generals and brevet generals to the Union and Confederate armies: John Adams, Richard Anderson, George Blake, Robert Chilton, Abraham Buford, John Buford, James Carleton, Samuel Chamberlain, Philip St. George Cooke, Patrick Connor, Henry Davidson, John Davidson, Richard Ewell, Thomas Fauntleroy, William Gamble, David Gregg, William Grier, David Hunter, James C. Parrott, William Dorsey Pender, John Davidson, Rufus Ingalls, John Pegram, Phil Kearny, Alfred Pleasonton, Daniel Rucker, Marcus Reno, Charles Ruff, Delos Sackett, William Sanders, George Stoneman, Samuel Sturgis, Edwin Sumner, Andrew J. Smith, Thomas Swords, and Joseph Wheeler. In addition, Jefferson Davis, the

president of the Confederate States of America, was a lieutenant in the First Dragoons, and cadet Ulysses Grant applied to serve as a dragoon officer.

12. See Allen Guelzo, *Gettysburg: The Last Invasion* (New York: Knopf, 2013) 139ff.

13. The critics cheered *Stagecoach* not just for its heavenly vistas and Monument Valley mesas but for a chase scene that made the movie "a genuine rib-thumper," in the words of an awed Frank S. Nugent in the *New York Times.*

14. Ernest Haycock, Jr., *On a Silver Desert: The Life of Ernest Haycock* (Norman: University of Oklahoma Press, 2003), 170.

Bibliography

Internet Sources

Carroll, H. Bailey. "Snively, Jacob." *Handbook of Texas Online.* Texas State Historical Association. http://www.tshaonline.org/handbook/online/articles/fsn07.

National Institutes of Health. Medline. Summer 2009. www.ncbi.nlm.nih.gov /pubmed/19684375.

Presidential and Congressional Documents

The description and value of the arms taken from a party of Texans, within the Territory of the United States, by Capt. Cooke, 1st Regt Dragoons, June 30, 1843, and deposited at Fort Leavenworth, Mo., January 8, 1846. 29th Congress, 1st Session. Senate Document 43, 1846. Submitted, and ordered to be printed, to accompany bill S. No. 37.

Marcy, William. *Letter from the Secretary of War transmitting the report, and map of Captain J. Allen, of the First Regiment of Dragoons, of his expedition of the heads of the Rivers Des Moines, Blue Earth & etc., in the Northwest, in compliance with a resolution of the House of Representatives of the 29th of January of 1845.* Doc. No. 168. Washington, D.C.: Government Printing Office, 1846.

Message from the President of the United States, on the Subject of the Mexican War, 1848. Congress Executive Document 60, Washington, D.C.: Wendell and Van Benthuysen, 1848. Serial 520.

Message from the President of the United States to the Two Houses of Congress, at the Commencement of the First Session of the Twenty-Third Congress, December 3, 1833. Washington, D.C.: Duff Green, 1833, serial 238.

Message from the President of the United States to the Two Houses of Congress, at the Commencement of the Second Session of the Twenty-Third Congress, December 2, 1834. Washington, D.C.: Duff Green, 1834, serial 266.

Message from the President of the United States to the Two Houses of Congress at the Commencement of the Thirty-First Congress, December 2, 1850. Washington, D.C.: Printed for the Senate, 1850. Serial 587.

Message of the President of the United States, Transmitting information on the Subject of California and New Mexico. 31st Cong., 1st sess., House Executive Document 17. Washington, D.C., 1850. Serial 573.

Reports of Explorations and Surveys to Ascertain the Most Practical and Economic Route for a Railroad from the Mississippi River to the Pacific Ocean, 1853–6, According to Acts of Congress of March 3, 1853, May 31, 1854, and August 5, 1854. Vol. 11, p. 37. Washington, D.C.: Beverly Tucker, 1855.

"Report of Major General Alexander Macomb." Attached to the *Message from the President of the United States to the 24th Congress,* 2d sess., no. 1, Senate Executive Document 2. Washington, D.C.: Blair & Rives, 1836.

Report to the President of the United States, February 16, 1832. Indian Office Letter Book, Box 2, "Letters sent, 1824–1908," M21.

National Archives, Washington, D.C.

Please note: "Entry" means a collection's number in the record group (RG) inventories published in the Archives. "M" followed by a number is the microfilm number for the collection in question.

Annual Report of the Commissioner of Indian Affairs for the Year 1848.Washington, D.C.: Wendell and Van Benthuysen: 1849 [not published as congressional document].

Dragoon Letter Book. Record Group 391: Records of the United States Regular Army Mobile Units, 1821–1942, Entry 612, Letters Sent, 1833–1906. 9W2: 29/9/3, vol. 1, *Letters Sent,* First Dragoons, July 24, 1833–December 13, 1839.

Emory, W. H. *Notes of a Military Reconnaissance from Fort Leavenworth, in Missouri to San Diego, California, including part of the Arkansas, Del Norte, and Gila Rivers.* 30th Cong., 1st sess., Ex. Doc. No. 41. Washington, D.C.: Wendell and Van Benthuysen, 1848.

Jackson, Andrew. Message to Congress, "On Indian Removal," December 6, 1830. Record Group 46, Records of the United States Senate, 1789–1990. National Parks Service. Last accessed October 20, 2014. http://www.nps.gov /museum/tmc/MANZ/handouts/Andrew_Jackson_Annual_Message.pdf.

Johnston, Abraham. "Journal of Captain A. R. Johnston," contained in Emory, *Notes,* Ex. Doc. No. 41.

Journal of the Executive Proceedings of the Senate, December 1, 1845 to August 14, 1848, Washington, D.C.: Government Printing Office, 1887.

Letters Received, 9th Military District, RG 393, M-1102.

Letters Received by the Office of the Adjutant General (Main Series), 1822–1860, RG 94, M569.

Letters Sent, First Dragoons: Records of the United States Regular Army Mobile Units, 1821–1942, RG 391.

Message from the President of the United States Communicating the Proceedings of a Court Martial in the Trial of Lt. Col. Frémont, April 7, 1848. 30th Cong., 1st Sess., Ex. Doc. No. 33, 1848.

Message from the President to the 31st Congress. Washington: 1850. Ex. Doc No. 1, Senate version.

Message from the President of the United States Transmitting Reports from the Secretary of State and Secretary of War with Resolution of the House of Representatives of the 7th February 1848. Ex. Doc. No. 60. Washington: Wendell & Van Benthuysen, 1848.

Orders issued by Brig. Gen. Stephen W. Kearny and Brig. Gen. Sterling Price given to the Army of the West, T1115.

Records of the Adjutant General's Office, 1780s–1917. RG 94. 1968.

Records of the Chief of Ordnance. Letters Received by the Chief of Ordnance, 1797–1988. RG 156.

Records of the Office of the Quartermaster General Consolidated Correspondence File, Fort Gibson. RG92, M206.

Records of the U.S. Regular Army Mobile Units. Entry 612, Letters Sent (1st Dragoons/1st Cavalry). Volume 1 of 20: 1st Dragoons, Letters Sent. RG 391.

Regiment of Dragoons, Semiannual Muster Rolls. RG 94.

Report of Thomas Fitzpatrick, September 8, 1847 in *Annual Report of the Commissioner of Indian Affairs for the Year 1847.* Washington: Wendell & Van Benthuysen, 1848.

Returns from U.S. Military Posts, 1800–1914. *[Fort] Leavenworth, KS; Aug. 1827–Dec. 1850.* RG 94, M617, Roll 610.

United States Army. Records of the Judge Advocate General. Proceedings of U.S. Army Courts-Martial, 1809–1890, Court Martial, Headquarters, 2d Military Department, in Adjutant General Order No. 24, March 20, 1843. File # DD213.

U.S. Army. Register of Enlistments 1798–1914. RG94, M233.

U.S. Department of State. Daniel Webster to General Juan Almonte, April 29, 1843.Appended as an exhibit in War Department, record of the Judge Advocate, Proceedings of a Court of Inquiry held at Fort Leavenworth, pursuant to General Orders No. 6, February 28, 1844. DD405.

U.S. Department of War. United States Army, Returns from Regular Cavalry Regiments 1833–1916, Regiment of Dragoons, Monthly Returns. RG 94, M744.

Unpublished Journals and Letters

Antes, William. Journal. Beinecke Library. Yale University, New Haven, Connecticut.

Baker, Matthias. Letters. Mexican War Collection 1846–1940. Missouri Historical Society Archives. (Also at Yale University.)

Clairborne, J. F. H. Papers. Southern History Historical Collection. University of North Carolina, Chapel Hill.

Dunne, William H. "Notes on San Pasqual," 1878. MS C-D 202. H. H. Bancroft Library Collection. University of California at Berkeley.

Dyer, Alexander. Mexican War Journal 1846–1848. Fray Angelico Chavez History Library. Museum of New Mexico History, Santa Fe.

French, Erasmus Darwin. Letter, Poway, California, July 7, 1887. H. H. Bancroft Library Collection. University of California at Berkeley.

Gillespie, Capt. Archibald, to Commodore Stockton. Report of the Battle of San Pasqual, San Diego, December 25, 1846. U.S. Navy, Gillespie Papers. University of California, Los Angeles.

Hitchcock, Ethan Allen. Letter to his brother. Hitchcock Papers. Library of Congress, Washington, D.C.

Kearny, Capt. Philip, to Gen. Winfield Scott, February 6, 1847. In authors' private collection.

Love, John. Collection of letters and documents at the Indiana Historical Society., Indianapolis, Indiana, and at the William Clements Library, University of Michigan, Ann Arbor.

Stevenson, James. Journal. Gettysburg College Library, Gettysburg, Pennsylvania.

Newspapers and Journals

American Star. Mexico City.
Arkansas Gazette. Little Rock.
Army and Navy Chronicle. Washington, D.C.
Army and Navy Journal. New York.
Army History. Washington, D.C.
Boon's Lick Times. Fayette, Missouri.
Buffalo Journal.
The Cavalry Journal. Fort Leavenworth, Kansas.
Deutsche Tribune. St. Louis.
Evening Post. New York.
Evening Star. New York.
Galveston Civilian and Galveston City Gazette. Galveston, Texas.
Jefferson City [Missouri] Inquirer.
Kansas Weekly Herald. Leavenworth, Kansas.
Little Rock [Arkansas] Gazette.
Military and Naval Magazine of the United States. Washington, D.C.
Missouri Republican. St. Louis.
Missouri Whig. Palmyra.
Nashville Banner. Tennessee.
Niles' Weekly Register. Baltimore.

Ohio Repository. Canton, Ohio.

Republican. Santa Fe.

Richmond Enquirer. Richmond, Virginia.

Santa Cruz Banner.

Times. New York.

Weekly Tribune. Liberty, Missouri.

The Western Mountaineer. Garden City, Colorado.

Books, Articles, and Dissertations

Abert, W. *Western America in 1846–1847: The Original Diary of Lieutenant J. W. Abert, who Mapped New Mexico for the United States Army.* Edited by John Galvin. San Francisco: John Howell Books, 1966.

Adkin, Mark. *The Waterloo Companion: The Complete Guide to History's Most Famous Battle.* Mechanicsburg, Pa.: Stackpole Books, 2001.

Alcaraz, Ramon. *Apuntes para la historia de la Guerra entre México y los Estados-Unidos.* Mexico City: D. F., Tipografia de Manuel Payno, 1848.

Almada, Francisco R. *Resumen de Historia del Estado de Chihuahua.* Chihuahua: Centro Libero La Prensa, 1955.

———. *Perfiles biográficos del General Angel Trías.* Chihuahua: Ediciones del Gobierno del Estado de Chihuahua, 1981.

Anonymous. *The Ordnance Manual for the use of the Officers of the United States Army.* Washington, D.C.: Gideon & Co., 1850.

———. "The American Occupation of Iowa, 1833–1860." *The Iowa Journal of History and Politics* 17, no. 1 (Jan. 1919).

———. "*The History of Fayette County, Iowa: A History of the County, Its Cities, Towns, & Etc.* Chicago: Western Historical Society, 1878.

Armstrong, Perry A. *The Sauks and the Black Hawk War.* Springfield, Ill.: H.W. Rokker, 1887.

Bailey, Lynn. *The Long Walk: A History of the Navajo Wars, 1846–1868.* Tucson: Westernlore Press, 1988.

Ball, Durwood. *Army Regulars on the Western Frontier, 1848–1861.* Norman: University of Oklahoma Press, 2001.

———. "Lt. Sylvester Mowry's Report on his March in 1855 from Salt Lake City to Fort Tejon." *Arizona Quarterly of History* 7, no. 4 (1965).

Barbero, Alessandro. *The Battle: A New History of Waterloo.* New York: Walker & Co., 2003.

Barry, Louise. *The Beginning of the West: Annals of the Kansas Gateway to the American West, 1540–1854.* Topeka: Kansas Historical Society, 1972.

Bauer, K. Jack. *The Mexican War 1846–1848.* New York: Macmillan, 1974.

Bayard, Samuel. *A Sketch of the Life of Commodore Robert F. Stockton.* New York: Derby & Jackson, 1856.

Baylies, Francis. *A Narrative of Major General Wool's Campaign in Mexico in the Years 1846, 1847 & 1848.* Albany, NY: Little & Co., 1851.

Beatie, Russel. *The Army of the Potomac: McClellan's First Command, March 1862– May 1862.* Havertown, Pa.: Casemate, 2014.

Becher, Ronald. *Massacre along the Medicine Road: A Social History of the Indian War of 1864 in Nebraska Territory.* Lincoln: University of Nebraska Press, 1999.

Benet, Stephen. *A Treatise on Military Law and the Practice of Courts-Martial.* New York: D. Van Nostrand, 1868.

Bennett, James A. *Forts & Forays: A Dragoon in New Mexico, 1850–1856.* Edited by Clifton Brooks and Frank Reeve. Albuquerque: University of New Mexico Press, 1996.

Bieber, Ralph P., ed. *Marching with the Army of the West, 1846–1848.* Glendale, Calif.: Arthur H. Clark, 1936.

Brackett, Albert G. *History of the United States Cavalry, from the Formation of the Federal Government to the 1st of June, 1863.* New York: Harper, 1865.

Breithaupt, Richard. *The Aztec Club of 1847: Military Society of the Mexican War.* Universal City, Calif.: Walika, 1998.

Brigham, Johnson. *Iowa—Its History and Its Foremost Citizens.* Chicago: S. J. Clarke, 1918.

Brown, John. *History of Texas, 1685–1892.* 2 vols. St. Louis: Becktold & Co., 1893.

Buhoup, Jonathan. *Narrative of the Central Division.* Pittsburgh: M. P. Morse, 1847.

Byliss, Francis. *A Narrative of Major General Wool's Campaign in Mexico in the Years 1846, 1847 & 1848.* Albany, N.Y.: Little & Co., 1851.

Carleton, James. *The Prairie Log Books, 1844–45. Dragoon Campaigns to the Pawnee Villages in 1844, and to the Rocky Mountains in 1845.* Edited and with an introduction by Louis Pelzer. Chicago: Caxton Club, 1943.

———. *The Battle of Buena Vista: With Operations of the Army of Occupation for One Month.* New York: Harper & Bros., 1849.

Carroll, H. Bailey. "Stewart Miller and the Snively Expedition of 1843." *Southwestern Historical Quarterly* 54, no. 3 (January 1951).

Carson, Kit. *Kit Carson's Autobiography.* Edited by Milo Quaife. Lincoln: University of Nebraska Press, 1966.

Catlin, George. *Letters and Notes on the Manners, Customs, and Condition of the North American Indians.* 2 vols. London: published by the author, 1841.

Chalfant, William. *Dangerous Passage: The Santa Fe Trail and the Mexican War.* Norman: University of Oklahoma Press, 1994.

Chamberlain, Samuel E. *My Confession: The Recollections of a Rogue.* New York: Harper & Bros., 1956.

Clarke, Dwight. "The Final Roster of the Army of the West, 1846–1847." *California Historical Society Quarterly* 43, no. 1 (March 1964).

———. *Stephen Watts Kearny, Soldier of the West.* Norman: University of Oklahoma Press, 1961.

Clausewitz, Carl von. *On War.* Translated and introduced by Michael Howard and Peter Paret. London: Everyman's Library, 1991.

Coffman, Edward. *The Old Army: A Portrait of the American Army in Peacetime, 1784–1898.* New York: Oxford University Press, 1986.

Cohen, Felix. *Handbook of Federal Indian Law.* Albuquerque: University of New Mexico Press, 1958.

Cooke, Philip St. George. *Scenes and Adventures in the Army or, Romance of Military Life.* Philadelphia: Lindsay & Blakiston, 1859.

_____. "A Journal of the Santa Fe Trail." Edited by William Connelley. *Mississippi Valley Historical Quarterly* 21, no. 1 (1925).

Couts, Cave J. *Hepah, California!* Tucson: Arizona Pioneers' Historical Society, 1961.

Croghan, George. *Army Life on the Western Frontier: Selections from the Official Reports Made between 1826 and 1845 by Colonel George Croghan.* Edited by Francis Prucha. Norman: University of Oklahoma Press, 1958.

Cullum, George. *Biographical Register of the Officers and Graduates of the U.S. Military Academy at West Point, N.Y., from its Establishment March 16, 1802, to the Army Re-organization of 1866–67.* 2 vols. New York: D. Van Nostrand, 1868.

Cutrer, Thomas P. "Algernon P. Thompson." *Handbook of Texas Online.* Texas State Historical Association. http://www.tshaonline.org/handbook/online/articles/fth15.

Cutts, James Madison. *The Conquest of California and New Mexico, by Forces of the United States in the Years 1846 and 1847.* Albuquerque: Horn & Wallace, 1965.

Davis, Jefferson. *The Papers of Jefferson Davis.* 13 vols. Edited by Haskell Monroe, Jr., and James McIntosh. Baton Rouge: Louisiana State University Press, 1991.

DePalo, William. *The Mexican National Army, 1822–1852.* College Station: Texas A&M Press, 1994.

De Peyster, J. Watts. *Personal and Military History of Philip Kearny.* New York: Rice and Gage, 1869.

DeVoto, Bernard. *The Year of Decision 1846.* New York: St. Martin's Press, 2000.

Dillon, Lester. *American Artillery in the Mexican War, 1846–1848.* Austin: The Presidial Press, 1976.

Dolph, Edward A. *Sound Off: Soldier Songs from Yankee Doodle to Parley Voo.* New York: Cosmopolitan Book Corporation, 1929.

DuPont, Samuel. *Extracts from Private Journal-Letters of Captain S. F. DuPont, While in Command of the Cyane, During the War with Mexico, 1846–1848.* Wilmington, Del.: Ferris Bros., 1885.

Elting, John R. *A Dictionary of Soldier Talk.* New York: Scribner, 1984.

———, ed. *Military Uniforms in America.* Vol. 2, *Years of Growth, 1796–1851.* San Rafael, Calif.: Presidio Press, 1977.

Esparza Terrazas, Eduardo. *Santa Cruz, Antigua region de los tapacolmes: Historia del la Villa de Rosales*. Chihuahua: Solar, 2004.

Fessler, W. Julian. "Captain Boone's Journal." *Chronicles of Oklahoma* 7, no. 1 (March 1929).

Flynn, John. "Reminiscences of Some Incidents in the Career of a United States Dragoon between the Years 1839 and 1844." *Texas Quarterly* 9 (Autumn 1966).

Foos, Paul. *A Short, Offhand, Killing Affair*. Chapel Hill: University of North Carolina Press, 2002.

Foreman, Carolyn Thomas. "General Richard Barnes Mason." *Chronicles of Oklahoma* 19, no. 1 (March 1941).

———. "Nathan Boone: Trapper, Manufacturer, Surveyor, Militiaman, Legislator, Ranger, and Dragoon." *Chronicles of Oklahoma* 19, no. 4 (December 1941).

Foreman, Grant. *Pioneer Days in the Early Southwest*. Cleveland: Arthur H. Clark, 1926.

———. *Advancing the Frontier*. Norman: University of Oklahoma, 1933.

———, ed. *A Traveler in Indian Territory: The Journal of Ethan Allen Hitchcock, late Major-General in the United States Army*. Norman: University of Oklahoma Press, 1996.

Gardner, Mark. *Edward James Glasgow and William Henry Glasgow, Brothers on the Santa Fe and Chihuahua Trails*. Niwot: University of Colorado Press, 1993.

Gilsan, Rodney. *Journal of Army Life*. San Francisco: A. L. Bancroft, 1874.

Goetzmann, William H. *Exploration and Empire: The Explorers and Scientists in the Winning of the American West*. New York: Knopf, 1966.

Gorenfeld, William. "Battle of Cieneguilla." In *Battles and Massacres on the Southwestern Frontier: Historical and Archaeological Perspectives*. Edited by Ronald Wetherington and Frances Levine. Norman: University of Oklahoma Press, 2014.

———. "Jefferson Barracks: 'I am Disgusted with the Duty.'" *Military Collector & Historian* 55, no. 4 (Winter 2003–2004).

———. "The Taos Mutiny of 1855." *New Mexico Historical Review* 88, no. 3 (Summer 2013).

Gorenfeld, William, and John Gorenfeld. "John Bull Shot Down His Gambling Pal, Soldier-turned-Gunfighter Langford Peel." *Wild West* (April 2011).

———. "Punishing the Paiutes." *Wild West* (December 2001).

Gorenfeld, William, and Tim Kimball. "Such is a Dragoon's Life: Corporal Mathias Baker, Company B, First Dragoons 1845–1849." *Missouri Historical Review* 105, no. 4 (July 2011).

Gorenfeld, William, and George Stammerjohan. "Dragoons vs. Comanches." *Wild West* (June 2004).

Grant, Ulysses S. *Personal Memoirs*. 2 vols. New York: Charles L. Webster & Company, 1885–86.

Gray, Alonzo. "Cavalry Tactics Illustrated by the War of Rebellion Together with Many Interesting Facts Important for Cavalry to Know (Part 1)." *Cavalry Journal.* Leavenworth, Kans.: U.S. Cavalry Association, 1910.

Gray, William F. *The Diary of William Fairfax Gray, from Virginia to Texas, 1835–1837.* Dallas: William P. Clements Center for Southwest Studies, Southern Methodist University, 1997.

Grbasic, Zvonimir, and Velimir Vuksic. *Cavalry: The History of a Fighting Elite 650 B.C.–A.D. 1914.* London: Cassell, 1993.

Gregg, Josiah. *Commerce of the Prairies, or, the Journal of a Santa Fe Trader, 1831–1839.* New York: Langley, 1844.

Griffin, John. *A Doctor Comes to California: The Diary of John S. Griffin, Assistant Surgeon with Kearny's Dragoons 1846–1847.* San Francisco: California Historical Society, 1943.

Grippaldi, Richard. "The Politics of Appointment in the Jacksonian Army: The (Non) Transfer of Ethan Allen Hitchcock to the Regiment of Dragoons, 1833." *U.S. Army History* 27 (Winter 2009).

———."The Best Possible Appointments Should Be Made: The Officers of the U.S. Regiment of Dragoons and Military Professionalism." Unpublished doctoral dissertation delivered at Temple University and the United States Army Historical Center, Carlisle, Pennsylvania, 2006.

Guelzo, Allen. *Gettysburg: The Last Invasion.* New York: Knopf, 2013.

Hafen, Leroy, and W. J. Ghent. *Broken Hand: The Life Story of Thomas Fitzpatrick, Chief of the Mountain Men.* Denver: Old West Publishing Co., 1931. Reprinted by University of Nebraska Press, 1973.

Hall, Thomas. *Medicine of the Santa Fe Trail.* Dayton, Ohio: Morningside Books, 1971.

Hallahan, William. *Misfire: The Story of How America's Small Arms have Failed our Military.* New York: Charles Scribner's Sons, 1994.

Hamalainen, Pekka. *Comanche Empire.* New Haven: Yale University Press, 2008.

Hamlin, Percy, ed. *The Making of a Soldier: Letters of General R. S. Ewell.* Richmond, Va.: Whittet & Shepperson, 1935.

Hannings, Bud. *Forts of the United States: A Historical Dictionary, 16th through 19th Centuries.* Jefferson, N.C.: McFarland & Company, 2006.

Haycock, Ernest, Jr. *On a Silver Desert: The Life of Ernest Haycock.* Norman: University of Oklahoma Press, 2003.

Heitman, Francis. *Historical Register of the United States Army, From its Organization, September 29, 1789, to March 2, 1903.* 2 vols. Washington, D.C.: Government Printing Office, 1903.

Henry, Guy. *Military Record of Army and Civilian Appointments in the United States Army.* 2 vols. New York: D. Van Nostrand, 1873.

Herrera, Carlos. *The Contested Homeland: A Chicano History of New Mexico.* Albuquerque: University of New Mexico Press, 2000.

Hildreth, James. *Dragoon Campaigns to the Rocky Mountains: Being a History of the Enlistment, Organization, and First Campaigns of the Regiment of United States Dragoons; together with incidents of a Soldier's Life, and sketches of scenery and Indian Character.* New York: Wiley & Lane, 1836.

————. *Recollections of the United States Army: A Series of Thrilling Tales and Sketches by an American Soldier Written During a Period in "The Service," since 1830.* Boston: James Munroe & Co., 1845.

Hoffman, Charles. *A Winter in the Far West.* 2 vols. London: Richard Bentley, 1835.

Hollingsworth, John. "The Journal of Lieutenant John McHenry Hollingsworth of the First New York Volunteers (Stevenson's Regiment) September 1846–August 1849." *California Historical Society Quarterly* (September 1923).

Howe, Daniel. *What Hath God Wrought: The Transformation of America, 1815–1848.* New York: Oxford Press, 2007.

Hughes, Willis. "The First Dragoons on the Western Frontier, 1834–1846." *Arizona and the West* 12, no. 2 (1970).

Hunt, Aurora. *James Henry Carleton, 1814–1873, Frontier Dragoon.* Frontier Military Series, no. 2. Glendale, Calif.: Arthur H. Clark, 1958.

Hurt, Douglas. *Nathan Boone and the American Frontier.* Columbia: University of Missouri, 1998.

Hyde, George E. *The Pawnee Indians.* Norman: University of Oklahoma Press, 1988.

Hyslop, Stephen. *Bound for Santa Fe: The Road to New Mexico and the American Conquest.* Norman: University of Oklahoma Press, 2002.

Irving, Washington. *A Tour on the Prairies.* Edited and with an introductory essay by John McDermott. Norman: University of Oklahoma Press, 1956.

Johnson, Curt. "The Decline of the Knight." In *The Cavalry,* edited by James Lawford. London: Roxby Press, 1976.

Kane, Adam. "James Carleton." In *Soldiers West: Biographies from the Military Frontier,* edited by Paul Hutton and Durwood Ball. 2nd ed. Norman: University of Oklahoma Press, 2001.

Kautz, August. *Customs of Service for Non-Commissioned Officers and Soldiers as Derived from Law and Regulations and Practised in the Army of the United States, Being a Hand-book for the Rank and Files of the Army, Showing What Are the Rights and Duties, How to Obtain the Former and Perform the Latter, and Thereby Enabling Them to Seek Promotion and Distinction in the Service of their Country.* Philadelphia: J. B. Lippincott & Co., 1864.

Kearny, Stephen W. *Carbine Manual, or Rules for the Exercise and Manouevres for the United States Dragoons,* Washington: Government Printing Office, 1837.

Keleher, William. *Turmoil in New Mexico, 1846–1868.* Albuquerque: University of new Mexico, 1982.

Kendall, George W. *Dispatches from the Mexican War.* Edited and with an introduction by Lawrence Delbert Cress. Norman: University of Oklahoma Press, 1999.

Keyes, Erasmus. *Fifty Years' Observation of Men and Events: Civil and Military.* New York: Scribner's Sons, 1884.

Latrobe, Charles. *Rambler in North America.* Vol. 2. New York: Harper & Bros., 1835.

Launius, Roger. *Alexander William Doniphan: Portrait of a Missouri Moderate.* Columbia: University of Missouri Press, 1997.

Lawrence, Vera. *Music for Patriots, Politicians, and Presidents: Harmonies and Discords of the First Hundred Years.* New York: Macmillan, 1975.

Lowe, Percival Green. *Five Years a Dragoon ('49 to '54).* Kansas City, Mo.: F. Hudson Publishing, 1906.

Mahan, Bruce. *Old Fort Crawford and the Frontier.* Iowa City: State Historical Society of Iowa, 1926.

Mahon, John. *History of the Second Seminole War, 1835–1842.* Gainesville: University of Florida Press, 1985.

Marquez, S. J. Joaquin. *Hombres Célebres de Chihuahua.* Mexico: Editorial Jus. 1953.

McCaffrey, James. *The Army in Transformation, 1790–1860.* Westport, Conn.: Greenwood Press, 2006.

Michno, Gregory, and Susan Michno. *Forgotten Fights: Little Known Raids and Skirmishes on the Frontier, 1823 to 1890.* Missoula, Mont.: Mountain Press, 2008.

Miller, Darlis. *Above a Common Soldier: Frank and Mary Clarke in the American West and Civil War, 1847–1872.* Albuquerque: University of New Mexico Press, 1997.

Mooney, James. *History, Myth, and Sacred Formula of the Cherokee.* Asheville, N.C.: Bright Mountain, 1992.

Moore, M. J. "Sketch of Capt. Benjamin Davies Moore." *Publications of the Historical Society of Southern California* 6 (1903–1904).

Munroe-Fraser, J. P. *History of Sonoma County.* San Francisco: Alley, Bowen & Co., 1880.

Myers, Harry. *From the Crack Post of the Frontier: Letters of Thomas and Charlotte Swords.* Fort Scott, Kans.: Sekam Publications, 1982.

Nesbit, Robert. *Wisconsin: A History.* Madison: University of Wisconsin Press, 1930.

Newman, John. "Henry Dodge: Colonel, U.S. Dragoons 1833–36." *Iowa Historical Review* 7, no. 3 (January 1891).

Nichols, Roger. *General Henry Atkinson: A Western Military Career.* Norman: University of Oklahoma Press, 1965.

Nolan, Louis. *Cavalry: Its History and Tactics.* Originally printed 1854; reprinted Yardley, Pa.: Westholme, 2007.

Nosworthy, Brian. *With Musket, Cannon, and Sword: Battle Tactics of Napoleon and His Enemies.* Boston: Da Capo Press, 1996.

Oliva, Leo, ed. *Confrontation on the Santa Fe Trail: Selected Papers from Santa Fe Trail Association Symposia at La Junta, Colorado, 1993, and at Larned and Great Bend,*

Kansas, 1995. Woodston, Kans.: Santa Fe Trail Association Publications, 1996.

———. *Soldiers on the Santa Fe Trail.* Norman: University of Oklahoma Press, 1967.

———. *Fort Scott: Courage and Conflict on the Border.* Topeka: Kansas Historical Society, 2008.

Onofrio, Jan. *Texas Biographical Dictionary.* New York: Somerset, 1996.

Ormsby, Waterman L. *The Butterfield Overland Mail.* Edited by Lyle Wright and Josephine Bynum. San Marino, Calif.: The Huntington Library, 1942.

Parkman, Francis. *The Oregon Trail: Sketches of Prairie and Rocky-Mountain Life.* New York: Library of America, 1991.

Pelzer, Louis. *Marches of the dragoons in the Mississippi Valley: an account of marches and activities of the First regiment United States dragoons in the Mississippi Valley between the years 1833 and 1850.* Iowa City: State Historical Society of Iowa, 1917.

———. *Henry Dodge.* Iowa City: State Historical Society of Iowa, 1911.

———. "A Journal of Marches by the First United States Dragoons, 1834–1835." *The Iowa Journal of History and Politics* 7, no. 3 (July 1909): 332–33.

Perrine, Fred. "Military Escorts on the Santa Fe Trail." *New Mexico Historical Review* 2, nos. 2 and 3 (April 1927).

———. "The Journal of Hugh Evans, Covering the First and Second Campaigns of the United States Dragoon Regiment in 1834 and 1835. Campaign of 1834." *Chronicles of Oklahoma* 3, no. 3 (September 1925).

———. "Hugh Evans' Journal of Colonel Henry Dodge's Expedition to the Rocky Mountains in 1835." *Mississippi Valley Historical Review* 14 (Sept. 1927): 192.

Peters, DeWitt. *Kit Carson's Life and Adventures, from Facts Narrated by Himself Embracing Events in the Life-Time of America's Greatest Hunter, Trapper, Scout and Guide.* Hartford, Conn.: Dustin Gilman & Co., 1874.

Pfanz, Donald. *Richard S. Ewell: A Soldier's Life.* Chapel Hill: University of North Carolina Press, 1998.

Pickerall, William. *History of the Third Indiana Cavalry.* Indianapolis: Aetna Printing Co., 1906.

Poinsett, Joel. *Cavalry Tactics, Part One.* 3 vols. Washington: J. and G. S. Gideon and Co., 1841.

———. *General Regulations for the Army of United States.* Washington: J & G. S. Gideon, 1841.

Prucha, Francis P. *The Sword of the Republic: The United States Army on the Frontier, 1783–1846.* London & New York: Macmillan, 1969.

———. *Great Father: The United States and the American Indians.* Lincoln: University of Nebraska Press, 1995.

Reed, Allan Millett, and Jack Shulimson, eds. *Commandants of the Marine Corps.* Annapolis: Naval Institute Press, 2004.

Reilly, Robert. *United States Military Small Arms, 1816–1865: The Firearms of the Civil War*. Highland Park, NJ: The Gun Room Press, 1970.

Rickey, Don, Jr. *Forty Miles a Day on Beans and Hay: The Enlisted Soldier Fighting the Indian Wars*. Norman: University of Oklahoma Press, 1963.

Rives, George. *The United States and Mexico*. New York: Scribner, 1918.

Robinson, Fayette. *An Account of the Organization of the Army of the United States, with Biographies of Distinguished Officers of all Grades*. 2 vols. Philadelphia: Butler & Co., 1848.

Rodenbough, Theophilus. *From Everglade to Canyon with the Second United States Cavalry*. Norman: University of Oklahoma Press, 2000.

————. *The Army of the United States: Historical Sketches of Staff and Line with Portraits of the Generals-in-Chief*. First published in 1896, republished New York: Argonaut Press, 1966.

Roemer, Jean. *Cavalry: Its History, Management, and Uses in War*. New York: D. Van Nostrand, 1863.

Rolle, Andrew. *John Charles Frémont: Character as Destiny*. Norman: University of Oklahoma Press, 1999.

Rutland, Robert, ed. "The Dragoons in the Iowa Territory, 1845." *Iowa Journal of History* 31 (April 1953): 156.

Ruxton, George. *Wild Life in the Rocky Mountains*. New York: Macmillan, 1924.

Salter, William. "Henry Dodge in the Black Hawk War." *Iowa Historical Record* 5–6 (1890).

Schmidt, Peter. *Hall's Military Breechloaders*. Lincoln: Andrew Mowbray, 1996.

Schubert, Frank, ed. *March to South Pass: Lieutenant William B. Franklin's Journal of the Kearny Expedition in 1845*. Washington, D.C.: Army Corps of Engineers, 1979.

Shalhope, Robert. *Sterling Price*. Columbia: University of Missouri Press, 1971.

Shirk, George. "Peace on the Plains." *Chronicles of Oklahoma* 28, no. 1 (Spring 1950).

Sides, Hampton. *Blood and Thunder: The Epic Story of Kit Carson and the Conquest of the American West*. New York: Anchor, 2007.

Simmons, Marc. *Murder on the Santa Fe Trail: An International Incident 1843*. El Paso: University of Texas, El Paso, 1987.

Skelton, William. *An American Profession of Arms: The Army Officer Corps, 1784–1861*. Lawrence: University Press of Kansas, 1992.

Smiley, Jerome. *Semi-Centennial History of the State of Colorado*. Chicago: Lewis Publishing, 1913.

Smith, George Winston, and Charles Judah. *Chronicles of the Gringos: The U.S. Army in the Mexican War, 1846–1848: Accounts of Eyewitnesses and Combatants*. Albuquerque: University of New Mexico Press, 1968.

Smith, Justin. *The War with Mexico*. New York: Macmillan, 1919.

Starr, Stephen. *The Union Cavalry in the Civil War.* 3 vols. Baton Rouge: Louisiana State University Press, 1979.

Steffen, Randy. *The Horse Soldier, 1776–1943: The United States Cavalryman: His Uniforms, Arms, Accoutrements and Equipments.* 4 vols. Norman: University of Oklahoma Press, 1977.

———. *United States Military Saddles, 1842–1943,* Norman: University of Oklahoma Press, 1973.

Stevenson, Stanley. "Expeditions into Dakota." Includes "Allen's Expedition in 1844" and "Sumner's Expedition of 1845." In *South Dakota Historical Collections,* vol. 9. Compiled by State Department of History. Pierre, S. Dak.: Hipple Printing Company, 1918.

Swanton, John. *The Indian Tribes of North America.* Washington, D.C.: Smithsonian Institution Press, 1952.

Sweeney, Kevin. "Thirsting for War, Hungering for Peace: Drought, Bison Migrations, and Native Peoples on the Southern Plains, 1845–1859."*Journal of the West* 41, no. 3 (Summer 2002).

Taylor, Alan. *The Civil War of 1812: American Citizens, British Subjects, Irish Rebels.* New York: Random House, 2011.

Thoburn, Joseph. "The Dragoon Campaigns to the Rocky Mountains." *Chronicles of Oklahoma* 8, no. 1 (March 1930).

Trask, Kerry. *Black Hawk: The Battle for the Heart of America.* New York: Henry Holt, 1996.

Troiani, Don, Earl Coates, and James Kochan. *Soldiers in America, 1754–1865.* Mechanicsburg, Pa.: Stackpole Books, 1998.

Turner, Henry S. *The Original Journals of Henry Smith Turner with Stephen Watts Kearny to New Mexico and California, 1846–1847.* Edited and with an introduction by Dwight L. Clarke. Norman: University of Oklahoma Press, 1966.

Tyler, Daniel. *A Concise History of the Mormon Battalion in the Mexican War, 1846–1847.* Salt Lake City, 1881.

Unruh, John. *The Plains Across: The Overland Emigrants and the Trans-Mississippi West, 1840–60.* Chicago: University of Illinois Press, 1993.

Urwin, Gregory. *The United States Cavalry: An Illustrated History.* Dorset, England: Blandford Press, 1984.

Utley, Robert. *The Indian Frontier, 1846–1890.* Albuquerque: University of New Mexico Press, 1984.

———. *Frontiersmen in Blue: The United States Army and the Indian, 1848–1865.* New York: Macmillan, 1967.

Van der Zee, Jacob. "Captain James Allen's Dragoon Expedition from Fort Des Moines, Territory of Iowa, in 1844." *The Iowa Journal of History and Politics* 11 (January 1913).

Van Zandt, Howard. "The History of Camp Holmes and Chouteau's Trading Post." *Chronicles of Oklahoma* 13, no. 3 (1935).

Von Alterburg, Hans. *Winning the West: General Stephen Watts Kearny's Letter Book 1846–1847.* Boonville, Mo.: Petitanoui Publications, 1998.

Watson, Henry. *The Journals of Marine Second Lieutenant Henry Bulls Watson, 1845–1848.* Edited by Charles Smith. Washington, D.C.: History and Museums Division, Headquarters, U.S. Marine Corps, 1990.

Watson, Sam. *Peacekeepers and Conquerors: The Army Officer Corps on the American Frontier, 1821–1846.* Lawrence: University Press of Kansas, 2013.

Wharton, Clifton. "The Expedition of Major Clifton Wharton in 1844." *Kansas Historical Collections* 16 (1925).

Wheelock, Thompson. "Journal of Colonel Dodge's Expedition from Fort Gibson to the Pawnee Pict Village." Reprinted in *News of the Plains and Rockies, 1803–1865*, compiled and annotated by David White. Vol. 4. Spokane, Wash.: Arthur H. Clark, 1998.

Whitcomb, Mary. "Reminiscences of Gen. James C. Parrott." *Annals of Iowa* 3, nos. 5–6 (April, 1897).

White, David. *News of the Plains and Rockies, 1803–1865: Original Narratives of Overland Travel and Adventure Selected from the Wagner-Camp and Becker Bibliography of Western Americana.* 4 vols. Spokane: Arthur H. Clark, 1998.

Wilson, R. Michael. *Tragic Jack: The True Story of John William Swilling.* Las Vegas: Stagecoach Books, 2001.

Winders, Richard. *Polk's Army: The American Experience in the Mexican War.* College Station: Texas A&M University Press, 1997.

Winthrop, William. *Military Law and Precedents.* Washington, D.C.: Government Printing Office, 1920.

Woodward, Arthur. *Lances at San Pascual.* San Francisco: California Historical Society, 1948.

Wooster, Robert. *The American Military Frontiers: The United States Army in the West, 1783–1900.* Albuquerque: University of New Mexico Press, 2009.

Worchester, Joseph. *A Dictionary of the English Language.* Boston: Brewer and Tileston, 1864.

Young, Otis. *The West of Philip St. George Cooke, 1809–1895.* Glendale, Calif.: Arthur H. Clark, 1955.

Index

References to illustrations appear in italic type.

Abby, George, 22, 56, 62
Abercrombie, John, 151
"act for the more perfect defense of the frontier" (1833), 23
Adams, John Quincy, 20, 21
Adams, Langdon, 350
Adams-Onís Transcontinental Treaty, 138–39
Adrian, Terry, 350
Adventures of Oliver Twist, The (Dickens), 3
African Americans. *See* slavery
Albert, James, Jr., 236–37
alcohol: consumption by dragoons, 256–59, 405n20; sale to Indians, 21, 105–6, 114, 119–20, 152–54, 203, 205, 399n44
Alipas, Dionisio, 268
"A Little More Grape, Captain Bragg" (Foster), 313
Allen, George, 98–99
Allen, James, *187*, 211, 213; cartographic expedition of, 158–59; death of, 232, 291, 357; leadership style, 147, 156–62, 210; in Mexican War, 157, 221
Almonte, Juan, 124–25
Alta California, *231*, 245
Alvarado, Francisco, 279

Alvarado, José, 255
American Fur Company, 199
American Star newspaper, 424n82
Ames Company, 97
Ampudia, Pedro de, 308, 316
Anderson, Robert, 26
Anderson, William, 79
Andrews (private), 408n71
Antes, William, 259, 365n15
Apache Canyon advance, 227–28
Apache Indians, 7, 170, 175, 242, 243, 347, 360–61
Arapaho Indians, 76, 78, 201, 204–5
Arbuckle, Matthew, 41–42, 72, 81, 116
Archuleta, Diego, 227
Archy, Nelson, 91–92, 221, 233, 237, 258
Arikara Indians, 76
Arlege, Jonathan, 301, 417n33
Armijo, Manuel, 123, 138, 220–21, 223, 226–27
Armstrong, Bezaleel, 225, 291–92, 357
Army and Navy Chronicle, 89, 98, 101, 379n111, 381n12, 386n86, 387n95
Army and Navy Journal, 371n105
Army of Observation, 194
Army of the West, 220; Apache Canyon advance, 227–28; march to California, 230–35, *231,* 244–48;

CPSIA information can be obtained
at www.ICGtesting.com
Printed in the USA
BVHW071836270123
657296BV00008B/784

9 780806 190969